"2005"

To the desk of
WA2WAI
thru M
from
W9RWN

D0934096

ACCOLADES FOR JEAN SHEPHERD

"The classic Jean Shepherd shows were less than an hour in length and they came on late every night... There'd be a commercial or two, a sardonic swipe at station management more often than not, a mordant throwaway observation or two about modern life. And then he'd kind of back into the program—a story. Jean Shepherd invented a form of radio storytelling to which all of us still on the air are indebted."   —Harry Shearer

"He was a tremendous addition to [*Playboy*] and a part of Americana, and I loved his work. I'm proud to have had him in our pages."   —Hugh Hefner

"The inventor òf free-form radio, shtick radio, hip radio, he worked pranks, philosophized, concertized on jew's harp, kazoo and nose flute, and was way, way better at radio than anybody else, then or now. And that might have been that, a gifted and amusing guy, and an off-beat asset to New York radio—except that he was an artist and an innovator, and one of the tiny handful of radio geniuses ever to exist."
—Daniel Pinkwater, *The New York Times Magazine*

"I used to see [Shepherd] all the time at the Limelight, where he and Jan Kindler would carry on, improvise, and we all would do spontaneous stuff together. Lord Buckley and Dizzy [Gillespie] and all in the jazz world loved Jean because he was such a great verbal improviser."   —David Amram

"In the evening, WOR gets further out. At 11:15 Jean Shepherd comes on, a brilliant and undisciplined night sprite. A sort of oral abstract expressionist."   —*Time*

"Listening to him was like a religious experience."
—Jules Feiffer

"Shepherd has the educated man's virtue of slowness, of taking time to reflect, and he does this in the process of his shows. Who else does this? Sahl? What he gives you is some carefully honed, brilliant, blade-like stuff which he's worked out beforehand... Shepherd is like a man quietly plumbing the depths of his own mind while sitting across from you at a party. It stays with you no longer. *It starts your own mind off.* One feels restored, an entire personality." —**Suzanne Kiplinger,** *The Village Voice*

"I first met Jean Shepherd on the South Side of Chicago on a hot July day in 1935. He was twelve years old and I was seven. I remember him as a skinny, freckle-faced, sandy-haired kid, quiet, sensitive, and pensive, always raising hell and always ready for a good fight. I did not know at that time of his part in the atrocious St. Valentine's Day Massacre, nor was this to affect our friendship in later years." —**Shel Silverstein**

"Jean Shepherd knew all the four-letter words. If he could have used them on the radio, maybe he would have. But since he couldn't, he rendered them unnecessary. His nightly suggestion that laughter is the only real defense against the shrapnel of life was memorable largely because he shared it in language and tone quiet enough that his voice could be heard." —**David Hinckley,** *New York Daily News*

"I don't think any sense of humor is funny. Rarely. Jean Shepherd is funny." —**Andy Kaufman**

"I had to get my Shepherd fix. He actually made you feel that you weren't alone... I think he had the best influence on my sensibility. And I think helped me kind of pursue that sense of being different, being an individual." —**Billy Collins, U.S. Poet Laureate, 2003**

"What I got of him was a wonder at the world one man could create. I am as awed now by his achievement as I was then." —**Richard Corliss,** *Time* **magazine senior writer**

"Ain't no one else ever gonna come close to what the man accomplished...in the dark...with a microphone, a kazoo and 50,000 watts!" —**Vin Scelsa, free-form radio broadcaster**

Jean Shepherd, master of radio, television, film, live performance, and the written word, in one of his "silly" moods in the 1970s.

EXCELSIOR, YOU FATHEAD!

THE ART AND ENIGMA OF
JEAN SHEPHERD

EUGENE B. BERGMANN

APPLAUSE THEATRE & CINEMA BOOKS ▦ NEW YORK

Excelsior, You Fathead!: The Art and Enigma of Jean Shepherd
by Eugene B. Bergmann
Copyright © 2005 by Eugene B. Bergmann
All rights reserved

Andy Kaufman quote from *Was This Man a Genius?* by Julie Hecht. New York: Vintage Books edition, 2002, p. 161. Harry Shearer quote from "A Voice in the Night," a National Public Radio two-hour tribute to Shepherd, 2000. Shel Silverstein quote from the liner notes to the LP *Jean Shepherd and Other Foibles*. Electra Corporation, 1959. "Excelsior" by Henry Wadsworth Longfellow from *Yale Book of American Verse*, edited by Thomas Raynesford Lounsbury. New Haven: Yale University Press, 1912. Excerpt from *The Realist* used by permission. © *The Realist*. Excerpts from the *New York Times* copyright © 1956 by The New York Times Co. Reprinted with permission. Definitions for "creeping meatballism" and "night people" on page 218 from *The Dictionary of American Slang* by Harold Wentworth and Stuart Berg Flexner. Copyright © 1960, 1967, 1975 by Harper & Row, Publishers, Inc. Reprinted by permission of HarperCollins Publishers Inc.

Book design by Mark Lerner

Library of Congress Cataloging-in-Publication Data:
Bergmann, Eugene B.
  Excelsior, you fathead! : the art and enigma of Jean Shepherd/Eugene B. Bergmann.
     p. cm.
  Includes bibliographical references and index.
  ISBN 1-55783-600-0
  1. Shepherd, Jean. 2. Radio broadcasters—United States—Biography. I. Title.

  PN1991.4.S52B47 2005
  791.4402'8'092—dc22

                          2004026320

British Library Cataloging-in-Publication Data
A catalog record of this book is available from the British Library

Applause Theatre & Cinema Books
151 West 46th Street, 8th Floor
New York, NY 10036
Phone: (212) 575-9265
Fax: (646) 562-5852
Email: info@applausepub.com
Internet: www.applausepub.com
Applause books are available through your local bookstore, or you may order at
www.applausepub.com or call Music Dispatch at 800-637-2852

Sales & Distribution
North America:
Hal Leonard Corp.
7777 West Bluemound Road
P. O. Box 13819
Milwaukee, WI 53213
Phone: (414) 774-3630
Fax: (414) 774-3259
Email: halinfo@halleonard.com
Internet: www.halleonard.com

Europe:
Roundhouse Publishing Ltd.
Millstone, Limers Lane
Northam, North Devon EX 39 2RG
Phone: (0) 1237-474-474
Fax: (0) 1237-474-774
Email: roundhouse.group@ukgateway.net

This book is dedicated to the memory of Jean Parker Shepherd, who gave so much of his real as well as imagined self to us all.

With thanks to my parents, Marjorie Crosby Bergmann and Benno Bergmann, who loved me enough to tolerate Shep and record him for me way back in the Legendary Time.

I hope this book will help my wife and kids understand why Jean Shepherd is so important to me.

EXCELSIOR

The shades of night were falling fast,
As through an Alpine village passed
A youth, who bore, 'mid snow and ice,
A banner with the strange device,
Excelsior!

His brow was sad; his eye beneath,
Flashed like a falchion from its sheath,
And like a silver clarion rung
The accents of that unknown tongue,
Excelsior!

In happy homes he saw the light
Of household fires gleam warm and bright;
Above, the spectral glaciers shone,
And from his lips escaped a groan,
Excelsior!

"Try not the Pass!" the old man said;
"Dark lowers the tempest overhead,
The roaring torrent is deep and wide!"
And loud that clarion voice replied,
Excelsior!

"O stay," the maiden said, "and rest
Thy weary head upon this breast!"
A tear stood in his bright blue eye,
But still he answered, with a sigh,
Excelsior!

"Beware the pine-tree's withered branch!
Beware the awful avalanche!"
This was the peasant's last Good-night.
A voice replied, far up the height,
Excelsior!

At break of day, as heavenward
The pious monks of Saint Bernard
Uttered the oft-repeated prayer,
A voice cried through the startled air,
Excelsior!

A traveler, by the faithful hound,
Half-buried in the snow was found,
Still grasping in his hands of ice
that banner with the strange device,
Excelsior!

There in the twilight cold and gray,
Lifeless, but beautiful, he lay,
And from the sky, serene and far,
A voice fell, like a falling star,
Excelsior!

—Henry Wadsworth Longfellow

"Stay tuned for WOR's resident genius, Jean Shepherd."
                    —Announcer at the beginning of a show

"I thought you'd kind of like to know how it is out there, gang.
Just keep your knees loose."   —Jean Shepherd

"Excelsior, you fathead!"   —Jean Shepherd

CONTENTS

PREFACE

RECORDINGS OF BROADCASTS PAST

Jean Shepherd commented on Samuel Beckett's play *Krapp's Last Tape* of 1958 at least twice during his twenty-one years on New York radio. He obviously related Krapp's act of speaking into a microphone—spontaneous communicating—to that of broadcasting and taping his own thoughts:*

> ...a piece called *Krapp's Last Tape*. It was the story of a man who tape recorded things as he went along in life... Now that's very different from making a diary, you know. A lot of people keep diaries. And a diary is an incomplete record, because when you sit down to write—you're inhibited. The fact of writing itself inhibits most people. The most *natural* form of communication is the voice. The very first thing that the Neanderthal man did is to communicate with his friend by voice—not by diary—or by memo...
>
> But *Krapp's Last Tape* was about a man who, every day, would record things on his little tape recorder. He'd sit there and he'd talk about his life. Now he didn't talk about the things that were happening like, "Today Normandy was

---

invaded." That kind of stuff—which is what people usually write. They get very pompous when they write in diaries. When you talk into the tape recorder you do something else, see. You're very personal, generally. So he talked about the things that he was thinking about during the day...

And one of the things that fascinated me about *Krapp's Last Tape* is this is *definitely*, in a very real way, a play about the story of my life. Most people say, you know, "That's a play about *me*," and actually it's not. It's about what they *think* they should be like. I know many guys who think they're Hamlet. They aren't. They just *think* they are. But not many people have recorded every day, forty-five minutes or so of their thoughts on life and existence and the passing scene.[1]

Yes, Shepherd thought a lot about what it meant to speak one's ideas daily, and to listen to and contemplate what those thoughts meant. He claimed to have recorded all his radio broadcasts, and WOR radio taped at least some. No one knows to what extent Shepherd may have gone back over his old material, although he commented on occasion that he had heard some of his old broadcasts. From a number of times when he spoke about previous performances, we know that his focus of attention was nearly always on his current activity rather than the past. He said what he thought into his microphone, and it was for others to receive the message as he spoke it. That is what his listeners were for, but that initial listening did not satisfy many. They recorded so that they would not miss anything, so that they could go back and hear it again (thinking about what he meant, enjoying it all another time), and maybe pass the tapes on to others.

It is Shepherd's act of speaking his "thoughts on life and existence and the passing scene" into a microphone, and the taping and being able to study the contents, that make this book possible.

A NOTE ON TAPINGS AND TRANSCRIPTIONS

No one knows whether all of Shepherd's shows were taped. Many of the tapes that were done may no longer be accessible or even in existence. Nearly all of the shows available are from listeners who taped at the time of broadcasts. Recordings made from one's radio are called "airchecks." There are many hundreds—maybe thousands—of Shepherd broadcasts preserved as airchecks. What other radio performer—what other humorist, what other talker—has had hundreds of dedicated acolytes recording and preserving his word?

Back in the late fifties and early sixties, my parents and I recorded nearly a dozen reel-to-reel tapes of Jean Shepherd broadcasts—and I still have copies of them. In addition, through rebroadcasts and purchases from an ever-increasing supply of mostly fan recordings made off the radio as mine were, I've now heard hundreds of hours of ol' Shep.

The transcriptions of Jean Shepherd broadcasts are mostly by me and, I believe, quite accurate. I have tried to retain the flavor of Shepherd's broadcast talk. As he was a master of "the long form," I have sometimes included material that precedes or follows the main subject matter, when it helps indicate the feeling of flow, content, and transitions. I have tried to incorporate some of the hesitations and repetitions natural in all speech of this sort, but on occasion, I have omitted some of those momentary lapses in live broadcasts that would only be disturbing in a printed text.

For timeframe reference, the original broadcast dates of transcripts appear in the source notes at the back of the book. These frequently derive from notations listeners made at the time of taping; many dates are confirmed by additional recordings from separate sources, and some by internal evidence on the tape (such as a date or news story). For radio performances before the live audience at a then-popular club in Manhattan, "Limelight" follows the date, and "syndicated" refers to broadcasts distributed in syndication. (Thus, these would have been created earlier—some making use of shows originally broadcast.)

Although titles exist for nearly every Shepherd show now available for sale or trade, he seemed not to have given titles himself—the person who originally recorded the show often gave a descriptive title which stuck, or the show's distributor, if he thought the title inappropriate, might have retitled it. Because most shows cover a variety of areas, titles provide only clues to the matter at hand. Most were a delightful collage.

NARRATIVE AND THEMES

Not only were individual shows a collage, but Shepherd's fictional life consisted of story parts collaged from whatever crossed his mind—and whenever it happened to occur to him—put together with exuberance and joy. Much as Lawrence

Durrell, author of *The Alexandria Quartet*, would have done, writing that he wished he could do a plot description in the first chapter of a story, and then be free of narrative obligations for the rest of the book, Shepherd did not present his life in a chronological narration. This also holds true for other material. Thus, a subject spoken about at any time during Shepherd's career will be found where it best fits the context. For example, a 1998 Shepherd statement regarding the 1956 *I, Libertine* hoax belongs with the 1956 *I, Libertine* material. I have aligned the real and the fabricated autobiography of the life and mind of Jean Shepherd in a framework that pegs his stories and themes to that rough narrative of his life as we know it. The theme chapters appear where they seem to best illuminate that narrative. For example, though the material overlaps chronologically, there is some cause-and-effect relationship between Shepherd's later radio days, focused in one chapter, and his branching out into other areas of entertainment, described in the following chapter.

The quotes from people who knew or were influenced by Shepherd were obtained through personal interviews—face-to-face and by phone—and emails to me. The subjects are more fully described and acknowledged (with their respective dates of correspondence provided) in Appendix A: Annotated List of Interviewees. The real-life narrative presented here has gained invaluable depth through the contributions of those who were interviewed for this book.

The endnotes provide pieces of information which add parenthetically to the story and if inserted elsewhere would have interrupted the flow of the main ideas.

Eugene B. Bergmann
New York
Spring 2004

ACKNOWLEDGEMENTS

I am especially grateful to Matthew Callan, who, while an editor at Applause Books, discovered *Excelsior, You Fathead!* through the website www.flicklives.com and championed the book with Applause's former CEO John Cerullo. (They are both big Shepherd enthusiasts.) Matt, with his varied interests in radio, jazz, and other areas of popular culture, his considerable knowledge of Jean Shepherd material, and his editorial eye, proved a valuable asset. He did research at WGBH Boston's facilities on Shepherd's television work, and he contributed several observations about that material, and offered other comments for this book. I appreciate what Matthew Callan and John Cerullo have done—without them, this book might not have seen the light of day.

My cousin and good friend, Raymond B. Anderson, got me to think more clearly about the crucial early chapters of this book and prodded me into probing more deeply into what Jean Shepherd said over the years. Regarding the entire book, he asked the right questions, clarified my thinking about organization and content, and helped me eliminate innumerable stylistic gaffs. I take credit for any remaining gaffs.

Special thanks to my long-time good friend Margaret Cooper for contributing her keen editorial eye at the eleventh hour.

Thanks to the college classmate (whose name I no longer remember) who first told me about the fascinating guy talking late into the night on the radio. Thanks to my friend Bill Hartland, who reminded me that I had made reel-to-reel recordings of Shepherd in the 1950s, thus jump-starting my renewed interest when Shepherd died in 1999. Thanks to numerous people who responded favorably to my early comments on Shepherd, thus increasing my enthusiasm—and leading me to write the book I knew should be written.

Special thanks for many assists—including comments, information, and audio dubs—go to Jeff Beauchamp, Jim Clavin, Max Schmid, and Lowell Thelin. Most of my transcripts were made from Max Schmid's "Mass Backwards" WBAI radio broadcasts, cassettes available for sale by him, and from the extensive collection of broadcast recordings available from Jeff Beauchamp's "The Jean Shepherd Project." Jim Clavin, with his Jean Shepherd website, www.flicklives.com, provides access to all the sources of Shepherd material. Flicklives also contains enormous quantities of other information, articles, etc., by and about Shepherd—this book is indebted to the online archives of Flicklives. Pete Delany's voluminous files of Shepherd material found on www.flicklives.com frequently provided necessary references.

Interviews, correspondence, commentary, and personal stories about Jean Shepherd are acknowledged for the following people: Bob Alden, David Amram, Fred Barzyk, Dan Beach, Bob Brown, Ron Della Chiesa, Billy Collins, Ed Fancher, Barry Farber, Mort Fega, Jules Feiffer, Helen Gee, Murphy Grimes, Hugh M. Hefner, Martin Jackson, Larry Josephson, Paul Krassner, Dan List, Norman Mailer, Bill Pasternak, Brian Pearson, Herb Saltzman, Scott Schwartz, Randall Shepherd, Herb Squire, Laurie Squire, Jerry Tallmer, Oliver Trager, Dan Wakefield, John Wilcock, and Pete Wood.

Interviews were taped with permission; as with the mail correspondence, the subjects understood that their words were going to be used in this book. As in any conversation, themes sometimes mentioned early on in an interview came up later in the talk. Where this ran counter to the presentation of an idea, the quoted material has been arranged to make a logical sequence. In no case has this, or the editing out of superfluous material, altered an intended meaning.

Ray Carney, author of several books about filmmaker John Cassavetes, *Cassavetes on Cassavetes*; *Shadows*; and *John Cassavetes: The Adventure of Insecurity*, provided information about the important role Shepherd played in launching Cassavetes' career (see Chapter 6). Carney maintains a website, www.Cassavetes.com, with additional information.

Shepherd would sometimes comment that he had received a piece of information from one of his "spies." Spies for this book who provided information and comments toward an understanding of the art of Jean Shepherd are acknowledged in the endnotes and include: Rich Badagliacca, Kerr Lockhart, and Brian Pearson. Thanks to all the members of shep@yahoogroups.com who shared information, opinions, and enthusiasm with the group—and thus, unknowingly enrich this book. And thanks to all of the Shepherd fans who taped, preserved, and made his programs available to the world at large.

A number of people and organizations helped me obtain images for this book without charge. For this, thank you to the following. Raymond B. Anderson took the author photo and provided it. Dan Beach provided his photo of Jean Shepherd, Leigh Brown, and Fred Barzyk. Bill Griffith provided his Zippy the Pinhead tribute to Shepherd. Donald A. Hamburg obtained permission from the Shel Silverstein estate to use the *Look, Charlie* playbill cover and the Shepherd LP cover drawing. Andy Paley gave permission to reproduce from his collection the Al Parker photo of Shepherd playing the jew's harp. Greg Potempkin provided his father Sol's photo of Shepherd in the Amazon. Random House, Inc. gave permission to reproduce the dedication page of the Doubleday edition of Shepherd's book, *A Fistful of Fig Newtons*. Random House registered "no objection" for the Ballantine Books cover of *I, Libertine*, and for the flyer advertising the book. Laurie and Herb Squire provided their photo of Shepherd, Bob Elliot, and Ray Goulding. WGBH Boston gave permission to reproduce the photo of Shepherd in his white hard hat. Special thanks to David Schmit of *Playboy* for helping make the connection for my interview with Hugh Hefner, and also for his persistence in helping me obtain *Playboy*'s multiple portrait of Shepherd, which *Playboy* provided without charge. Thank you to Jim Clavin, who provided higher resolutions than I had been able to obtain for many of the images used in the book.

Other images were paid for. The sources for several images were either defunct or beyond efforts made to contact them, or the images fall within the category of fair use, such as flyers. For those organizations that either refused permission or required fees that were outrageously beyond reach—thanks for nothing.

Thanks to Allison, Evan, and Drew—my wife and sons—who have endured the last four years of my obsession with Jean Shepherd. It ain't over yet.

Mainly, of course, we all have to thank Jean Shepherd, who taught us to say EXCELSIOR!

INTRODUCTION

[Jean Shepherd's voice, outrageously dramatic and ironic, accompanied by bombastic orchestral music.] Undaunted, slightly ridiculous, unbelievably fatheaded—and yet at the same time curiously noble—as he fights forward... Mankind, we salute you![2]

GEE! THE GUY WHO WROTE THE MOVIE *A CHRISTMAS STORY*?

A Christmas Story!—that movie we watch every year at Christmastime about the kid who wants a Red Ryder BB gun and nearly shoots his eye out? Based on his stories? And he created the movie? That's his voice narrating it? And he wrote other great stuff, too? Wow! What else did this guy do?

Well, he did many things. Jean Shepherd produced entertaining and memorable work in many media. He was the originator and finest master of "talk radio."[i] (This book will demonstrate it.) He wrote prolifically—dozens of stories and articles for *Playboy* and other publications, many collected in books that remain in print and bring joy and laughter to thousands. He created several television dramas and several original television series, including *Jean Shepherd's America*. Although The Great American Novel may only be an elusive grail, the latter may arguably be The Great American Television Documentary. He made comedy LP albums and performed live for scores of thousands of adoring fans at Carnegie Hall, Town Hall, and on college campuses all around the United States. More than any of his contemporaries, he remains a vibrant influence on the thinking and psyches of those who knew his voice in the night.

JEAN SHEPHERD—THE VOICE-IN-THE-NIGHT GENIUS

Jean Shepherd (July 26, 1921–October 16, 1999)[3] was a genius, a unique master of talk and sound on the radio. What did he do that created a fine art out of the humble medium of radio? How was he different—and superior—to the subsequent, widely popular performers of talk radio, who reach audiences of millions with their call-in formats and shock tactics? What was the nature of Jean Shepherd's complex art and why did he abandon radio and his not quite as vast, but surely more devoted, listeners? Although he also created works of high quality in other media, what combination of historical, technological, cultural, financial, and personal factors caused this radio loss—a tragedy not only for America's cultural life, but, indeed, for Shepherd himself?

Although radio had some music, a few interesting dramas, a few well-done comedy shows, and some little-kid adventures that lasted into the 1950s, by the time Jean Shepherd came on the scene,[ii] the golden age of radio as a dominant force in American life had nearly ended. Then he arrived, telling his stories and riffing his themes on the radio between the mid-1950s and 1977, speaking to each listener as no one else in any medium had ever spoken to me or you or anyone else—as a single, separate, intelligent being. Everybody else merely *performed*—for a mass, undifferentiated audience, and we didn't believe a word of it. For Jean Shepherd listeners, each person out there in the dark was that one and only one engaged with him in the illusion of an intellectual interaction—a dialogue. Listeners felt they were members of a small band—a secret society, an in-group—of those who *knew*, who *understood*. Jean Shepherd was a real, reliable, giving-it-to-us-from-the-depths voice in the night, who, by exploring his own life and sensibility in the process of living, entered the listener's own inner world by entertaining the finer parts of his mind and emotions.

There was the sense that this highly knowledgeable, perceptive person was discussing things with you as an equal. If he disparaged people for their ignorance, it was usually those in the control room. If some young listener hadn't followed his instructions in contacting him, or some such, that kid was put down unceremoniously and trampled on, but this was rare—Shepherd usually restrained himself. That there was a Shepherd who had to be restrained—and kept hidden from the public eye when possible—was a fact most Shepherd fans did not know in his lifetime and wouldn't have wanted to know. The Shepherd they knew was no angel, but he was the good old playful Shep, nevertheless.

> I feel very playful tonight. So be careful. Can you tell it? This is—this is, believe me—for the benefit of those of you who don't know what this is all about—this is my *dangerous* phase. This is a very dangerous time, when I'm feeling like this. [Pause.] I'm as likely as not to get fired before midnight— when I get in this mood. It only happens, I'd say, once every six weeks. So get your friends on the phone. And say, "Shepherd's playful tonight. He's going to get fired before midnight."[4]

As a creator, Shepherd fought battles all his life—and many of them he did not win to his satisfaction. He was fired several times for talking too much during his programs (and not playing enough music). He battled radio administrators who didn't understand him and did not give him enough respect. He battled the sponsors (fights that he usually picked himself) and his station's commercial-time salesmen, who neither understood him nor liked how he demeaned their clients on the air. He felt disadvantaged by the ads, which, proliferating in later years, disrupted his style. He battled his engineers, most of whom gave him no attention or respect, and who, in his eyes, inadequately engineered his shows.

He battled television, which stole his audience, undermined radio (his prime medium), and failed to provide him with recognition and the success he deserved within it. He battled most of his coworkers and business associates on innumerable issues he found important—somehow they did not always agree with him. He battled inadequacies in his fellow Americans, who failed to fully comprehend and appreciate his talent (except in that composite Shepherd work, the movie *A Christmas Story*).

He battled some flaw within himself—a persistent negativity—that helped prevent his even greater success. His flaw, possibly not a debilitating factor in many people, was part of the Shepherd enigma. Clearly Shepherd was not a simple person—in fact he was not even just one person.

Herb Saltzman noted that, "You had to call him Shep. He loved that. That was his term for himself." Jean Parker Shepherd frequently used Parker as his last name as a cover for avoiding detection in public—his short story persona was Ralph Wesley Parker. But name changes were superficial. To many of his radio listeners, Shepherd was simply referred to as Shep. But this Shep was at least three people.

First there was a real Jean Parker Shepherd that an ideal biography would uncover in an ideal world—an accurate, historical Jean Shepherd, not found in this book or anywhere, in part because throughout his professional life he hid this truth and confounded the attempts of others to discover it. Therefore, this is not a straight biography of Jean Shepherd. Yet biography is only a grasping at an entertaining and probable hunch—especially unreliable if combined with an attempt to analyze a creator through comparison with the creator's work. Even more perilous when trying to understand the slippery relationship between truth and fiction, as they interweave in what Shepherd gave as his life story. Some biographical information is included for comparison and contrast. The comparisons are interesting and the contrasts can be devastating.

Along with that first, biographically based Shepherd, the second and third Sheps, crafted by Jean Shepherd, artist and fabulist, are ones you will find and know in *Excelsior, You Fathead!* The second Shep persona was the storyteller who artfully conflated bits of the true Shepherd into the concocted biography of his life ("I was this kid, see..."). The third was the Shep who spoke on the radio, the perceived here-and-now Shep, whom his listeners knew, giving real ideas and perceptions through his on-air persona.

A number of people who had close personal and professional contact with Shepherd contribute their comments and memories here of what the real Jean Shepherd was like for them. Some of this experience and knowledge presents a far different person from the one people familiar with his art probably expect. Unexpected and only suggested through faint clues in Shepherd's work. It is an image far less pleasant. Far darker. Far sadder. Not a pretty picture. Not one fans might want to know and accept. As with a book, so with the artist—don't judge either by its cover. One hopes that the art of the artist is the more important and longer lasting.

JEAN SHEPHERD—RADIO GENIUS

Other than some very short programs in various time slots,[iii] Jean Shepherd's earliest New York nightly broadcasts ranged deep into the early hours in extemporaneous, and thus unpredictable, forays into streams of consciousness. Shepherd gave us hundreds of finely nuanced, strikingly detailed stories that we never doubted were true—and he devoted even more of his on-air time to elaborating the range of his perceptions with insight and metaphor.

Entertainer, observer of quirky humanity, commentator on the world around us, extremely funny guy, humorist who understood what foible-filled mortals we are. Shepherd's broadcasts encompassed many themes, and his talks can be categorized in a variety of ways. He segued from one topic to another, blending ideas to such an extent that many times one can't easily pin down a particular riff. He had endless variations on his themes, repeating himself less than one might expect in such a long career. There was a continual elaboration and enrichment with new detail, a continuing, entertaining funniness as well as wit, and his listeners found intellectual pleasures in apprehending his mind at work.

Later, he broadcast Saturday mornings, Saturday night live at the Limelight café, and for over sixteen years, in forty-five-minute, week-nightly soundings of his inexhaustible fund of stories, anecdotes, and commentary.

Each of his broadcasts, either with one theme or with many interwoven themes, was part of a complex collage that, when placed within a gigantic frame, acts as a self-contained fragment participating in the overall picture of what Jean Shepherd was. Because only a portion remains of his thousands of broadcasts, and only a portion of those remaining could be contained in a book, the mosaic has white spaces. If the pieces have been well chosen, the resulting collage can stand for the whole.

Shepherd talked about nearly all possible subjects and had an opinion on all of them. Whatever the topic at hand, his style was never dull. Gerald Nachman's *Seriously Funny*, a study of over two dozen "Rebel Comedians of the 1950s and 1960s," describes Shepherd on the air: "The bemused voice, whether chortling slyly or in full maniacal cry, was by turns self-mocking, seductive, manic, querulous, and reflective. There were digressions, footnotes, parenthetical jokes, random observations, and stories within stories, augmented by an occasional sound effect or snatch of music."[5]

Because he was so enthusiastically taken to heart by his listeners when he spoke highly, seriously, and at great length—or even mockingly—of those products and services he cared about, his listeners would throng to stores to buy them. Herb Saltzman, his radio general manager at WOR, says that Shepherd's creative ad-libbing with jingles and promotional copy was a seminal force in establishing Miller High Life beer in the eastern half of the country (Saltzman had brought the beer to New York in his earlier capacity as the station's merchandising manager); and Bob Alden, one of the radio time salesmen, referring to Shepherd's energetic talk on behalf of an audio components store, describes seeing "a steady parade of people coming in to buy what he was talking about" the following day. With this kind of emotional attachment from his listeners, what heights would Jean Shepherd have reached in the mass media on a national scale, given the all-pervasive satellite, syndication, and internet distribution that broadcasts lesser talents today?

SHEPHERD'S CAREER AS AN ARTISTIC WHOLE IN CHAPTERS

This book is the only extensive account of Jean Shepherd's creative career, and as such, it works toward several related ends. It documents and describes what he produced in many media, and it is an appreciation and analysis of what he accomplished. And, importantly, it attempts to impart to the reader some measure of the great pleasure Shepherd's art gave to his audiences.

Using transcriptions of Jean Shepherd radio broadcasts and material from other media, I describe his artistic career as a whole in an attempt to grasp the unique artifice of his constructed art and persona in a biographical framework, using the range of his stories, ideas, observations, and themes in chapters arranged within that chronology.

Part I illustrates Shepherd's formative years (as he chose to present them to us, through what he would have the listener believe was merely his remembering of them). He talked about his childhood in the Midwest—the world of childhood he remembered and invented in such rich detail—wonderful, and yet overlaid with the struggles, crises, and disillusionment he goaded us into recognizing as parts of every life. His army life was full of humorous situations, sometimes with the threatening consequences inherent in adult life. His early radio days were fraught with the tribulations of apprenticeship. Always, he spoke with humor, often with simultaneously discordant effect.

Part II describes Shepherd's continued interest in the nature of humor and the history of radio—his roots—and the intensity of observation that he brought to his art. Observation that could reveal the significance of what we might otherwise dismiss as unimportant minutia, much like looking at a drop of pond water in a microscope and finding it teeming with life—fascinating to observe because of the shape and movement revealed, some specks of which might keep you well or make you awfully sick. Here was the foundation—the heritage and endowment—he used to such forceful and entertaining effect throughout his career.

Part III illustrates the first great burgeoning of his power as he began his New York radio broadcasts—the free-form improvisational compositions of jazz in words. The creative force of jazz dominated his early style as he explored for himself, and his listeners, the wide world open to him. The power and effectiveness of his intimate style and commentary led some to refer to his early audience as an underground cult of Night People—with whom Shepherd concocted one of the great literary hoaxes of our time.

Part IV. How did Jean Shepherd create this entrancing concoction that kept generations of listeners awake way past their bedtimes, with radios glued to their ears? On the radio, he had only sounds and words—tools that he used to almost magical effect.

Part V. Beyond the stories, to what purpose did he use radio? This section delves into his dichotomous view of his world (cynical/joyous, pessimistic/life affirming), his wide-ranging observations, his critique of America, his often-confrontational attitude toward others, and his encounters with the moneychangers in the temple of his art.

Part VI. The pursuit of greater respect, renown, dough, and additional outlets for his art produced a broadening of his professional endeavors (an effort begun even in the earlier parts of his career), including a wide range of writing, such as the astonishing *I, Libertine* literary hoax, and his "novel," *In God We Trust: All Others Pay Cash*. He wrote articles for many diverse publications, extensively for *Car and Driver*, and short stories for *Playboy*, which honored him with its annual best humor award four times.

Most prominently for many of his fans, Shepherd continued talking on the radio throughout the 1960s and up to 1977, mostly in forty-five-minute nightly excursions into his world, the form becoming tighter, the level of artistry and enjoyment remaining exceedingly high. Gems from this period include a Shepherd "lesson" regarding human limits illustrated with forays into Mark Twain and Morse code and, in a radio essay demonstrating his concerns for American society as well as his powers of observation, his eulogy occasioned by the assassination of President John F. Kennedy.

In other media, Shepherd made recordings, created several television dramas and series including what may be the Great American TV Documentary, *Jean Shepherd's America*, and made movies based on his published fiction, the best known of which is the popular film of the kid who nearly shoots his eye out with his BB-gun present, *A Christmas Story*.

Part VII. The final chapter of a unique career is a festive wake—a celebration, told to a funky jug-band tune, a summation of artistic success, disappointment, personal failure, and an enigma. By the time of his death in 1999, Jean Shepherd had created works still visited by thousands through radio rebroadcasts, recorded broadcasts on cassettes and CDs, his films and television, his writings, radio and written tributes, an email group, and on web sites.

Toward what great unachievable goal did Jean Shepherd's creative life point? Understanding Jean Shepherd's career reveals the all-too-common tragedy of the innovative artist not sufficiently appreciated in his time—of a creator who knew how good he was, and who repudiated his most glorious creations toward the end of his life. As the title of one of his records put it, *Will Failure Spoil Jean Shepherd?*

ME AND SHEP

This is not a coldly concocted project. It is a book written by a specific individual who has a special relationship with Jean Shepherd—as do tens of thousands of other listeners. I provide as much information as seems appropriate—but I also interpret—and all interpretation has elements of taste, biases, and feelings. Although most of the book is in third person, the personal "I" sometimes appears. Considering the kind of special one-to-one relationship that Jean Shepherd's unique radio persona inspires, I expect that he would have wanted no less.

I knew Jean Parker Shepherd. I like to think I still do. We had these deep conversations throughout the entire time I festered as a youth on the east side of New York City. Actually, I didn't fester, but only sometimes thought I did because ol' Shep used to claim that *he* festered as a kid. Shep festered on the South Side of Chicago, but the eastern side of New York City's five boroughs where I grew up is just a place called Queens.

As a kid in the higher reaches of grammar school and early high school, I had the good fortune, along with countless others, to encounter *Mad* comics, which opened a kid's eyes by making fun of our culture's assumptions, clichés, fads, fancies, and popular arts—just at an age when a kid first begins to realize (but has not yet fully articulated) that the world constructed by parents and other adults has inconsistencies. In college, I found Jean Shepherd. There he was on the radio entertaining and expanding my mind. He was there as an older, wiser brother—a mentor, whose way of thinking affects me still. Most gratifyingly, I find that what he had to say remains as thought provoking and entertaining to me now as it was when I was a feckless youngster (no, I was not at all "feckless,"—that's just another Shepherdism to describe his own childhood). Jean Shepherd is a gadfly and humorist for all ages. To quote a listener, "He makes us think about stuff."

Let me tell you about the first real conversation we had. It must have been in late 1956 or early 1957. I called the station (WOR AM and FM) and asked to speak to him. People did that—it was an extension of what already seemed to be a dialogue. He would talk to listeners off-air during long newsbreaks. Finally, there he was on the other end of the line. I was nervous. I have no idea what he or I said, except I know that my end was shaky and inconsequential. His end was polite. Period.

On the second occasion, we spoke face to face, and I managed to keep up my end. It was at a gathering later referred to as "The Marboro Episode." Marboro was a bookstore chain in New York City. Shepherd had suggested that his listeners meet him at one of the Midtown branches. I think that as nonbuyers, we were cluttering up the premises, and after a while, we were asked to leave. Some of us regrouped with him on the balcony of the nearby Horn and Hardart Automat. I boldly approached him, pen and paperback copy of his book, *I, Libertine* in hand. The conversation in its entirety went something like this:

"Would you sign this for me, please?"

"Sure."

I still have the deckle-edged, black-and-white photo that I took. He is signing my book, which I treasure. On the back of the photo, I had written the date of the episode, April 8, 1957.

Although in fact we spoke only those two times, it had always seemed that he was speaking directly to me during all his broadcasts. There was that sense of intimacy. We had so many "conversations," from the deepest mental explorations to the joys of trivia—a true meeting of minds. It seemed as though he and I would talk for hours at night, but in these discussions, I never got a word in edgewise. He did all the talking—he really knew how to dominate a monologue. He was in studioland, and I was listening to him out there in radioland on my maroon plastic Zenith AM/FM radio with the big simulated gold dial.

After the early 1960s, we lost touch. Maybe it was partly my fault, partly his. All I know for sure is that we both had changed. We'll get into that later. Recently I've gotten to know him a lot better, beginning when I read his obituary in the *New York Times*, and realized that I'd lost an old friend. It was then that I recognized how much he had meant to me—and means now. And how important his art is to American culture.

ENIGMA AND BRICKBATS

> WOR is making available instant Jean Shepherd pills. That's
> right, and they'll be sold through the John Gambling Show in
> the morning. Yeah. And the McCanns will talk about it after
> the frozen asparagus moment. Just before the Campbell's Soup
> instant. Yeah. All you do is take this pill and all of a sudden,
> your eyes start lighting up and your talons start growing and
> man, you *swing*.
>
> Instant Jean Shepherd. Of course, be careful, there's a ter-
> rible letdown. It always happens to *me*. I mean, you don't
> think that I'm Jean Shepherd *all* the time, do you? Oh no.
> Ohhh, by George, you oughta see who I am sometimes![6]

The title of the notes on the jacket for Shepherd's first comedy
LP, though obviously written to fit the bizarre text by Shel
Silverstein, became more truth than may have originally been
intended: "Jean Shepherd—the Man, the Myth, the Enigma."[7]

Because of what Jean Shepherd created on the radio and in
other media, many thousands of fans saw him as hero, mentor,
and role model for creative urges and personal integrity. In the
high quality of his work, the joy he provided, and in the ways
about perceiving the world that he inspired and nurtured, Jean
Shepherd was worthy of such ardor. Barry Farber says that Jean
Shepherd was the same in real life as he was before the microphone.

It was too easy for his listeners to assume that this good old friendly Shep was just a regular guy. Interviews and other research reveal a more complex picture. Jean Parker Shepherd, as with so many artists of all types and eras, "was at once brilliant, enigmatic, creative...and boorish; he was always fascinating."[8] So remembers Dan Beach, who met Shepherd in 1959, worked with him as production coordinator on several of his television projects, and remained a friend for over forty years. With a disturbing consistency, a less appealing persona emerges from the biography Jean Shepherd did his best to conceal.

Memories from those who had personal contact with him confirm many of Shepherd's positive qualities. But memories fade, details consciously or unconsciously alter, and information from informants can be difficult to assess. One might think a real or imagined harm influenced negative comments, or there might have been some personal vendetta leading to false and malicious responses. Yet, this less appealing image came not from individuals who experienced only one side of Jean Shepherd. A pattern emerged from comments by people in different fields, none of whom knew one another. Pieces from this darker pattern have not been diluted or expurgated; they are transcribed throughout the book. Added to the mosaic of Shepherd's art, they combine into an inescapable enigma.

Some who love Shepherd's work, and find that it had a strong positive influence on their lives, express an understandable viewpoint: they don't want knowledge of the negatives of real life to decrease their enjoyment of the art. A creator's life and the art are two separate things in their minds.

This may be true. And yet the artistic persona of Jean Shepherd was such a special creation, one that relied in great part on the feeling of verisimilitude to the real Shepherd, one that insisted it had some real inkling into the human psyche, that some reckoning of the "truth" would seem called for, even if "truth" is too strong a word and is sometimes unpleasant. Ignorance may be bliss, but children's naiveté evolving to a more realistic and complete knowledge is a sequence that does not offer regression. Innocence is ever so pleasant, but leaving Eden for a more unsettling understanding is part of the tragedy and triumph of being a fully human adult. Shepherd insisted on it. He urged listeners to observe and accept even the painful:

> **I mean, anyone who looks at life with a cold, unprejudiced agate eye of truth must realize that life is basically in *extremely* bad taste.[iv]**

He insisted that we face the truth with that agate eye:

> Something that bothers me is to find a man who—who will walk away from things which are going on because he doesn't like them. This is—this is wrong—you should stand and look... And if you do stand off and look enough you'll begin to have this great love of it all, which is an undeniable thing.

"Love of it all" may be too strong. Jean Shepherd urged listeners to be strong and clear eyed. What one sees in him is the greatness of art and a darker, deeper human story about a major creator of our time. Would knowing some of Shepherd's private life adversely color enjoyment of his work? Knowledge is worth a little pain. Maybe knowing enhances by adding another color to the spectrum of our understanding of life in general and Jean Shepherd in particular—increasing, through wonder and awe, our appreciation of what he accomplished. To use Shepherd's favorite philosophical entreaty, a metaphor taken from baseball, the sport he loved above all others, keep your knees loose—and be ready to dive into the hole.

FOIBLES: THE REAL JEAN SHEPHERD

[Spoken over the opening theme, in a mock-dramatic imitation of the 1950s *The Shadow* radio adventure.] Yes, the secret powers which I have been given by a visitor from another planet have enabled me to hold you hypnotically night after night, to cloud your reason, to befog—to continually becloud your mind so you don't know which end is up.[9]

According to Dan Beach, who knew Shepherd professionally and as a friend for decades, "Trying to make a point with Shep was useless; he entertained no ideas other than his own."[10] From this report and similar comments from others who knew him, it appears that Jean Shepherd, in his life as in his art, was a dedicated monologist. How fortunate for him and for his radio audience that his life in art found outlet in the one-way communication tool of a microphone. (In his live broadcast performances in the 1960s from the Limelight café, any unasked-for attempt at interaction from the audience was met with a harsh rebuke.) With his microphone, Shepherd shut off all but the input he chose to allow. With it, he controlled the expression of his inner life and the materials of his real and invented biography—his feelings, prejudices, beliefs, and his view of the world.

Jean was probably born some time in July, between 1921 and maybe 1926—the reality was private. According to his death certificate, he was born in Chicago on July 26, 1921.[v] He grew

up on "the South Side of Chicago" and on Cleveland Street in
Hammond, Indiana. Maybe as a kid, he had friends named
Flick, Bruner, Schwartz, and so on.[vi] Although he told hundreds
of stories about his kidhood, the extent to which the tales were
true to the "real" Jean Shepherd is difficult to discern. His adolescence is almost a blank record. He spent time in the Army
Signal Corps during World War II, and a few semesters in college.

He got out of the small-town, small-minded, intellectually
limited world of the midwestern mill town. He found (nearly)
free rein in radio in smaller cities; jobs that eventually led to the
big time—New York City—where he did a night-long radio program. He wrote articles and books, made records, did live performances, created several television series and movies, and
acted in plays. He was an acknowledged master of the arcane art
of *Kopfspielen*.

He lived in various locations in and around the New York
City area and was married several times, once to an actress and,
finally and most enduringly, to his producer. He was a man of the
world—with a taste for exotic cars, fine food, travel, and friends
in the arts.

He retired to a small island off the coast of Florida. On
October 16, 1999, at 78, he died.[11] He kept his private life as private as he could. The *New York Times* obit referred to him as a
raconteur and wit and quoted his closest friend of his final years
as saying he had no survivors. His two children subsequently
indicated that they were survivors.[12]

Jean Shepherd had a persona that listeners felt they knew very
well indeed, but they were wrong: "The factual record shows
that Shep..." "But his kid brother in later years said..." "People
who knew him said that..." "Shep tells us on the radio that...and
he also tells us that..." The real Jean Shepherd? Occasionally he
took on (only for a few moments) the persona of one of his created characters, with appropriate voice, such as the effeminate
Mr. Chucky, and the "little old lady" who frequently wrote in
complaining about his broadcasts. When reading little strange-
but-true news items, he became a self-important Walter
Winchell–type character named Grubbage. Sometimes he just
introduced himself with a fictitious name and then went on as
himself:

Grubbage here.
I'm friendly Fred.

This is Uncle Fred.

This is Skeezix.

This is Clark Smathers.

This is Uncle Wiggly.

My name is Harold Everyman.

Harold Monolith here, rising like a single block of
granite.

Hello gang, this is King Kong here.

This is old Ben Watanabee here, yowsa, yowsa, yowsa.

This is Allie Khan, and we'll be back again immediately
after 14,022 hours have passed. And we'll be back
tomorrow at five minutes past nine for the insignificant
hour. For those of you who love impedimenta and
effluvia, stay tuned for—speaking of effluvia—for Ed
Pedit who follows in just a moment. He speaks very
fluent effluvia.

In a program titled "Fake Shepherds," Shepherd read from a
Rutgers University article about someone who impersonated
him at a personal appearance:

> I might as well tell you the truth about this thing. There is
> no Jean Shepherd. Jean Shepherd is a composite name. It's an
> entertainment concept, and there's actually a *stable* of Jean
> Shepherds. I am the fourth one. I work Mondays and
> Wednesdays and the other Shepherds work Tuesday. There's
> one who works—I never met the one who works on
> Thursdays. Tall skinny guy. And there are six Jean Shepherds
> that have been beating out there in the bushes and playing col-
> leges.
>
> Now you see what I'm telling you? [Talking to someone in
> the control room.] I just tell you the truth—and do you buy it?
> No. Okay, that's all I can say. I mean, the truth hurts.[13]

> I suppose a lot of you people are wondering why I'm
> talking like this. [Talking about people who do good, skillful
> jobs substituting for others.] Well, I'm not actually Jean
> Shepherd. I'm a guy who wrote him a letter. I told him I did a
> great Jean Shepherd imitation. And I've been doing the show
> for the last three nights. He's coming back tomorrow night. It's
> the first time I've been on radio. There's nothing to it.[14]

Jean Shepherd told the story of his life and mind on radio, in writing, television, and movies. Only part of it was true to fact—all of it was true to the artistic construct he wanted listeners to perceive as the persona "Jean Shepherd." There was a rock bed of verisimilitude consisting of incidents and events from his real life—he gave what could be simply and easily believed, always with a profuse richness of minute, idiosyncratic detail that drew listeners in and convinced them that his tales were nothing less than the truth. One always believed Shep. He told it so believably, so intimately, that he seemed to bare his life, soul, and beliefs to each of us alone. Shep was our best friend and confidant in the quarter-to-three AM openness and intimacy of a bar or a dorm.

His stories contained stuff we knew was true, or easily verified, that melded seamlessly into each increment toward the unlikely and unbelievable. We did not know where to draw the line. We did not know there was a place for a line. We did not know that a line had any need to be thought about. Worst of all—no, best of all—there was no identifiable borderland where a theoretical line might accurately have been drawn. A "line" was too rigid a metaphor for trying to separate the meat from the bread in Shepherd's *chef-d'oeuvre* meatloaf.

What about his "autobiography"? As Henry Miller once told a friend, "I had a thousand faces, all of them genuine."[15] In *Lying: A Metaphorical Memoir*, Lauren Slater wrote, "This is my tale, and I have written it over and over again, and, depending on my mood and my auras, the story always seems to change, and yet it always seems true."[16] Will the real Jean Shepherd please stand up? The true story of Jean Shepherd, creator, is not the chronology of his life, but consists of what he said in more or less spontaneous flight—a sound collage constructed across decades—which is to say, the life of his mind as artist. In *Design and Truth in Autobiography*, Roy Pascal says: "In the novel, everything is tightly bound, everything is closely related to the theme. Now this is true in part in autobiography. Henry James repeatedly speaks of everything in his life 'signifying,' bringing some accretion of understanding and insight, a continuous, almost imperceptible assimilation."[17]

Jean Shepherd's stories of his childhood always signified, but as "truth" they were especially suspect. How truthful were the details of his anecdotes and philosophical homilies? Did he make most of it up just to illustrate some life lesson—just to tell a story? Was *Field and Stream* really a great literary influence on him, as he once claimed? Or had he transformed and amplified some hint from his past into a parable to illustrate that any vicarious tale that takes one away from one's drab everyday life, providing much-needed fantasy, becomes indeed, an important part of dealing with one's world?

Shepherd told fables for our time. He was a weaver of tales and parables, ones that may or may not have been partly true to fact. Was his radio material more likely to be true than his written work? Were his earlier short anecdotes more likely to have been true than the later material, when maybe he'd used up so much of his biography that he *had* to make up more? Given that his observations and commentaries gave so many clues for ferreting out the bogus in all of life, it is indeed an irony that he manipulated the facts of his *own* artist's life. His real life was none of our business—our business, and his, was his *art*.

Although one might presume that he never articulated a belief he did not actually hold, one might take cognizance of some contradictions—maybe the belief he articulated at any one time more suited his current monologue; maybe he forgot what he had earlier believed; or, over time, maybe he changed his mind. One example is his comment from a broadcast that he did not much follow the funnies; at another time (a *Village Voice* article) he said that his moral outlook was significantly influenced by such funnies as *Little Orphan Annie*.

"I'LL NEVER FORGET..."

> I'll never forget one time, I'm a kid about—oh, I must have been in about in the eighth grade. [Pause.] In fact, I know it was eighth grade because I remember the teacher who read this story to us.[18]

That "I'll never forget" was a favorite ploy of Shepherd's to convince us it's true, combined here with another technique for convincing us of the truth—he would often hesitate as though unsure of a detail, and then suddenly "remember"—thus in his narration confirming the detail for himself, and so very artfully confirming for us its veracity.

What was the nature of Jean Shepherd's memory? He conjured up a profusion of details into such a reality—he "remembered" so much—that listeners should logically ask how so much could happen to one person. Likely, much of the remembering was not of specific incidents, but of the ways life happens

to all of us—the truly seeing and being able to report back per-
ceptively and inventively, the being alive to experience—the
"signifying" that Henry James spoke of and Ernest Hemingway
worked so hard to put in his work.

When one speaks of the "truth" in Shepherd, one deals with
at least three kinds of lies.[vii] Type A was fictional art told as
truth. Type B was Shep denying a truth or creating a lie to con-
found those who would confuse his art with his biography.
These first two were the province of Jean Shepherd as artist.
Type C was the bald-faced lie Shepherd told about himself for no
apparent reason other than that it might better fit the image that
he wanted to project, such as whether he graduated from college, when he was in the army, and whether he ever had children. This type-C bald-faced lie is the province of a
psycho-biographer, who might discover to what extent type-C
lies might become an inseparable component with types A and
B. It's one of those conundrums that some biographers thrive on
and give the rest of us migraines.

What was "truth," what was hyperbole, what was downright
fabrication? Kid brother Randy—yes, he had a kid brother,
Randy. Friend Flick—yes, there is a photo of Flick's Tap and a
photo of Flick in Shepherd's high school yearbook. Hohman,
Indiana—we know he lived in Hammond, not too far from
Hohman Avenue. Yes, he really lived on Cleveland Street.[19] And
what more perfect concoction for the ironic workings of his
mind than his claim that his primary education had been at a
school named for Warren G. Harding, someone regarded by his-
torians as one of the more inconsequential of our presidents? As
he put it in his 1985 talk to a ham radio convention, "We did not
realize this, at the age of twelve—we were going to a school
named after the worst president in history." Surely the name of
this school was one more dry, fictional joke on the theme of the
apparently powerful/actually ineffective—until one sees the
photo of the sign in front of an otherwise undistinguished two-
story building in Hammond: "Harding Elementary School." We
have been confounded by fact.

He told it as though it were true. We believed it, yet in his
book disclaimers, and in later years, he said it was all made up.
Reports say that he hid many important facts of his life even
from his wife. Did he dislike having people delve into his personal life? Was he just being ornery in denying the *truth*? Did he
feel it was more of an art if it were all made up? Was it a mix that
can only be evaluated as *creative*?

In a talk at Fairleigh Dickinson University in 1967, Shepherd said that "Flick, Schwartz, and Brunner were real people...there are three characters that run through—you see I work on the air as a short story writer—literally. I take people out of my past or I put them and use them as composite characters just as any good writer would. You don't write out of a vacuum. And Flick, Schwartz, and Brunner are real people. I used real names, but they're not really *exactly* like they are in the stories. I've taken other—naturally, I've taken other characteristics." This seems to be a straightforward and reasonable description of the creative process—one contradicted by Shepherd in other interviews, when he claimed that those same people never existed.

Barry Farber, who shared an office at WOR with Shepherd and became his friend, interviewed him on the air on June 26, 1975. Describing his stories as allegories, Shepherd said, "In America they think they're memories about boyhood and they never are. None of these stories, by the way, are based on any of my own memories. None of them are based on any—the families are all—I've created a mythical family—like—like Faulkner created a mythical county."

The story has it that when *In God We Trust: All Others Pay Cash*, Shepherd's strung-together compilation of seemingly true childhood stories,[20] appeared on the *New York Times* bestseller list, he called the *Times* and insisted that they switch it from the nonfiction to the fiction category. The listing in either category remains elusive, but the easy confusion between truth and fiction remains the issue.

Often, in the middle of some apparent hyperbole, Shepherd exclaimed, "This is the truth, I'm not exaggerating." Often his listeners had good reason to question the literal veracity of his word—especially within the context of fantastic or hard-to-believe details. At other times he knew nobody was going to believe the details—for instance, when he described his Warren G. Harding grammar school as being made out of balsa wood and silly putty. Ah, yes, what is "truth"? Did we settle that one in our freshman or sophomore year?

What can we know about someone who constantly, in public, invented his past and present life, who constantly told stories—fictions about his life? Shepherd's disclaimer in his 1972 book, *The Ferrari in the Bedroom*, possibly giving us the answer as forthrightly as he cared to at the time, says that "Large parts of the following are fiction; other parts based on fact. Still others are pure mythology. Some characters are real; others are figments of a harassed imagination. To the real, I apologize. To the others, the back of my hand."[21]

Shepherd was not the only monologist ever to sit at a table and talk about himself—and make a living at it. Others followed this public journey into self-absorption and analysis. For example, Spalding Gray, twenty years younger, sat before audiences performing his theater pieces. His performances, according to an obituary, were "closely observed autobiography, performed in a style that alternated between conspiratorial whispers and antic screams as he roamed through topics large and small."[22] An appreciation of him comments, "He was not above bending the sequences of events so that his life would, in the retelling, conform to the narrative structure he was building."[23] Spalding Gray's refashioning of his autobiography certainly bears resemblance to what Shepherd began doing on the radio several decades before. Both of them shared a pattern used by other artists in their own ways: refashioning of their autobiographies to suit artistic purposes.

The following reference in *The American Humorist: Conscience of the 20th Century,* by Norris W. Yates (1964), suggests a close-to-home precedent for Shepherd, someone who combined fact with large portions of fiction. It refers to Kin Hubbard of Brown County, Indiana (active 1904–1930). Every year from 1906 until 1930, Hubbard published volumes about a character he had created named Abe: "Hubbard's version of Brown County was actually a composite of the real Brown County, which lies in south central Indiana, and of Bellefontaine, Ohio. Certain names of buildings, such as Melodeon Hall, and many of the names of Abe's acquaintances, usually altered in part, were based on actual buildings and names in Bellefontaine."

Of course, this is common. Literature is filled with novels using parts of the author's real life more or less transformed into the fiction. Ernest Hemingway and Henry Miller are two prominent American examples. Far less frequently encountered was Shepherd's mode of action—he fabricated a fiction with such illusions of verisimilitude that he convinced us of its autobiographical truth. Some autobiography! Like Escher's drawing of an artist's hand in the act of drawing itself.[24] He invented it. The Jean Shepherd persona became what he invented.

In the following, he explained why he told his stories as if they had all really happened to him.

> Never grab a guy's elbow and say, "Hey, boy did I hear a
> great joke—Hey, did you hear the joke about..." You've
> already lost him.[25]

On Alan Colmes' 1998 call-in show more than twenty-five
years later, Shepherd gave what was very likely his "final" interview, and probably told the truth about his fictions:

> I'm an actor, you know, and I want my stuff to sound
> *real*. And so when I tell a story, I tell it in the first
> person—so it sounds like—by the way, to tell a good
> story—in the first person—that it sounds like it actually
> happened to me. It didn't. It's a story I invented but I put
> it in the first person so it would sound like—you
> know—a narrative—the guy telling the story. And,
> when I did this stuff people took me literally. They
> thought these things happened to me.[26]

Decades after his radio broadcast had ended, Shepherd, while
apparently admitting his subterfuge, seems to be putting the
onus on his listeners for believing it was true: "They thought
these things happened to me." The real cause of the misunder-
standing is the skill with which Shepherd had plied his art.
In *Understanding Media*, Marshall McLuhan writes:

> Jean Shepherd of WOR in New York regards radio as
> a new medium for a new kind of novel that he writes
> nightly. The mike is his pen and paper. His audience and
> their knowledge of the daily events of the world provide
> his characters, his scenes, and moods. It is his idea that,
> just as Montaigne was the first to use the page to record
> his reactions to the new world of printed books, he is the
> first to use radio as an essay and novel form for
> recording our common awareness of a totally new
> world of universal participation in all human events,
> private or collective.[27]

> Hey, why do I enjoy doing this show so much? What's the
> matter with me? I can't figure it out. You know? You know, it
> bothers me sometimes because—you're supposed to, you
> know, you're supposed to look at your work as work. No, I'll
> tell you this is, uh—you know, the Protestant ethic—causes me

a little problem at this point and—really. The other day this guy interviewed me. He says, "You must get very tired. Always thinking of new things or trying to do stuff every night on your show and all that."

And I said, [Shep speaking in mock solemn voice] "Yes, that is true. I get extremely tired." And he said, "Uh—yes, it must drain everything out of you. I just don't know how you can continue to do this—you know, producing forty-five minutes of stuff every night. Most nightclub comics, they got twenty minutes of material which they work—you know—milk like a cow—around the country for years on end. You must really— it must be a terrible strain—it must be an awful lot of work." [Shep, mock solemn.] "Yes, yes, as a matter of fact." And of course there I am having trouble with the Protestant ethic, see—I have to pretend.[28]

Although Shepherd felt he had to pretend to the interviewer, his listeners knew he enjoyed his broadcasts. He had such a laid-back conversational style, and it did seem so easy for him to just sit down at the mike and talk. However, in planning at least the outlines of his programs, Shepherd worked hard to create the illusion of ease. Shepherd the artist was a deceiver.

He told at least three versions of his father's frustrated attempts to undo a pair of apparently inextricably linked nails. The familiar Chinese nail puzzle. Once, he said his old man unbent them with pliers, in another version, his father flattened them out with a hammer, and still another time he sawed them apart. All *three* can't be true. Did his father have a set of nail puzzles, or two sets, or three—or none at all? If he had a set, did he unbend it, saw it, hammer it—does it matter? Shepherd's point was not how his old man "solved" the puzzle. Maybe it was another invented Shep-tale, dramatizing his attitude toward his old man while commenting on his inevitable failures. Using his old man, he applied a new metaphor: undoing Chinese nail puzzles as the American Everyman's false triumph over inevitable defeat in his ceaseless battle with reality.

As books sometimes make use of an ancient tale, updating it to give a sense of a universal human situation (such as James Joyce did by having Leopold Bloom recapitulate the adventures of Ulysses through an ordinary day in Dublin), Shepherd's old man three times unknowingly reenacted Alexander the Great's solution: Alexander did not untie the baffling Gordian knot, but sliced it with a sword. If Shepherd's listeners didn't get the historical metaphor, or didn't think Shep had the reference in mind, to make it clear, at the end of one broadcast featuring the nail puzzle story, he referred to Gordian knots. Shepherd used metaphor and he used memory:

> But why I happen to be able to pull it out of my vast Koda-chrome file—busted-up slides of memory, is because, one, it happens to be my profession. You know, my job, the work that I've chosen in life, is mostly, totally, introspection—and then transmitting it out. That's what an artist does, really. He pulls things out of his memory and his—and his perceptive nerve endings, and he tries to pour it into some form where he can tell the other people—"see what it is." It's what Norman Mailer does, it's what all people who attempt to interpret life do—whether they're doing it on the radio, or television, movies, newsreels, sculpture, or scratching it in the sand, or writing dirty words on the subway. They're all trying to say—*it*. Whatever it is. Nobody can quite grab ahold of it and say why they say it, but they do—and that's it. Squirrels do not write short stories. They do not. There has been no recorded instance of a bear sitting down, taking his felt tip pen in hand and starting out—"Call me Ishmael." Never. [Laughs.] Man yes, bears no. It's one of the great differences between man and beast.[29]

Yet, Jean Shepherd worked at *really* making it seem to be truth—his was not a one-time skit. It was a continuous, one-on-one con game (other than when he admitted the fiction in the almost never read disclaimers in the front of his books). And although he did not tell his tale in chronological fashion as in a straightforward autobiography, the most powerful case for the seeming verisimilitude of what Shepherd said was that to such a large extent he maintained a coherent story of his life and thoughts throughout his long career. What was considered his incredible memory was in large part an act of remembering details, feelings, and situations—close observation—and using them all in his fictional invention. Jean Shepherd had it both ways: he had us believing it was all true, so we were more personally involved in it—and he could make up whatever he wanted, because after all, it was all fiction. He combined invention with introspection into some kind of exquisite Gordian knot. In the *Realist* magazine interview of October 1960, Shepherd said:

> I got a call here a couple of weeks ago from a doctor who is a well-known psychiatrist in town and is a lecturer at one of the universities here. And he said, "You know, I've been listening to you for three years, Shepherd, and it might be of some interest to you to know that I feel you're the most completely analyzed man I've ever met." Apparently, this is a great compliment from an analysis man.
>
> And then I got to thinking about it, and I thought— well, you see, what I do on the show, I guess, makes people wonder about me—the psychological problems involved. I am always looking for my own motives within me, trying to *extend* those motives to find out why other things happen, why *other* people do things. Freud, for example, when he came up with his most important work in the late 19th century, it was by looking at himself—not other people, but himself—and *then* looking at other people.
>
> I don't think it's pertinent to my work as to whether I've been analyzed or not, but I will say this in all truthfulness: that my work is probably as great a purgative as any analysis could ever be, and more, because you can really be truthful when you're talking into a faceless microphone instead of to a living individual, an analyst.

Most who are familiar with Shepherd's work admire his ability to remember. They think he remembered the details of what happened in all the stories he told. But what was truly extraordinary was his ability to remember so many bits and pieces from the past and present, which made his monologues seem real through their detail. Actual remembering was not a simple act with Jean Shepherd; it was a major tool of his creativity.

> **Do you ever have the feeling that half the stuff you remember just didn't exist at all? That you sort of made it up? [Here, more than in most cases, he is obviously talking to personnel in the control room.] Or in some nutty way? You mean you don't have that problem ever, Herb [Squire, his engineer]?**

> You mean you—you really *believe* that everything you remember actually *happened?*[30]

In the above excerpt, he seems to be musing aloud directly to people in the control room (knowing, of course, that his words are also going out over the air), rather than just stimulating the minds of anonymous listeners. It just might be that this idea was not quite a production of the Shepherd-constructed persona, but rather an oblique projection of a real Jean exploring the issue. Whatever the case, Shepherd here contemplates the truth and falsity of memory (and, by implication, his own "remembering" as a storytelling device). Maybe Shepherd was not always sure how much he was making up and was suggesting that to some extent we all create our memories. Certainly, it seemed for Shepherd that memory is a baffling mix of conscious and unconscious fabrication. Thus it will never be fully possible to separate Shepherd's reality from his performance—or indeed, from his everyday talk. As Shepherd's friend Bob Brown puts it, "He had the ability to weave things that really couldn't possibly be true—in conversation. He was a difficult guy to know where reality stopped and fiction began. What he saw—or whether he saw it literally or whether he saw it in his mind—became reality for everybody around him."

Just as Shepherd often told stories about himself and others on his show and in interviews as though they were factual, several times he used television to story-tell rather than act as historian, the role that the situation would seem to have required. Two such projects stand out.

The first, a video history of the Chicago White Sox, which Shepherd narrates, consists of two rather distinct formats. He is onscreen from time to time describing his personal interests in baseball, and especially in the White Sox. During the documentary footage sections, he narrates what sounds like a script written to reflect the straightforward history of the team. When history reaches the first All-Star Game in the major leagues (at the White Sox's Comiskey Park), with Babe Ruth hitting the first home run in an All-Star Game, one sees the Babe hit it as Shepherd tells us that his father and Uncle Carl were at the game and his father just missed catching that ball, lunging, and then landing empty handed in a woman's lap.[31]

One imagines that most innocent viewers of the documentary think this really happened, but one should think again.

Shepherd aficionados may recall the similarity to his radio story told in 1966, of his father booing Yankee pitcher Marius Russo from the upper deck in left field. Of course, in retaliation to the old man's raspberries, "Marius Russo hit a home run that almost decapitated the old man!" Shepherd continued, emphasizing the story's veracity, "So help me, I swear...but I am here as a witness to tell you that my old man lost a ballgame—against the New York Yankees." Another and better-known "true" story was that of the old man taunting that other Yankee great, Lou Gehrig, who responded by aiming a home run ball into the right field stands, just missing Shepherd's father. Reflecting on all these stories, some will recall the interview after Shepherd's radio days in which, asked to tell about his father and Lou Gehrig, he responded in a moment of truth, "Don't forget, I'm a storyteller, not a historian."[32] One wonders if, when producing the television documentary about the Chicago White Sox, Major League Baseball and the Sox organization were sufficiently aware of that.

The second project was the television show *Home for the Holidays: A History of Thanksgiving*. First aired on the History Channel in 1994, Shepherd appears for only a minute, right after a narrator discusses Norman Rockwell's *Freedom from Want* (the artist's famous 1943 *Saturday Evening Post* illustration depicting a family Thanksgiving dinner). Shepherd begins speaking: "As a kid I got a job selling the *Saturday Evening Post* [with the *Freedom from Want* picture in it]. And I remember one day—as clear as a bell..." In 1943 Shepherd was a twenty-two-year-old "kid" whose 24/7 job (according to official records[33]) was not selling magazines door to door but tapping out code in the Army Signal Corps.

So Shepherd consciously presented his fabrications as truth, while on the other hand he would complain that supposed historical records did not adequately convey life's little realities:

> ...this show about George Washington. All these people wrote me [long letters] about how I could read a book—it says read this book and it'll tell you how Jefferson was, and I say *booj*-whaa, *booj*-whaa! I have never known—I have known many a person that has been written about in contemporary accounts. In fact, it's funny, I knew Malcolm X, and I might as well tell you that, I knew Malcolm X, but he does not come out, in any of the interviews or the paper accounts that I have read about him. He just isn't the way he is described. The way

the newspapers describe him. That is, in person. When you're sitting down having a cup of coffee with Malcolm X.

I've known other people who've been written up in newspapers, and they never are—and even in very serious books—in short, I don't believe the written account of the person can ever quite capture that person.

I still wonder how George Washington really was—when he was putting his teeth in in the morning. You know—putting on his socks. He's got to go off to another hard day in the Revolution. He's sitting in his tent. Well, of course he has had hard days in the Revolution. He's sitting in his tent, you know. It's about the second or third year of the Revolution and he's sitting in his tent.

They've been chased all over New Jersey, you know. And it looks like things are going from bad to worse, and now they're going even from worse to worser. And he's sitting in his tent, and he's pulling on his socks, and the wind is blowing in underneath the cot and he hears a couple of guys griping out there and another guy—fistfights breaking out there among the riflemen, and he puts his head in his hands and he just sort of rubs his temples for a minute, you know, before he puts his wig on, says, "Oh boy, what a can of peas we've opened up! What a can of *peas*! Oh jeez, oh man!" And these things are never brought out—not in the contemporary accounts of him.[34]

The biography, whether of someone like Washington, or the autobiography—what in Shepherd and some others could be termed the "created self" and the "performing self"—is a tricky and subtle business of simulation.

> ...the human urge to recreate the world, be it through the imaginative transactions of art...or the grinding gears of memory. This rage to simulate reality...[35]
> —**Michiko Kakutani**

Why did Jean Shepherd take for his subject his own life, feelings, and observations? Why did Shepherd simulate reality through embellishment and lies? Certainly part of the reason was his enormous ego. In addition, as his work was to be incessant talk, perhaps he had to have the broadest possible field to work in—the world outside plus his world within. It would be nice to put all Shepherd's stories and comments together in a seamless web. But the pieces inconveniently overlap at different angles. The same threads produce different webs (and, crucially, these inconsistencies—minor though they are—cannot be accounted for by the vicissitudes of memory). With Jean Shepherd, how can one tell the portraitist from the artistically constructed self-portrait? Were there times when Shepherd could not tell them apart? For his audience, they were almost always the same.

As his flow was in part extemporaneous, like a jazzy riff, it appeared that he was merely bringing forth facts out of his past and recent observations. In reality, Shepherd was creating his life—the art, with variations on a theme—in the act of performing it. In his 1971 book, *The Performing Self*, Richard Poirier discusses how certain artists—especially writers—contemplate themselves in the act of creation. Their art is a performance—a "self-discovering, self-watching" act. Poirier quotes Norman Mailer's thoughts on Hemingway: "The first art work in an artist is the shaping of his own personality."[36] Many writers have worked a near-mythic transformation—among poets, Walt Whitman did it, as did Robert Frost, and James Dickey reveled in it, writing, "One finds that the mode, the manner in which a man lies, and what he lies about—these things and the *form* of his lies—are the main things to investigate in a poet's life and work."[37] The massive Dickey biography is subtitled *The World as a Lie*. Jean Shepherd was just such a creative liar and a performing self—primarily in the ephemeral art of radio.

Shepherd's creative lying is never more delightfully developed than in stories of his childhood. Although in his early days in front of a microphone Shepherd speaks less of these days than he would from the mid-1960s on, in many of his most captivating extended stories he portrayed himself as a kid on the South Side of Chicago and in the contiguous Hammond, Indiana. We are about to enter the wonderful world of childhood, full of the trappings of nostalgia. But it is a Jean Shepherd kidhood of shattered illusions and nearly shooting your eye out. A kidhood where the stink of steel mills and being hoodwinked by Little Orphan Annie are not at all the nostalgia one might expect.

PART I

FORMATIVE YEARS

The real Jean Shepherd (as well as the fabricated Jean Shepherd) begins learning about life while growing up on the South Side of Chicago and in Hammond, Indiana. He learns that you have to be tough to survive kidhood and even tougher to survive the army. He learns a lot about the craft of radio in his early, pre–New York years.

CHAPTER 1
TOUGH TO BE A KID
Growing Up in the Midwest

> "I'm this kid, see."
> —Shepherd, beginning many of his childhood stories

As is common in much storytelling, Jean Shepherd made use of his childhood tales to express his attitudes about life in general:

> Well, tonight I decided, before we got on the air to try—
> 'cause I'm so tired of books where they talk about how beau-
> tiful it is—"Your happy days are childhood days!" Forget it.
> These are the scariest days of a guy's life, and you know it. But
> we never admit it. And I can remember—one of the things that
> I will carry forever, and I think most kids today miss this,
> because schools are almost all devoted to one thing—don't
> make the little lout feel insecure. When, as a matter of fact,
> that's what he needs more than anything else. Because I believe
> this is an insecure world. I mean, you know, that's the way life
> is. Lightning bolts, thunderstorms, hail, Mack trucks, fistfights
> in the dark. The whole scene. But when a kid gets out of
> school today, he's not prepared for it. Well, I came out of
> another world.[1]

Shepherd frequently talked of being from "the South Side of

Chicago." That city received almost no attention in his childhood stories other than being the place one sometimes visited
either for fun, or to root for the Chicago White Sox as they lost
a baseball game. He commented that the White Sox were losers
and the team of the working class, while the hated Cubs, from
the north end of the city, were winners and represented the
higher income brackets.

Matthew Callan comments, "In his earlier broadcasts and TV
appearances, he tended to say he was from the South Side rather
than Northern Indiana. Many of his favorite jazz artists (Lee
Konitz, Lennie Tristano) and authors (Nelson Algren) were
Chicagoans, coincidentally or not. Chicago's history as a boiling
pot for early jazz (Louis Armstrong, Bix Beiderbecke, and others
honed their skills there) had a lot to do with Shep's lifelong love
of this music. His boosterism for *Playboy*, aside from the fact
that they published his stories, had much to do with the fact that
it was published out of Chicago."

Shepherd grew up in the adjacent city of Hammond, Indiana,
which he often referred to on the radio. (In his writings, he conflated various nearby places into "Hohman, Indiana."[i]) He lived
with his parents and little brother, Randall, at 2907 Cleveland
Street in the Hessville section.[2]

One might expect that a commentator on nearly all aspects of
life would deal with the psychological, economic, and social
impact of an area dominated by steel mills and refineries.
Shepherd, however, never spoke about big business vs. the little
man, management vs. labor. His comments mostly related to the
intimidating and ugly environment:

> Now, if you're living amid four million square miles of
> refineries...are you aware that the entire northern half of
> Indiana is coated thickly—encrusted, in fact, like the bottom of
> a Humphrey Bogart–type tramp steamer—with barnacles?
> That the entire northern half of Indiana is encrusted with
> refineries? Did you know that? You didn't? Well, you're getting
> a little lesson here in contemporary geography—see.
>
> As a matter of fact, Standard Oil is an Indiana company.
> Standard Oil of Indiana—you've heard that? Well, where the
> hell do you think Standard Oil of Indiana is? Utah? Well, it's
> all over northern Indiana.
>
> And as far as the eye could see, you see these silver tanks,
> and you smell this great drifting effluvia of a—of kerosene and
> low grade insecticides. They make insecticides out of petro-

leum. How would you like to live within a half mile of the biggest insecticide plant in the Western world? And they would test it every couple of days by shooting it up in the air and seeing how many things fall down. [Laughs.] I mean, that was the scene, see. And between the refineries, of course, would be dotted picturesque steel mills. And what glued all of it together—some of the most colorful and some of the most unforgettable used car lots and junkyards ever created by man.[3]

Although he frequently referred to the mills as well as to his working in them, his were but summer—not career—jobs. He made a point of noting that—as his father worked in an office at the Borden Milk Company[4]—his was a white-collar background. It is clear that the real Shepherd family and the created Ralph Parker family were white collar. He talked and wrote about what it was like to be a kid growing up in a lower middle class family, growing up in the 1920s and 1930s in America. In the first chapter of *In God We Trust: All Others Pay Cash*, he described Hammond/Hohman: "It clings precariously to the underbelly of Chicago like a barnacle clings to the rotting hulk of a tramp steamer." He also said that if Carl Sandburg's Chicago was the "City of the Big Shoulders," then Hohman had to be that city's broad rear end. The way he told it, the town had Lake Michigan on the north and steel mills roaring into the night on all other sides.

It was not only the environment that was polluted—the esthetic soul was undernourished, as Shepherd put it in *In God We Trust*, "Mr. Doppler operated the Orpheum Theater, a tiny bastion of dreams and fantasies, a fragile light of human aspiration in the howling darkness of the great American Midwest where I festered and grew as a youth."

Shepherd was named Jean after his father, whose sister, so it is said, had admired the Victor Hugo novel *Les Miserables* and suggested that her baby brother be named Jean after the main character.[ii] Jean was sensitive about being given a name that in the United States is usually reserved for girls. In various broadcasts he said he disliked being called Jeanie by his parents; in one he talked about a grammar school teacher who, on the first day in class, insisted his name must be Gene; and in another, he mentioned the time he was assigned to a girls' gym class. In his movie *A Christmas Story*, he narrated how his alter ego, the kid Ralphie, was given a pink bunny suit for Christmas by a distant aunt, because she always envisioned him as a tiny tot and thought he was a girl. The adult Jean's buddy, Shel Silverstein, reportedly noted Jean's problems with his name in his lyrics to the song made famous by Johnny Cash, "A Boy Named Sue."[iii]

In the August 28, 1965, Limelight broadcast, Shepherd commented, "You know how it felt to grow up all of your life, with the name Jean? Spelled with a J? Listen, I fist-fought my way through every grade in school. How do you think I got so aggressive? So wiry?"

This specific reference to himself was often Shepherd's way of taking the particular and implying its wider relevance. When asked why he talked "so much about how it was like when you were a kid," Shepherd's response gave a clue to indicate that autobiography was not his underlying focus: "Because...I'm really making a comment about how it is *now*."[5]

> When I'm on the air, quite often I'll talk about when I was a kid. I'll discuss the time—maybe I was ten years old and I wanted a BB gun or I wanted to—who knows what, you know—I wanted to get the Little Orphan Annie secret society decoder pin. And people listening to me—older people generally—will suspect that I'm making it up. Because most people, when they get a certain age they have a tendency to completely forget their lives. As a matter of fact, I suspect that many people today in, you know—the twentieth century—there are fifty million things going on, five thousand television shows a day and five hundred newscasts a day—[have trouble] remembering even last Wednesday. And yet it's exactly the opposite. I think that as most people get older, they have a tendency to erase their lives—they rarely even remember the fact that they were a kid. And so, for that reason, I use childhood as a point of—I suppose you might say—common communication. It's the one thing we've all had.[6]

Henry Morgan, like most listeners, was obviously duped into believing that in Shepherd's kid stories the broadcaster was telling autobiographical truth when he once commented about Shepherd, "He has talked about that youth of his in such detail that I suspect it lasted about forty years."[7] All the more extraordinary is the fact that Morgan said this in 1960, only four years into Shepherd's twenty-one-year career on New York radio. Morgan, like so many listeners, seemed to believe that Shepherd's stories were supposed to be autobiographically true.[iv]

That the stories were not literally all true can be recognized by noting, as did Morgan, that there were too many stories to cram into anyone's childhood. Besides, who could have that many interesting episodes in one lifetime? Also, Shepherd told the same stories with changes over the years, often substituting contradictory material. Yet, with each telling, Shepherd related it so convincingly that listeners fell hypnotized into credulity.

One imagines that Shepherd remembered *what it was like* to be a kid and projected that into mostly made-up stories, some of which had fragments of fact. It's not quite that clear cut, however. He probably remembered in good part what it was like *for him* to be a kid, and remembering more general attributes and universalities of childhood, he was able to project his adult attitudes upon them in his fabricated tales—his fabricated autobiography. They weren't all just humorous tales—he could project his ideas within that form. Roy Pascal describes the autobiography of the poet (of the creative person), as showing "the evolution of his mode of vision in terms of his successive engagement with the world."[8] We have to keep remembering that with Shepherd we shouldn't assume he was giving us autobiography—maybe he was just telling us a story.

People have always responded strongly to Shep's childhood stories. On the surface they contain reminders of stuff one used to do, or seems to remember doing—in other words, nostalgia. Shepherd found it frustrating that people failed to go beneath that surface to the dark core of his tales—the nearly inevitable point—that life is tough, especially for a kid. At the beginning of his first New York television show, he said, "It took guts just to *be* a kid on the South Side of Chicago."

Chicago was a center of radio broadcasting in the 1920s and 1930s, and this may have stimulated young Jean's interest in radio. Several radio programs for children began in the early 1930s, before Shepherd was a teenager. Two of them are associated with Shepherd himself: *Jack Armstrong: All-American Boy* (premiered July 31, 1933), because of his claim that he played the young friend of Jack on the radio,[9] and *Little Orphan Annie*[v] (premiered April 6, 1931).

Little Orphan Annie figures in Shepherd's kid-hood because he told a story about one of their premiums. *Little Orphan Annie* was a kids' radio adventure program, advertised by Ovaltine, the chocolaty drink mix. At the end of the program, the announcer, Pierre Andre, gave the secret message in coded numbers that required a decoder to understand. It was the most important part of the program for little Shep. In order to obtain a decoder, one had to send in the inner foil from a container of Ovaltine, and he lived in a non-Ovaltine neighborhood. In one version of his story he gets a can as a present, and in another version he finds an empty can that has been tossed out in another neighborhood. He sends in the label, gets the secret decoder, and anxiously copies down the secret message, letter by letter, which reads: D-O-N-T F-O-R-G-E-T T-O D-R-I-N-K Y-O-U-R O-V-A-L-T-I-N-E.

No! As little Ralph/Jean put it, "A crummy *commercial!*" At a kid level, he was learning about real life in America.

On another occasion, the Mechano set that he gets as a present has just three pieces—a set only big enough to make a T-square. Disillusion set in early. As with his other subjects, Shepherd used his kid stories to explore what were painful lessons about life. Lessons about what nostalgic adults remember only as a happy, innocent kid-garden.

Shepherd talked about his adventures as a kid with friends such as Flick, Schwartz, Bruner, and Gruber. Although Shepherd made numerous contradictory statements over the years as to whether or not these and other childhood characters actually existed, evidence (including the Hammond High School 1939 yearbook with pictures and descriptions of some of them) shows that many of them did, though this does not prove that the specifics he told about them were fact rather than Shepherd's fictions. Many of these stories appear in the books *In God We Trust: All Others Pay Cash* and *Wanda Hickey's Night of Golden Memories—and Other Disasters*. He also talked about his school days. He attended the Warren G. Harding grammar school and graduated from the local Hammond High School in 1939.[vi] From time to time he commented that, having a last name beginning with *S* and seating usually done alphabetically, he sat toward the back of the classroom where he couldn't hear the teacher well or easily read the blackboard. Even in later life situations, he was relegated to near the back of the line—Shepherd frequently suggested how some autobiographical detail of his life also formed some easily overlooked significance in many lives. Observing that some educational tidbits with seemingly no practical use remain lodged in his brain, he noted that "Bolivia exports tin."

His first appearance before an audience:

> I attended more pageants. For those of you who are interested in my debut, I made my debut in show business in an oral hygiene pageant. I played "bad breath." [Laughs.] No, no,

> I'm wrong. I'm just being rotten here. Actually what I played
> was "decayed tooth." That's the truth. They had me all
> dressed up in a thing—that was a decayed tooth, and Dawn
> Strickland played a toothbrush, and Jack Robinson played a
> squeezed tube of toothpaste. I'll never forget that, and [laughs]
> Alex Josway played "mouthwash." And I remember reviews
> came out the day after in the Warren G. Harding grade school
> *Daily Bugle.*[10]

Jean Shepherd's stories were an unfolding of the sensitive
person growing up in Midwest, mid-twentieth-century America
—growing up American—growing up being alive to experience!
He transformed his childhood into a fiction that depicted the
American reality—one that did not match the standard-issue
illusion—a reality in which being a kid had its pleasures but
being tough was a necessity, a reality that was not picturesque
but rather ultimately disillusioning, because that was the way
the world worked. He seemed to feel there was a lot to grow up
from and grow out of:

> I come from a long line of people who live by calendar art.
> Now I have to frankly admit that in the home when I was a
> kid—I don't know whether you come from a family like I did,
> but I'm going to tell you the kind I came from. We never once
> to my knowledge ever bought a picture. I don't recall our
> family buying a picture. I don't recall anybody in our family
> ever really going to an art museum. I can remember going to
> museums, but they always had bones of dinosaurs and stuff in
> them, you know, and once in a while we went to a museum
> where they had a lot of old Fords—that kind of stuff. But I
> never—I can't recall going to an art museum as a kid.[11]

LIFE AT 2907 CLEVELAND STREET

Shepherd's stories often related his first confrontations with
unpleasant realities—in the form of other kids, parents, shop-
keepers, teachers, bosses. Despite the problems, the issues all
seem to be minor ones—minor bullies, minor embarrassments,
minor kid-type problems. It is the implications of these stories
that give them wider significance for all of us. For example, one
gets the impression young Jean ate almost nothing but salami
sandwiches, and for supper, meatloaf, mashed potatoes, and red

cabbage, the commonplace food of the common American, lacking culinary interest—it will be this lack of a sense of adventure and imagination that will be a major impetus in nudging a slightly older Shepherd out of his childhood restraints. Just wait till the end of this chapter when he gets a taste of snails.

Randy was the stock kid brother, always depicted as annoying, always hiding under the daybed, runny-nosed and whiny, playing the turkey in the Thanksgiving pageant. It's a logical bit: to the older kid, the younger brother must always seem a whiner and annoying—it's an easy tag to hang on him. Shepherd does little with the kid brother theme other than putting him down—it might be that Shepherd felt jealous that brother Randy seemed the more athletic of the two. Consistent with this is that Shepherd often depicted himself as overweight and obsessed with the sedentary obsession of ham radio. It is also said that some of Shepherd's athlete-based stories, and some others,[12] derived from the adult Randall's talks with the adult brother Jean.[vii] Whatever the sibling rivalries, the real-life adult Randall remained behind in Hammond, working for the milk company,[13] and later running a limousine service.

His mother always seemed to wear a red, "rump-sprung," chenille bathrobe, sometimes with a bit of "petrified egg" on one lapel, and was often described working away over the sink with a Brillo pad.

> I'll never forget sitting next to my mother's knee. She had this huge, giant, wonderful old granite knee. Had these handholds. I can remember standing next to my mother's knee. I was about five or six years old, and she said, "Son, always keep your eye on the subject." Well, I didn't know what she meant of course, you know. But I do remember she had this great knee. So tonight's program will be developed along the lines of—"Let's all honor knees for a change." We've had enough trouble with subjects, predicates. We've had enough trouble with—you know—the surface things. We've gone through all the surface things. And it seems to me that we can do something else tonight.[14]

During his first New York television appearance, Shepherd said:

> You see it starts way back. Let's take me. It started in my childhood. I grew up next to my mother's knee. She had this—

this great big beautiful granite knee. Oh, it's a great knee. And I grew up next to it. Sitting there in the shadow. Rich, deep, comforting shadow, and my kid brother's on the other side, see. We got hanging straps. We're sitting there. And once in a while she'd give us these words of advice, "Jean, you got to make dough. You got to make dough." I was only five years old. I didn't know what this meant, you know. "Jean, you got to make dough."

It isn't like that now, you know. In fact just the other day I was going past this store here in town where they sell all these progressive toys, all these progressive things for progressive people, these free-form puzzles, these amoeba-shaped beach balls, all that stuff for the progressive kids, and right there in the window is a big plastic knee. It's called the Plasto-Mom. You see, it's for mothers who get careers but who want their kids to have rich, full childhoods. And this big, beautiful plasto-knee has a recording in it. And this recording plays words of motherly advice recorded especially by Ma Perkins. You see, for the kids. And right there in the kneecap is a seven inch TV screen. And this Plasto-Mom comes in six decorator shades and is washable—and has a wedgie.

I'll never forget my ma saying, "Ya got to make dough, Jean." Kids don't get that kind of advice anymore. They don't get that kind of background.[15]

Here, Shepherd flirts with nostalgia. He seems genuinely fond of the memories and to have had a mother's knee to snuggle up to in the "good old days." At the same time, he undercuts the notion with the comic image of the handles the little kids held. We have his take on the cliché of parental advice—money as the great American obsession, even directed toward a little kid—and the absurdity of the bogus solutions offered by the best technology money can buy. And the allusion to modern mothers who fail to nurture except through a ridiculous gadget. Mothers, he seems to suggest, were always thus.

Shepherd derided his father in many anecdotes and stories. "My old man" was well-meaning, but somewhat dull witted and pedestrian. He loved his car and constantly had trouble with it. He loved air shows. He loved the Chicago White Sox, who were perpetual losers. In one story, his father won a prize, a lamp with an illuminated lady's leg–shaped base, and was so proud of the thing that he just had to have it centered in the living room window—until Shepherd's mother "accidentally" broke it while dusting. Of course, his old man had those three ways of "solving" the Chinese nail puzzle by destroying it. It seems that the old man was not much of a thinker and only gave a kid advice, unknowingly, by example.

> He never offered much advice, my father. He never really offered any advice that I can pull out of the great—I'm always amused—not only amused, I'm always a little bit—I feel a little inferior. These guys I read all the time who write autobiographies and it seems that people were always saying great things to them that affected their lives.[16]

One is supposed to learn from one's parents, but little Jeanie only seemed to find negative lessons in the old man's actions. Sometimes, as in the following, it got really bad. It's hard to believe Shepherd would make this up and let us think it's the truth. Talking as Gerry Mulligan's jazz played underneath, Shepherd said he, himself, could have been a great jazz musician. Whether the truth or fiction, there is something essential going on here. Jean Shepherd, expressing how important jazz was to him, expressed an important longing that would forever be unfulfilled:

> He was lucky enough to have an old man who bought him a baritone sax when he was nine. My old man bought me a pair of shoes. With a pocket for a knife in the side. He immediately disarmed me. He says, "No kid's going to carry a knife in his shoes in my family." So I went around with a clothespin in that pocket—with the flap buttoned down. It looked like I had a knife. I'll never forget the time Esther Jane finally reached over across the aisle, unbuttoned the flap, says, "Can I see your knife?" and pulled out the clothespin. It was when I began to hate my old man. It has not stopped since. [Laughs.] All right, so it's twenty dollars an hour it costs. I mean it's good for laughs. A twenty-dollar laugh is a better laugh than a three-dollar laugh. Especially when you're laughing at yourself, you know. [Laughs.] And your old man. And everybody around you.[17]

Shepherd's hostile comment about his old man giving him utilitarian shoes instead of a creative boost gains significance when one considers the profound importance of jazz in his New York City life and work in the mid-to-late 1950s. But Shepherd's resentment of his old man had at least one other source, where truth and fiction stared at each other through Shepherd's looking glass. In his introduction to the published script of his TV movie, *The Phantom of the Open Hearth*, Shepherd reported a conversation with James Broderick, the actor playing the fictional old man.[18] In a personal reference the actor may not have been aware of, and certainly one most readers would not have known, Shepherd asked the actor what he thought happened a year after the movie ended, and then told him: "Okay. One year to the day after Ralph's prom, in fact the week of Ralph's high school graduation, the old man comes home, announces he's leaving the family, and takes off for Palm Beach with a twenty-year-old stenographer with long blond hair and a Ford convertible. They never hear from him again." Although one might see this as simply Shepherd's attempt to have the actor put more depth into his portrayal of his father, Fred Barzyk relates that Shepherd told him that his father left their family for a secretary at the office, commenting, "I think it was one of the *major* blows in Shepherd's life—why he had such a damaged ego in many ways. Everybody reacts differently to different kinds of losses. When his father sat him down and said he's leaving his mother, it really—it was real pain for Shepherd. And eventually he said he was his father's son."

So Shepherd never got to play jazz like the greats. But, while still a kid, he encountered the crucial interest that would lead to his adult career in radio. As he once put it, he "found a higher calling." Shep also commented, "I became, at the age of ten, totally, maniacally, and for life I might point out, completely skulled out by amateur radio."[19]

Indeed, Shepherd at a young age (which depended on the version of the story he was telling) got his amateur radio license.[viii] His frequent use of the common glass radio tube designation "6SJ7GT"[ix] for almost any technical object that came to mind served as a little reminder of his early radio days, and his life-long involvement in amateur radio. As a teenager, Shepherd would be sending Morse code ("continuous wave" or CW) every night on his ten-watt transmitter, commenting in a broadcast that his ham radio was "the joy, the light of my life." He said that his boyhood experience in amateur radio helped him get started in his first radio jobs, leading him to high school broadcasts and then local sportscasting, that included part of a summer season for the Toledo Mudhens baseball team. A knowledgeable Shep enthusiast and amateur radio operator, Lowell Thelin, emphasizes the importance of ham radio for developing Shepherd's style before a mike and comments that on amateur radio, one often floats from topic to topic in a way that Jean Shepherd was to make his own stream-of-consciousness style:

> There have been many observations that Shep appears to be talking to the listener on a one-on-one basis. I also felt that Shepherd was talking just to me and think now that this effective technique may have been strongly influenced by his amateur radio beginnings. With ham radio, you often talk to just one other person and you can say all sorts of things to test the reaction of the operator at the other end. I suspect Shepherd carried this practice further by directing his broadcast to the studio engineer to get an immediate response.[20]

Fred Barzyk, talking to steel workers at Inland Steel during a shoot for *Jean Shepherd's America*, asked what Shepherd was like when he worked there as a teenager. They said he was incredibly shy, quiet, glasses—nobody would have ever known. "He had an insatiable desire to talk—but he was shy in public. What gave him voice was his ham radio. And to his dying day he always got on at night to be able to talk. This was his way of getting the demons out."

Even as a kid, maybe without exactly understanding it yet, Jean Shepherd had found a way to escape the confines of the "howling darkness of the great American Midwest." With his ham equipment, he was communicating with the big world out there.

One part of that big world beyond home was work. Shepherd mentioned several early jobs he had as a kid, such as helping friend Flick clean up his father's tavern after a Friday night. He talked about a high school summer job working for a surveyor laying out lines for dredging out the Little Calumet River. He told a few stories about working in a steel mill (once as a mail delivery boy), including one about his first day there.[x] He had gotten the job through his ham radio contact with the boss, Mr. Galambus:

> I remember—speaking of first days—I suppose the most—
> the most—vivid first day that I have in my mind, is the first day
> I ever worked in a steel mill. You know—again, this is a matter

of perception and myth and reality, dream, and the *logique*. What does a steel mill seem to you to be?

If I say to you "steel mill," what do you think of in your mind? How do you see it? Do you think that you've even *approached* it? Do you think you've even scratched the surface of a steel mill? Well, let me tell you about the first day—and remember this—I lived within a mile and a half of most of my adolescent and childhood life within—within a mile and a half of the greatest steel mills in America. So logically I should know about steel mills, right? Logically, since most of the people who lived in the neighborhood worked in steel mills, steel mills should not come as a surprise to *me*.

Well, let me tell you about that first day. I remember this so vividly that it's—it's as though it was some kind of a lithograph—even better than that, a steel engraving hanging in this lone corridor of my room. This room of the mind, with lights properly placed so they can be seen clearly. And I hardly even think of it—I never look at it. Like a picture that's in your house, that you never look at—it's always there, you know. You walk in and out of the room and there's this thing hanging. And you never look at it. Once in a while you look at it and suddenly say, "Yeah, yeah, yeah, *Aristotle Contemplating a Home of Buster*. Yeah, there he is." You know. And—and suddenly hits you again and again, and maybe one day you get so tired of the picture you throw it out! But you never can *really* throw it out, 'cause it's always somehow hanging in your memory. That first day...

And so I'm sitting in this bus, and it's going GRRRRRRR! and I see outside these windows. I don't want to appear eager, you know. That's the worst thing when you get into a terrible foreign country or a strange world, is to let everyone know that you're not a native.

And so I'm sitting but I'm looking out—casually, you know. And I see these great buildings on either side, so close that you could reach out and touch them with your hands. Big, square cutouts in the buildings, and I could see enormous ingots—BOOM! BOOM! BOOM! Back and forth! Sparks. And it sounded like—to the ear, which was not trained—it sounded like there was nothing but a continual *scream* cutting the air. A great, great *scream*. Of all the machinery—everything all together. And I'm sitting. Oh!...

I finally arrived in the stores. And I'm sitting there and here's a man come out. He says, "I'm going to fit you with

safety shoes, kid. I see you got a note from Galambus. You got
to get to work." The stores where they give you safety shoes
and goggles. I say, "Well, what am I gonna do?" "I don't know.
It's none of my business, kid. Hah. You work for Galambus
over there. You're working for Galambus over in Stationary
Shipping, I don't—note says. Don't come to ask me about it.
It's not my problem, kid. You get safety shoes and goggles."

And I walked out of the stores with a big pair of safety
shoes that were forty pounds each, a pair of goggles—and
sound rose and rose and rose and rose—it was screaming and
hollering around me. [End-theme music begins.]

I had nowhere to go. No place to go. I had no point of reference, and I went into a doorway where there was a telephone. I picked up the telephone and I instinctively dialed
zero. And I got this voice on the phone. It was the operator. The
plant operator.

I said, "I want to talk to Mr. Galambus, please."

"Mr. Galambus?"

I says, "Yes, Mr. Galambus, who is the superintendent of
the rolling shop."

"Oh, yes, Mr. Galambus, of course, sir." She thought I was
a big man.

I get Mr. Galambus. I say, "Hi, Gil, hi, Gil, this is W9QWN
[the ham radio connection that landed him the job], ha ha, I'm
over here in the 2AC, Gil. Please come and get me. Oh oh oh."

Well, twenty minutes later I'm in the Stationary Shipping
Department. And that was only the beginning. [Pauses.] That
day I learned something very important. I haven't discovered
yet what it is. [Theme music up to finale.][21]

One thing Jean Shepherd learned was that, even if you were
in close proximity to some part of the world, you would not
have a realistic perception of it unless you immersed yourself in
it—participated in it. Then it would always be part of you, like
a steel engraving in the room of your mind. He may not have recognized it then, but the finely scribed engravings of his memory
would be crucial elements in his creative method. He also
learned that life out in the real world was scary, and that you'd
better be wearing the appropriate safety shoes and goggles.

His steel mill stories were each sharply engraved little lessons
in life. Stories about a tornado that touched down, about
drinking with the men at the local gin mill after the shift on his
first day, and about being given, at the age of sixteen, a sample

of Mail Pouch chewing tobacco. It seemed like "molten lava going down," but the physical sensation was not the point of telling it. Shepherd gives us one of his oft-repeated themes:

> Very few people ever talk about the way life really is lived. Like I say—Have you ever tried chewing tobacco, Roger? How come? I thought you wanted to taste all life has to offer. [Laughs.] Well I'm serious, you know. We're only in this vale of tears for a short time and there are just so many things available and yet most people will at about the age of five—they'll glom onto two or three safe things. Like they'll eat canned peas and chopped steak they discovered at the age of eight; they'll eat that [laughs] and I'll be damned if they'll eat anything else—for the rest of their life till they're seventy-four years old. They won't try anything else.
>
> Let's take another experience. The tried and true is the greatest debilitator, the greatest hang up, that I suspect that the average one of us—everyone of us walking-around types have—to fight against, and—you have not tried chewing tobacco? Well let me tell you something about chewing tobacco. I'm a kid, see, and going through a terrible—for those of you who are squeamish, I'm going to warn you, this is not a story for women and children. It is definitely not a story for—. [Laughs.]
>
> I'm a kid, see, and one thing about being a kid, see, is you have not established all the various rules yet, by which you are going to live your life, or let us say, by which you are going to destroy your life—which is even better—closer to the point. And you're walking around. You're sweating—now from the very earliest days when you are a kid, you are controlled by your old man—by your family, see—you emulate them—for the first couple of years. And so, if your mother says, "Yeesh!" every time somebody mentions broiled liver—I wonder how many people today think that they don't like things—they absolutely believe they do not like liver because their mother went "Yeesh sheesh!" every time it was mentioned. And they've never tried it.[22]

Shepherd repeated over the years that we are being held back by custom and fears. The limited mentality of his early environment had done its best to hold him back. Fearing an unusual taste is but symptomatic of everything young Shepherd confronted.

He began realizing that there was life beyond what he was used to, what other people accepted and promoted and controlled you by—beyond childhood, beyond what he would soon recognize were the limitations of living in Hammond, Indiana. There was the time he picked up Esther Jane Albery in his Ford convertible and took her to the prom:

> The night of the prom. I'll never forget it. It was announced that it was to be in formal. Well, I don't know if you know how the word "formal dress" hits Hammond, Indiana. I mean, their idea of formal dress is *pressed* overalls. I'm not kidding. It's a steel mill town, you know, and on Sunday a guy would take out his Sunday overalls and walk around, you know? And he—I can remember guys with their Sunday safety shoes on. Well, they'd polish them, you know—they'd wear 'em.
>
> And you oughta see a guy with his Sunday blue work shirt on. And they wear it—they even have Sunday ties. You get them at Sears Roebuck and they're made out of linoleum. And they're black, you know, and they snap on. So these guys would walk around on Sunday. They're all dressed up. You'd hear the starch cracking in their knees. You know—crack crack. That was the idea.[23]

At the rental place, trying on a tuxedo:

> There I stand in my tennis shoes. And there I stand in front of the mirror, you know. And I walk back, and I look at it. Now I knew what life was about. It was that moment that I began to get bugged with Hammond, Indiana. You know, that brief instant.[24]

There, trying on the tuxedo, that special formal clothing as a symbol of a change from adolescent schoolboy to a more formal adulthood, the young Shepherd stands before a mirror—he sees himself as he is, and is struck by an image of himself in Hammond with which he is not happy. The prom itself is a symbol of transformation toward what might be the rest of one's life. The prom is not a night for golden memories but a portent of potential disasters. At the end of the published script of Shepherd's television film, *The Phantom of the Open Hearth*, Ralph (Jean's alter ego) returns from a memorable and disastrous prom night and heads wearily up the stairs to bed. Shepherd, the film's narrator, says [and we read italicized screen directions], in what may well be an essential expression of his worldview:

> The male human animal, skulking through the impenetrable fetid jungle of kidhood, learns early in the game just what sort of animal he is. The jungle he stalks is a howling, tangled wilderness, infested with crawling, flying, leaping, nameless dangers.
> [Through this all we continue to hear "Good Night, Sweetheart" and see Ralph climbing the stairs.]
> He daily does battle with horrors and emotions he will spend the rest of his life trying to forget or suppress. Or recapture. His jungle is a wilderness he will never fully escape, but those first early years, when the bloom is on the peach and the milk teeth have just barely departed, are the crucial days in the Great Education of Life.

The Hammond High yearbook has a photo of Jean as a senior, and the following description, referring to his tuba playing, bass playing, and his interest in cars, planes, and sports. And Hammond's institute of learning, in an ironic, final kick in the face, misspells his last name:

SHEPHARD, JEAN
Senior band and orchestra / Hi Y / Automobile Club /
Aeronautics Club / Football

One Shepherd story that masterfully chronicles his discovery-fueled childhood goes as follows:

> Well, here in America it's very different, and — the idea, you know — of rising out of this meatloaf world is just sort of automatic — you try to do it. So, anyway the groovy thing about going to school in a lot of ways is hardly anybody knows where you came from. [Laughs.]
> I was going to college and of course I was barely scraping on — my end was tough. I've got this one suit, this one sport coat. And so I got to know a couple of chicks — people there — and I never talk much about things. And one night this girl — very elegant girl with long blond hair asks me — she says, "Would you care to come to dinner tonight — my home? We're having a few people over, and I think it would be kind of fun."

I said, "Yeah." You know, I'm always very glib with my ad-libs. "Yeah."

So she said, "Have you ever been out to the place?"

I said, "No, I haven't."

And she gives me this address, in this town—where the school was. And I knew nothing whatsoever about it.

So I said, "Okay, I'll be there."

And she—"Oh, don't bother to dress, or anything like that, just—you know."

I said, "Yeah, fine." I didn't realize the import of this at the time—"Don't bother to dress." Don't bother to dress. So, that night I put on my J. C. Penny sport coat and I put on my Sears Roebuck pants and I've got on my new shirt. You know, the one with the pearl buttons that light up. And I've got my tie that my Aunt Glen gave me for graduation from high school, and so I go walking down—cooling out there—towards this place.

Well, as I walked, the houses got bigger and bigger, and the lawns got broader and broader. Until they were so high—the lawns—that you couldn't see the house anymore! And you knew you were really in the big time when the house was so far back on the lawn that you just saw nothing but trees and this winding driveway—Ohooo boy! [Laughs.] Well anyway, to make a long story short—

I now joined the gathering. In this *fantastic* house! Oh wow! They had white pillars in front of the door and they had this big brass knocker that you just go bonk! Bonk! And it was shaped like a lion. And you grabbed this thing, you drop it— clunk! Clunk! And this guy comes and opens the door.

And I say, "I was invited to dinner."

"Of course, come right in." And in I go!

He says, "Shall I take your hat?" My hat! "Your coat, please." If he took my coat I'd have nothing. So I says, "No, that's all right."

So I walk back in through. I followed him, and now I'm in this room. These people are all standing around. There were about maybe fifteen or twenty people, and here was Nancy, this girl, and her sister, Dolores, but Nancy was something else, man. And so here's Nancy, and she says, "Oh, Jean! How wonderful you could come!"

And so, she came running over and she kissed me! See, I— this was not in *my* strata of society. One doesn't do these things, you know. This whole idea of just running up and kissing somebody—we had to have a big thing like a game of post office or something—to pull that one off.

So she comes right over and she kisses—"Oh! How good of you to come!" And she kisses me.

I says, "Yeah, hi, Nancy."

She says, "Here, would you care for a—James, please." And James comes over with a big tray with drinks. And there are these tall, skinny glasses, you know, the long, skinny stems? So I didn't—I had never really held one of those glasses, so I grabbed it and it tipped over! Instantly! [Laughs.] And down it goes, all over the floor. She says, "Oh, I'm sorry."

And with that everybody's rushing and all this running round. So James says, "Excuse me, sir." So he brushes off the furniture, where I spilled all the goo-goo all over it. So I take another one of these things, and I'm walking around. It's a martini, see.

So—I had never had a martini before—our family—the only thing my old man used to talk about once in a while drinking—the only thing he ever talked about in the way of actual drink was—he used to say, "How about some booze?" Now we didn't ever have any actual names for them—it was just called booze. And—then he had a thing—once in a while when he was really putting on the dog—as he would say—he would have a thing called "a highball." Now a highball means that you put booze in a glass, and then you pour in ginger ale. That was [laughs]—that was what a highball was.

So I've got this thing—martini, see, and it tasted terrible—like I was drinking some kind of strange chemical. Ohooo! Wow! Had this little olive bobbing up and down there. I liked the olive, so I reached in and took the olive out and I crunched—it was the first olive I ever saw in my life that had an *almond* in it. So, whole new things were opening already, see—yeah—it was stuffed with an almond! So, I'm walking around with these people, and suddenly they all move like a herd of cattle. They say, "Oh—it's time for dinner. Oh oh oh oh."

We move into the next room and we're all sitting down at this big, beautiful table—white tablecloth and the crystal and linen and all that. I sit down and—gee, you know, food—I don't know what's going to happen here. And then it came!

Nancy, sitting next to me—she said, "Have you had—have you had any of the fresh escargot this season yet?"

I said, "What? Oh yeah." I said, "Well, yes, yes, it's a good season, hee hee." You know, faking it all the way. And the next thing I know, in front of me is this plate of something which had always been rumored in our house. That people somewhere, someplace, ate. And we never really believed it! And whenever it was mentioned they ate these things—it was universal—"Oh, ugh! A plate of snails! With the little forks. Oh my God, snails!"

Snails! Ugh! And instantly inside of me—my meatloaf insides were immediately saying, "Oh, ugh, oh my God, this is all fantastic!"

And Nancy—she takes one of the snails and she says, "Oh, these are so wonderful." She takes one out, you know, and I see how she does it. She takes this little fork and she fishes one of these things out, and it comes out, and it looks strange, you know—like a little black snake or something—see. She pulls it out—she goes, "Oh!" Here was this beautiful girl. What am I going to do? I can't chicken out, see.

So I says, "Oh, they look very good, hee hee." I take the little thing and I'm feeling sick inside. My little fork, and—fish it out. I put it in my mouth—I go, "uuushup!" Oh my God! Oh my God! Oh my God! It was fantastic! It was fantastic!

[Closing theme trumpets start.] It was fantastic! I tasted this—it was so good I couldn't believe it! Well now—then I went the other way—I made a total pig of myself. I—kiwkiwki-wkiwghkiw! I ate all the snails up so quick—I mean they were gone!

And then the lesson hit me. I looked around. I saw all these other people—they've been doing this all of their lives! They weren't surprised at snails. And then it began to sneak in on me—what other terrible stuff did I learn at home? What other things do I think are awful? Just because it was back in the kitchen that way, you know? I ate the snails and late that night when I got home, I'm lying in the dormitory room and I would feel those snails—you could taste them. There's an aftertaste. And I—I began to suspect that night there was a fantastic, unbelievable world out there. And I was just be-gin-ning to taste it! Just beginning! God knows where it would lead![25]

The escargot story seems so perfect and the moral so pat—and it worked so well to cap off Shepherd's coming of age chapter in his "radio novel." The craftsmanship—the artistry he put into it! Building up the image of himself as the unsophisticated bumbler—awkwardly dressed, never having been to such an affair before. The terrible, strange chemical taste for him of the first martini he had ever had, spilling the martini, never even having seen the exotic snails he described as little black snakes. (Are those snakes descendents of the Garden of Eden's first tempter enticing him into a delectable world beyond innocence?) He felt sick inside at the thought of eating one. All the way through that third exclamation of "Oh my God!" Shepherd had listeners convinced the response to snails would be disgust. Even more powerful then, the revelation—"It was fantastic!" Finally, the easily overlooked significant metaphor for remembering the lesson of the escargot—easily overlooked because it was so natural and appropriate on its literal level—there's a lingering, an aftertaste on the palate, just as knowledge that there is a wider world will linger in his mind. An epiphany that "there was a fantastic, unbelievable world out there."

Jean Shepherd as a youngster had seen what it was like in the Midwest, and it was not for him. Years later, as a reporter in *In God We Trust: All Others Pay Cash*, Shepherd's stand-in, Ralph, returned to his "despised hometown." He met Flick in Flick's Tavern. Throughout the book, in the short tie-in chapters with Ralph in the bar talking to his old friend who had stayed behind to tend his father's bar, while Ralph had escaped to the big city, Ralph frequently took the opportunity to disparage Flick—not to Flick's face—no, in Ralph's reportage which we read. Flick is the guy who remained—limited in outlook and in mind, who had to be told about what was now second nature to Ralph, who comments:

> ...forgetting where I was I said:
> "Pure Pop Art."
> Flick paused in his glass polishing.
> "Pure what?"
> It was too late to back out.
> "Pop Art, Flick. Pure Pop Art. That jukebox."
> "What's Pop Art?"
> "That's hard to explain, Flick. You've got to be With It."
> "What do you mean? I'm With It."
> I sipped my beer to stall for time.
> "Flick, have you ever heard of the Museum of Modern Art in New York?"
> "Yeah. What about it?"
> "Well, Flick..."

Thus ended the chapter. Ralph implied in the book that his New York world had its superficialities and limitations, but it was obvious where he, Ralph, now found home. Toward the end, he commented, "I looked again at my Rolex. For some reason I didn't quite recognize it at first as belonging to *my* arm, and to be honest I wasn't sure that it *was* even my arm. Somehow, that sleeve and that watch all belonged in New York. Another world. Back there they probably would not even believe there *was* such a man as Flick. Or Stosh, or Kissel, or Yahkey. They'd probably figure I made 'em all up." Shepherd toys with the reader here—Shepherd, who had for years been telling it as though true, says in the book's disclaimer and in interviews that it is fiction, but here has the fictional Ralph/Shep say it's true. We don't know how many of the details are true, but the effect it conveys, however, is unmistakable—he did not feel comfortable going home again.

Even though he had a fund of funny stories about being a kid, Jean Shepherd rejected what it was like to grow up in the Midwest. As an adult, in retrospect, he could see the unpleasant meanings of some of his kid experiences, and could convey them to listeners, readers, and viewers. As he told it, by the time he reached high school, he began understanding his experiences not only later, but also in the act of living them. He could see that there was something beyond the smokestacks. Beyond midwestern schooling, he would see another world—that of military service. You see other people and other places and you get another kind of education. Although most of his army stories are light and funny, not all his experiences are as amusing in reality as they might seem when told in retrospect. The army is a world of riding home on a troop train sleeping on a dead soldier's coffin, but nobody wants to hear that kind of unfunny truth. Sometimes in Shepherd, the unpleasant truth is found between the laughs—the army is a harsh school, learning how not to let 'em do it to ya.

CHAPTER 2

"HANG LOOSE, SON. DON'T LET 'EM DO IT TO YA"
Army Life

Compared to Shepherd's kid stories, the army tales were a more direct confrontation between the adult world and the individual. They were sometimes about serious problems, and often darker, more bitter, wry, and even touching. They exposed a more dismal and depressing side of Shepherd that he may have wanted to explore more extensively in his live, on-air introspection and self-analysis, but this darkness evidently provoked too much negative feedback from listeners. He said he received letters complaining about that dark side of some army tales—usually he kept these stories light, or kept his darkness off center stage.

Jean Shepherd told army stories because the army was an area he was familiar with, providing a whole world of possibilities. He could use the army to spin his yarns and endow it with universal themes he found in the rest of life:

> For those of you who were ever in the army, I'd like to point out—very quickly—the army has not changed. You know, one of the reasons why army stories have a certain universality is because there are very few things in life—there's gravity—maybe—there's the moon, there's the ocean, there are maybe

lions—these are unchanging. These things stay the way they
are—always. And one you must add to this list is the army.[26]

Shepherd played his jew's harp over the opening theme music
of a January 13, 1971, broadcast titled "Private Sanderson." He
described the characteristics of Private Sanderson, a "basic yard-
bird" from Tennessee, a hillbilly career soldier who constantly
got in trouble, and who avoided doing much of anything. One
day Sanderson was reassigned and walked out of the barracks
and out of Shepherd's life, with these words of warning: "Hang
loose, son—don't let 'em do it to ya."

Most GIs endure army life by trying to avoid letting 'em do it
to them. The real-life Jean Shepherd spent a few years in the
army, saying he was in the service by the time he was eighteen.
According to official records, Shepherd entered the army in July
1942 (when he had just turned 21), near the beginning of World
War II, and because of his radio background, spent time in the
Signal Corps, in part at Camp Crowder, Missouri. He attained
the rank of T/5 (similar to corporal) and was discharged on
December 16, 1944. (As a silly alternate military occupation, he
said in one broadcast that he had been in the handle platoon of
a mess-kit repair company, the insignia of which was "mess kits
with crossed forks on a background of SOS."[xi])

The army was early, alien terrain, where one reacted and
learned, usually under stress. In the army, Shepherd learned
something about life—but not what the army expected him to
learn. He told many army stories, and maybe some parts of
them were true. Many of these tales do not appear to have the
explicit points found in the escargot story or those of the nail-
puzzle Gordian knots. Many seemed to have no special message,
yet, as always, his storytelling style, with its profusion of
amusing details, built-up images, and tone of voice, provided the
entertaining texture he was a master at conveying. If, in addition, an army story had a lesson, he did not usually point it out
directly, so the "lessons" noted are not his, but one listener's
interpretation.

Shepherd once described a cartoon he had made up: A man
enters an eye doctor's office and exclaims, "I'd like to see a little
less clearly, please!" Apparently, the man sees more of the
world's foolishness than he cares to. This relates to an episode
given the title, "Army Glasses." Shep tells how he received his
army-issue glasses and found that he couldn't see out of them.
The army was a blur—life was a blur. Probably for Shepherd,

the army was better that way. Lesson: What an organization such as the army does to you is make you see (perceive the world) less clearly in some ways (it could make you blind!), and make you see more clearly in other ways.

In Morse code class, several of the participants, including Shepherd, having been yanked out of the Signal Corps through a bureaucratic error, were past masters, but for their amusement, and with hostility toward the obtuse bureaucracy that had subjected them to the demeaning, elementary class, feigned incredible difficulties learning code. Lesson: Do your best to befuddle the authorities. It's a good way to vent hostilities about anything and everything connected to your indentured servitude in the military.

Shepherd described learning to climb thirty-foot, sixty-foot, and ninety-foot poles for attaching Signal Corps lines. It was scary. One of his fellow privates fell off, and though we do not learn what happened to him, it couldn't have been good. Shep went up a pole, looked down despite the warning not to, and also fell. Ten days later, he woke up in the hospital, alive but a casualty. His sergeant visited and, referring to the accident, in a stern, admonitory voice said, "How are you Shepherd? Keep your knees tight!" Those familiar with Shepherd's philosophy of life know that his prime directive was that in order to react to all life situations one must remain flexible—"Keep your knees loose." He nearly died because this army activity had required the opposite of all he knew about human survival—he had failed to keep his knees tight.[xii] Lesson: Once you start upward, don't look back, and don't expect that the normal precepts of life apply in the army.

In the barracks, the GI in the next cot had a fancy ivory manicure set, which he used frequently. When he disappeared (how or why not indicated, but probably AWOL), the sergeant, upon going through the man's personal stuff, asked Shepherd what the set was for. Shep knew nothing about the missing soldier, but gave the sergeant a description of the use of the manicure implements. From then on, as he had bunked next to the missing GI, and could explain the use of arcane objects, he was looked on with suspicion. Lesson: In the authoritarian mind, there is guilt by proximity and by the possession of unusual knowledge.

One of Shepherd's barracks mates died and the man's relatives came to collect his personal property. Feeling it to be a nice idea, they gave Shepherd the man's stationery and shoeshine set as a remembrance. He felt uncomfortable with the stuff and tried to abandon it. Someone found it and he was called into the orderly room, where it was returned to him. Lesson: When handed a bit of life's sadness, you can't just walk away from it.

A catalog of Shepherd broadcast tapes includes many army-related stories, many told during broadcasts from the Limelight café. The simple, descriptive titles are not Shepherd's, but give some sense of the variety of army story subjects. "Hey, gang," Shepherd would say, "do you want to hear an army story?"

4th of July in the Army
Another Army Story!
Army Casual Company
Army Days
Army Fun
Army Glasses, VD Film, Troop Train Ernie
Army Grease Trap
Army Induction Physical
Army Life
Army Payday
Army Phrases
Army Ping Pong
Co. K: Captain Cherry Bugs Out
Code School
Company K Eggs
Company K: Pole Climbing
Forced March Through the Ozarks With Gasser and
    Gruber
GI Party
Laying Wire from the Air
Laying Wire in the Swamp
Lost Three Day Pass
Love at the USO
More Army Stories
Morse Code Seduction
The Poetic GI
Private Sanderson
Realism: Co. K and the Movies
Rude Noises on Co. K Latrine Duty
Shermie the Wormie
Signal Corps Special Order
Soldier of Fortune, Army Aptitude Test
Theme for Signal Corps
Weekend Pass

The radio story told during a Limelight Café broadcast known as "Troop Train Ernie" was later made into the short story "The Marathon Run of Lonesome Ernie, the Arkansas Traveler," which appeared in Shepherd's book, *A Fistful of Fig Newtons*. In it, one of Shepherd's buddies, Ernie, gets off the troop train at a stop to buy beer at a local stand. The train starts up, and Ernie can't quite make it back on board. The image of Ernie, who may be still running to catch that train years later, makes this one of Shepherd's best-loved army tales. Some of Shepherd's army stories appeared in *Playboy* but not in books published in his lifetime. In contrast to the prosaic, merely descriptive names given to his stories by those who taped them, as per his other *Playboy* stories, Shepherd created humorous, quirky, eye-catching titles, such as "The Secret Mission of the Blue-Assed Buzzard" (September 1967);[xiii] "Banjo Butt Meets Julia Child" (December 1968); "Zinsmeister and the Eighter From Decatur" (January 1970); and "The Unforgettable Exhibition Game of the Giants Versus the Dodgers, Tropical Bush League" (May 1971).

From those titles, one can imagine that they are attached to funny stories. As for darker army tales, Shepherd describes some listener reactions:

> Whenever you do a show—you seriously talk about things that *are* bothering you, you'll get dozens of letters saying, "What is this lecture? Come on, guy, when are you going to tell about when you were a kid. [Laughs.] Come on, get back—tell us a wonderful story of when you were in the army," you know, and so forth.
>
> You know what's interesting—whenever I tell an army story that *really* deals with the war, people get *very* bothered and write angry letters—and yet they want me to tell army stories. Like the time I told the army story of riding back in the train. Riding back in the train *sleeping* on the coffin of a dead Pfc. This *bothered* a lot of people. And why? Well—war is war, you know? And really, it is what Sherman said it was. Rip Torn in combat to the contrary. McHale to the contrary. War really is that.
>
> And maybe we've created our own—maybe we all secretly want it. Maybe Man wants and desires, and hungers after Hell as much as he hungers after Heaven. Since it's easier to produce Hell, he whips it out whenever the hunger gets a little too strong. I suspect there may be something to that—but then again, this makes the whole problem very complicated.

It can't be dealt with in a three-line bit by Lenny Bruce. It can't be disposed of in one single fantastic insightful comment by—uh—Mort Sahl. Right, gang? How about let's all sing a folk song about it, heh? Who wants to play the guitar? I'll sing tenor.[27]

Despite the tendency for the miseries of life—even army life—to fade from memory, and more of the benign or fun things to remain, Shepherd did his best to remind us of how it really was, even when the story told on a Christmas Eve concerned the relatively minor discomfort of pulling guard duty in the cold and rain:

And I remember my last go 'round; my last trick was at six o'clock in the morning. Two-hour trick. And the guy comes around, and he drove off in the mud, and as he drove off in the mud, he says, "Look," he says, "take it easy, soldja'. Oh by the way, merry Christmas."

I said, "Merry Christmas, sir." I could see the glint of his wet first lieutenant's bars on his wet raincoat, and I had the vague feeling—he didn't like it any more than I did. And somewhere, someplace, he too, is probably saying, "It's Christmas Eve. Thank God I ain't in the army!"[28]

Shepherd told one story about just getting out of the army. Back home, he is maneuvered into a date with a minister's daughter, apparently to help him adjust to life away from the crudities of the military. Surely, this would provide an example of nice, normal, civilian life. She takes him to a wild honky-tonk bar, where she is obviously a regular customer. That she gets falling-down drunk seems evidence, as Shepherd frequently pointed out, that no matter who you are and where you are, the essence of human behavior remains a constant.

The army and college life (of which he said very little, other than in that important story of epiphany regarding snails for supper) provided experiences moving Shepherd away from the limited world of Hammond. The Army Signal Corps was certainly an appropriate place for Shepherd, who was obsessed with communicating in one way or another all his life. As early as his adolescent ham radio passion, and his radio broadcasting jobs as a teenager, Shepherd, through these means of communication, had already encountered wider worlds beyond what he felt were the severe limitations he grew up with—he had already escaped.

After the army, he used the GI Bill to go to college. Although he sometimes claimed he graduated, at other times he said he didn't.[xiv] Shepherd's education derives more from actual experience and extensive reading on his own than from formal education. By the early 1950s, referring to this period of apprenticeship as "when I was a tadpole," he is knocking around from one "salt mine" radio job to the next. He is Friendly Fred and other personas, he hears the siren call of Alaska, and feels the irresistible tug toward the Big Apple.

CHAPTER 3
WHEN I WAS A TADPOLE
Early Radio

Shepherd said that he became involved in ham radio as a kid, and that this helped lead him into broadcast radio work. He once referred to ham radio (his voice one-on-one with an invisible listener out there) as "a higher calling." The term evokes a religious experience, and considering Shepherd's early sense of being suppressed, and his need to find the path to fulfillment, radio indeed, could be called his salvation.

PORTRAIT OF THE ARTIST AS A TADPOLE

Shepherd's life in radio as a tadpole, as he referred to it (tadpoles, as the reader will remember, are the limbless larval stage, after hatching, of what will become a fully operational frog), had begun when he was a young ham operator, and developed into several more advanced forms of broadcasting in his high school days. Elaborating on his claim to have acted in the kids' radio serial *Jack Armstrong: All American Boy*[xv] on the PBS special "Three Worlds of Jean Shepherd," he said, "I was playing a kid—a toady even then. I played Jack Armstrong's best friend— I played the guy that always said, 'Jack! There's smugglers coming! What are we going to do?'" He also said he was a sportscaster in high school and did some other radio work then.

Here are possible elaborations of this:

> I figure we'll all have a lot to answer for. And one of the things I'll have to answer for is a dismal quarter season spent doing the play-by-play of an improbable ball team—you won't believe it—of an improbable ball team named the Toledo Mudhens.[29]

> I remember one night, I used to do a radio show when I was a kid out of a bar. I was doing a remote. I was an announcer working—I was in school. Actually in high school at the time. We did a remote from a bar in Calumet City. It was a lawless town and I can tell you some stories about that some time. Radio in a lawless town.[30]

> Well, one time I'm working at this little radio station, I'm a beardless youth of 18. It was a one-man radio station. I was— I operated the transmitter, an old Western Electric, I sold time over the phone, I pulled records, I did every radio show from morning till night, from 7 AM to 7 o'clock at night when we went off. We were on only 12 hours a day. I did everything.
> I had a different character and a different name for every radio show that I did. In the morning I was a sort of Don McNeil character, you know—"Ho ho, hello everyone, we're going to read our favorite prayer for you now and don't forget it, folks, in just thirty seconds it's going to be march time— time for you to march around your old bed there. The time is now 7:36. The temperature is forty-one degrees. This is Friendly Fred."
> I'd go on like that for two hours, you see. And at eight o'clock Friendly Fred would say, "We'd like you to stay tuned for the news with—with Mr. Grubbage. H.G. Grubbage, who follows in just a few moments. So long, folks, we'll see you tomorrow [sings] la la la la la la la la la"—my recorded theme would come on. Then I would have my announcer voice: "WKLUCK Algonquin, Illinois, where iron meets coal in the heart of the Fox River Valley. Next, H.G. Grubbage and the news. Mr. Grubbage is brought to you each day at this same time by your favorite White Castle. Now here he is, H.G. Grubbage and the news."[31]

With this background, thinking the world of radio wide open to him, Jean Shepherd moved to Cincinnati in 1948 where he worked for three radio stations. He said he broadcast opera from Cincinnati, and claimed to have been emcee on "a show out of the Midwest called, *The Ohio River Jamboree*," with hillbilly music, on which he sometimes played the jew's harp.

At WKRC Cincinnati (1948) he was a "disc jockey," and was fired for too much talk, not enough music. After agreeing to play more music he was back, only to be fired again for the same reason. At some point, when management realized his popularity, he got to talk as much as he wanted. This talk/music conflict apparently happened at two Cincinnati stations. The less talk/more music syndrome would bedevil Shepherd in New York, too, where he would be fired from his late-night program for not playing music. Good ol' Shep!—and good young Shep!

At WSAI Cincinnati[32] (1948–1951) he did remotes from a restaurant, Shuller's Wigwam. (A photo of Shepherd broadcasting in the restaurant, with the sign overhead, is one of the earliest of him at work.) At WCKY Cincinnati (1948), he was listed as an announcer. Reportedly, he was married for the first time,[33] briefly, during this period. In September 1950, his first marriage apparently over, he married Joan Warner, a University of Cincinnati graduate. They had two children, Randall, born in 1951 (named after Jean's kid brother), and Adrian, born in 1957.

In a mid-1960s program, Shepherd referred to an announcer of a one-man, 250-watt station as a "full-combination man," as he had been in his early days:

> Let me say this about it. I may sound like it's very funny, but it's a *very* difficult profession. It's a profession that has thousands of little ins and outs. You have to be *extremely* flexible... [Radio] is a medium that has *never* been recorded. They've written books about the theater, they've written books about the movies, they've written books—no books about radio. None. And to me it's the most romantic of all the media. *Fantastically* romantic medium. I'll tell you some night.[34]

Yes, it sounds appropriate, and familiar, this image of Shepherd playing all the parts—the voices—his listeners believing he was many different people. But it was just young Shep creating illusions, carrying listeners along on threads of sound. Shepherd played Friendly Fred, he played Grubbage (we'll hear more from Grubbage later on in the program)— Shepherd was whoever he wanted you to believe he was, because you couldn't see him, and he could use his imagination and an invisible presence to do whatever he wanted. This modus operandi of full-combination men just doing their jobs was a technique Shepherd would later use to artistic effect as he explored the possibilities of the radio medium.

I WANNA GO TO ALASKA!

Now, further words from young Jean Parker Shepherd. From time to time, he read a poem about humans slowly moving along an evolutionary path: "When you were a tadpole and I was a fish/In the Paleozoic time/And side by side on the ebbing tide/We sprawled through the ooze and slime."[35]

> When I was a tadpole, I got an offer. I'd just gotten out of the army, see. I'm telling you some—some past, real-life history. I got out of the army, see. I'm sluggin' it out in these miserable classes in the origins of English words and phrases. I'm sluggin' it out in courses called Latin 1 and 2, Organic Chemistry 101B, and I'm sluggin', you know. I'm going through this real world. And at night I'm working in a radio station, see. I'm doing all these things. I'm doing these things—and slowly, by tiny, tiny inchings, my fame grew.
>
> I began doing the English cut-ins on a Lithuanian man-on-the-street broadcast. That was just a first run. After that, I was given my own program. A program that was heard every morning at 5:30 AM. A program of Elmer Rhode Heever hymns—recorded—in which I did the commercials in between. But it was my first program. I was beginning to inch my way up and up and up. Inch by inch. Moment by moment it looked like any day now—the next assignment I was Cousin Jean on a hillbilly teenage program when I had to talk like this. [Imitates accent.] I was beginning to really feel it. I mean, you know, I was "tearing a side."
>
> Well, one day I got a fatal—a fatal special delivery letter... I was just beginning to see that there was a world out there. I mean that there was something beyond Western Avenue. I was beginning to understand that—that out past Howard Street there was something. And that if you went out the other side of the municipal airport, there was something out there. Over beyond the lake—the big old lake there was—Ohhh!— Babylon! I was just beginning to understand this, see. And I

got—and it was beginning to erode me, you see. This city is the worst seducer in the world. It erodes. It cuts and digs and grinds and makes you into little things that finally you begin to read magazines like *Esquire*, and *believe* New York is like that...

Well, anyway, slowly but surely the strings are being drawn and I didn't realize it, and I get this special delivery letter which I opened. The special delivery letter said, "Dear Mr. Shepherd, I own a string of radio stations in Alaska. Four of them. Juneau, Anchorage..." Ohhhhh!—I can't even!—I mean, you know? Four of them! "We would like you to come up and run our Juneau radio station. We will provide you with a cabin." A cabin! [Shepherd bangs on his table.]

Now here were the terms of the deal..."furthermore, we will"—speaking of wild offers and the timberline, this is WOR AM and FM, New York. Boy, we are in the wilderness. That's another story. Another kind of wilderness. I mean, there is a wilderness within a wilderness within a wilderness, you know. Just as there are many mansions, there are many wildernesses and many gods. And boy, we are in a wilderness now! I mean it's a dark, dark one. [This is only one of many disparaging remarks Shepherd makes over the years about WOR.]

...Well, nevertheless I read this thing—and I was excited. "See—look at this, guys!" And every one of these guys who were doing things like the Elmer Rhode Heeber Gospel Hour, and guys who were doing the English cut-ins on the Croatian Hour. All of them looked at me, "What are you doing this ridiculous thing for?"

I says, "Well, look at this, look at this—Alaska! Alaska!"

"Alaska! Are you insane? Are you out of your mind, you fool?"

I says, "But it's Alaska. I mean Kodiak bears, salmon so big that they jump up and nip at your fanny! I mean, it's fantastic!"

They say, "Are you out of your mind?"

I says, "No, look around. Listen. Here we're in this little dark radio studio with the liana vines growing up the side, and the old—the old Wayne King records that we play over and over and over again." And in the middle of this, the music playing in the background was Bing Crosby singing to a ukulele, singing about blue Hawaii and every once in a while they would get up and make an announcement to the effect

that "Bing sings every day at this same time." On record. Old
record. He's telling me I'm insane 'cause I wanna go to Alaska!
I says, "But why? Alaska, fellows!"

Three of them looked at me with one eye, and all three of
them said, "If you go anywhere, man, the only one place to
go—New York! I mean, the Big Apple—that's the *big* time!
You can stand right next to Andre Baruch, right up there with
Frank Gallop, with Kenny Delmar!"

And all the while the Bing Crosby record was going, "You
and me, and blue Hawaii da de a do do do do." We didn't have
three dollars between us. Or one decent suit. It goes on and on.
I'm sitting there and that—I looked at this letter and I tell you
what I did. I looked at the three guys and I said, "You're
right!" Ohhh.

Oh, I would love to go to Alaska now—I mean—just fantastic. I'd love to go to Alaska. I mean really. Hawaii—nah. I
mean this sounds like a gigantic Nedicks stand with false, you
know—with reeds hanging down. Papaya juice on every
corner. And all the real estate operators. But no, I mean,
really—really Alaska! What have I done? What have *you*
done? [Here Shep is speaking to his engineer—and, by extension, to his listeners.] Don't laugh at Shepherd! What have you
done, you clown? Look at us! Look at us![36]

Shepherd knew that New York was the worst seducer in the
world—you needed to get there, and when you got there, you
wished you were in the wilderness. He moved to KYW in
Philadelphia, and broadcast from a hotel ballroom. His last
Philadelphia shows on KYW,[37] January 23 and 24, 1953, are the
earliest two broadcasts yet to have surfaced on tape. Here was
already evidence that his broadcasts were not standard—either
disc jockey, or anything else:

> I welcome adverse criticisms as much as I welcome a pat on
> the back, because the avowed purpose of my program is not to
> please, but to begin trains of sequence, to begin trains of
> thought, and certainly if people do not agree with what I say,
> that is just as valuable as a person who does. Because you have
> to begin a train of thought. Do you follow my reasoning
> there?...
>
> But KYW has been the most satisfactory radio position I
> have ever had and all the time I have been on KYW, and that has
> been since April 1951—and you don't know [how] unusual this

is, I have never had one word of advice from the front office. Not one, not a single word. There hasn't been a single note that came down and said, "What was the idea of that Sanskrit sequence last night?" There wasn't a single note like that.

That is the most valuable thing in this world—that is rapidly losing, by the way, rapidly losing its imagination because it's afraid to have one. And it is rapidly losing its belief in other people. I'm talking about the guy next to you. Hence, speech as a free thing...

I wish to thank all of you people who have been listening to us and I'm very sincere about it and this is not being funny, because I realize it takes listening, and I realize that many things that I do might not be good listening, and I'm the first to admit that, and I'm also the first to say this—probably not the first, but I'm probably the only one on 50,000 watts to say it, that there are many things that we attempt that do not come off, but I do feel that a few things do come off, just a few, but if a few of them do, I think that the wasted shots in the dark are worth it as long as the few do come off.[38]

On those two broadcasts, he seemed like a brash young kid feeling his oats, knowing he had talent. He was energetically, youthfully strong, with the power of being on the verge of full flowering. From what he said he seemed to have been experimenting with the medium—and this always results, in every art form, in some attempts that do not come off. If a painting, the artist could paint over it or destroy it—on live radio, every attempt, good or bad, was out there and one had to live with it. Shepherd moved to WLW, another Cincinnati station (1953–1954), and a listener on WLW remembers:

> ...being absolutely fascinated by hearing the iconoclastic, stream-of-consciousness "ramblings" (and I do not use the term pejoratively) of that voice during the wee hours over my old Crosley table model. As I recall, the broadcasts came from some sort of nightclub or bar, and there was the sound of patrons conversing and the tinkling of glasses or tableware in the background. The only specific I recall is that Shep at that time periodically launched into tales of his experiences as a T/5 while in the army.

Pete Wood, who later was to meet Shepherd in Philadelphia,

remembers hearing him in his earliest Cincinnati days:

> He started out stream of consciousness and the
> problem was he was so much so that he had an
> extremely limited audience. Those people couldn't
> understand him... What amazed me was the man's
> breadth of knowledge about things. So I envisioned the
> guy had all kinds of notes that he worked from.

Wood, who lived in Philadelphia, remembers when Shepherd
began broadcasting from there. Wood decided that he had to
meet him. He drove to the office building around midnight and
went up. He walked into the radio station, not encountering
anybody. There was a lighted booth back to one side and there
sat this guy doing this radio program, and obviously it was Jean
Shepherd:

> I was very forward. I walked back in and waited till
> he had a commercial or something and he came to the
> door and opened it and said, "Hello, can I help you?"
> And I said, "Well, I was just going by and wanted to see
> if I could meet you." And you know what this guy did?
> He said, "Well, come in and sit down." Now this was a
> tiny radio booth and I sat down there. And he said,
> "You'll have to excuse me, I'm going to get back on."
> And he went on with this stream of consciousness pat-
> tern. And I was totally amazed because there were no
> notes! The guy was working from no notes at all! And I
> thought, how in the world could you go on all night into
> early morning, with no notes! With these tremendous
> details! That's what struck me. And he was playing his
> collection of jazz records, because he had an incredible
> collection of very old, obscure jazz.

Shepherd did a television show for Cincinnati's WLW-TV called
Rear Bumper. He acknowledged liking to dress up in costume
for it[39]—armor, a cowboy outfit, etc. One can imagine that just
as he used the full potential of the radio medium, with television
he was quick to explore the visual possibilities, expanding them
for comic effect, possibly in a somewhat similar style to that of
Ernie Kovacs. Shepherd talks about one such show:

I came to New York as a television performer and I worked in television for a long time before I got to town. And how I got on the radio is a long story itself, and suddenly I found myself on the radio, and with listeners, and people began to say, "This guy—what could he—he couldn't do anything on television again—it's part of a separate world."

I remember one time I'm doing this TV show and I look out—2 o'clock in the morning I'm on and maybe 1 o'clock, something like that. I followed *everything*. When the whole rigmarole of the day on television was over, when all the hollering, and the guys selling the storm windows, and the movies staring Miriam Hopkins disappeared, and Bert Parks had disappeared and the whole crew had paraded through our lives, suddenly I appeared at the end of everything. In fact, it was the only show that was ever—that was regularly broadcast *after* the sign-off announcements. Really. I came on after—*after* "The Star Spangled Banner." It was kind of like a disclaimer. They didn't want me to come *before* "The Star Spangled Banner." [Laughs.][40]

Jean Shepherd's program followed the national anthem—he was an American, but he had already been told that he was not part of the crowd and no one was to salute and stand at attention for him. He did have a small, loyal band of listeners, but—his apprenticeship over—he was moving on. He had come from Indiana, from the Midwest, where he had roots, and he was lured toward the intellectual and broadcast center of New York City.

Beyond his tadpole experience in his early radio days, with what sources of nourishment and knowledge was Shepherd equipped to create a name—and a persona—for himself? He enjoyed and studied the Midwest storytelling tradition and style, and though he would on occasion be a stand up comic, the tradition he knew and loved is not one of joke telling, but rather of extended stories that create a narrative environment for insights he wanted to convey. These stories entertain, amuse, and instruct through context and humor. He looked back toward Mark Twain, George Ade, W.C. Fields, Jack Benny, and the dry, subtle, everyday humor in radio's Vic and Sade.

What is the nature of these roots? Why not jokes?

PART II

HERITAGE AND ENDOWMENT

Shepherd studies the art of humor—its history and its uses. With this knowledge he will be able to exploit his fine talent for observation—expressing what he sees in himself, his countrymen, and the common humanity around him.

CHAPTER 4

I CAN'T TELL A JOKE
Roots

By the time he reached the Big Apple, Jean Shepherd had absorbed much about the nature of radio, storytelling, and humor. What were Jean Shepherd's roots? Although there was variation and even contradiction in his comments on many subjects over the decades, there is considerable information in his own words that gives a good idea of his overall beliefs and makes it clear that he knew what he was doing in his crafts of storytelling and humor.

> I have a rhetorical question I would like to ask that came about—some guy wrote me a note here, see, and he said, "Shepherd, you know everybody's been influenced by things in their life." He said, "Who and what influenced you?" And this guy's writing a paper or something. It's very embarrassing having to answer a question like that. What do you say, you know?
>
> I mean, you know? If you want to be really pompous—if you ask, like—if you ask a guy like Mailer, he'd come up and tell you, "Well, I was influenced by Herman Melville and Camus and Jean Paul Sartre." But I don't know how to handle this, and, I have to approach it very delicately here tonight. I might as well tell you what I was influenced by—very strongly.[1]

He went on to say that he didn't believe most people were strongly influenced by the movies, even though movie critics claim people were. Several times over the years, he discussed comic strips, saying contradictory things about their influence on him. On other occasions he did, in fact, discuss influences:

[Opening theme begins, Shepherd starts speaking.] Well, I see here we have now a letter from the English Department of the University of Virginia. It says, "Dear Mr. Shepherd: Can you please tell us what your primary literary antecedents and your literary..." Yes, sir... God, I love these official letters—tell us what your influences were when you were a kid, you know. [Laughs, theme ends.]

My literary influence. Well, I'll tell you, that's a very sore point with me, I must admit. As a writer and a person who has had more than a few things appear in print, the question is—you know—what your literary influences are always is rather embarrassing to me because, every time I pick up an interview by some other author, he always has these fantastic influences, like. Kurt Vonnegut always says something like, "Dostoyevsky, *War and Peace*." I mean, you know? Norman Mailer always says, "Well, I guess it was the great tragedians that first influenced me." I wish I could say something like that. I—I wish I could say it was *Captain Billy's Whiz Bang* that influenced me, but it didn't. [Laughs.]

But, nevertheless, as an observer of the scene, I can only say that I have always admired people who can honestly say that they were influenced by Dostoyevsky. Or they were influenced by the great tragedians. I honestly, as a writer, can't say—I'll tell you I—you notice I'm shilly-shallying here. Now the reason I'm shilly-shallying is that I approach with some trepidation the admission of what I really was influenced by. Now there are people who have written to me and said, "It's obvious from your style of writing, at a very early age you were influenced by the Montgomery Ward summer catalog." That's not true...

So, nevertheless, I can honestly say that I was never influenced by Dostoyevsky, I was never influenced by Hemingway. Now, I read all those people [laughs]—of course. I listen to, I defer to *no* Mailer or Kurt Vonnegut—in lying about my past. I will—no way. But I will tell you what influenced me more than most other things. Now, when you were a kid, what did you read?... [Shepherd kids around a bit with obviously fake influences.]

Now you know when you—when you get back to your early influences—how can I tell them that one of my earliest *literary* influences was a commercial! One of the very first things I actually learned as a kid. I learned the song that goes like this, [sings] "Pepsi Cola hits the spot. Twelve full ounces, that's a lot. Twice as much for your money, too. Pepsi Cola is the drink for you. Nickel nickel nickel nickel nickel nickel nickel nickel nickel nickel." Okay. That was a profound influence on me. In other words, I was influenced by the slob world around me far more than Dostoyevsky ever influenced me...

I saved my money every month so that I could buy a copy of this magazine that came out every month. I not only read this magazine, I *memorized* it. I read the ads, I read the front, I read the back, I read—I even read the little print up in the front, you know? That says, "Our main offices, circulation offices." ...What was this magazine? Okay. You ready for it? *Field and Stream*... And as a kid, I loved this magazine so fantastically, because, I guess it was—it described a world so unbelievably alien to the world that I lived in that it seemed excruciatingly desirable... [He goes on to contrast this world of nature with the junkyards and steel mills of northern Indiana.][2]

STORYTELLING

[Newscaster at the end of his news: "And now here's Jean Shepherd." Shepherd's theme music begins.] Heh heh heh, oh yes. Yes, indeed. [Spoken ironically, affecting a leer, which is rare, because Jean Shepherd's programs almost never even border on the off-color.] Now you come sit on my knee, baby, and I'll tell you some fantastic stories. Heh heh heh heh heh. Yes, you just sit here right on my knee. There, yes, indeed. And now it's story time. ["De de de" along with the music. "La de de da *dee* la *dee*," etc.] Yes, all the thrill of victory and the drama of defeat [almost exactly quoting the opening announcement of a TV sports program]—will be yours for the next fun-filled, scintillating moments.[3]

Jean Shepherd told hundreds of stories on the radio over his twenty-one years in New York. His stories of his Indiana childhood and his life in the army are what many remember most fondly about his work. He is often compared to Mark Twain and James Thurber, both midwestern storytellers. Shepherd's stories usually built up slowly, with sharp, humorous, and extended detail. They usually contained some explicit or implied life lesson. On those occasions when the substance or point might be weak, one was still carried along on the richness of the telling—Jean Shepherd was never boring.

> There's a particular type of storyteller, which has practically disappeared. As a matter of fact the whole idea, the whole technique and texture of storytelling is practically a lost art in the United States and in fact, in most places in the world—the idea of the storytelling...
> I feel that I was very fortunate in coming from the Midwest, particularly—if I had not come from the Midwest, I doubt very much if my profession would be the profession I have chosen. But the idea of the storyteller is a kind of, in a sense, a holdover from farm tradition. Not necessarily the frontier tradition, but the farm tradition, and it has to be the farm tradition—that in most cases—the isolated farm tradition, and so the idea of a storyteller—a storytelling session was in a sense almost a theater of the time.
> Now the reason that I brought this up is that the technique of speaking that I used just a moment ago is a standard storytelling voice projection technique. There was a very special way of doing it. W.C. Fields used to use this technique occasionally. It was a kind of technique—he would speak like this, you see [Shep imitates Fields' voice]—"It was a long, cold, hard day in January. I had seated myself in the second seat in the parlor car of the train that was bound for Peoria, Illinois..." The story went on and on and on—[laughs] do you want to hear the rest of it? It's a technique of ad-libbing.[4]

Shepherd, as here, sometimes enjoyed discussing his techniques. Obviously, he found his abilities a pleasure to behold, and he enjoyed passing along the details of his craft. He wanted to be sure that his listeners understood that he was not just rambling on—in his work he exercised that craft with considerable skill, which they might have taken too lightly.

> I came across an old book, a paper book of recitations, and you know, it's interesting, in a sense, how our—how close to a frontier society we really are. In a little less than fifty to seventy-five years ago, the recitation was really the prime, and

the only—outside of religion—means [garbled] a form of release, a form of escape from the daily struggle, which was unceasing—the struggle for existence. The recitation was the only form of literature—the theater—that many of them knew in the early days. There were no touring companies of theater people. And so, the recitation became—and was—the chief source of the theater literature and that wild wonderful strange world of the imagination that existed out there beyond the last row of the trees...

And the reason I'm bringing this up tonight is because, in a sense, the work that I do every Sunday night, and Saturday morning too, the work that I do, is a form of recitation, a form of imaginative drawing upon our own life and our own emotions to paint a picture in a sense, of something that most of us don't feel day by day. And I have a great sense of empathy for the early recitation artists and monologists.

And these were just generally people in the community who learned two or three recitations, and every time there was a gathering of the community, a social affair, Charlie would be called upon to give his famous recitation, his recitation of "Life Is But a Game of Cards," which was one of the great recitations, or maybe give his famous recitation of "The Ace in the Hole," which was a great recitation, or—I'll read some more of these that you might be interested in. Of course, one of the most famous was "The Face on the Barroom Floor."

Now all these recitations had one thing in common: they were very emotional... [Shep reads several about hobos.]

Many of the recitations were based on actual news stories, things that people heard about—in this way they resembled—kind of resembled the ancient troubadours—carried a story around—it became news. It was a form in a sense, of the folk tune... And most of the recitations or at least many of them were a kind of evangelistic, do-it-now-while-you-can—because all [garbled] every man's life there's a sense of a kind of always wasting. Don't you feel like you're wasting ninety percent of your life? Well this is an old, old problem, the wasting the life, so naturally there would have to be a recitation.[5]

Recitations, fables, and parables all contain a moral and they are all forms of storytelling, which Shepherd used. He could tell stories endlessly. When Jean Shepherd told a story, or just an anecdote or fleeting little riff, what was he doing?

He told it as though it really happened to him.

He almost never dealt with sexual matters—except in occasional veiled and relatively innocuous references. Yet he never seemed to be puritanical.

He used striking images, colorful and unexpected adjectives and adverbs, amusing metaphors, and obvious exaggeration.

He often used reality in quirky ways.

He often built up to his point in a roundabout way, with seemingly tangential anecdotes.

Usually he tied it all together, often he explained his meaning—he gave a life lesson at the end. Tying together and life lessons were truer of his later radio work.

Possibly most of the true stories and most of the fictions he presented as true were fables for our time—telling more truth than one might at first imagine. In a 1960 *Realist* interview, he said, "About when I was a kid, most of those things are done as a parable. Literally as a parable. It is not true, let's say, that my mother stood near the sink all of her life. This is a parable."

He repeated various themes. In an early broadcast, although the culmination of the story is that his baseball batting slump had been caused by tight underwear, he talked about returning to ideas:

> This is a story I've told, so don't turn around and say, "Shepherd's told this before." It's an important story. This is a leitmotif. You know what is it a leitmotif?—that keeps weaving in and out of my life, you see.[6]

HUMOR

> I've often said and I still maintain this—that the big difference between humor and satire—I shouldn't say satire, I should say humor and comedy—is the longevity of humor versus the short-term value of comedy.[7]

His habit of distinguishing between humor and comedy has several causes. In the first place, there *is* a difference as he defines them. What is perhaps most important, he considered humor as he practiced it a higher form because it dealt with insights into human nature, whereas comedy almost always relies on superficial wisecracks. Finally, he wanted to distinguish himself from the then-current "seriously funny" comedians such as Mort Sahl, whose renown he envied and, moreover, felt was *his* due. In the October 1960 *Realist* interview, he spoke at length about humor:

> Well, comedy is a process whereby you're *aiming* at making a person laugh, and the end product is the laugh. With humor, however, the laugh happens to be the byproduct of what you're doing. Comedy, which does not say anything, is very funny and we laugh at this. But humor, that says something about a specific situation and really makes a point, is highly resented...
>
> If you want to make a point it's often not funny, but on the way, the examples you use to make your point *are* funny; now if you stop before that point is finally made—most of these guys would be terrified of going on for five minutes without anybody laughing; that's why it's like this [*snap, snap, snap*]—one-liners.
>
> The problem is, a humorist cannot *stop*—when he has something to say, he wants to say what he has to say—and if the laugh comes up, it's a byproduct of what he's saying. It's his *attitude* that makes people laugh, often, but *not* his end point...
>
> This is another thing about a humorist—he's very serious about what he says. Invariably. You don't think Bertrand Russell's kidding around? You don't think Mencken wasn't serious about what he said?

As a student of humor and his historical predecessors, Shepherd often talked about what he found funny. He talked of Laurel and Hardy, Groucho Marx, and H. L. Mencken, the great debunker, and he spoke on-air with that master of surreal wit, S. J. Perelman. He spoke about the early-twentieth-century midwestern humorist, George Ade, and sometimes read an Ade story. In the following March 20, 1960, anecdote, he bluntly separates his style from that of common tellers of jokes:

> I call this person—the person answers; it was a woman... A middle-aged woman. I finally get in touch with her, and she was laughing uproariously when she picked up the phone. I said, "What's going on?"

She said, "Nothing, nothing. Someone just told me a joke. Nothing. It's all right."

I said, "What is the joke?"

. And she said, "Well, it's not a very good joke. I'm embarrassed. I can't tell a joke." Then she broke into laughter again.

I said, "Tell me the joke."

And she said, "No, no, I'm embarrassed. I can't tell a joke." Then she broke into laughter again.

I said, "Tell me the joke."

And she said, "No, no, I'm embarrassed. I can't tell a joke..."

I never did find out the joke. And when I got her on the phone and she said that—when she said, "I can't tell a joke, it embarrasses me to tell a joke," I had this little thrill as though someone had touched a bad tooth somehow or someone had kicked my elbow in the wrong place, because I can't tell a joke either. I guess it goes back to early childhood. There are guys who tell jokes, and those who don't. I am not a teller. I can see the humor in the world. I deal in humor but I can't tell jokes. I have never told a joke successfully, ever.

Shepherd talked about "one of the most truthful interviews" he ever read, about an English sea captain who after decades, said he hated the sea—the interviewer claimed the captain was joking. Shepherd obviously thought about his own form of truth telling:

"Man was joking." What man? How does he know that? Oh, the *World Telegram* will not admit that he was saying the truth; they have to pretend that he was joking—oh yeah? [Laughs.] The *World Telegram* has to prove its case to me rather than the other way around. Believe me. [Laughs.] Ah— you tell the truth and everyone has to say, "Oh, he was only *kidding*."

You see, that's what happens—just a little trick you learn in life—the more truthful you become, the better you get by with it. Because—one, nobody believes—nobody believes it when they hear it. And two, when they *do* hear it and believe it, they have to then make it sound like— "Oh, he's just kidding," or "He's a kook," or "What a phony—take him out."

Now, whether or not you can argue the—whether or not you can argue the truth of what the man said is totally beyond the point—everyone has to make it into a joke—ha ha—you're kidding—and that's why—now *World Telegram* in its own little stumbling way has hit on one of the great facts of humor. This is one of the reasons why Voltaire, when you read him, always sounds like he's jokin' around—you know—he's sayin' funny little things—ha ha.

And—Jonathan Swift—Houyhnhnms and all those Wahoos and Yahoos and—"Oh, he's just kidding." Gulliver and that—just funnies, little funnies, and Lewis Carroll—oh funnies, funnies, funnies. All kinds of little funnies. Like, you know, the funnies.

And the poet has learned this—many, many centuries ago—you know? That—the deeper you dig—the more you can become [enter "cheap guitar music"]—truthful. As long as they don't listen carefully.[8]

Many people have tried to describe humor. E. B. White: "Humor at its best is a kind of heightened truth—a super-truth." And Irvin S. Cobb: "I concluded that what Mark Twain was saying to mankind as a humorist was this: 'Look what fools we are, and I at the head of the proccession!'" "Humor is meant to blow up evil and make fun of the follies of life," said Will Cuppy.[9] What did Jean Shepherd understand by humor?

For example, I got a letter from a kid. Now here—here's a typical example of a kid—who is beginning to see his world. Now I'm going to give you a classroom example of a person who sees the great dichotomy, the great contradictions, and in one way—the enormous bits of humor in our life. It's just in-built, see.

Humor has been defined many ways. One of the good ways, one of the best ways in a sense—and yet there is no real definition of it. Any of you have a dictionary out there to look up the dictionary definition of humor? Just look up "humor" some time, and see whether it covers what it is you feel—if it explains to you why you laugh. If it explains to you what humor really is, a really evasive thing—because no one has ever really successfully explained it. Yet, to a person who works *in* humor, there are certain things that do—in a way— that do their part of it and are part of the overall, let's say, recipe of humor.

And one is, the great difference between—the life we live and the way we think we live it. [Here Shep refers to one of his major themes—how we all delude ourselves and do not take enough advantage of life's possibilities. It is one of the

themes described in a following chapter on his philosophy.]
This can be illustrated by somebody like Charlie Chaplin
who always had the grand manner about him. He would take
off his gloves in a very fastidious series of movements—just
beautifully fastidious. He would take his gloves off. He
would dust off his coat, and he puts a carnation in his lapel.
And you, sitting back from the whole thing can see he's a
totally hopeless individual.

Here's another example of it. Shel Silverstein's famous cartoon. It shows the interior of a prison cell. Very famous cartoon
that again illustrates, I think, very perfectly, the difference
between the dream and reality. And you, as the outsider can see
both the dream and the reality, and so you find it funny... [The
cover of one of Silverstein's books of cartoons, for which
Shepherd wrote the introduction, shows two bedraggled pris-
oners shackled to the wall, not even touching the floor, as one
says to the other, "Now here's my plan."[10]]

Well, you know, this is the thing—now here's an example of
the kind of humor that's in your life, you see. It's always in
your life all the time, all the time, all the time. It's here—it's
absolutely inescapable. Every place you look. There's an old
photographers' axiom that says, "There's a prize-winning
photo within five feet of you." This is true. There is all the
humor in all of mankind, all the sadness, all the greatness, all
the gladness, and all the idiocy of all the man—is within five
feet of you. Just look around.[11]

Again, in April 1960, while talking about H.L. Mencken's
four-volume work on the American language, he talked about
humor:

Many people feel that the language—any language—that a
people use—is the real key to the philosophy by which they
lived or died. That the more exact a language is and broader a
language is—obviously, the more sophisticated a society
was—that the people were involved in. And it is interesting to
note that I—well, I think that—at least half the people who
are involved in cataloging our language today are concerned
over the fact that the language seems to be suffering a decline—not that slang is coming into it—this is not what we're
talking about. But that actual words have been so subverted
to the point that they are almost completely meaningless.

Of course the most are words—are such words—many of them are being done this way and being used this way by the advertising world. How many miracles do you see a day on television? Demonstrated in twenty-second spots? The word "miracle" you know, is a—is a—very, very exact word and it's a word that has ramifications of its own. It has very little to do with a new soap—actually. It might do you good to look up the word "miracle." As well as to look up the word—has anybody got a dictionary out there—they can look up the word "humor" for me. I'm curious to see what the actual definition of humor is—that is given in one of the more official type books of definitions...

The interesting thing about it is in the middle of it all, the dictionary throws in a line from an artist—as part of its definition. They have a line from Thackeray. And it's a definition of humor. Here's what Thackeray said, in the middle of the dictionary: "I should call humor a mixture of love and wit." That's the definition as given in—what is this? Webster's New International Dictionary, Second Edition, Unabridged. It weighs thirty-eight pounds. And so I guess that makes it stand. ["Stand" is a rare Shepherd play on words.][12]

Here are other definitions of humor that Shepherd would probably have agreed with[13]:

True humor springs not more from the head than from the heart—It is not contempt; its essence is love. It issues not in laughter, but in smiles, which lie far deeper.
—Thomas Carlyle (1795–1881)

The world is a perpetual caricature of itself; at every moment it is the mockery and the contradiction of what it is pretending to be.
—George Santayana (1863–1952)

Wit may be a thing of pure imagination, but humor involves sentiment and character—Humor is of a genial quality; dwells in the same character with pathos, and is always mingled with sensibility.
—Henry Giles (1809–1882).

The Henry Giles definition is close to what Shepherd called

true humor. This idea will occur again in our studies later in the semester—take notes and underline it each time it reappears. As Shepherd might have said, if Horace Walpole hadn't said it first, "The world is a comedy to those who think; a tragedy to those who feel." In that regard, the *Village Voice* reviewer of Jean Shepherd's book of short stories, *In God We Trust: All Others Pay Cash*, suggested that Shepherd's "cynicism" was a cover for refusing to feel anything.[14]

Shepherd's earlier work seemed more humorous, while as the 1960s moved along, he more frequently used lampoon, burlesque, and satire. This seemed especially so in much of his written nonfiction. Possibly, he felt the need to use a different mode in a different medium. Maybe for his casual articles he found hostility easier to do than humor, or he felt that the audience for written funny stuff expected more of a punch. Even his later radio work, though, sometimes lacked the tolerant attitude of earlier days. Frustrations in his career may have contributed to this—as we encounter his later discontent, we will understand better why the tone of his work changed.

The tradition of hostile, yet witty, commentary on America's citizenry and customs has a rich and vibrant history. Mark Twain in the nineteenth and early-twentieth century made Americans laugh at themselves as he criticized them. Ambrose Bierce ("Bitter Bierce") savaged all mankind with his harsh descriptions and ironic definitions. Then, beginning the decade before Shepherd was born, and continuing throughout his impressionable youth, H.L. Mencken smote the American booboisie with the bludgeon of his scorn. Shepherd knew this tradition and occasionally mentioned these three men, but he lavished most praise on an American comic writer, lesser known today than the foregoing, George Ade, whose sardonic humor was popular during the late nineteenth and early twentieth century.

Shepherd, writing in the extended introduction to his compilation of fables and essays by the early-twentieth-century writer George Ade, *The America of George Ade*, says of one essay on Indiana midwestern, nonprofessional humorists, "Almost all of their humor is of the school of Futility rather than the school of Tall Tale of earlier frontier days. Futility, and the usual triumph of evil over good. Which is another name for realism."[15] Ade's tales rely heavily on irony, satire, and sardonic humor, in which the upright innocent comes in second to the shrewd realist. Ade's focus on the foibles of the common man, the theme of futility, the clear-eyed, straight-faced expression of Ade's intelligence, and his use of slang—unusual in literature of the time—all seem to have attracted Shepherd's admiration. After recounting a story, Shepherd comments:

> The important thing here is that these were real people. Aunt Mary and Yaller-Eye were not fiction, and what happened to them really happened. It is wise to note that the man who told the story obviously loved both of them. This is a characteristic of all true humor, and particularly of Ade's. The philosophy of Ade is a reassuring one, since everywhere there is the deep compassion of a man who has been there and seen it.
>
> There are no heroes or noble figures in Ade. All are subject to the same trivial emotions and continual tiny frustrations, rich and poor alike. Ade, as has no one, before or since, chronicled the Great Unchronicled. Those who are totally unimportant. So profoundly insignificant that they hardly exist so far as literature is concerned. Those to whom nothing ever really happens. No tragedy or comedy. No romances or Great Loves. Those who settle for what they get and quietly move on. Which means most of us, in the end.

Here we see Shepherd fascinated by the minor people and events he frequently spoke of as signifying more about our common humanity and our time than most people realize. Shepherd enjoyed quoting odd, overlooked little newspaper clippings. As he would say—that was where the true history of our time was.

After another description of an Ade piece, he wrote, "What happened to her? You guess. But whatever did or did not happen is exactly true to life. This is a key to Ade as well as any other true humorist. Ade always maintained that he was not a humorist but a *realist*." It seems clear that Shepherd wrote all the above about Ade because he was thinking about the similar nature of his own work.

RADIO'S GOOD OLD DAYS

Shepherd's high regard for the potential of radio led him to discuss what radio could do and what it had accomplished in earlier decades. Michele Hilmes' book, *Radio Voices: American Broadcasting, 1922–1952*, focuses on the period corresponding

to Shepherd's childhood as well as his earliest years in the
medium and deals with radio's importance to "the real heart and
mind of America." Hilmes quotes Gertrude Berg:

> "I want to talk about the America I've discovered on
> the air—Radio America. Columbus discovered just a
> rock-ribbed continent, but if you want to discover the
> real heart and mind of America, you've got to look for it
> on the air! The programs of all the broadcasting compa-
> nies are like mirrors held up to America's soul. They
> reflect what people are asking to hear and wanting to
> know."
>
> With the same warm tone of buoyant Americanism
> that characterized her thirty-year serial, *The Rise of the
> Goldbergs*, Gertrude Berg editorialized for the
> *Cleveland Press* in 1933. Her article expresses the kind
> of sentiment about radio broadcasting so frequently
> heard in its first two decades; a utopian rhetoric tied to
> nationalism that glorified radio's special properties and
> emphasized its uniquely "American" character. More
> than any other medium, radio seemed in its early days to
> lend itself to association with ideas of nation, of
> national identity, to "the heart and mind of America," its
> "soul..."[16]

As Jean Shepherd was growing up in the 1920s and 1930s,
radio was the dominant medium. Most Americans listened to
news, music, commentary, quiz shows, stories—all on radio. In
Raised on Radio, author Gerald Nachman (who went on to pen
Seriously Funny: The Rebel Comedians of the 1950s and 1960s,
which includes half a chapter on Shepherd), writes that from
radio "I learned much of what I knew about honor, romance,
justice, evil, humor, manhood, motherhood, marriage, women,
law and order, history, sports, and families." Nachman also
noted that "the direct, unfiltered sound of the human voice, like
voices over a telephone on some nationwide party line, com-
pelled you to pay attention." He could have been thinking of
many kids listening to Shepherd when he continues, "There
was—still is—a mystique to radio unlike that of any other entertainment medium. Its intimacy amounts almost to secrecy.
People tend to listen to radio alone. Listening in—eavesdrop-
ping—is such a private, vaguely stealthy, literally undercover
act. You can take radio to bed (as I still do) and listen to it in the

dark. As a boy, so as to shield the glow of the dial on school nights, I would throw the covers over the radio..."[17]

Those were the good old radio days—there were original stories in addition to those adapted from films and theater, there were famous theater and movie stars, as well as many actors and actresses working primarily in radio in the various plays, and dozens of serials, both for adults, and for children. The Lux Radio Theatre, the Philco Playhouse, the Mercury Theatre of the Air, most famous for Orson Welles' 1938 Halloween broadcast adaptation of *War of the Worlds*, which created panic among thousands of the self-deluded, who, having tuned in late or were not paying enough attention, believed Earth was being invaded by Martians.

As television invaded the scene, radio began to collapse as a dominant force. In *Radio Voices*, Michele Hilmes writes:

> But contrary to some assertions, it was not advertiser abandonment of radio that motivated the rapid removal of network assets from the old medium to the new: rather, networks made a deliberate policy decision to concentrate development in the new technology, where sales potential was vast and regulatory conditions favorable, at the expense of radio... As radio waned as a national medium, networks broke down and local stations found themselves increasingly on their own.[18]

Radio made a few attempts to stay alive as it had been, such as *The Big Broadcast* of 1950, featuring big stars, and later, NBC's *Monitor* ran all weekend, featuring spots by Shepherd, and by Bob and Ray, but nothing stopped the decline. Jean Shepherd mourned the loss of radio's special qualities:

> It's sad that a whole art form grew to fruition and suddenly disappeared. It would be as if somebody had invented painting and great painters had flourished for—oh, maybe twenty years and then everybody forgot about painting because everyone discovered ceramics. Or they discovered sculpture and—they—they just completely from that day on—because radio can do things that television and the movies and the stage can never do. It plays with the imagination and the mind [in a way] that I think no other medium can ever approach.
>
> Yet the whole idea of radio acting—you know some great radio actors who in their field were as fine as, and in many

cases even better than, anybody performing on Broadway, anybody performing in the Shakespearean repertory today. Some great actors rose to become really fine artists in the field of radio back in the 1930s and early 1940s. And the whole—the whole canvas is gone now. The whole thing is gone. It's really a shame because this was a fine medium and is—it's as though there was a big sleeping giant out there. A huge, sleeping giant that's lying out there, that one time people hunted, that one time excited people and has now long since somehow been forgotten by the people.

And it's lying out there in the jungle there, just—just completely untouched as though it's a whole new mind-land, let's say, a universe of the—of the psyche is lying out there untouched, and will be untapped. It's interesting how it's ignored even by the most important types of people that—as far as radio is concerned it hardly matters what you say on radio. Even though there are thousands of people listening to radio—millions—every day—it hardly matters what is said on radio because the official journals don't really take cognizance of it. They never do. Somebody puts on a little bitty Off-Broadway show with twenty-five people in the audience and four people in the cast—they will get columns of print and type in the *New York Times*. On the Sunday page too, you see.[19]

Vic and Sade

Shepherd often referred to a 1930s and 1940s radio show called *Vic and Sade* that might (inadequately) be referred to as a situation comedy. This fifteen-minute program concerned a small family, talking of everyday small matters in small ways in a small town in the Midwest. It had a dry, unforced wit that required close attention. Shepherd was amused by the program's focus on mankind's obsessions—giving disproportionate importance to trivial matters. For example, one of the character's extensive washrag collection. In 1976, he wrote the foreword to *Vic and Sade: The Best Radio Plays of Paul Rhymer*, in which his appreciation for *Vic and Sade* came through in a variety of ways that related to his own work:

Most work done for the mass media is highly perishable by its very nature. Unfortunately, also by the very nature of mass media, the mediocre and the banal tends to outlive the truly creative and original. The "Lone

Rangers" and "Green Hornets" are forever dredged up
as examples of "The Golden Age of Radio," while
unfortunately the true gold is mentioned rarely, if at
all... but Smelly Clark's Uncle Strap taking his lady
friend to Peoria for a fish dinner somehow got me where
I lived. Maybe it was because Paul Rhymer created *true*
humor. He did not deal in jokes, but human beings
observed by a sardonic, biting, yet loving mind. The *Vic
& Sade* scripts are not only still fresh and funny, but are
absolutely recognizable as an authentic picture of
American life which persists in millions of homes
today... Another thing that amazes me is Rhymer's wild
and subtle imagination. Wild in the sense of being
totally unpredictable, and subtle in that he touched at all
times on the faint vein of madness that runs through all
of us. He rarely went for the obvious; hence he preceded
the Theater of the Absurd by decades. In fact, it is my
opinion that in some ways he is far closer to Ionesco in
spirit than he was to Thornton Wilder, who sentimental-
ized American life in a way that Rhymer's sense of irony
refused to allow...

Another example of Rhymer at his surreal best is the
little gem called "Caramels on a Hot Day," in which we
find Rush, as he puts it, "stirring up a little excitement"
by sitting on the front porch, making round balls out of
square three-for-a-penny caramels. Think about that for
a moment. A hot day, caramels, and boredom. This is
exactly what a kid does do, squatting on a front porch
in the heat of summer, but who thinks to build a fifteen-
minute drama to be broadcast to millions out of that
dynamic situation? Better yet, who but Paul Rhymer
could pull off such a feat, or would have the courage to
do it even if he could? Rhymer obviously was very sure
about his work in a medium where that kind of security
and self-knowledge is almost nonexistent...

Most contemporary writers for mass media simply
feed a series of one-liners to their characters, go for the
cheap laugh, and hope that no one is the wiser. Rhymer,
in contrast, wrote *dialog*; succinct, spare, yet with an
absolutely true ear for the rhythms and inflections of
American speech. This is much easier to talk about, or
discuss in class, than to accomplish. Obviously, Rhymer
was a very gifted listener.[20]

Jack Benny

Shepherd loved the unique quality of pre-1950s radio. When comedian Jack Benny died, Shepherd did a tribute and took the opportunity to comment on the joke style of comics he tended to disparage—those who got the easy laughs with one-liners—especially the various topical comics of the 1950s and 1960s who made it big with the public and the media. The wisecrack comics of which Bob Hope, of the older school, had been a consummate practitioner. Shepherd very rarely if ever wisecracked, and, as he said, he did not often tell jokes—they were a lower form of funny. Shepherd honored Benny—and simultaneously made an important statement on his own style of humor:

> Most comics today don't have much in the way of actual technique—they have material. Material is not the same as technique...this is the thing about Benny. Benny combined of course, talent—he was a talented man. But more than that, he also had great technique. And he had *guts*. [Laughs.] Now, what I mean by that. Well, the one thing that most comics today—let's say of the Don Rickles school—and I'm not putting Rickles down, but this is a different school. Let's say, the George Carlin school or the Morty Gunty school. This school—the one thing that they're afraid of *most* of all, is a moment of *silence*. [Laughs.] That would kill 'em. [Laughs.] So they just constant—it's like a machine gun. This is called the "scatter gun technique." In fact, they'll lay out in one minute—they'll tell thirty one-liners. That's a fact. That's why they all talk [mimics fast talk] you know it's all—it's a machine gun technique. So that if nine jokes fail out of ten, they've still got three laughs in a minute.
>
> Benny used the long pregnant pause, and he was a *consummate* radio performer—to begin with because he knew how to use the medium very well. Probably the greatest radio comic that ever lived. No question about it. He knew how to use the medium, he—he had very subtle modulation of his voice—he knew how to just turn a phrase, just with a slight—slight—almost a—a twitch of the eyebrow as a phrase is going by you, and he could get laughs on absolutely zero material—which always baffled many other comics—because Benny—Benny—his was the humor of *attitude*—which is *not* the same as the humor of situation...
>
> There was very little written about *Benny*. Benny was a private man, obviously. There was not much—you didn't see

> Benny appearing much in Earl Wilson's column. Benny did what he did and he walked away. And that was all there was to it. A curiously self-contained man.
>
> [End theme begins.] ...certainly is one that I think changed a lot of people in America. Certainly influenced me—no doubt about it—no way to get around it.[21]

And just as Shepherd here responded to Jack Benny's dry style and use of sound and silence on radio, he also commented that Benny was a private person—Shepherd must have felt a common bond with Benny, considering that he also kept much of his real self private.

Fred Allen

Shepherd said that he knew Fred Allen. Fred Allen's comic wit remained on the air for many years, his programs contemporaneous with Jack Benny's. Allen was sardonic, critical of society and of radio itself. He paid the price—his network's timid censors blocked him constantly and he fought them as hard as he could. Shepherd was also a social critic, and a battler against the constraints of radio's administrative and commercial forces. The title of one of Allen's books, which discussed his radio work, must surely have resonated with Shepherd: *Treadmill to Oblivion*.

Henry Morgan

Henry Morgan broadcast what seemed an extemporaneous and freewheeling style in 1940s and later radio, on *Here's Morgan*. Morgan seemed more scripted, with a very penetrating mind and wit—one's idea of the clever smart-ass friend, sure to come out with the wise-guy clever remark, who constantly made one's mind do double takes. A consummate pro with the verbal sword, whose thrust was not *touché!* but a slash that drew gushers of blood. He was acerbic, he was opinionated, and he was hostile toward "the powers that be." He was wonderful.

Herb Saltzman said that Shepherd "thought he was much better than Henry Morgan. Henry would add to it on the air—exchange blows. But Henry was one thing, [Shepherd] was another." Morgan had accused Shepherd of being anti-Semitic because of a remark Shepherd made on the air about a Hollywood producer he named "Manny," and Saltzman said, "He wasn't. I do not think he was anti-Semitic. He was—you know what he was—clearly he was jealous [of the success of some 1950s and 1960s comedians, many of whom were Jewish]."

In 1960 interviews, Shepherd and Morgan acknowledged listening to each other's programs, and Shepherd said he was a great admirer of Morgan's: "Morgan did some of the best stuff I ever heard on radio." Shepherd also commented, "Incidentally, one of my wonderful childhood memories is hearing Henry Morgan."[22] However, in 1971 during an Overseas Press Club conference, asked if his radio program was influenced by Morgan's earlier radio shows, Shepherd claimed that Morgan was not broadcast to the Midwest when he was growing up. Shep said, "No, Henry Morgan did not influence me." With Jean Shepherd, as we know, the truth was hard to come by, and searching for it in interviews is especially perilous.

Some of Shepherd's predecessors, Vic and Sade and the other people on that program, Fred Allen, and Jack Benny had the advantage of seeing some audience as they performed in the radio studio. Henry Morgan, probably the closest earlier radio peer of note, seems to have been nearly alone in the studio as was Shepherd. Shepherd would seem to have preferred to have had more of a visible audience than his engineer toward whom he could project his monologues. Maybe this is part of why he would so much enjoy his live broadcasts from the Limelight café in the mid-1960s. At the Limelight and at his hundreds of other live performances, his ego could feel the "sense of power" he refers to in the following excerpt. The sense of isolation during his studio broadcasts must have been distressing:

> But radio shows go on and on—many of them—many of them are very, very worthwhile. But that's beside the point. What I was trying to say here was that perhaps the sense of power that is evident in working before a live audience with a man—before a live audience—the sense of power, and the kind of two-way communication—this is not obviously—not often felt in radio. I know that I don't often feel it. In radio. In the sense that there is a great crowd out there—it's just not there for me. When I work, I work in a—in a vacuum. In a closed, sealed room.[23]

Although Shepherd spoke of his sense of isolation in the studio—the lack of two-way communication (ironic, in that his listeners felt so strongly their closeness to him), his not having audience interaction may well have been a great advantage to his style, a subject discussed later regarding his live Limelight nightclub radio broadcast performances. Note should also be taken of early complaints by Shepherd that his medium, radio— and thus, he himself—did not enjoy the respect he obviously thought it deserved. Forthcoming chapters deal with this lack of critical and financial rewards—both of which probably influenced him to branch out and eventually leave radio.

But here he is, struggling up the mountain slope, approaching the heights of radio broadcasting—the important medium of his youth. What could one talk about and tell stories about with humor in radio—and in other media? The easy and obvious laugh is one thing, but identifying the subtle human foibles, through close observation and understanding, requires a turn of mind that appreciates what many find unimportant—trivial. And trivial they may be, but these little cracks underfoot, in the very foundations upon which we walk, are evidence of underlying irresistible forces however invisible they may be to most of us. For Jean Shepherd, with his odd-angled insight and penchant for telling us the way it is, trivia is not trivial.

CHAPTER 5

CRACKS IN THE SIDEWALK
Close Observations

TRIVIA IS NOT TRIVIAL

"I'll award the brass figlagee with bronze oak leaf palm to the first person who can tell me..." The brass figlagee, with its made-up silly word, is a Shepherd invention, poking fun at the world of real awards given for real accomplishment. Shepherd awards it for a manifestly minor feat of knowledge and memory. Every Shepherd listener heard that request for a piece of trivia many times. Within the same sphere of humanity's array of foible-filled activities, there lies the peculiar fascination with trivia, the often arcane and frequently inconsequential detail. Shepherd, with his pleasure in details, and his insistence that there is often more to life than most of us perceive, delighted in showing off his knowledge and his ability to make unexpected connections. It has been suggested that he originated the use of the word as used today to designate the minor, nonessential facts of our existence. When he asked for a piece of trivia, it might be from an old radio show, music, literature, some product or the jingle associated with it, or any common object or occurrence out of the recent past of American culture. Of course, we see that, for him, the minor often signaled the major.

Trivia represents the culture of the common man, with whom

Jean Shepherd had an uneasy love/hate relationship—because the common man is the dominant stuff of American culture, the frequent subject of his humor, and because he was both the harshly critical observer and the self-aware participant enjoying the foible. Big ideas and high culture are not the concerns of the common man—it's the little things that define his life. Besides, these little things dominate not just the common man's thoughts, but occupy more of everybody's time than most are willing to admit. He once commented that rather than concentrating on great thoughts, even the best of us are too often deeply preoccupied with what kind of gas mileage we get.

In a 1960 *Realist* interview, he said, "I'm intrigued when *I* get hung up on trivia. I'm fascinated—all of a sudden I'll wake up and say, 'What am I doing this here for?—for twenty minutes I've been sitting here doing the *New York Times* crossword puzzle, and I should be out being *dynamic* or something.'" With a mingled tone of disdain and obvious pride, he frequently said, "Why do I *remember* this stuff?"

He saw blandness foisted on America by the media and the mediocre—the surface values—but was amused by the widespread oddballness, the funkiness that seemed just out of sight (or society tried to keep out of sight—it surfaced in the small news notes). He saw the common man's quirkiness as a vital part of our nature—that part of us that keeps us *alive*, from just being a cog in the machine.

When Shepherd offered to award the brass figlagee for the correct piece of some obscure information (and he seemed chock-full of this information), the implication was that knowing the tiny piece represented knowledgeable familiarity with its surrounding gestalt. It represented the ability to make connections from a vast mental storehouse of information (not the result of a college education, but of his intelligence and far-flung interests).

"Straws in the wind," trivia's kissing cousins, are the quirky, minor events (often found in newspaper column fillers—news notes) that can reveal more than we would imagine about ourselves. For Shepherd, these peculiar events are the substance of the life most of us live most of the time, but we tend to dismiss them. He found these news notes, or his "spies" (friends and listeners) sent them to him. He described an account of a dead camel found in an Indiana front yard, and commented that "the average American who's brought up on movies and TV shows and novels, believes that they're far truer—than real life. Therefore, he does not believe the stories out of real life. I'm sure that a lot of you listening to this story about the camel say, 'Aw, come on, what—are you *kidding?*'" Sometimes, when the news note was in "bad taste" or when his in-studio people showed signs of disbelief or seem to be offended, he sometimes replied, "I don't *make* the news, I just *report* it!" He summed up his attitude toward the absurd minor news notes with "We're living in par-less times," which, in the context, meant times without par, but could easily have also meant parlous times.

He loved the easily overlooked detail that the Dr. Watson in all of us misses, but in which Sherlock Shep discovered significance: "The reality of what we really are is oftentimes found in the small snips way down at the bottom of things." A marvelous example of this was his observation about the gravediggers, which he described at the end of his beautifully composed eulogy of John Fitzgerald Kennedy, broadcast right after the President's funeral in 1963. (See a partial transcription in Chapter 17.) Shepherd commented that, as the burial ceremony at Arlington concluded, and the cars of the funeral procession were already wending their way back to Washington, two men in their work clothes were briefly visible in a lower corner of the TV screen. As Shepherd put it, they were there to perform the inevitable—burying the coffin in the earth—and that this was the common end of all of us, not just of the average man, but even of presidents. He said that the camera quickly panned away, maybe because this bit of reality was too much to take.

> I'm a constant observer of cracks in the sidewalk. I like to see how these cracks go back and somehow they make patterns, you know. They—they make shapes. I like to look at the sides of old buildings where you can see old signs that have been erased. Old movies and ancient stage plays and—and old advertising campaigns that fizzled out like all of them do in the end, you know. Of course, this has never been and never will be listed on the "Big Board" of human achievements. But—some of us get hung up on one thing, others get hung up on another...
>
> Now stop a minute here, madam, *stop*—these little bits of trivia—you begin to see that they do have a universality and some kind of a deep, sinister meaning. Because I have a suspicion—within the heart of man, there lies this beautiful, irreverent creature. This creature that is constantly going—[spitting sound] *pitooy!*—you know, right out of the corner of

the mouth, and chews a very cheap brand of chewing tobacco. Never smokes anything that has any kind of a filter on it at all, and has been known to blow its nose in its sleeve.

This is the only side of man, of course, that really has any actual value. And is the side of man we are always pushing down, constantly. And—and the more a person becomes aware of this, the more a person works hard to prevent anyone from knowing he or she has this side. And so they develop all kinds of little tricks—mannerisms of walk, official looks on the face, wobbling jowls, all sorts of things that denote and connote in our time—respectability.

But nevertheless you cannot beat it down—it rises—it rises—that little creature shall—*pitooy!*—shall rise again—ha! [He speaks of news stories about "big" events and important people quoted.] Back and forth go these gigantic balloons, and all the while, you're having a problem with your knee, you know. All the while, you continue to catch the cold of your soul. It's sniffling. Every once in a while this creature goes pitooy!—hah pt—*pitooy!*—it's chewing tobacco like mad.[24]

Now you just heard Lester Smith do the newscast. Didn't you? Now this is called news. Well, it is, I suppose. Actually, all it does is describe events. The real news would be news that described people. I mean—what is happening to people? This would be the real news. 'Cause I mean all these events are forgotten. Everybody forgets the events, you know. I mean, can you tell me what events you were swinging with in 1947? That you sat there and said, "yeah, yeah, tch, tch, tch tch"—you can't, you know? They're gone. But if we could somehow capture the *essence* of people. Now I have prepared a newscast of items that I removed from the newspapers within the last five days, of the real news of what mankind is doing... [He goes on to read quirky news items.][25]

Did you read this little news note the other day? Only in our time!—believe me—I am collecting a million of these things and I am putting them in giant file cabinets which I will bury 200 feet deep six minutes before I finally kick off. This is going to be my own time capsule. Has nothing to do with newsreels of Elsa Maxwell. Has nothing to do with filmed interviews of Jack Parr talking to notables. Just, you know, kind of an attempt to preserve what it was *really* like.[26]

Sometimes he read the little news items in his own voice, and sometimes he assumed a Walter Winchell–type demeanor of the self-important newscaster:

> And now, ladies and gentlemen, it's time for the real news program with H.G. Grubbage, world commentator, author, lecturer, gourmet, man about town, bon vivant, and seer. Now Mr. Grubbage reports every evening at this same time with the real news. The news behind the news behind the people. Now, here he is, Mr. Grubbage.
>
> [Shep assumes the official newscaster-type voice.] Good evening, Americans everywhere! Grubbage here. A woman passenger became so incensed yesterday when a Lexington Avenue bus failed to stop at the corner where she wanted to get off, she whipped off one of her shoes and she hit the driver smack in between the shoulder blades—twice. [Dixieland music starts.]
>
> And now more news. A disappointed television viewer took revenge yesterday. Armed with a twenty-one pound sledge-hammer, he went to the shop where he had bought his defective set, and smashed every television set in sight.
>
> [Shepherd reads several more strange news notes.]
>
> And so you have heard it. The news of people as they are. Good evening, Americans, and before we leave you this night, we would like to provide you with our thought for tonight: sit it out—it might work out after all. Grubbage here. Good night. [Dixieland.]
>
> [Shep returns to his real voice, and after a few more words, continues.] Oh boy! Those were real news notes. You want to hear more? Oh no, no. It's hard enough to face the facts, you know. To face things the way they really *are*, without facing things the way they *really* are.[27]

At the end of a group of Grubbage news notes: "I have the feeling, of course, that—that we have a tendency to put these little notes aside and say, 'None of—of course, this is the trivia.'" Says Shepherd, "*Oh yeah?*" [Laughs.]

> We have a little note here from the silly section of the *New York Times*. That's the section in the last part of the paper where the real stuff is happening. You know I—you can read the *New York Times* all you want hour after hour. Read the

editorial page—you get nothing but all these platitudes. "We should think good, we should love each other." All that. [Laughs.] Nothing to do with the way it really is—fistfights, nitty-gritty world. And it's only when you get way back at the back part of the page, you know—where it says the surplus values that are available. And stuff you can buy in the silly section in the weekend section of the *Times*. For example, do you know on a recent one you could have bought yourself some surplus 88-millimeter mortars? That make—uh—souvenirs, it says, "For the *collector*." Well, it's also kind of fun to lob a few mortar shells over to the next apartment house—nice to see how the *action* is going.[28]

ODDBALL EVERYWHERE

Once again, you know that life in the Midwest is continuing as it always has. And shall always continue.[29]

Is there something especially strange about Indiana that led Shepherd to think about trivia, cracks in the sidewalk, and oddballs? One might check out several real books available at the local online bookstore: *Indiana Curiosities: Quirky Characters, Roadside Oddities, and Other Offbeat Stuff*, and *Oddball Indiana: A Guide to Some Really Strange Places*. Then browse through *Oddball Illinois*, followed by *Oddball Wisconsin*, *Oddball Colorado*, and who knows where the list might stop? Maybe, as Shepherd undoubtedly suspected, it's not Oddball Midwest, but Oddball Everywhere.

Regarding life as rendered in art, Shepherd had the same objections as he did about the "important" news events which crowd out the infinity of minor commonplaces that fill most people's lives most of the time. This undated segment was played on the WOR tribute to him:

It first hit me when I went to see—I was—at this time I was working in the Actors Studio. I was in the Actors Studio for a while. They were always doing these scenes, see—from new— you know—from plays and stuff guys were working on. I was even working on one myself, and once in a while I'd get this strange sensation, you know—I've never seen anything like this actually happen in real life. It only happens in *drama*. It's called "drama." And people live one way in drama and real *life* is another thing.

So I went to see *Virginia Woolf*. Remember that? I never heard any man and wife argue like that in *real life*. Not about that kind of stuff. So I figured, well, drama was one thing, life was another. Literature is one thing, life is another. Movies are one thing, life is another. I wonder what would be—what would happen if they ever came together? If a guy ever made a movie about what life really is. I mean, it would be totally inconclusive. [Laughs.] Absolutely no—just a lot of sort of aimless talk—sort of—sort of fooling around. A lot of talk about absolutely irrelevant stuff.

Yet, it would be the only stuff that *is* relevant! In other words, the relevant stuff is only talked about in movies, films, and plays. The *real* stuff that we're concerned about is talked about in life. Like endless discussions about how much gas mileage you get.

Just as the trivial piece of information and the minor news item are representative of the little pieces of everyday life that constitute most of our existence, so is the style—the ways we deal with tiny occurrences—the substance of what we are. Seeing the minutia of events and the bits of style, and being able to transmit them in one's art, was a talent Shepherd prided himself on. He read a clipping about a man in Lima, Ohio, who caught a bullet from a small-caliber pistol in his teeth. Describing the opening of an imaginary play, he took the "little house half way up in the next block" line from the announcer's opening description of the neighborhood in *Vic and Sade*:

> A simple midwestern apartment, just like that little house half way up in the next block that everyone grew up in... *Where* did he catch it? Between his *teeth!* Then he *spit it out!* Now that's what I call style. You know, speaking of this, oh yeah, I've always said, "Just put down what you see, what you hear around you." Seriously. And you have got *genuine* drama.[30]

During the same broadcast, he plays some bouncy piano music, and speaks in ironic tones:

> Will you please give me some—uh—*style* music, please, please? Excellent, excellent. That's superb. Style. Picking them

up and laying them down—at precisely the correct moment. Timing. The delicate, suave essence of the beautifully modulated nuance. Timing. Style. That is what life is. It is all. It is the distillate of being. The waft of the aroma of the far lost and forgotten fields. The gardens of yesteryear. Time, place. The moment. The instant of the spinning cosmos. The long dusty road of eternity. So one must learn how to pick them up and lay them down—with style—with élan—with savoir faire—with a—a spirit of implied—*whoopee!* Yes. Bring it up there. Cha cha cha *cha*. That's enough.

You are listening to the most stylish cat in the business right now. You're damn *right!*[31]

NOSTALGIA

One might find connections between trivia, straws in the wind, and nostalgia—they all seem to involve a sentimentalizing of the superficial and a simpleminded concern for minor matters. That Shepherd often talked about the trivia and the straws and also about his childhood left him open to accusations of being nostalgic. Despite there being a few grains of truth in the charge, Shepherd always denied it vociferously.

> Long John, you misquoted me fantastically last night! Long John on his program said, "Jean Shepherd is always talking about how great things were in the old days." I have never *once* said that! Have I? *Never!* In fact, I am constantly saying quite the opposite. It was *rotten* in the old days. [Laughs.]
>
> You just won't admit it. Often, when I describe how rotten it was, this is mistaken for many people for saying it was good. Interestingly enough, any time you mention something that happened beyond—past 1953—they say, "Oh, those were the days, oh, those wonderful days!" You can hear the sound of cud chewing from block to block as people say, "Oh, *those* were the days." And they're not listening to anything you're saying. You're saying, "Rotten, *rotten*, they were *terrible*, rotten—up to my neck, oh!" you know.
>
> I have a feeling the Earth is covered with a thick layer of viscous liquid. There is a common street corner name for it. I cannot discuss the name here at this point. I think all of you know what I'm talking about. It's not really a liquid. But it's a thick coat of it.

And—and man's talk, man's constant hoopla consists merely of making various formations of this particular, vast liquid cloud that is getting thicker and thicker on the Earth. He piles it up in pyramid shapes, and then he makes it into interesting various other types of symbolic shapes. Moving it back and forth and all the while he refuses to concede that the material he's working with is bad from the beginning.

Time, tide, and the affairs of man shall contrive to undo him. It's as though the world has a vast zipper, and somehow it's left it unzipped in a very crucial and very embarrassing time. That's another story.[32]

My work, I think, is anti-sentimental, as a matter of fact. If you really read it, you realize it's a putdown of what most people think it stands for—it's *anti*-nostalgic writing.[33]

The trouble with talking about the past is that people assume the speaker is being nostalgic. People usually think of "the good old days." Shepherd built up elements of the past, but then contrasted the illusion with a twist—the reversal at the end, in which reality denied the sweet image. People seem to regard Shep's reversal as "just a little joke," just as the newspaper reporter did not believe the ship captain who claimed to hate the sea. Jean Shepherd was plagued by this misconception throughout his career, and he hated it. He said that most people think the past was wonderful and the future is going to be even better, and it's just the present that stinks.

So we're not talking about nostalgia, friends. Get it out of your *skull*. Stop it! We're not talking about the old days—get it out of your bean. Stop it. We're talkin' about l-i-i-f-fe. Life. You *dig*, Keith? You dig? There ain't nothin' like it. It's the *only* thing we all got. And the *best* thing we all got.[34]

Oh by the way, the only man who can have *any* breadth at all, incidentally, in this world—in any world—is one who *does* remember his youth. In short—has a sense of the history—of the time in which he has lived. That man who remembers yesterday in the office is the man who knows something about today in the office. I'm not speaking on behalf of nostalgia here at all. Oh no! I'm speaking of jungle cunning. I'm speaking about the—the tiger, who, after having been shot several times, learns about shooting—and knows how to move

easily and gracefully in those long winding pathways. The
man who forgets his youth is rapidly on the way, and towards
becoming an interesting sort of psychopath.[35]

Regarding bits of apparent nostalgia from some of Shepherd's
stories, it was not that he got a secret decoder ring from the
Little Orphan Annie Show, but that instead of spelling out some
great message, it was a lousy Ovaltine commercial. It was not
that he got an air rifle one Christmas, but that it nearly put his
eye out. It was not that movie theaters once gave out free plates
to the women, but that, after receiving nothing but gravy boats
week after week, the frustrated women threw the china back at
the theater owner. It was not that his old man won a contest, but
that the prize was a slob-art lamp shaped like a woman's leg.

There was some nostalgic pleasure in some of Shepherd's stories (especially if one floated on the surface of such stuff in the
movie, *A Christmas Story*, or only paid attention to his truly
nostalgia-laden end-narration in two of his later video dramas).
Mostly that is our fault, not Shepherd's. We were seduced by our
erroneous impression of "good old days" in his stories and had
difficulty realizing that ironic deflating of the illusion was the
main point.

> **Ron Della Chiesa:** He hated the word "nostalgia."
> ...He said it wasn't nostalgia. "What is nostalgic about
> the Depression?" But he was able to evoke that era in a
> way—as a storyteller—that I think a lot of people
> related to, and I think that was a big part of his humor.
> That there is humor *in* nostalgia. And satire. But I think
> he envisioned himself much more as a satirist than
> somebody who is just reminiscing. *Bitter* satire. He once
> said to me, "Satire is the greatest putdown."
>   So I think that the line you draw is between people
> who listened to him and laughed in a humorous way
> over the nostalgic aspect. I think that he really envi-
> sioned himself as a sort of [Voltaire, author of *Candide*]
> or a Jonathan Swift, whom he admired—*Gulliver's
> Travels*—he always talked about that.

Even Shepherd's publishers, for their own reasons, sometimes
worked against his stated beliefs. Of the twenty-three short stories that *Playboy* published, the first seven were labeled as
"memoir" or "nostalgia." The remaining ones, except for two

that were untagged, are more properly described by *Playboy* as "humor." The back cover of the paperback edition of his book of stories, *Wanda Hickey's Night of Golden Memories—and Other Disasters* refers to Shepherd's "nostalgic Americana."

During the Alan Colmes interview in December 1998, Jean Shepherd spoke (whether honestly or in denial, we can never know) about his attitude toward his radio days, which had ended twenty-one years earlier: "No, I don't reflect on my past. I've never been a guy that, you know, was involved in his past—so, no I don't—that was one big long gig, and I enjoyed it and felt the audience enjoyed it—and when it came time to leave and go ahead and make movies, and get out—move up a rung, in other words—I did it—without a glance backwards." What we can probably accept from this is that he claimed he never allowed himself to sentimentalize the past, and that his constant attitude was one of concentrating on the present and future.

Ah, those were the good old days, when you couldn't say "shit" on the radio (but had to refer to "a common street corner name for it.") And, ah, now come the good old nights. Jean Shepherd arrives on the New York radio scene. He has his background, skills, special talent for observation, and idiosyncratic viewpoint. What better time to let 'em all hang out then, when the day-people mentalities are barricaded, asleep behind their privet hedges. When it is so late at night that there's no one in the place except you and Shep.

We have all the time in the world and no place to go except in the limitless expanse of our skulls. We can roam, we can amble, we can stop and cogitate whenever we find something. We can circle around stuff, play variations on its themes, and improvisations on its chords—all that jazz. We are the Night People, and Jean Shepherd has started to play with our minds.

PART III

THE GREAT BURGEONING

In New York City, Shepherd combines introspection, imagination, and improvisation in jazz-extemporized riffs—and becomes a man of the world in the Big Apple.

CHAPTER 6

NIGHT PEOPLE AND ALL THAT JAZZ
Earliest New York Radio

Jean Shepherd, with his strong interest in what makes humor important and, indeed, funny, and his strong bent toward the quirky details in the life around him, was ready to reach for all the intellectual pleasures of the cultural capital of the world in his time—New York City.

People everywhere at all times, for the most part, have been conservative, pedestrian, philistine, nonintellectual. Ask H.L. Mencken, ask Jean Shepherd. But the years following World War II were something special. Countrywide, Americans who came of age in the 1950s have been called "The Silent Generation" of conformists with insipid taste and stagnant minds—yet destined to lead the free world. And the hinterlands had always been the spiritual home of the vapid masses. To some budding intellectuals yearning to breathe free, what more backward zone than that flat, corn-and-cattle Midwest that Jean Shepherd fled?

The Depression and the war over, chrome and tailfins proliferated along with togetherness and suburban housing, and President Eisenhower presided with a fatherly, secure smile. "Under God" became part of our pledge. McCarthyism spread the fear of being different.

Of course, not everything could be solved by "the power of positive thinking," and the 1950s were not all silent. And there was "the Bomb," Communists under our beds (loyalty oaths and blacklisting), and the Korean War. Many of the social, intellectual, and artistic issues that found wider expression in the following decades began to surface by the mid-1950s. As Jules Feiffer observed in the June 15, 2003, issue of the *New York Times Magazine*, "The culture was reinventing itself under a patina of conformity." Existentialists (beginning in Europe, which had felt more directly the nightmare of wartime destruction) questioned the efficacy of simply thinking positively altogether. Artists who fled the Nazis gathered in New York, energizing American art. There were the Beats, sick humor, *Rebel Without a Cause.*

Sexuality reared its provocative head more openly with Kinsey's *The Sexual Behavior in the Human Female* (1953); *Playboy* magazine began publishing (1953); Grace Metalious published her novel of small town sex, *Peyton Place* (1956); and the contraceptive known as "the pill" was invented (1957).

Those surrounded by the Silent Generation, but who sought to explore and exercise their creative urges, found enclaves in big cities (including Chicago), but the goal of most of these people was New York City—Manhattan, the center of the bubbling intellectual, literary, musical, and artistic life. Author Dan Wakefield (originally from Indiana), in his film documentary *New York in the '50s*, put it, "You were freed from your background." And "people came to New York to escape the Eisenhower Age." As Wakefield said, talking about Greenwich Village's Sheridan Square, "There was no such place like this in Indiana."

Jean Shepherd was aware of and involved in the dramatic, exciting, and sometimes disturbing changes in 1950s and 1960s America. Besides the civil rights movement, there was concern about conformity and the "rat race," and the increasing influence of television's "vast wasteland." Urban folk singers were engaged in political and social protest. There were dramatic changes in the arts, such as Abstract Expressionism exemplified by the abstract "drip" painting of Jackson Pollock, who listened to jazz while working. It was an exciting time to be involved in the creative life.

[Shepherd is playing parts of the overwrought narration to the musical recording celebrating New York City, "Manhattan Towers."] "The seven million keepers of the flame." That's a real romantic idea, and yet, you know, curiously enough, there *is* some of that romanticism still in New York.[1]

New York was the center of the word—not only written, but spoken—the communications hub. People of Jean Shepherd's generation and inclination knew radio as a major medium—one with potential to do great things, to project ideas—in which a wide range of talented reporters, news analysts, comics, character actors in radio dramas—talkers all—were a vital force. Shepherd must have recognized the possibilities within himself for conquering radio and the other media in which he felt he had talent. But his timing was bad—he arrived in New York during the same period in which radio's consequence and the wide diversity of its broadcasting were already declining because of the expanding of television's vast wasteland—which was changing the way people accepted written and spoken words in general, and traditional stories in particular. This was also the time of another massive attack on traditional radio—rhythm and blues would broaden its appeal in the mid-1950s, becoming multiracial rock and roll. Elvis Presley was performing the crossover act that would spread rock and roll throughout the American consciousness and radio airwaves.

When Shepherd began broadcasting for WOR in New York in 1955, American cultural life was changing drastically, and his personal life also changed. His son, Randall, remembers what it was like to have his father leave the family, and the emotional stress it caused him and his sister:

> **Randall Shepherd:** Jean was already living away from our house most of the time, seeing Lois Nettleton [the actress]...coming home from time to time to pick up clean shirts my mother Joan was still ironing for him. He would talk his way back in with a line how it was going to be different from now on, he was going to stick it out with Joan and me.
>
> [Randall says that Jean left the family for good by 1957, not knowing that his wife was again pregnant. They were divorced in 1957.] Jean didn't just walk out the door and never return. For a couple of years he would put in an infrequent appearance as a father figure. I say figure because he really didn't have much heart in it, parenthood wasn't something he had the listening skills for,

to be able to empathize with a kid. For a couple of years after the divorce he would store his Morgan during the winter in our garage at Princeton, NJ. He would stop in to pick the car up, or drop it off, and while he was there he would ask us what we were doing, what's new, but he was more interested in talking about himself, and what he was doing. Living in Princeton, Adrian [Randall's sister, born after Jean left] and I had an annual emotional Gordian knot to deal with because he would do his show at the University [annually, 1966–1996], the posters would go up several weeks in advance, and we would wonder if he was going to call, and he never did. As we got older, we'd go to the show and try to see him afterward, wait out the hoard of well wishers, hoping to get a word with him ourselves. We were good show business children, we never identified ourselves. Joan [their mother] taught us that you didn't want to embarrass Jean in front of his audience, he would devour you. So we would wait, until finally he'd give us the slip, or say he'd call, but we'd never get any time with him.

Jean Shepherd sought to end most of his connections to his past, except for the creative memory and inspiration he used in his work for the rest of his artistic career. In a 1972 broadcast he commented, "Now oddly enough—I have never felt any sense of involvement in the country from which I have come [the Midwest]. My only involvement—from the time I've been a living mature person—has been with this city of New York. This is my home. I do not consider myself an out-of-towner."

Wherever he had lived, all media of self-expression fascinated him, and nowhere was the word—in all its forms, especially the written word—more important than in New York. No wonder Shepherd felt right at home.

The written word produced numerous books of social and literary import. Conformity was analyzed in at least three books that drew national interest: David Riesman's *The Lonely Crowd* (1950); Sloan Wilson's *The Man in the Gray Flannel Suit* (1955); and William H. Whyte's *The Organization Man* (1956).

Aspiring writers were coming of age at a time when modern literary writing (think Hemingway, Faulkner, Wolfe, dos Passos) had great force on the consciousness and dreams of youth. Influential literature included Norman Mailer's *The Naked and the Dead* (1948); J. D. Salinger's *The Catcher in the Rye* (1951);

Samuel Beckett's play, *Waiting for Godot* (first produced in 1953); William Golding's *The Lord of the Flies* (1954) with evil children, a contradicting of Salinger's vision of childhood purity corrupted by society; Allen Ginsberg's *Howl and Other Poems* (1955); Jack Kerouac's *On the Road* (1957); and Norman Mailer's *Advertisements for Myself* (1959), which included his influential and controversial essay, "The White Negro," first published in 1957. Author Dan Wakefield wrote:

> In New York the word was most honored, most pow-
> erful, most brilliantly imagined, created, and produced,
> by writers and editors and literary agents, the newspa-
> pers, magazines, and publishers of books, gathered on
> one single island, which made us love it and believe in it
> all the more. Here was the place where more writers
> lived than anywhere else on earth, more even than in
> Paris... The writers who produced the words that moved
> us were our heroes and heroines, our stars and guides,
> their works our texts for study and debate not just of lit-
> erature but for life, the very meaning and understanding
> of it, in fact the conduct of it... And where else would
> you have the chance of seeing and hearing so many of
> them, if not in New York in the fifties?[2]

Of course, words can be used in many ways, and certainly the carefully honed prose of literary figures first comes to mind. In addition, a more unconventional approach was gaining in strength and influence during the postwar period. This was the technique of expressing one's thoughts directly at the moment of their conception, in a technique known as improvisation.

After World War II, improvisation was in the air, greatly inspired by jazz improvisation. Jazz groups had begun merging the races and quitting the white man's Big Band swing for a more individual, subtle, difficult, cooler, wilder "bop"[i]—the antithesis of silence and conformity, with, according to dictionary definition, "rhythmic and harmonic complexity, improvised solo performances, and a brilliant style of execution."[3]

The writing of the Beats, and Jack Kerouac's seemingly extemporaneous prose in particular, was certainly influenced by jazz. Shepherd claimed to be the radio talker listened to by the characters in Kerouac's *On the Road*, and though this reference has yet to be substantiated, that he wanted us to believe it is enough to indicate where his sensibilities were.

People such as Henry Morgan (whose style sounded improvised) with his wry wit had been on the air for years; beginning
in the 1940s, Bob Elliott and Ray Goulding, starting with much
improvisation, honed their radio act and remained around for
decades. During the early 1950s,[ii] when Jean Shepherd was
working in Cincinnati and Philadelphia, doing early versions of
his unconventional and improvisational broadcasting, a
Chicago improvisational group, the Compass Players, opened,
followed by the Second City and the Premise.[4] From these, several Chicago-based individuals and teams (and people from
other areas of the country) began appearing in small clubs, a
new generation of comedians doing work that appealed to a
more adventurous audience. These new comedians mostly wrote
their own material—giving them more of an image of expressing
their own thoughts and feelings—as opposed to traditional
comics who told standard jokes, many of which were produced
by hired gag writers. The new material was often more improvisational, satirical, topical—often making cutting and sophisticated commentary with frequent shocks of recognition leading to
laughter—on politics, social situations, interpersonal relationships, sex, and death.

Among the new comedians were Mort Sahl, with the day's
newspaper as a prop, commenting wryly on politics; Mike
Nichols and Elaine May exploring personal relationships; Shelly
Berman with his telephone, covering angst and neurosis; Lenny
Bruce digging deeply into sexuality, race, and other previously
taboo areas for standup comedy. There were Stan Freberg's
parody recordings of customs and commercialism, Bob
Newhart's insecurity, Jonathan Winters' improvisatory imper-
sonations, Dick Gregory, Tom Lehrer, Bill Cosby, the widely talented Steve Allen—some gaining great renown through highly
popular long-playing records and appearances on major television shows by the late fifties, and television's visual genius Ernie
Kovacs, among others. These new comedians became nationally
known, with all the glamour and financial rewards that accom-
pany instant stardom. Mort Sahl, in fact, made the cover of
Time's August 8, 1960, issue.

Before national audiences, their material, though having the
feel of improvisation, was generally carefully honed and
rehearsed. Most of their material had a forceful punch line every
few seconds (almost a necessity for television), something that
Jean Shepherd did not have and did not consider an appropriate
part of his style. His style required more extended time for elab-

oration and a more contemplative response, neither of which was as conducive to mass-media appeal as the shorter and somewhat scatter-shot approach of most of his contemporaries.

Shepherd also began making comic record albums. The first, 1959's *Jean Shepherd and Other Foibles*, had a routine, "Controversial Noncontroversial Comics," in which, without naming names, he made fun of what he implied was their lack of significant content. He derided the publicly accepted notion that the new comedians dealt with controversy, while envying the renown that these other comics had achieved:

> One of the most interesting things of the twentieth century—particularly here in America, is the noncontroversial/controversial comic—the Philosopher! The Great Humorist. And this type of comic works in these little places that are like caves. These places where there's a guy sitting there wearing a pair of black glasses, playing a tenor horn. Nobody says much of anything. They just sort of sit around at the tables.
>
> And about every hour or two the great man walks out on the stage. And he's always dressed very casually. Kind of Beat, you know. Like an old pair of chinos, an old worn sweater. And he has this bitter look on his face. This very special bitter look that says, "I *know*." He walks out, usually has a prop of some kind—maybe it's a telephone, maybe it's a newspaper. And he walks on and he looks down at the assembled followers. These people don't have fans, by the way, they have *acolytes*. He looks down into the darkness and the acolytes are waiting for the word.
>
> The silence begins to grow. And he looks with this kind of casual look, as though it's building up—this anger. Then finally it comes out and he says, "Governor *Faubus*." [Uproarious laugh track.] The word is beginning to come and they feel it! "Adlai *Stevenson*." [Laugh track.]
>
> *Now* he's beginning to really swing. He's really giving us the *truth!* Waves his hand for silence. His face has assumed the bitter look of the tea that General Yen long ago himself drank deeply to the dregs. Disgust is evident. For the entire world, all of the things—everything that he sees—"*Ike!*" [Laugh track.]
>
> This is his last and his telling capper—"Heh! [Pause.]

Golf balls!" [Laugh track.] The *New York Times* says,
"Hard hitting! Solid! The truth at last is being delivered."

Bitter tea indeed. What Shepherd failed to recognize, or chose
not to, is that much of the new material did indeed deal with
controversial matters, and that properly used one-word free
associations can evoke nimble mental connections that make
amusing and relevant points about the subject at hand. The one-
word joke also entertains by giving the audience a glow of satisfaction in having been quick witted enough to make those
connections.

Shepherd's recordings did not sell as well as those by others,
and he remained more of a cult figure despite his successful
forays into other media. In a 1968 article, Shepherd is quoted
comparing his longer-lived humor career with the shorter ones of
his contemporaries:[iii] "Look at the big comics of just a few years
ago—Shelly Berman, Bob Newhart—the ones with just one joke.
Look what happened to them."[5] He had the opportunity to comment directly about the leading serious comic—as happens frequently in the book-reviewing game, a peer (read "competitor")
is often chosen, and Shepherd got to review Mort Sahl's
memoir/justification book, *Heartland*,[6] for the October 3, 1976,
New York Times Book Review. Sahl stuck his chin out from time
to time in the book, and Shepherd took the opportunity to
pummel it. Repeating his complaint about "Controversial/
Noncontroversial Comics," Shepherd suggested that he,
Shepherd, was not alone in discovering a serious flaw, writing in
part, "There were detractors, of course, who maintained that
Sahl had merely mastered the trick of stringing together one-
liners that *seemed* to be cutting and revealing of an inner truth."[iv]

Those familiar with Sahl's work might well disagree with this
attack.[v] But Shepherd's continued focus on his view of what constituted the higher and more lasting form of humor has prevailed—he did not rise as high in the popular consciousness, but
he remained funnier and more relevant regarding universal
human foibles, because he never pegged himself much into the
topical culture and psychological currencies. He would have a
more lasting career than most—their material was more dated in
content and attitude, while his material continued to deal with
the unchanging human condition. An extended *New Yorker*
review by Adam Gopnik (May 12, 2003) of Gerald Nachman's
Seriously Funny commented about most of the over two dozen
comedians discussed, writing that forty years after, "we cannot

laugh quite as easily at Nichols and May or even Lenny Bruce as we do at Chaplin or Keaton, because their subjects are too narrowly circumscribed."

Ron Della Chiesa: He was always an enigma. And he carried the burden of his talent being usurped by people like Woody Allen. If you look at some of Woody Allen's work there's a connection—*Radio Days*, for example. And one of the things that used to recur constantly in my discussions with him—a lot of people who were in New York used to listen to Jean and cull their material from his radio show.[vi] He complained about that a lot. And when you consider the fact that he was on—three or four hours a night?—in those early days. And probably there's no question there were people listening, and he would see *his* ideas show up in sitcoms, show up in comics' nightclub acts...

A lot of it was lack of recognition for his talent—that he became a cult. He became well known among people who knew Shepherd's work, and who revered him as a cult... He would say to me, "What do you mean *a cult*, Ron?" He would be offended by that, as opposed to being universally known, like a Steve Allen. So there's a problem he had there, I think, adjusting to that.

Herb Saltzman: He said, "It's tough not to be Jewish and funny in New York." [Saltzman indicates that Shepherd felt it was hard to be accepted by the New York intellectuals.] He was both. He was not Jewish and he was very funny. He lamented the success of Henry Morgan, Mort Sahl, Lenny Bruce, Shelly Berman—those kinds of guys went past him with a surge of comedy in the sixties. So Shep was bitter about that in those days.

Another "comedian" around in the 1950s, was the little-known, jazz-based, far-out cult figure, Lord Buckley. Buckley played jazz joints in California, Chicago, and New York, among other places. He dressed like a lord and spoke like a hipster. Some who only heard his recordings assumed he was Black. Supposedly, Shepherd and Buckley knew each other and admired each other's work. Oliver Trager, who wrote the book on Buckley, *Dig Infinity!* in part describes Buckley's style as having "innate musicality" and a "deep use of obscure vernacular."[7]

> **Oliver Trager:** Buckley, like Shep, was a major league raconteur—a man who could hold an audience enthralled for hours with his buoyant charisma, grand sweep of vision and language, and plain old down-home storytelling that brought you back to caveman space of hanging around the fire bewitched by shadows flickering on the walls...
>
> I realized that both men were strolling down similar word-jazz paths... And both were hip, and hip enough to let the listeners feel as though they were being inducted into a special world, secret society style. They were able to paint the big, mythic picture and allow you to feel you had a place in it but kept it real down-home, down-to-earth at the same time.

THE LEGENDARY TIME

It is said that Steve Allen, having seen Shepherd's pre–New York late night TV show, *Rear Bumper*, recommended him to be the host for NBC's *Tonight Show*, but he wasn't hired.[8] This story, disseminated by Shepherd, may well not be true (reportedly, Allen did not remember it years later)—but if it was, one can imagine that NBC TV would have recognized that the young Shepherd was too independent to be tamed by the conservative sensitivities of a high-profile broadcast; too unpredictable to keep TV producers and sponsors comfortable; and too ego centered in his need to express himself to be comfortable sharing the spotlight with a nightly parade of sofa guests.

Shepherd claimed that he came to New York City to do television and theatrical work and only took a radio job to fill in while looking for other performing work. When he arrived, though television was in the ascendancy, WOR dominated New York talk radio,[vii] including the early-morning John Gambling dynasty, Martha Deane, Arlene Francis, the various married couples who chatted on the air for hours: the McCanns, Ed and Pegeen Fitzgerald, Dorothy Kilgallen and Dick Kollmar. In this company, Shepherd was indeed a strange newcomer—an oddball.

During Shepherd's early broadcasting at WOR, February 1955

to January 1956, he had weekday and Saturday afternoon time slots, varying from an hour and a quarter to almost three hours. From June to December 1955, he also did fifteen-minute, late-afternoon, weekday shows. No examples of this material have yet surfaced.

This was the legendary time—from early January through mid-August 1956 he broadcast nightly from 1 AM to 5:30 AM, and then into 1960, Sunday nights from 9 PM to 1 AM. These were the times of the "night people," a major literary hoax, firings, protests, rehirings, invectives hurled into the night, and involvement in the progressive jazz scene. He sometimes played complete jazz recordings on the air.[viii] In 1956, he began writing columns for the *Village Voice* during its early days. In 1999, Jerry Tallmer wrote in a typescript for the *Villager*:

> It was, to my own best memory, Edwin C. Fancher, the founding publisher of the *Village Voice*, who came into the musty little office at 22 Greenwich Avenue one morning and said he'd been listening half the night to this crazy after-midnight guy on WOR AM who talked about this, that, and the other thing, including his boyhood, and baseball, and fishing, and chewing gum, and comic strips, and other Americana, without any script at all.
>
> In short order, Ed hunted up Jean and invited him to come in and write for us—an occasional column about anything that happened to be on his mind.
>
> Which he did. But Jean, a man of many parts, not only took Ed up on the offer, he soon was doing everything he could (through his radio show and otherwise) to put not just the *Voice* on the map but Greenwich Village itself, and everything about the Village that he loved (freedom, imagination, unsquareness) and hated (elitism, intellectual snobbism, phoniness).[ix]

Early shows on WOR AM and FM were broadcast not from the New York studio, but from the transmitter in Carteret, New Jersey. WOR engineer Herb Squire remembers hearing this about the transmitter broadcasts: "It was a cost-saving thing that RKO General had—'We've got to do a night show. We could cut back money and save expenses of the studio. We'll have the transmitter engineer run the board.'" Shepherd described this period a few years later:

It is unbelievably hot in that building with that 50,000-watt
transmitter going and no ventilation at all. I used to sit out
there wearing nothing but a pair of shorts, and work all night,
just slave all night, trying to dredge things out of my mind...
Well, I'm out there late, working two, three o'clock in the
morning and I'm dealing with this little gray furry creature,
the id, the ego, the super ego, and all the rest of the layers, you
know, and I'm digging and digging and digging.[9]

Sometimes listeners called, usually talking to him off the air
during newsbreaks. Of those calls he took while on the air, most
resulted in only Shepherd's voice being heard as he responded to
the listener (these call-ins were usually elicited by Shepherd to get
response on some issue he was discussing). Occasionally one
heard a listener's voice—usually unintelligible, occasionally
understandable. All these phone calls together amounted to a
miniscule percentage of his on-air time—Shepherd never did
what anyone today would think of as a call-in show with the
public on the air rambling or ranting incoherently. Several
people who knew Shepherd indicate that one constant caller,
named "the Listener," was Shepherd's girlfriend and eventually
his wife, actress Lois Nettleton. Jerry Tallmer explained, "He
kept talking through the night to 'the listener,' the listener—that
was Lois [Nettleton]. I'm sure that's who it was. Maybe nobody
documented it, but I always assumed that was Lois. Because of
the way he—it was like talking to his girlfriend. The tone of his
voice." According to the Internet Movie Database (IMDb.com),
under the biography of Lois Nettleton, "She was the first caller
to Shepherd's late-night program on WOR AM. He answered the
call on the air, and she became a frequent guest, known as 'the
Caller.' Together, they created the call-in radio show."
　　Some listeners wondered if he prerecorded shows. He taped a
few shows before going on a trip, and said, "I was on tape last
night, which doesn't happen often." This appeared to be true, at
least until his final WOR radio days. He said it was important for
his listeners to understand that the occasional prerecorded
broadcast was just as spontaneously delivered as the "live"
ones—spontaneity was an important part of Shepherd's radio
art. This seemingly casual style required the appropriate venue,
time frame, and audience. Students, isolated, doing their homework, or after homework, constituted just one such audience.
During those very late night hours, Jean Shepherd talked to
people who—for whatever their reasons, work or tempera-

ment—were up late. This nighttime aura of the world slowing down, a time to relax and contemplate, was the perfect setting for Shepherd's special radio theater, for doing improvisation.

> You see I worked late. I had a radio show I used to wind up about two o'clock in the morning. [Actually 5:30 AM.] It was then I began to know something about the night world of the— of the whole panoply of it all. And you know, incidentally, it has bothered me so much what has happened to the term "night people," which I have always regretted coining. This was a term that I coined, and I will stand accused and guilty of it. And I notice that people have taken it up and used it to cover all sorts of sins of omission and commission. It has nothing to do with Walter Winchell's world of bus boys—nothing to do with Walter Winchell's world and Damon Runyon's world of cab drivers. This is not the night people that I'm referring to.
>
> I'm talking about people with that wild tossing in the soul that somehow makes them stay up till three o'clock in the morning and brood. They might get up at seven the next morning and go to work—but that ain't—that isn't what their life is about. Not a bit of it. And I began to know something about this world and be part of it—as a matter of fact, always have been philosophically and finally I became not only philosophically but every other way involved in it. And so to me generally the world is not what it is until it's three or two or one o'clock in the morning. It begins to have a sharp focus to it. It has nothing to do with metabolic rates either. This is another story, too.[10]

Night people live with a mindset separate from the conventionally driven, work-a-day lives of most of us. Night people might be artists, jazz musicians, students, or others who prefer that different kind of world—those who just don't fit in— because some of them, a Jack Kerouac or a Jackson Pollock, might even suffer a dark night of the soul. Columnist John Crosby, in the August 8, 1956, *New York Times*, quoted Shepherd: "There's a great body of people who flower at night, who feel night is their time. Night is the time people truly become individuals, because all the familiar things are dark and done, all the restrictions on freedom are removed. Many artists work at night—it is peculiarly conducive to creative work. Many of us attuned to night are not artists but are embattled against the official, organized, righteous day people who are completely bound by their switchboards and their red tape."

During the Alan Colmes interview of December 1998, Colmes commented, "You were talking about that three o'clock in the morning—the way they thought versus the way people at three o'clock in the afternoon thought. That was a great—I thought that was a great hook." Shepherd responded, "Yeah, it was. And it's very valid. It's very true. It's the difference between Democrats and Republicans." (Offhand political comments such as this were not common for Shepherd on the air during his broadcasting years.)

The overnight programs lasted only five and a half months, followed by Sunday broadcasts 9 PM to 1 AM from September 1956 to mid-1960—a total of four and a half years.[x] These first New York years had a crucial place in the development of Shepherd's art. More so than later programs, these longer, late-night broadcasts had a slow, casual, laid-back, free-floating association of ideas, philosophy, and bemused commentary. One such commentary led to the international dissemination, in many newspapers and magazines, of the caper known as the *I, Libertine* hoax.

Shepherd talked about how night people were different in various ways from day people. One was that day people believed in lists: if something was on a list—a bestseller list, for example—because lists are official repositories of truth and authenticity, it must be believed. He said that in a major New York bookstore he asked for a book he knew existed, but the clerk, looking it up and not finding it, said it could not exist. Shepherd was inspired to action! He suggested on the air that polls and bestseller lists were perverse, artificial constructs that people took too seriously. What was the mindset that depended on lists—that found it important to have read the books on lists? A bogus book by a bogus author would have to be fabricated to undermine the apparently solid ground of the public, bookstores, distributors, and list makers—all those day people out there. Listeners called in suggesting titles, and *I, Libertine* was chosen. The author would be the fictitious Frederick R. Ewing, former British commander and civil servant in Rhodesia, known for his BBC broadcasts on eighteenth-century erotica. (The preceding is the myth, based on evidence and anecdote. The story is undoubtedly true in outline, and in most details, but better knowledge of the episode awaits discovery of a tape of the broadcast.)

Listeners went out and asked for *I, Libertine* at bookstores.

Bookstores checked with distributors. Official-type people were perplexed—if so many people were asking for the same book, it must have existed. Why wasn't it on any of their lists? Students in on the gag wrote erudite book reports on it and phonies at cocktail parties began claiming they'd read it. It was banned in Boston (purportedly, a listener working for the Archdiocese of Boston put it on the list of proscribed books as a joke, and nobody caught it before the list was published). Airline personnel took the hoax overseas and asked for it. It "made best-seller lists," so it is said, though proof of this has not been found. A society columnist claimed to have had lunch "with Freddy Ewing yesterday."

Eventually, science fiction author Theodore Sturgeon and Shepherd put together a real *I, Libertine*, published under the nom de plume Frederick R. Ewing by Ballantine Books in fall 1956. The September 16, 1956, *New York Times* review says, in part:

> Nevertheless, readers who enjoy their genealogy served with sex, and unraveled at a twentieth-century tempo, will find much to their taste in this bebop minuet... *I, Libertine* has been termed by *Publishers Weekly*: "The hoax that became a book." Originally, the hoax was launched by Jean Shepherd, an all-night disk jockey who sent his listeners (the Night People) into bookstores in quest of a "classic" that did not exist. Mr. Ewing came to the rescue—i.e., the book was co-authored by the team of Shepherd and Sturgeon. *I, Libertine* is history once over slightly.

The jacket photo reproduced in the review, that of Shepherd as a dissolute Ewing, was simply titled, "Jean Shepherd." In keeping with the nature of the enterprise, the book signing was held not at some prestigious book emporium, but (as seen in a photo accompanying a January 1957 article in *Saga* magazine) at the Times Square Liggett's drugstore. Copies of the book are now high-priced collector's items, and the *I, Libertine* affair is considered a major literary hoax. Sadly enough, the vast majority of people today are still vulnerable to their dependence on official lists.

With a similar irreverence for conformity, Shepherd also refused the disc jockey routine image of a bit of talk between records. As Herb Saltzman relates, "The boss was then Bob

Leder—couldn't stand Shepherd. Bob Leder was a commercial guy—strictly. He was very full of himself...he took over the radio station in...April or May of '56 as I recall."

I'll never forget the time. Mr. Leder came in. He says, "Jean, I've got a surprise for you." And ten minutes later, I'm out. [Laughs.] It's a fact. Some of you might remember that fiasco. The great firing.[11]

WOR station management complained that he didn't play enough music and was "not commercial." Management believed that more people would listen to a program that had more music. Of course, management did not understand his style, and his cult following was not considered important enough to generate sponsorship. The vicious circle in this is that late-night programs of whatever kind could not draw much sponsor interest. The issues came to a head in August 1956. Here is an exchange between Alan Colmes and Shepherd during the 1998 Colmes interview:

A.C.: You got fired in the middle of a show in the middle of the night, didn't you—they pulled—didn't they yank you off the air at WOR? They wanted you to play music and stop talking so much at one point?

Shep: Oh, that was so early on, that was like when I first came to New York and there was a guy who was the manager of WOR, named Bob Leder, and he was a strong-willed tyrant, and he was a classical boss—even had a bald head. Smoked cigars. The whole boss thing.

A.C.: Probably wore a pinky ring.

Shep: And he insisted that I play music. I said, "For God's sakes, Bob, everybody in the business is playing music. They don't need any more music. What they gotta hear is a voice once in a while." And he said, "You'll play music tonight or you're gonna leave." And so I played no music at all that night and sure enough, they yanked me.

A.C.: In the middle of the show?

Shep: Well, it was about—yeah, it was about the middle. Okay.

A.C.: Well, it was some time during the night. They didn't let you finish your broadcast, did they?

Shep: Oh, no. I was delighted.

A.C.: You were delighted?

Shep: Well, I knew what would happen. We knew that they were going to get a tremendous negative listener response, which they did. In fact one editorialist in New York, who was a writer for the *New York Times*, at the time said that, you know, "There's a Mr. Leder on WOR, and I think in the future, he's going to be known as the only guy who fired Shepherd." He said, "He'll be infamous for this act." Anyway, it worked out.

A.C.: They really came to their senses.

Shep: And later they called me in—they said, "We want you to go back on the air," and I said, "Look, I'll play records only when I want to use the record as an underscoring of what I've just said, or perhaps mood music, but I'm not going—I'm not a disc jockey. So don't reduce me to that status."

One of the good things about being on late at night is that there is more freedom and less meddling from commercial interests. One of the bad things is that if you "can't attract enough sponsors" at that hour (or at any hour), you're not "commercial." If you're kept on the air, the station is sustaining you: you're "sustaining." When Shepherd was about to lose his program, at least in part because of a lack of sponsors, he came up with an amusing ploy. According to the *New York Times* of Saturday, August 18, 1956, Shepherd was cut off the air during his broadcast for urging his listeners to buy a brand of soap, which was not a sponsor. This *Times* article did not name the brand—it was Sweetheart Soap. After thus being fired in mid-performance, Shepherd was quoted as saying that he wanted to prove he could sell soap, and he hadn't thought that anyone would mind.[xi]

WOR soon faced unexpected responses from two fronts. The first, as reported in the *New York Times* on Sunday, August 19, 1956:

Mr. Shepherd's final broadcast was to have taken place last Monday morning. The night before, four hundred of his followers met to protest his dismissal. Like Mr. Shepherd himself, his followers are not ordinary. They are members of his cult of Night People who function after sundown when the conventional Day People have retired. Their number includes students, artists, performers and just dreamers. Some of them are admittedly impractical fellows who regard the do-it-yourself movement with loathing. They met before the shell of the burned-out Wanamaker Building in downtown Manhattan because of the "Charles Addams feel" of the location. Their passive protest caused no serious problem for the police. After hearing a mildly worded talk by Mr. Shepherd about the baleful results of commercialism, they dispersed quietly.

On the second front, Sweetheart Soap volunteered to sponsor Shepherd, proving that he could sell soap. He returned to the air. Shep described the Sweetheart Soap incident:

> I'm sitting out there wearing a pair of Fruit of the Loom jockey shorts and—and when it happened the temperature was a hundred and forty degrees. It was August. I'll tell you even the date of it. I will award the brass figlagee—I won't tell you that—if you guys are really collectors of trivia of our time. What was the date of the night that the axe fell?
> Well, you don't know. Someone else will. I will ask you another question. I had just gotten out of my mouth—I had just said, "All right, gang, let's show 'em there *are* a few klutzes out there to listen to this drivel at night. That there *are* a few of the great unrecorded. All of you go to your grocery store tomorrow and ask for..." It was not a commercial. No commercial—it was just a measure of defiance.[12]

Shepherd's defiance of his general manager makes sense in relation to his desire to express himself in humor as an art form, and in his obsession with talk. Talk was not just something he liked—numerous people who knew him noted that he seemed possessed:

> **Helen Gee:** He was quite a name already [by about 1955–1958]—among young people—high school students. I was aware of him and I guess he strolled into the Limelight at some point, like a million other people... And then of course he discovered that I was a good listener. So I would sit. He did give the Limelight publicity on his radio program. He would talk not about the photography, which disappointed me, but about the beautiful *waitresses*... So I was a captive audience, I would sit

there at the table and he would talk. And if I turned on by accident the radio that night, I would hear what I had been listening to, so in a way he was sort of trying out his programs. I would sit there and smile—I, in deep grati-tude, of course—and he would go on and on and on.

I often thought that I could go into the kitchen, I could go to the bathroom twenty times, do anything, and he wouldn't notice that I've gone because I was just a pair of ears to Jean. And then I'd come back and sit down again and say, "Oh my God, now it's one in the morning—when can I go *home*?" And Jean would be still going on.

Asked if she became very friendly with Shepherd, she responded, "Yes, very much so. As friendly as you could be, because there was never any kind of intimacy—I don't mean man-woman, or anything like that. I just mean the intimacy of friends. I never felt that with him, because he was really quite removed, in his own world. And very much *of* himself. Very self-involved. He did not want any competition of *any* kind. So I just kept my mouth shut. I enjoyed talking to him—I couldn't under these circumstances. But I *liked* him."

HOLDING A "MILL" AND OTHER ACTIONS

Helen Gee liked Shepherd enough to endure his talk and to withstand the sometimes unexpected invasion of her Limelight shop and gallery by his listeners, in what was called a "mill." These were one of Shepherd's gently disruptive tactics: he some-times suggested that listeners meet in some public location and "hold a mill"—that is, move around aimlessly and talk softly without revealing a purpose, to unnerve the unwary. These mills instigated by Shepherd have their echo in the gatherings called "be ins" of the 1960s and the "flash mob" fad of late, in which groups of random people, contacted by cell phone or other elec-tronic means, gather briefly to disconcert the unwary, then dis-burse. Among those mills reported:

At the Limelight Photo Gallery and Coffee Shop

Helen Gee comments that Shepherd's following "was extra-ordinary—these young people. Every now and then he would announce on the air—too often as far as I as concerned—that he was going to have a mill at the Limelight." Gee says that

Shepherd announced these without her permission. "Oh, I *dreaded* it." She says that because the space was large, and his millings were fairly successful, he wanted to broadcast from there, but while she owned it, she never let him because she wanted the focus of the Limelight to be on the photo exhibits, which showed work by most of the major photographers of the day. Gee continues talking about Shepherd's Limelight mills:

> I just tolerated them, because of Jean and the publicity he gave. And he would give a date. Everybody dreaded it. The waitresses dreaded it because all these young people would come, and [the waitresses] were all stiffed—they never left a tip. They would not order either. So the evening was just ruined. And I just had to sit there and tolerate it. All these young people. The regular customers would stay away. They didn't want any part of that.
>
> And Jean, before these events—he would come in quite early. He was so afraid—he was so insecure, this guy. I know it's an overused word, but by God it applies to Jean. He would come in early and he'd look around and see whether anybody was there yet. And he was so nervous. I'd be sitting in a chair waiting for this goddamn event. And he would look in and he'd quickly depart. He wouldn't see anybody and he'd come back later, looking even more nervous because, "Isn't anybody going to come?" He was so nervous that I felt that he'd have a breakdown if nobody came. Like, you're giving a party and nobody comes. He'd check in and check in, and finally a little group would come in, and another group and another group, and before you knew it they were milling around.

The Burned-Out Wanamaker Building
(August [12?], 1956) At the time Shepherd was fired, the *Times*, as noted above, had commented on the Wanamaker Building meeting as a "passive protest."

A Midtown Marboro Book Store
(April 8, 1957) After a while, the management asked the milling throng to leave and some, at Shepherd's suggestion, gathered with him at the nearby Automat.

In Washington Square Park

To fly box kites about 3 by 5 inches in size, on a Saturday afternoon, reported in "The Art of Milling, or Go Fly a Kite" by Alan Bodian in the *Village Voice*:[13]

> Jean Shepherd, in sports coat and open collar, appeared and mounted the ledge [of the Washington Square fountain], and the throng, at least a thousand strong, closed in on him. Shepherd raised his hands and exhorted his followers to calm down. It soon became apparent that Shepherd has two kinds of admirers: the "let's-mill-quietly" clan and the "let's-mill-at-any-price" clan.

Bodian reported that, as the "let's-mill-at-any-price clan" ultimately prevailed in an unruly fashion, Shepherd departed, taking off in a flaming red Isetta sports car.

At other and sillier times, Shepherd suggested that many people run to one side of a building to tilt it or that they jump up and land at the same time to move Manhattan Island.

MONOLOGUE/DIALOGUE; SHEP EXTEMPORE

The less-structured broadcast style Shepherd employed in this early period, with its stream-of-consciousness fits and starts, instilled a feeling that he was conversing just with each listener individually. And doing it very casually. It seemed to be an exceedingly intelligent and entertaining conversation (even though in reality, except for very limited exceptions, it was a one-way monologue). In later days, retaining the one-on-one feeling, but with a little more formality, he referred to what he did as a "performance." Although it was that, performance is too limited a description for the very personal mind-and-soul-searching talk he delivered nightly.

We don't know to what extent Shepherd prepared or had notes or had a script or rehearsed for his broadcasts (either the early ones or the later ones). What his engineers, coworkers, and other observers all tell us is that he had nothing with him in the sound booth, or only a few notes, maybe a news clipping, a couple of items appropriate to the themes he intended to deal with—but never a script. Barry Farber noted that "his stories always came out right on the button. Never had a script or anything. *Good Lord!* Don't ever use the word 'script' anywhere in your book! Jean would be so offended. Everything was off the top of his head."

> **Fred Barzyk:** I had been with him before he did his radio shows and he'd be talking about everything— *never* did any preparation. He said it was all up here anyway [pointing to his head].
> I really did consider him a jazz musician with words. He said, "The steel mill. I know that tune. Let's see what it does tonight." "Grade school—oh yeah, oh Flick. Let's talk about Flick." Or somebody would get him angry, and he would be—creeping meatballism—so that was a *theme* and then he could go do ten, fifteen shows but he never knew where it was going to go. Though as a storyteller there was always a beginning, a middle, and an end. What happened in between were sometimes pure riffs.

During his long, more diffuse, early broadcasts, in all likelihood he had some ideas with a thread, which he then put together on-air, often going off on his delightful tangents. Shepherd the alchemist had his own secret mix of the planned and the extemporaneous. One could liken this style to skiing downhill on one's self-created course, where you give yourself leeway to move within the course over bumps and hollows as the mood fits—where the goal is not speed or final destination, but the pleasure of the journey. Shepherd's thrill—and the listeners'—came from the exhilaration of instantaneous response to unexpected scenery or icy patches along the trail. He used a different metaphor on June 16, 1957: "You have to look at this as kind of a blank sheet of paper stretching out till one o'clock in the morning. The trick is how to fill it." One might also liken Shepherd's style to jazz improvisation. On Shepherd's last Philadelphia broadcasts, way back then, he talked of the potential in radio for the unexpected—the extemporaneous:

> Do you recall a program that I—In fact most people in radio still talk about it as a classic. Do you recall a program that used to be on—afternoon? The star of which—three people really. Groucho Marx, Basil Rathbone, and Madelyn Carr—a very peculiar combination. Well, it was called *The Circle*. You might remember it. It was sponsored by a big dairy company. And the reason that this particular radio program is

considered a classic among radio people is that this was about the last example of the really freewheeling comic being allowed his head on a radio program. It would start out with a script—and this is really the truth—it is not press agentry, because of what happened—they would start out with a script—everything was under control, you see. Basil would be on one side of the mike, and Madelyn would be on the other. The orchestra would be there, and Groucho would be in the middle. About five minutes they would stick on the script, and Groucho would see his opening. By the time the program was twenty minutes old, there was nothing but pandemonium in the studio. No one outside, no one listening on the radio could understand what was going on. And it would wind up that what Groucho used on that program were things that really— well, this was really a freewheeling program—this was really a freewheeling comic in his own medium.[14]

Shepherd rebroadcaster and archivist Max Schmid comments, "I don't think that the kind of pandemonium that Shep referred to would have been possible, as this series, while trying to appear unstructured, was as scripted as any other show of the time—the networks wouldn't have it any other way." (Unless Groucho and his peers had the clout to insist on it.) What is crucial is that Shepherd apparently believed *The Circle* had this extemporaneous aspect. If *The Circle* was not extemporaneous, but seemed so, then it was similar in nature to some of Shepherd's own material. His early radio work was probably improvised with only a few signposts along the way. His later, finely organized programs were probably somewhat more thought out, though from what is known, none with a script.

AND ALL THAT JAZZ

Working with just a note or two but no rigid script is what 1950s jazz contributed to the essential style of Jean Shepherd. As Dan Wakefield puts it, "Jazz was *the* music of New York in the fifties, at least of literary and artistic New York." Regarding "The San Francisco Renaissance" of the 1950s, Albert Goldman in *Ladies and Gentlemen—Lenny Bruce!!* writes, "The exaltation of jazz among the white American middle classed reached, during these years, its final apogee. So widespread was the jazz cult that even *Time* broke down and put the fuzzy face of Thelonius Monk on its cover... Perhaps the most deliberate approximation to the jazz esthetic in another medium was the characteristic art of the North Beach Beats—poetry and jazz."

Author and jazz critic Nat Hentoff writes, "It is unavoidably personal music, John Coltrane, who created new ways of hearing as well as playing jazz, told me, 'The music is the whole question of life itself.' Other players have also emphasized that what you live—and how you live—becomes an integral part of what you play each night. Jazz, then, is a continuing autobiography... As the prodigious bassist and bold composer Charles Mingus told me: 'I'm trying to play the truth of what I am. The reason it's difficult is because I'm changing all the time.'"[15]

As Shepherd's life and career advanced, it is obvious that he also changed all the time. This became evident in his forays into many media, his alternating between good guy and not-so-good guy, and in the ways he even changed appearance—seen in photos of him over the decades. This trying out of different riffs in every aspect of his life—this improvising temperament— clearly placed Shepherd in the world of jazz. Those who first encountered Jean Shepherd's work later in his radio career may not have been aware of the very strong jazz element in his life and work. Shepherd's connection to jazz was a major influence on his most innovative form.

Remember in Chapter 1, when listening to Gerry Mulligan, Shepherd lamented not having been given a musical instrument so he could have been a great jazz musician: "He was lucky enough to have an old man who bought him a baritone sax when he was nine. My old man bought me a pair of shoes." He coulda been a contender!

On the air, he played music by itself and as ambience under his talk. He played recordings by Dave Brubeck, Sidney Bechet, and Stan Getz, all current modernist jazzmen. At least as early as 1955, and to a lesser extent as his time frame became shorter and earlier in the night, he sometimes played primitive, earthy jazz recordings, such as that June 16, 1957, opening, with the 1930s "Blues I Love to Sing," and played parts of the same cut on later programs. He played the great Gypsy guitarist Django Reinhardt and his group more than once (obviously enjoying the music immensely) and two cuts from an old record, *Louisville Stomp*: the instrumental "Banjoreno" and the instrumental plus vocal "Boodle-Am Shake"—announcing neither title nor players of either, just letting the "hairy vitality" rise up out of the ether and make its statement.[16] To get some idea of the "hairy vitality" and "funky" quality of these two pieces, try to picture a small parade of amiable, glaze-eyed, numbly-yet-rapidly strumming banjo players and the thumping and the thudding of a mouth-blown jug uttering endless flatulence—musical farts.

Jean Shepherd into the Unknown with Jazz Music

Jean Shepherd played jazz recordings on his show and, in an early demonstration of his strong predilection for working as a jazz performer, he recorded with a group in the 1956 LP *Jean Shepherd into the Unknown with Jazz Music.*

This full-length record, made during the time of his overnight broadcasts, presents Shepherd performing in a jazz idiom with words-plus-music dialogue—which he used in such effective ways during the longer-length, late-night programs before the 1960s.

Into the Unknown also allows an early glimpse of some of the techniques, themes, and catchphrases Shepherd would use throughout his radio career. The record begins with a trumpet fanfare and a dominant harpsichord playing a comic version of the opening of his theme song, "Bahn Frei." Other instruments on the record include flute, oboe, bassoon, and celeste, which contribute to the strange and fascinating effect the record's com-poser-arrangers Mitch Leigh and Art Harris describe as "unusual compositions and arrangements [that] are among the first to blend the 'classic' with 'jazz.'"

As Shepherd did so frequently, he begins speaking over the theme: "And a tiny figure appears over the twentieth-century horizon, beautifully dressed in his ill-fitting sports coat, especially selected for this auspicious occasion, and you note the placard: 'Will travel—honest, reliable, sober, industrious, *in hoc agricola conc, in est spittle louk*, motorists wise Simonize.' Strange, peculiar, elliptic world. He mounts the podium. Glances to the left, glances to the right, exuding confidence—the twentieth-century man, striding into the future."

The record's seventeen cuts alternate between Shepherd with background jazz and jazz interludes by themselves. In the final piece, the harpsichord and other instruments again do a bouncy, tinny, funny rendition of his theme as he finishes with a coda including "I got my job through the yellow section," echoing his gently ironic commentary throughout the disc on the social and commercial world. With a few phrases such as "and here I am working my way through the undergrowth," "hardly even begun to scratch the surface," and "I'll never forget" intro-ducing yet another version of the *Little Orphan Annie* secret decoder story, we hear on this record—for the first time so far encountered—some of Shepherd's familiar themes and variations, and we realize how early in his New York radio career he had developed his unique style.

The Clown

Shepherd was a good friend of jazz double bassist, Charles Mingus. In 1957, Shepherd and the Mingus group (bass, piano, tenor sax, trombone, drums) recorded the improvised piece "The Clown," with narration by Shepherd.[17] It starts with a relentless beat of seven descending notes, a galumphing beat like a waddling pachyderm. People laughing. Shepherd narrating, "Man, there was this clown, and he was a real happy guy—a real happy guy. He had all these greens, all these yellows, and all these oranges bubbling around inside him. And he had one thing he wanted in this world. He just wanted to make people laugh. That's all he wanted out of this world. He was a real happy guy."

Music with narration over it. Shepherd continues about how, instead of laughing at some planned piece of slapstick mishap, people begin laughing when some unplanned accident occurs, such as when the seal gets sick, or the clown falls on his face, really hurting himself. Several minutes of music alone. Then he describes how the clown changes his act to include hurtful "accidents" to himself—the crowd loves it, and he is becoming more successful. Shepherd says the clown now has "Lot of gray in there now, lot of blue." A backdrop falls on him—it hurts him deep down—the crowd laughs uproariously. Shepherd says, "Man, he *knew* now! He really knew now!" and he ends the piece: "William Morris sends regrets."[xii]

The record company ran an ad in the *Village Voice*, connecting "The Clown" to the Beat writers, saying that the recording, "with its improvised narration by Jean Shepherd in a jazz setting, unpremeditatedly has played right into the jazz-cum-poetry movement out in San Francisco... This development helps to explain in just what way ours is a beat generation."

Blues I Love to Sing

When considering why Shepherd's earlier work seemed more innovative and fascinating, think about the following. One of the pleasures in experiencing art of any kind is observing how the creative mind worked to produce the (traditionally) carefully composed piece (whether a painting, a sonata, a poem, a story).

All of Shepherd's material gave this joy. In the writing and later broadcasts one saw how his mind *worked* to produce the art. In the early freer form, one had more of a feeling of somehow participating with him in the wonder of his mind in the process of *working* at that very moment. With Shepherd, the listener was engaged *in* the moment, and in anticipation of what was to come, the content of which Shepherd was aware of only a bit sooner and more clearly than the listener. It's comparable to the thrill of downhill skiing or the excited anticipation of what might be around the path during a slow amble through unfamiliar terrain.

One has to be in the appropriate mood for almost any artwork—for example, if one goes to a movie and expects a fast-moving film such as *Dr. Strangelove* and instead is confronted with *2001* or the Andy Warhol fifteen-minute movie called *Eat*, which shows a man eating a piece of fruit in an almost empty room—one won't be happy. To appreciate *2001* or the Warhol, one has to be in an almost Zen-like, contemplative mood, letting the film flow over you without expecting kinetic excitement. One has to appreciate the moment-by-moment jolts of mental pleasure, and, overall, the coherence of its being tied together by a unique and entertaining sensibility.

Now imagine yourself, tired, and it's getting late, maybe on a Sunday night. You have nowhere to go—or you're on a dark two-lane road heading home, seeing only your headlight beams ahead, the gravel on the side of the road, and a solid wall of trees at the edge. And Jean Shepherd will soon be on the air. He will be in this cool, even, slow mood, but his mind always moving along ahead of you, and you never know what gentle syncopation will move through the dark, what free-floating bluesy riff will flow.

Read the following slowly. Slow way down—go with this slow and even flow. Think of the funkiest early Louis Armstrong or Bessie Smith, or a small black combo, with tinny acoustics and a cheap turntable for your old 78s, and maybe some cheap booze and acrid, punky smoke—and you're in a mood to listen to a set-'em-up-Joe-I've-got-a-story-you-oughta-know kind of weaving intoxication woven by a kindred soul. You will be buoyed up on a stream-of-consciousness sound and bits of wit that give you confidence that you will be carried along, your mind joggled and jiggled and richer for the ride. And you will smile, and nod your head—yes, oh *yes!* He's taking you somewhere you've never been, but feel you have—or should have been—and the jazz of it has you in its funky thrall.

Get in that mood, and you're ready for early Jean Shepherd. The commercials, the newscast, and the station identification are over. Shepherd's theme music is about to start—it is by Eduard (a lesser known) Strauss—a "William Tell Overture" type, three-minute, lightweight, self-important, operetta-racing-course-prance tune.[18]

> [Opening theme starts, then Shepherd's slow, even, knowing, irony-tinged voice over the theme.] Yeah, and high on the mountaintop, the giant voice rings out, "Stay tuned." Oh, oh, what a come on—what a message from the heights of Parnassus. [Shepherd's voice is quiet and pensive, as though carrying on, ever onward despite the odds.] A tiny figure, tattered and torn, can be seen moving across the barren landscape. A giant load being pushed before him. And a sign reads enigmatically, "Will travel—anniversaries, weddings, an occasional banquet our specialty. Supermarket openings by job lots. Honest, reliable, sober, industrious, square jawed, weak kneed, lily livered." Stay tuned, friends. [Theme ends.] Yes—Excelsior!
>
> Stay tuned, the lily-livered of the world. We'll be here until one o'clock tomorrow morning, pursuing what mankind has always pursued. In the fashion that he best sees it at the moment. Now that, of course, has been the problem that many of us have pondered back and forth—this business of what mankind has always pursued...
>
> It seems to me that we can do something else tonight—we can—it's summer, you know. It's summer, really [old jazz has begun slowly, under], and it's too bad that you're listening to the radio. It is, really.
>
> We can only extend our hand in quiet, sympathetic good will, to those of you who are forced to, you know—ahaaa—look at—all this wonderful time, all this wonderful weather, all this stuff all around and here we sit. I'm here and you're there. I'm in studioland. Studioland has a peculiar kind of sterility about it—which we will discuss later on, after 11:15, when we touch upon the sterility portion of our program. And you're out there in radioland, where things are lush and green, where things grow—out there where people do things—like send in box tops, answer questions, write letters of protest. You're out there in radioland—the *real* world. The real world. Ever

occurred to you that what you have out there is real? What we have here is—is all *artificial!* False! Ridiculous! *All* of this stuff! Don't you believe *any* of it! *Any of them!*

You're out there in radioland, aren't you? You see, that's what I mean—all this is unreal—false—*sterile!* How can I escape—how can I become one of you? Out there? I've heard all kinds of stories about what goes on in the outside. All sorts of stories. I don't believe any of them, though. I can't. I can't let myself believe them. If I do, everything I have here will crumble here in studioland. Gotta cling to something. To dreams—belief or two.

Jean Cocteau said, "Destroy the dream, you destroy the man." So, you know—hang onto a few things. I have to think that nothing happens out there. But I know it does, little box-top sender-inners. All you people out there in radioland. It's too bad it's the way it is. I'm here and you're there. Ah, gladly would I, indeed—oh, but yes.

[There is a pause, and then Shep, apparently in an act of self-encouragement, continues.] Who's for beach lotto tonight? [He speaks with mock enthusiasm.] This is a *great* beach lotto night! Who's for beach lotto tonight? About four o'clock in the morning. Seven thousand, five hundred and eighty-two people—we might even make the sports pages. [Funky old jazz behind never stops.] Can't you see yourself in the lineup? The lineup—sixteen columns long. There you are, you see. You scored two goals last night at Jones Beach in beach lotto. *Ahooo!*

[Back in a contemplative mood.] Isn't it pitiful the way I sit here and spin these poor little glass dreams? [Song ends.] Oh! Play it over again, fellows! Once again! That's it, play it over. We have nothing but time here. Spinning all those poor little idle dreams. You know? Sort of? It's sort of like it's a jigsaw puzzle. They took a couple of the pieces once—you know— and didn't bring them back.

I have a friend who has—you're not interested in my friends, are you? 'Course not. That is the secret of it all— *you're* not interested and I'm not. I am not interested in my friends, nor are you. Ok? Fine. Now we're on a good, solid, equitable basis. You don't like me, and I don't like you. And it's just as well that I'm here in studioland, and you're in radi-oland. [There is a tinkly piano going under all this.]

So let us entertain no further notions. I am no good! The secret is—neither are you. So let's not have any of this business here. You know? You keep your opinions to yourself, I'll keep mine to myself. And we'll get this thing going here, baby.

Heh—don't you miss magic? Really? Weren't those the great days when we used to have magic? Am I still insufferable? *Huh!* You people don't know the *meaning* of the word—yet.

Isn't this *great*? Listen to this crowd in the back—*listen* to that! Hear that? You don't always have to say everything you mean, you know. Listen to this bass man—he's great! You don't always have to say everything you mean. That's where you make your mistake—you always try to say things. *Ahaa!*—that's great!—*listen to that!* [Piano, bass.]

Isn't that great?—yeah— [Laughs.] Has a certain hairy vitality about this thing that most of us lack today. [Trumpet blows a nitty-gritty riff.] Yes sir, that's my baby. No sir—no, that's—sorry, that's another program. [Hums along.]

Ever tell you about the time that I wrote the message on the inside of a Baby Ruth candy wrapper? And floated it in a Castoria bottle down the Chicago River? Castoria. [Laughs.] Is there anyone out there who is willing to cry for us now—for it? No, you don't float anything down the Chicago River—it flows *up* the Chicago River. They reversed the direction of the Chicago River—they really did—it's one of the mammoth achievements of mankind. [Music fades to a close.] Ohhh—that's great! Great! Great! Ohh! [Laughs.] That's just the way I feel tonight!

Hey—play another cut on that side, will you? And hold it in abeyance. The one—the cut I want you to play is, "Blues I Love to Sing."[19] Hold it in abeyance. We use this occasionally when things look the way things look tonight. I have this terrible, terrible, terrible, awful feeling. It's not really frustration—it's a kind of borderline—a case of immense disappointment or something. Here it is, June, it's springtime—it's almost summer, isn't it? The sixteenth, isn't it? Summer will be here in four days—five days. It's June. All these people—everywhere, are stretched out for millions of miles—one after the other, bumper-to-bumper, sitting there with their radiators overheating.

Isn't that a wonderful feeling, though? The June air? [Laughs.] It is, though. I came over the bridge there, by Yonkers? I don't know what the name of that bridge is—and I was stopped for a moment—traffic was slowing up and the windows were open in the car—since it's a Triumph TR3 it's wonderful, you know—I'm sitting there with all this—this June air around me and—and—I could hear the muffled curses of the populace—just quiet, muffled—wonderful spring sound. And you could hear them lowing in the bushes once in a while. And it just gave me a feeling of warmth, a feeling of well—almost—it's the feeling you get from reading Dostoyevsky—you know—a feeling of being one of this great mass of humankind—all marching to the brink—and it's nice—it's nice and warm—to know, you know, there's this great crowd.

All—you know, jostling each other with their ill-fitting sports coats, all moving slowly toward the brink. Muttering muffled curses under their breath. In this quiet June atmosphere. Isn't it wonderful to be alive? Take a deep breath. Long, deep breath—*Ahhhh!* Now, say after me, "It's *great* to be me!" [Laughs.] I know. I know. [Laughs.] You see, it doesn't work, does it? [Music, the same funk as before starts quietly, with a raspy trumpet.] Nothing works—well—I wouldn't say *nothing*. Stay tuned for our magic phrase department—guaranteed to work—children cry for it, babies cry for it.

[A gravelly voiced woman begins scatting a slow blues with a bump-and-grind beat. One pictures her as a big, black, earthy, all-knowing woman crushing you to her ample bosom and smothering you with love in her embrace. Her voice is raspy like the trumpet's.]

Ohhh—yeah, baby! Can't you see this—can't you see this queen leaning over your shoulder and saying this stuff in your ears, you know? Listen? Ohh—come on, baby, I got to finish this hamburger. [Laughs.]

Ever been to one of those joints where the people walk around tables and they sing to you? It's a terribly embarrassing thing. I'm in this joint one night with this girl, we're eating a plate of spaghetti, and there's this guy who plays cheap guitar. And he comes over and he hangs over the table, see. He has been eating garlic and he's playing this guitar, and he's doing "La Paloma"—sort of a South Chicago–type "La Paloma." And he's playing the guitar and the spaghetti tasted terrible and the "La Paloma" was awful too—and you're not again, I can see it—that interested in my—I don't blame you. But can't you just see—[Singer on the record interjects, "Oh, but you're killing me!"]

It's just the way I am, baby. [Laughs.]

[Singer: "Ohhh!"] *Ohhh!* You see what I mean? There's a

certain hairy vitality about this that all of us lack today. We're
kind of poured out of a plastic mold. Each of us. Let me say a
polyethylene mold—it's better than just plastic. Or styrene, for
the low, lost types.

Yes sir, that's my baby. No sir, don't mean maybe. Yes sir—
that's—my—baby—now. Baby! [Laughs.]

See—it doesn't work—nothing. You got to wind it up. You
got to have the key, you see—stick it in the side where the
socket is and wind it just as tightly as you can. Not *too* tight!—
you break the springs—wind it up [Singer gravelly, grating,
with that earthy, serious, syncopated beat.] and—wouldn't it
be incredible if this world turned out to be actually only this
big ball with a key sticking out the side of it—and they forgot
to wind it? For the last ten thousand years, we're running
down?

[Gravelly voice increases in volume.] There she goes! Yes
sir, that's my baby... [Her voice continues—"That's the blues, I
love to hear" she sings plaintively, fading, slowly ending with
a gentle cymbal finish.]

That's what I need. Once in a while—since everybody has
the feeling, generally, that things aren't going well—you
know—kind of eroding—I have a few things that I do—for
those of you who—I guess it's a—no, I guess it isn't a form of
Positive Thinking, it's a form of—I suppose you might say,
"mental hypocrisy"—No! No! *Not that!*—I mean, a sort of a
form of a—mental hopscotch—uh—I have a phrase—once in
a while when things get terrible, I pull out this letter that a guy
wrote to me a couple of months ago. It's headed "The office of
Jean Shepherd," and it does some great things. It hasn't done
anything for me yet.

Know what the trouble is, don't you? You know what the
trouble is, don't you? I have a feeling if—a kind of a feeling of
dissatisfaction—with me tonight. No, not with me, really, *with
the things*. Seriously, here it is, it's Sunday night. *What am I
doing here?*[20]

What Shepherd appears to be doing here (in just the first ten
minutes of his three hours and forty-five-minute program) is
improvising. His word excursions are often described as "riffs,"
a frequent jazz term that has been appropriated in the field of
speech. The word refers to part of a larger music or sound composition, in which the performer, inspired by the major theme,

moves away from it—or moves around it with variations, or in a related tangent. Similarly, in a monologue, the speaker branches off from the main topic of his talk, into an extended, usually improvised excursion on a related topic or stream-of-consciousness sequence. The listening pleasure resides in following a nimble mind down an entertaining path.

John F. Szwed in his book, *Jazz 101*, writing of improvisation, said something that, if we switch the idea to Shepherd's technique with words, seems relevant: "Bebop of the 1940s was sensitive to the limitations of the pop and blues forms and often rewrote the melodies, retaining their harmonies only as a basis for providing a string of solos. The revised melody was then simply restated at the end of the piece in order to signal the ending."

Jean Shepherd was sufficiently engaged in the jazz world that he was offered a number of outlets to show off his expertise. He began writing a series of columns titled "Jean on Jazz" for *Audio* magazine in 1956—a total of three have been verified, appearing in March, July, and August. The introduction to the column indicated that the writer heard Shepherd in the summer and fall of 1955 on Saturday afternoon radio from 3 to 6 PM, talking about jazz in an informal yet informed way. Other recognition of Shepherd's engagement with jazz was the opportunity given him to emcee important jazz concerts.

Shepherd was the emcee for concerts (several connected with the *Village Voice*) featuring some of the most important jazz musicians of the time. The Saturday midnight concert, June 15, 1957, at Loew's Sheridan in the Village, began after the last movie. The flyer advertising the event features him prominently as the "narrator." The *New York Times*, review of June 17, 1957, referred to Shepherd as the emcee, who also improvised to the Charles Mingus Quintet performance of "The Clown."

> **Ed Fancher:** [Art d'Lugoff, who organized jazz concerts] came to the *Voice* and said, "I'll put together a jazz concert for you. And you won't make any money but you'll be able to sell advertising. Special advertising." So we said okay, what the hell. We were dead broke. And he got Jean Shepherd to agree to emcee it at Loew's Sheridan Theater. It was a big theater— [according to the *New York Times* about 2,500 seats]. He had some of the biggest names. The biggest name of all was Billie Holiday.

Jerry Tallmer wrote of the occasion:

> It was in fact Jean who at 3 AM, the police deadline hour, announced to a packed crowd that had been sitting for seven hours in that theater... "Ladies and gentlemen, I'm happy to inform you that Billie Holiday is now in the house." A great cheer went up—so I'm told—because at that moment of Jean Shepherd's huge, risk-taking lie, Billie Holiday, rushed from a gig in Philadelphia, was being conveyed up to Loew's Sheridan from the Holland Tunnel and Canal Street at 65 or 70 miles an hour in a car driven by me. But then, as on his radio shows, Jean always worked without a net.

Shepherd talked about another jazz performance during a broadcast:

> I had a very interesting experience this afternoon, and it will continue all throughout the summer. We have Sunday Afternoons at the Vanguard. On Seventh Avenue in the Village, and they pick up at 4:30 and this afternoon I was there, and Stan Getz and his quartet were there and we had a great time till about 7:30. I made snappy snide remarks, and Getz made great remarks on his tenor.[21]

Shepherd also emceed a jazz concert in Central Park featuring Billie Holiday. Donald Clarke, in his book about Holiday, reported additional performers in this July 1957 concert: Gerry Mulligan, George Shearing, Dave Brubeck, Erroll Garner, and Lionel Hampton.[22]

The *New York Times* of December 9, 1957, opened its article about a concert two days earlier featuring Charles Mingus, the Jazz Modes, and Anita O'Day with "The 'night people' who follow the radio broadcasts of Jean Shepherd assembled Saturday at midnight at Loew's Sheridan Theatre to hear a jazz concert presided over by their leader."

Jean Shepherd knew jazz intimately and used it on his program. Jazz as statement, interaction, and response. Obviously, this cannot be described adequately in words on paper, and, indeed, took a variety of forms. The "Blues I Love to Sing" sequence was a Shepherd interaction with the music. On another program, undercutting the straight commercial of Nat "King" Cole singing a jazzed-up version of the pop song "Let's

Do It" in a jingle for a beer—Shepherd, over the recording, did his own musical riff. Shepherd used jazz techniques in word improvisations in a more extended way than did the little theater pieces that became popular in Chicago and New York in the 1960s. He made compositions in word and sound. When you heard him speaking with a sense of timing, beat, a certain rhythm, with pauses (with or without music)—interacting, extending the performance with words apparently discovered in the moment of their articulation—the total ensemble he created was jazz performance.

PRESENTED BY JEAN SHEPHERD'S NIGHT PEOPLE

Shepherd's jazz performances on the radio were monologues. He did not often work with other people. Only four people are known to have been Shepherd's guests on-air.[xiii] In 1957 or 1958, he spoke with humorist S. J. Perelman (despite the potential for great dialogue, the result was stilted, probably because Perelman was a writer, not a talker). He also talked on-air with radio playwright Arch Oboler, playwright and cartoonist Herb Gardner, and actor John Cassavetes.[23]

Ray Carney, professor of film and author of several books on John Cassavetes, writes in *Shadows* that Cassavetes "had been on the show many times" and he asked to be a guest again, ostensibly to talk about the new film, *Edge of the City*, in which he acted.[24] Cassavetes had been conducting classes in acting, with an interest in improvisation. He developed an idea for a film, to be called *Shadows*. He tried to promote it, with no responses. When he and Shepherd talked on the air (a Sunday night in February 1957), Cassavetes said he could make a better movie than *Edge of the City*. Author Carney reports that Cassavetes said, "If people really want to see a movie about *people*, they should just contribute money." Shepherd's listeners mailed and hand delivered over $2,000. As Carney puts it regarding the contributions, "Cassavetes' career as a fundraiser, producer, writer, and director was launched." Cassavetes and his crew made the film. Shepherd appeared for a moment as a nightclub patron, and Cassavetes acknowledged his crucial support in the film's opening credits, right after the actors' names[25]: PRESENTED BY JEAN SHEPHERD'S NIGHT PEOPLE.

Carney's comments on Cassavetes' interest in improvisation and his self-promotion tactics lead one to think that Cassavetes and Shepherd shared some personal and professional traits. Just

as Shepherd told apparent truths in his performance, only to
have many of his stories eventually confirmed to be fiction—and
his statements on-air and in interviews regarding simple factual
matters about himself often having been shown to be untrue—
Carney, in his introduction to his book, *Cassavetes on
Cassavetes*, writes:

> In many cases Cassavetes consciously and deliber-
> ately shaded, suppressed or embellished the truth.
> Sometimes (as when he lied about his height or told
> people he majored in English at Colgate) it betrayed an
> insecurity. Sometimes (as when he told interviewers that
> the final version of *Shadows* was improvised[xiv]) he did it
> for PR reasons...
>
> When he spoke with interviewers a few years later,
> Cassavetes exaggerated or outright lied about many
> aspects of the production [*Shadows*], bragging that he
> had shot the film in forty-two days, that most of the
> footage was "grabbed" on the streets of New York, and
> that the movie was entirely spontaneous and impro-
> vised... Much of the final version was scripted and all of
> it was carefully, meticulously planned.[26]

The end title of *Shadows*, the final version, stated, "The Film
You Have Just Seen Was an Improvisation." Truth and fiction,
improvisation and scripted—there were ways of defining each
that Cassavetes and Shepherd deviously shifted at their wills to
satisfy personal and artistic imperatives.

Among Shepherd's imperatives was to be in total control of his
creative world. Any lessening of that control was met with firm
resistance. His attitude could be encapsulated in the lyrics of the
Sinatra song "I Did It My Way." Thus, an extended commentary
expressing gratitude to others for assisting him in his struggles is
a rare opportunity to observe him humble.

Long—But Important—Parenthetical, Unexpected, Atypical, Not-to-Be-Repeated "Personal Remark" Expressing Shepherd's Gratitude to Listeners and Sponsors

> Hey, you know, I want to say this. May I make a personal
> remark before we go any further? And I have never done this.
> Ah—as you probably are aware, this show has had a stormy
> career. And don't—don't ever accuse Shepherd of getting com-

mercial, because if Shepherd was commercial, he would be on late night television all night with Elsa Maxwell sitting on one side and Genevieve on the other—he ain't.

As you obviously see, he ain't. [Laughs.] If you look back over what is called commercial in this business—generally it is what appeals to the most number of people at the greatest amount of time, and sells the most jazz. Unfortunately, this program has never done any of those things. And all I can say is this. Something I haven't said ever. About four years ago [August 1956], many of you listeners remember the big incident of the show being taken off the air when I was on late night—used to be on seven nights a week and the listeners wrote in, and got us back.

None of this was hoked up, there was no publicity involved, there was a lot of stuff went on behind the scenes that someday will make a very interesting story. But—I can say this—without the listeners who did what they did, I would never be working in New York today. It's a fortunate—or unfortunate fact—whichever way you happen to look at it. And I can only say this. This is a personal remark. I must thank people who have listened to me for years, because it is quite obvious that quite often it must be difficult to listen to me. Many times, I obviously get very boring. Writers get boring for many pages but you can skip the pages, you know? Hemingway bores me many times, but he also exults many times. I recognize that I must be very boring, and I must often-times be lying fallow when I shouldn't be, because what I do is difficult in one sense. That a writer, you know, when he has a bad day just stops writing for a while. You never see that. That part of him. You don't read the stuff he throws away, or that his editors knock out. You only read that which is finally culled, and the danger of what I do, obviously, is that you hear the good and you hear the bad. [Laughs.] There's no way for me to say, "Forget that last half hour, that was awful." Well, it's a fact, I know that there are many half hours that are awful, and I'm the first to admit it.

But I hope that in some small way that there are moments that are good. I have enough ego to believe that there *are*. And to the people who have stuck over the years and who listen—I can only thank you—because I am very selfish about what I do. I do it because it's important and necessary for me to do it. I'm not one of these performers who will get out and say, "Thank you one and all for being such a wonderful audience."

No, this is not what I'm doing. I'm thanking you for sticking with the bad moments and the bad periods, which obviously I have many of— [Laughs.] In short I—you know, I'm very very—grateful. That's all. I hope in the next year or so I will be able to enlarge my scope. And don't think that if I go on stage with my material, which is in the offing—I'm scheduled to open in *New Faces* in spring—that it will be any different. I go because I have been around too long to do—a—to do something merely because I have been given the opportunity to do it. I will only do it if it is being done the way I must say what I have to say.

This is again, not a statement of braggadocio; it's a statement of fact. Because somewhere along the line I have discovered that men live—and die. And they live and die regardless of whether they have been on the Jack Parr Show or not. They live and die. And they don't die any happier—either—under one condition or under another. Now death is never funny. It never comes incidentally, it never comes too soon, nor it ever come too late. You know people always say about a death, they say, "You know, he—too bad, he—he's better off." Nobody's ever better off. [Laughs.] I refuse to accept it. Speaking of death, this is WOR AM and FM. [Laughs.] I couldn't resist it. [Big laugh.]

And—I feel—I feel that if maybe I was nineteen years old I would not feel the way I feel. I would have learned to do my tap dance well, and I would learn my jazzy jokes and would have made the nightclub circuit—which is the easiest circuit, by the way, to make. Having worked in clubs, I can say that most of the guys I've known, have material bits which they—if you were to say to the average one, "Do all your stuff," you would have heard him all in twenty-five minutes, or maybe forty—at the most. He has said his all. And I could have done this. But that's another story. In exchange for the decisions that I have made, I must say that I feel very grateful for the people who have stuck. Because it is so easy to fall into a routine, and when a person does, this is safe. It's easy to fall into a series of things that he knows will get laughs. For example, if I were to do the show that most people will seem to think they want me to do, I would begin—I would read Fu Manchu, then I would hurl an invective, then I would tell the story about the starlings. Then I would tell the story about Miss Shields, then I would hurl another invective. Then I would read "The Face on the Barroom Floor," and apparently, I would do this show every week. [Laughs.] And by the end of the third week you would be back there watching Loretta Young.

I can tell you this. And I would have slowly died, and would be out somewhere, someplace, telling jokes in a nightclub. I'm not about to do this. But this is a personal policy statement here, and I hope you accept it as that. That I must say, thank you for sticking around when I have been terrible. [Laughs.] I will not thank you for listening when I've been good. That's been *your* fortune. [Laughs.] I will be that much of an ego— because it hasn't cost you a red cent. But I will thank you for sticking around through the mires and the muck—which must come awful fast sometimes. Which I know do. Sometimes after I finish the show I am so low, I am so deep in—in depression, that I can hardly—I can hardly look up to the top of the building where the big sign says, "If you never see another movie in your life, you must see this one." I don't even see that sign. And—these are facts, and, I can say thank you, you know, for sticking when the going has been sticky. It has been.

And speaking of sticky going, we have with us Worth Perfume, our final sponsor for tonight. And by the way, this is another thing I want to say. That no radio program, and in fact *anything* today—I don't care whether your name is Faulkner or not. You would never hear of Faulkner unless he sold books. This is an unfortunate fact of the matter, my dear. If you—if you want an interesting experience, just take your favorite novel, open it up, and look inside the flyleaf and you will see it says three dollars and ninety-five cents. Somebody is getting that dough. And I can say that there is nothing today that comes to you cheaper than that which you get out of your radio. This is a fact. Generally, it is cheap, too, for that reason. An unfortunate fact, too.

But I am most grateful—not only to the people who have listened to the program, and you'll never hear me say this again, so listen. I am most grateful to the people who have been brave enough, and courageous enough to sponsor the show. Now I say courageous not in the sense of me doing a controversial show—in the sense that it is quite obvious I ain't gonna sell a lot of goods. That in itself is controversial—in our business. And people like Marlboro Cigarettes, people like Goggomobile—and I know that oftentimes in a four-hour show you say, "Why does this guy have to do a commercial?" Well, my dear, it's because if I didn't, there would be no show at all. And you could sit out there on your duff and listen to Joanie James records. Or—and I might point out another salient fact—I don't think Geraldine Page works for nothing. I think when you walk through that box office you plunk down some good hard coin. Hardly anybody ever goes to that box office and says, "I don't know why I have to pay for this stuff—this is art." Art my foot! You pay for it and you pay hard for it. And when you go into the Museum of Modern Art they have a box office that you pay for—when you walk through there. It is an unfortunate fact of our world.

And these poor little one-minute commercials that come through about every forty-five minutes on the show seem to irritate people more than the forty-two dollars they'll plunk down for a tenth-rate musical [laughs]—of which there is hardly any other kind—these days. Yet it is one of the strange and salient facts of our world.

I'm just—by way of this—I don't send out Christmas cards. I haven't sent any Christmas cards to the people at work. And I haven't sent any Christmas cards to the Paper-book Gallery. I haven't sent any Christmas cards to Marboro Books. They haven't sent any to me either. And the only thing that they have done, which is the most important thing—for all of us—I mean, I assume a few of you listen—and I do it—is that they have picked up the charge of admission through the whole year. And I am very grateful to them for that.[27]

Wow! Talk about an extended thank you! We won't get one of those again. By 1959, Shepherd had a lot to be thankful for. He had experienced an extraordinary amount of creative and personal pleasure. Within a very short period upon his arrival in New York (seemingly months or less, in 1955), he had immersed himself as a creative participant in the underground, the avant-garde, and the experimental arts as a disturber of equanimity and conventional peace. Within a year or so, Jean Shepherd began his extemporaneous "all-night" radio broadcasts, was fired, rehired, causing on occasion a ruckus; perpetrated the *I, Libertine* book hoax and brought the actual book into existence; wrote a series of columns for the early *Village Voice*; and wrote his defining "Creeping Meatballism" article for *Mad*.

In the world of jazz, he began a column of jazz commentaries; was master of ceremonies for a number of jazz concerts; recorded his first album, *Jean Shepherd into the Unknown with*

Jazz Music; and narrated his thirteen-minute improvisation to Charles Mingus' "The Clown."

Jean Shepherd is truly out of what he thought of as the limited world of the Midwest. He did not wait an instant—from the moment he reached New York City, from the beginning of the "Night People" period, he was grabbing at life—and turning it slowly in his hands so that listeners saw what he saw in it—through his broadcasts, his listeners could imagine that they could also taste it. Jean Shepherd in New York was living on the heights as leader and as creator. He had achieved his dream. And he wanted more—other far-flung activities engaged him as a Man of the World. Excelsior!

CHAPTER 7

AND I WAS JUST BEGINNING TO TASTE IT!
(A) Man of the World

The Big Apple, home of the arts, the land of "golden promise," as Shepherd put it. He had come a long way from Hammond, and a long way from his first taste of escargots in college— from what was his early taste of a world beyond meatloaf. Now he could indulge his ravenous appetite for experience. Fine food and drink, sports cars, travel. He traveled widely— both geographically and in the broad range of his activities and intellectual interests, making up for the time he'd served as a child, as a T/5 in the army, and as a broadcaster in the provinces.

Of course, wherever he lived, at least in retrospect, Shepherd could create a more interesting and significant experience out of what to others might seem to be meager material. But he had reached Manhattan, "The Enfabled Rock." He was really there!

He took in and mastered not only the big things but the small things—like where to get the best shoeshine or haircut— the trivialities that represent a knowledge of how to live intelligently and well in the big city. Shepherd experienced the wider world. In his first book of collected stories, *In God We Trust: All Others Pay Cash*, the interchapter scenes with Flick in his hometown tavern show the man of the world Jean/Ralph returning to write about his hometown. Flick, with his limited mind of a person who never left, stands in sharp contrast with Shepherd in New York:

> I was in the East. The effete East. The East of golden promise. What was it that Thomas Wolfe used to call Manhattan? "The Enfabled Rock." And I was here. I mean we're all here. Do you realize how—how *fortunate* we are? We are the fortunate few. I mean, out of the billions of people who live all over the world, do you realize how lucky we are? That we're here, that you're you. Just think who you could have been! Oh! Boy, you break out in a cold sweat when you realize how lucky you are to be so—you know—[said ironically] so real and right... I'm the New Yorker now, you know. I would just like to know—just—just for purposes of my own particular statistics—how many people are living in New York— how many Manhattanites are people who have—let's say they are immigrants from—Iowa or from—Ohio—Utah. Millions and millions. You have no *idea* what a terrible lure this place is to people who live outside of this place.[28]

Shepherd felt himself to be a real New Yorker. Over the years, he said he lived in New York City's Upper East Side, East 57th Street, the Lower West Side, the East Village, and the West Village. From some time in the 1960s until about 1977, he lived in the West Village in a townhouse. In the *New York Night* one-hour television documentary hosted by Long John Nebel (1968), Shepherd narrated the Greenwich Village segment, partly from his Village apartment, partly walking the Village streets. Greenwich Village certainly seemed a most appropriate location, given its aura of the unconventional, of the artistic and the literary.

Yet, despite how obviously Shepherd gloried in his life, he kept a considerable part of himself private—not just from his listeners but even from his close associates. Jerry Tallmer says, "I don't think we [publisher, writers, and friends at the *Voice*] ever found out where he lived—he was very mysterious about that." Tallmer said in an article, "It's funny, Jean was certainly a Greenwich Villager...but I do not know if he ever lived in Greenwich Village or, in fact, where in New York he lived. Fancher [*Voice* founder] doesn't know, d'Lugoff [jazz concert promoter] doesn't know. McDarrah [*Voice* photographer] doesn't know. Nobody knows."[29]

"Nobody knows" is a recurring theme regarding much of the

real Jean Shepherd. Despite his constant talk, some of Shepherd's experience of life was not to be shared with friends— it was too precious because it was the very stuff of his art and he apparently protected and preserved it for that use. Helen Gee has commented, "He was really quite removed, in his own world." As several of his friends have noted, if he did talk about these experiences with them, he was sometimes testing out a riff in a dry run for his art of radio broadcasting.

Only through considerable research and asking the right questions (despite Shepherd's best efforts to hide) will "nobody knows" be modified to "well, we do know *some* things." Some things we can feel confident in knowing are a few of his openly expressed appetites for pleasure, including eating and drinking. As in virtually every activity he talked about to his listeners, his purpose was not just to convey information, but to comment about it in a way consistent with his overall attitudes.

FOOD AND DRINK

Even in food preferences, Shepherd not only indicates his delight in good food, but takes the opportunity to disparage the culinary limitations he had left behind:

> My mother came all the way out—I took her to this fancy restaurant—she came all the way out from the Midwest. Do you know what it's *like* in the Midwest, any of you? Have any of you ever sat down to a meal in the Midwest? In a midwestern restaurant? Well here, I figured that she had come out of the desert.[30]

In an April 1960 broadcast after just returning from Europe, Shepherd spoke of his love of good food, describing how both excited and sad he had been on his last night there, and how he had decided to have the best meal he could get, and how much he enjoyed being alive and savoring it!

Despite his close association with the jazz, Beat, and Village scene in the late 1950s and the 1960s, there is no indication that Shepherd indulged in drugs or excessive drinking. At most, nicotine held *some* appeal for him. In fact, on the air, primarily directing his comments at the psychedelic culture of the 1960s, he disparaged any such use because the joys of everyday life gave surpassing pleasure.

MODES OF TRANSPORT

Shepherd not only enjoyed food and drink, but modes of propelling himself—usually at considerable speed. He spoke of the first car he'd had as an adolescent—the first instance of his being dominated by a machine. He frequently spoke of the joy he had in the act of driving his vehicles over the years, whether it was a scooter, motorcycle, Rover, Riley, Austin Healy, Jaguar, Peugeot, Fiat, Triumph TR3, MG-TD, or the rough-hewn, traditional, connoisseur Morgan sports car. Some of these brands were sponsors, and he gave glowing, personal recommendations. On one program, he described how he would race to arrive on time for his Carteret, New Jersey, broadcasts in 1956, claiming he once crashed his Porsche sports car into the transmitter's three-foot-deep cooling pool. In another broadcast, he said he had driven his Porsche at 140 miles per hour on the Jersey Turnpike. Shepherd seemed not only to enjoy all kinds of experiences, but to add the unpredictable thrill of danger to the mix, as Helen Gee recalls:

> He invited me to ride on his motorcycle. What a mistake. I thought he was going to kill himself—or me. [He drove] very fast...he'd swerve and I was hanging on. And he did have an accident at one point. And he also didn't see too well. He was wearing contacts. He was one of the first people, I think, to wear contact lenses—or so he told me... He kept boasting about his contact lenses. Vain. Oh, very vain... He came in one day smiling, "I've got contact lenses," and told everybody, because he liked to be first on everything.

As in all activities, he seemed to insist on experiencing cars and other vehicles with intensity. He also prided himself on his expertise in all areas that captured his fancy. Dan List, *Voice* automotive columnist, remembers, "He knew a lot about the cars, no two ways about it." From 1971 to 1976, at the request of the *Car and Driver* editor, he wrote a wide-ranging monthly column for them. He attended and announced a variety of sports car and stock car races, and liked to pal around with car racing enthusiasts, including cartoonist Charles Addams, out on Long Island, New York.

For over a decade—from the late 1950s to the mid 1960s—he emceed the annual *Village Voice* Washington Square sports car rally. Jerry Tallmer remembered in the *Villager* article that "to

help promote the new newspaper, as well as one of his own particular enthusiasms, Jean—and auto-nut Dan List—thought up
and produced, if that's the word, a series of auto rallies in which
all sorts of wonderful antique cars and modern sports cars
would chase their way, or wend their way, through the twists
and turns of Greenwich Village, ending up in the Sheridan
Square to which the *Voice* had by then moved."

Shepherd piloted his own single-engine plane. One is
reminded of the barnstorming flying shows he said he went to as
a kid with his father. Occasionally on a radio broadcast, he
talked about the thrill of flying. One of his *Jean Shepherd's
America* half-hour television episodes features him flying his
own small plane.

Shepherd's long-time friend Peter Wood remembers Shepherd's broadcasts from Philadelphia in 1951 when "he would go
on the air in this more or less cocktail lounge/dining room, and
he had a standout booth there and he would do his broadcast for
about three hours. I think it went till two o'clock in the
morning. He would talk to people or kibitz, and so on, and
everybody could sit there and hear this patter." Wood remembers
that a lot of the fellows from the Air National Guard would go
there after Guard practice: "They'd all fill up that room to hear
Jean Shepherd talk about airplanes, because he had wonderful,
wonderful stories dramatized, about World War I fliers in
France. And he would talk about the Red Baron, and describe all
the maneuvers and preparations, and the weather, and he would
just make it so real."

TRAVEL BROADENS ONE

In addition to traveling intensely on his own wheels or wings,
Shepherd took trips all over the world. In a 1972 broadcast
describing his recent trip to Australia, he said he started traveling in 1957 and in that year had gone around the world. He
then talked about the importance of travel:

> If you ever have any doubts about spending any money on
> traveling, friend, forget it. I'm serious. The people that I always
> feel sorry for are people who are old and are about to depart
> this mortal coil, who have never traveled. Who have never
> really seen the world. And it doesn't take a lot of money, you
> know. Really doesn't, because it's amazing how people tend to
> spend a lot of money on junk.[31]

Jean Shepherd emphasized that being in new places promoted new ideas, new ways of perceiving our world. Travel unplanned—all the simple things should be noticed, especially because they are of a different order from the simple things at home. He usually described his visits upon his return in a series of broadcasts, and sometimes played recordings made on site. Most of his travel was for pleasure, though a few times he went on assignment. Among other places, in 1958, he traveled to Lebanon for the U.S. Navy, for which he did the narration for a documentary film on the U.S. forces landing there; in 1960, he was in Germany and Guantanamo Bay, Cuba; in 1963, he was in the Negev Desert, Israel. In 1964, he traveled to the British Isles and toured for a week with The Beatles for his interview with them for *Playboy*. In 1965, he was in Australia.

That same year Shepherd agreed to substitute for fellow WOR broadcaster Barry Farber, going in his place to Peru's Amazon headhunter territory "delivering candy to the natives."[xv] Farber had won a raffle at a Luden's Cough Drop promotional party and the prize was 500 pounds of cough drops and candy to be delivered to his favorite charity.[32] Farber chose to help missionaries in the Amazon—the Indian tribe's chief had been his radio guest a few weeks before. They had only recently stopped their headhunting custom. (Yes, this is the story.) Shepherd, a public relations man for Luden's, a photographer, and a translator spent several days with the tribe. (During one program devoted to the trip, he played a tape of himself playing some music with the Indians.) On the night he returned, he described an aspect of what he considered his role in life:

> I went to the headwaters of the Amazon. I was there. I am a trained reporter. Those of you who listen to me know that. My life has been devoted to absorbing sights and sounds and listening, and I am going to try to give you in the next couple of days—maybe the next week or two—my impressions of what I consider probably the high point of my life so far as adventures and experience is concerned. [He says that the trip started in part as a bit of a lark, but that they soon realized it was very serious business.[xvi]] I'm not going to appear, incidentally, as an anthropologist on any of these shows—an expert. I'm appearing as an artist who has seen something and would like to transmit his impressions to you.[33]

Yes, most important was to transmit his impressions, as he

continued to do in his other trips, such as 1969 in Agra, India. In early 1972, he described his trip around the world in seven days, which he took to see what such a whirlwind tour would feel like. In 1975, he described St. Patrick's Day after his second trip to Dublin, Ireland. He traveled widely in the United States, including to sites for his *Jean Shepherd's America* television series, and for scores of live performances at colleges and elsewhere. Although he admitted that he was a tourist, he avoided official tours:

> I've never taken a tour in my life. I just walk around and dig the scene, see. And when I see a dirty, rotten, crummy, smelly alley, I go up it. I mean, if I feel like going up that alley, and if I don't, I don't. I see a lot of country and I see a lot of the world this way.[34]

Shepherd, always noticing his surroundings, going up a real or metaphorical alley, urged listeners to be keen observers because it engaged them more fully in life. What an intense need he had to experience and to *know!*

> As far as I'm concerned, travel—I have found travel to be one of the most—oh—use all these clichés, but it *is* the one thing I find that really, truly, does give me a kind of a final sense of involvement and satisfaction.
>
> I love the sensation of being completely removed from my known environment, and just looking out—just being able to walk through a street that is—that is completely unknown to me—to look at people who are unknown, to go into a place that is unknown—a restaurant to look at—the sky is unknown.[35]

As with all Shepherd commentaries, he related the specific to one of his continuing themes. The following comes from a program on Tel Aviv and the Middle East:

> You know the one thing I think keeps most people from really enjoying travel—in fact enjoying life itself—is groundless fear. I wonder where we develop these fears—early in our lives. The fear of strange smell, for example, you know? How many people have these fears? The fear of strange food. Yeah, that's right! The fear of strange names. Just the name, for example— Tel Aviv sounds foreign. It sounds vaguely dangerous. I sup-

pose most people would feel better if it was called Circleville—
you know—or Littleton, or some name that you can handle
like that.

Yet I do feel that fear—groundless fear—keeps most people
from actually—genuinely enjoying their lives. I'm talking
about fear of all kinds. Sexual, aesthetic, and—we could go
further and further and further until finally you don't know
where it ends.[36]

Shepherd seemed to be a fearless traveler, but neither travel
nor anything else quenched his thirst for fulfillment. Just before
his Peruvian trip, corny, silent-movie-type piano music in the
background, he speaks mock melodramatically:

Deep down inside of me there is a little violin playing that
says, "Yes, why, why me? Why am I a Flying Dutchman, forever sailing over the seas—the seven seas of this benighted
globe? Always looking, always searching, always hunting
[jew's harp twang now and again] and never finding?"[37]

He wanted to see everything, know everything, go everywhere. Listeners might have thought that Shepherd was just
making a pointless little funny about "always looking and never
finding," but, remembering his talk about the sea captain who
hated the sea and was *serious* about it, the reader can understand that Shepherd's comment about never finding might have
been a serious statement from a man who seemed to constantly
seek out an elusive something from life that he felt he could
never quite grasp. Always the urge, but apparently never the
complete satisfaction of having all his heart's desire. Little
wonder that, when not at the microphone, he frequently exhib-
ited the unhappiness and hostility that can result from intense
frustration. That frustration might also account for his forays
into so many activities and such creative fields as the visual arts.

VISUAL ART

Jean Shepherd obviously had a great interest in the arts in general, and expressed a special interest in photography and drawing.
His outline-style ink drawings appeared with his *Village Voice* articles, on the back of a paper Prexi Restaurant place mat and in
two of his own books of stories and articles. As might be expected, his drawings are usually full of minutely observed details.

Helen Gee comments, "The amazing thing about Jean is that whatever he decided to do he did rather well... He decided to draw and he drew very well... And he used to draw on napkins and I think I have somewhere, some of the napkins too... He wanted to become an artist. An artiste." But, though enjoyable to glance over, the drawings do not result in any profound revelations, possibly because they do not involve his master ability with words. On the other hand, sports, another passion of his, provided a wider field for him to describe and deal with in metaphors.

SPORTS AND STUFF

Shepherd's coworker, Barry Farber, remembers, "He used to come in [to his WOR office], I don't know where the hell he played—come in all sweaty, with real equipment—gloves and everything. And he loved baseball stories... Baseball was one of his loves."

Shepherd frequently used sports metaphors—usually baseball—saying he played sports in his youth, had been a professional ballplayer, and had done play-by-play broadcasts for the minor league Toledo Mudhens. In New York, he transferred some of his interest from the Chicago White Sox to the New York Mets—both teams steeped in the frustrations of humankind's ever-futile striving. He said that his 1964 play-by-play of the World Series between the New York Yankees and the St. Louis Cardinals, for the Armed Forces Network, was the first such satellite broadcast. The *New York Times* writer who interviewed him for an article at one of these games picked up on Shepherd's love of "seeing things as few others see them."[xvii] The article continued, "Thus, though he was only one among 67,101 customers at Yankee Stadium, he spent the afternoon looking not only at the players on the field, but also at the players in relationship to the customers, and both groups in relationship to the stadium, and the stadium in relationship to Western civilization."

As with all that interested Shepherd, he related baseball to his overarching, philosophical themes—here, baseball as metaphor—"In the great baseball game of life, what position do you play?"[38] And what better than the corny uplift/putdown poem of the hero who strikes out:

> Once a year, every year, almost at this time—we do "Casey at the Bat." "Casey at the Bat," I believe, is probably as close to a true American classic as you can get.

[After several short diversions and a tinkling player-piano rendition of "Take Me Out to the Ballgame," and saying, "My father was an insane baseball fan," he continues.] This piece has a peculiar kind of artful artlessness about it. It embodies so many difficult attitudes. The attitude of—if you got up to go. That's very real, you know. There's always a few guys who *do* get up, no matter what's going on. No matter what ballgame. I'm not even talking about baseball—life itself.

A few get up to go. And who remains? Just the rest. Sitting there with the hope that burns eternal in the human breast. The faithful. Knowing full well it's not going to work, because two clowns are coming up. Still, they can't tear themselves away. It's that nutty thing that's inside of people, you know? Nothing to do with baseball. It's that thing...

[After reading "Casey at the Bat," as the end theme music wells up, Shepherd ends his riff.] So you have to pick 'em up where they are. You have to do what's got to be done. A man's got to sometimes get out there and just—do what a man has to do. Just keep your knees loose, look up into that sun, go back there as it's drifting back towards the fence. Move easily. Make sure that you judge for the windage. Drift a little to your left. And just stand there and wait.[39]

As far as the New York Mets were concerned in the 1960s, all a fan such as Shepherd could do was shake his head at their "aggressive ineptitude" and "wait-till-next-year" mentality. At the start of a season, he announced that the Mets were thirty-seven and a half games out of first place. Then, in 1969 when they won their first World Series, he devoted an entire program to them:

One of those things that happen so rarely in the world of sports—and in fact, in the world of anything! A hundred to one shot hardly ever wins in *any* field. I'm talking about your office, I'm talking any situation that involves competition between human beings, turtles, and thoroughbred horses. That hundred to one shots are exceedingly rare. And as a matter of fact, in professional sports, where a hundred to one is being kind to the teams—that are a hundred to one. In professional sport, it's not only rare, it is almost an impossibility. And the Mets did it. And they did it magnificently! There was no luck involved. You know, a lot of people say luck—no, no. There was just too much *great* play that went on to be luck.[40]

He mourned the loss of something essential to the game in late 1965, speaking of the effect of humidity and wind in a ballpark:

> Have you noticed that down in Houston, for example, they are building a stadium down there—which is an indoor baseball park?
>
> Now what does this mean? To most people this seems to be progress, but in fact, what it really is doing is eliminating baseball. Part of—yeah—in the elimination of rain and weather, you're eliminating baseball.
>
> Now—now any good ball player will tell you, one of the most important facets of baseball is an outfielder drifting back under a fly ball that's being carried by the wind. This is a skill; this is part of the game. It's difficult. To catch a fly ball in a high wind—that's drifting it back toward the stands—or bringing it back in from the stands—and this is part of the game.
>
> The pitcher, for example, uses wind in pitching—are you aware of that? That a hard crosswind is very valuable to a certain kind of curve ball pitcher...
>
> Therefore, they have removed from baseball the game's actual life's blood. Actually, they've taken the blood out of the game now.[41]

In this perception of the seemingly minor—we are shown how the inconsequential represented matters of greater importance. Shepherd's observation used subject matter as a metaphor for ourselves and as commentary on human activity—"taken the blood out of the game" described an insensitive intervention that degraded what had been a subtle combination of forces between nature and people that many of us would not otherwise recognize. Shepherd perceived more in his various activities, and thus enjoyed them more than most people enjoyed their enthusiasms—and he conveyed this perception and knowledge to his listeners.

Shepherd enjoyed himself immensely as a man of the world, pursuing his private enthusiasms, and communicating those enthusiasms to his listeners. New York, more than elsewhere, was the place to enjoy private pleasures, and to engage in the arts. He immersed himself in an impressive variety of professional pursuits and his renown began to expand among those involved in the performing arts. He gathered a large group of

creative friends in those various arts he enjoyed. They appreciated Shepherd and worked with him on various projects. Some
of these encounters were quite successful. Some others caused
what could be called "people problems." As long as his activities
and creative acts were under his control he did fine. Dealing
with other people, as it is with everyone, could be a problem.
Other people have their own needs and priorities, whether they
are one's peers or, as with Shepherd, when they are the increasingly large hordes of "fellow sufferers" known as fans. For
some, it's tough to deal with other people.

CHAPTER 8

AND I WAS JUST BEGINNING TO TASTE IT!
(B) Dealing with Other People

The scene shifts from the more individual pleasures of Shep to the worrisome problem of interacting with others—not only with creative associates but also with listeners, whom Shepherd would on occasion refer to in his broadcasts as "vast hordes," a group not satisfied just to sit and listen from afar but which in increasing numbers insisted on changing his monologues into dialogues. Dealings with fellow creators were usually more positive experiences. As Dan Wakefield writes, "David Amram, the jazz musician and composer I used to hear play at the Five Spot, says, 'There was a cross-pollination of music, painting, writing—an incredible world of painters, sculptors, musicians, writers, actors, enough so we could be each other's fans.'"

Through the late 1950s and the early 1960s, Shepherd had expanded his activities and professional friendships. Among these activities: he created and starred in his Off-Broadway theater piece, *Look, Charlie* with Herb Gardner, Shel Silverstein, Lois Nettleton, and others; he appeared onstage in *Smalltacular* and *New Faces of 1962*; he appeared in the plays *A Banquet for the Moon*, *Voice of the Turtle*, and *Destry Rides Again*; he performed solo at various venues, including One Sheridan Square; he did two comedy LP records—*Jean Shepherd and Other Foibles*, and *Will Failure Spoil Jean Shepherd?*;

he appeared on several television shows and did his own short-lived Jean Shepherd television show; he narrated a couple of short documentary films; he edited and wrote an extensive introduction to *The America of George Ade*, about one of his favorite humorist precursors; and he starred in a popular comic magazine, *HELP!*, in a seven-page photo story printed in the September 1961 issue. The editor's preface said that Shepherd "has the distinction of being practically ubiquitous in New York these days."

A *New York Times* news story of August 13, 1956, states, "Mr. Shepherd, a rather shy, professorial young man, has built a quietly fanatic audience among self-confessed eggheads, college students, artists, performers, semiprofessional intellectuals." In photos at this time, sometimes wearing the regular glasses he would soon forsake, Shepherd looked shyly professorial. (He seemed less shy from the early 1960s onward.)

There were many people in Shepherd's personal and professional life. A number of topical comedians who had nationwide reputations listened to him. More than one of them who listened, Shepherd complained, stole his material off the air and from his nightclub performances, and many others had been "influenced." Although it seems a tradition for comedians to complain that other comedians steal their jokes, Shepherd, in the increasingly inconsequential medium of radio, would seem to have had more than average cause to complain, when those making it big in the culture at large stole more than just jokes from him, but humorous ideas and situations—the substance of what he considered his loftier creative form.

Many well-known people whose work he admired were friends and listeners.ˣᵛⁱⁱⁱ Composers George Antheil and John Cage, jazz greats including Charles Mingus. Other friends included cartoonist and playwright Jules Feiffer, radio playwright Arch Oboler, S. J. Perelman, Steve Allen, Johnny Carson, Ernie Kovacs, Fred Allen, Jack Kerouac (when he died, Shepherd delivered a broadcast tribute), and many others. Sometimes he read Feiffer's weekly *Village Voice* cartoon on the air. Shel Silverstein, Herb Gardner, and Jean Shepherd seem to have been especially close during the late 1950s and early 1960s. Silverstein, in an interview in 1963, is quoted, referring to "my closest friend, Jean Shepherd."[42]

[In a kidding voice.] What do you want *Shel*? What do you *want*? You want *what*? You wanta be on the radio? What you wanta say, for crying out *loud?* [Pause.] Okay, Shel, say hello to everyone. They're all waiting out there.[43]

Shepherd comments in his foreword to cartoonist and writer Shel Silverstein's cartoon book, *Now Here's My Plan*, "Shel is the only continuously funny man I have ever known."[44] Silverstein's 1961 book, *Uncle Shelby's ABZ Book: A Primer for Tender Young Minds*, proclaims, "This book is affectionately dedicated to Uncle Shelby's old comrade, Jean Shepherd."[45] Silverstein did the artwork for Shepherd's 1959 record, *Jean Shepherd and Other Foibles*, and wrote the extended, bogus memoir for the liner notes, a paragraph of which is:

> After his flight from Orly Airport in a stolen biplane, Jean arrived in Detroit on the verge of complete mental collapse. Olga was gone and he was depressed. The others—Ernie Hemmingway [sic], Gertie Stein, Picasso—had already achieved a degree of recognition and still there was no word from the Guggenheim Foundation. And so, after three years of starving with his Orange Period, Jean was forced to accept the "conditional" hospitality of the aging Duchess "L." Jean asked me if I had heard any news of Henri and I lied and said that I hadn't. He told me that Henri had deceived him and that he was completely disillusioned with circus life in general. I tried to cheer him up. I pointed out that the accident was unavoidable and that Borili's wife did not hold him at all responsible—Jean, nevertheless, felt a tremendous guilt because he had been driving. We had some more wine and then Jean asked me if I had any word from Clarence Darrow. It was here that I first suspected that the absinthe was taking its toll on Jean's brain. Darrow had been dead for the past five years.

That Shel wrote "A Boy Named Sue" in response to Jean's complaints about having a girl's name may never be confirmed, though it seems consistent with Shel's humor and treatment of his old pals. In 1959 Shepherd created an Off-Broadway show—according to the program (sketches and text drawn by Silverstein), "Jerome Kretchmer and Dorothy Love Proudly Present Jean Shepherd and Rabble in...*Look, Charlie: A Short History of the Pratfall*. Created, conceived, written, directed, inspired, perfected, head thumped, ballyhooed, and worried over by Jean Shepherd." The whimsical program notes indicated the participation of Shepherd doing head-thumping music, Silverstein, friend Herb Gardner juggling, actress Lois Nettleton, a pit orchestra, and a jazz band.

At about this time, as one of Shepherd's rare on-air guests, Gardner described his cartoon characters, "Nebbishes." In probably the best known of these images, two Nebbishes sprawl on chairs face to face, feet up on a low table, as one says (expressing the illusion of potential improvement that Shepherd must have responded to), "Next week we've *got* to get organized." Herb Gardner did the liner notes for Shepherd's 1961 LP, *Will Failure Spoil Jean Shepherd?*[46] Soon, however, the Shep and Herb friendship would be over.

Silverstein seemed to continue to be a good buddy, through available evidence, but Herb Gardner's relationship to Shepherd deteriorated drastically following the creation of Gardner's *A Thousand Clowns*. Although not following the details of Shepherd's life, the main character of the 1962 play and 1965 movie, Murray (played by Jason Robards), has enough of Shepherd's traits and is described clearly enough to be recognizable. Murray is a nonconformist whose brother says about him, "There's only one thing that really bothers you—other people— the enemy." Murray says, "Gee, if most things aren't funny, Arn, then they're only *exactly* what they are. Then it's just one long dental appointment, interrupted occasionally by something exciting like waiting, or falling asleep."

In a manner seemingly borrowed from the Shepherd custom of "hurling invectives," Murray frequently hollers ironic commentary toward the world at large. Also, just as Shepherd, mentorlike, wanted to expand the perceptions of his listeners, Murray says about his precocious twelve-year-old nephew, "I want to be sure he sees all the wild possibilities. I want him to know it's worth all the trouble to give the world a little goosing once you get the chance." A salacious statue of a curvaceous woman in the movie echoes a familiar Shepherd story featuring a lamp shaped as a woman's leg. As leitmotifs woven among other allusions in the movie are two songs which Shepherd frequently used for ironic effect: "Stars and Stripes Forever" and his favorite, the sung, hummed, and played, "Yes Sir, That's My Baby."

Shepherd has been quoted as saying, "They've stolen my life!" Until the final scenes, Shepherd could well have enjoyed the tribute, but that was not the problem. Jules Feiffer and Paul Krassner each remember that Shepherd's resentment ended the friendship between Gardner and him.[xix] He must have hated seeing himself as Murray in the final scene, suited, in mid-commuter-sprint, freeze-framed like a dead butterfly pinned to a board—no longer free, forced to compromise and conform. Compromise and conforming would be damning descriptions for Shepherd, but there is evidence to support the truth of the portrayal—his radio style changed with the shorter length after mid-1960, his style became more organized, with less-improvised, laid-back jazzy riffs, but with more commercials and adolescent adherents. He began riffing less as an equal and more frequently as a mentor. The changes did not destroy Shepherd's art—to his eternal credit, he found ways to accommodate artistically to his new situation—but Herb, his old buddy, went too far in condemning the partial metamorphosis, which occurred somewhere during the period when *A Thousand Clowns* was written.

Others spread tributes to Shepherd far and wide. Shepherd claimed that screenwriter Paddy Chayefsky asked him for permission to use a variation on his "hurling invectives" for his 1976 film, *Network*, about television news becoming entertainment. In a scene forming an important element of the film, the television newscaster, apparently suffering a nervous breakdown, tells his audience to "get up out of your chairs. I want you to get up right now and go to the window, open it, and stick your head out, and yell, 'I'm as mad as hell, and I'm not going to take this anymore.'" His viewers proceed to do just that.

In a different kind of theft, borrowing, or homage, a strong case can be made that Jack Nicholson in *The King of Marvin Gardens*, a 1972 film, plays a Jean Shepherd–based character. Nicholson is a late-night radio monologist who talks about childhood incidents and other personal experiences. Although the character and his monologues are far more morose than Shepherd, and totally lacking in Shepherd's humor, the connection seems strong. Especially as we are shown that Nicholson on-air, using metaphor, speaks in allegories and alters the facts of his reminiscences for his own artistic purposes—just as Shepherd did. The Nicholson character is referred to as "an artist" and is known as "The Philosopher."

These films were made during the period when Shepherd spread his considerable talents and ambitions into various mass media. The future at that time seemed open to much wider recognition for him. The fact that he would fail to achieve the greater renown and rewards that should have been his destiny during his life, despite the promise and possibilities and numerous limited successes, must have increasingly stuck in his craw. It must have been difficult to be around him at times, especially to have lived with him.

MISOGYNY? LIBERTINISM? MARRIAGE?

According to Herb Saltzman, "He was, in his mind, that guy—the libertine [main character in the hoax book *I, Libertine*]. In his mind Shepherd was a latter-day version of the swashbuckler Errol Flynn. That's his view of himself."

> Traditionally in Chinese astrology, the year of the rat is a good year for business... Now what else is it? Well, it is also a *bad* year—and I don't suppose this will surprise many of you—a bad year for marriages [laughs], which puts it there with all the *other* years.[47]

"I found out about that marriage trap early," Shepherd once said, yet married four times.[xx] Reportedly for a very short time in his youth, then to the mother of his two children, then to actress Lois Nettleton. Herb Saltzman suggests that Shepherd's misogyny played a role in Nettleton's eventual departure. (His subsequent marriage to Leigh Brown will be discussed in a later chapter.)

Actress Lois Nettleton is listed in the program of Shepherd's *Look, Charlie* in 1959. They married in 1961—a union which ended six or seven years later.[xxi] Mention of Lois Nettleton with Shepherd occurs in Helen Gee's book about her Limelight Gallery, and there is a photo of them together. Considering the abundant testimony that Shepherd did not treat Nettleton with much respect, it is sadly appropriate that the photo shows his face, but only the back of Nettleton's head.

Jerry Tallmer says, "Lois was a *gorgeous* woman—and Jean was so detached." Ed Fancher comments, "Lois Nettleton—an absolutely gorgeous, wonderful, beautiful person. Unfortunately, that marriage didn't last, and I think it was because Jean was a little too self-involved." Jules Feiffer complains that "when I was with them, Jean only wanted to talk about himself and his own ideas, while Lois would ask about *me*."

Helen Gee: He was so concerned about his reputation and himself, he couldn't stand *any* competition. Even from a woman. And [Lois] was getting to be well known as an actress. She was a very good one. And she was a lovely woman. So she would come in with Jean. And I always thought of those Japanese women that followed their husbands behind. Because that was her attitude. The Great Man sat down, she pulled up a chair next to him, looked at him with great, adoring eyes, and he held forth. He never introduced her even after he was married. I don't even know how I found out that he was married... He never introduced her as his fiancée or his wife. I thought it was so demeaning.

Women certainly seemed to be a problem for Jean Shepherd (other than his mother in her red chenille bathrobe bending over the sink with her Brillo pad). Jean's problems with Lois were undoubtedly many faceted. Barry Farber, from the perspective of a coworker, remembers, "Whenever he was hurting because of something, he made no secret of it, and sort of passed it on as a sermon. He was married to a *beautiful* actress, Lois Nettleton, for a brief time [six to seven years]. And one day he came into the office shaking his head, and just said, 'Don't ever get yourself into a situation where your woman's making more money than you are.'"

Herb Saltzman: She was a lovely lady. I thought she was—in some ways—almost too nice for him. He was jealous of those [comedians who made it big in the 1960s] and I think that that obsession and that jealousy was the thing that tore Lois apart. She is a very gracious lady—actress. And then the call of Hollywood came and she couldn't resist. She went to Hollywood to do a movie—and stayed. Beyond that I didn't pry. It was a painful period he couldn't talk about.

Nettleton was quoted as saying that she had been family oriented and Shepherd had not been. From a newspaper article in 1977, when the subject of the marriage came up: "'I'd rather not talk about that,' she stated with ringing finality."[48]

Although Nettleton would not talk for publication about her marriage, and Shepherd would only show his distress in private at the time his marriage was apparently disintegrating, veiled references may have surfaced on his broadcasts. During this period he would sometimes sing on-air an ironic, mock-melo-dramatic version of "After You've Gone." (After you've gone/ And left me cryin'/After you've gone/There's no denyin'/You'll feel blue/You'll feel sad/You'll miss the dearest pal you've ever had.) Was he asking her to stay? Was he hiding his sadness in a bit of silliness? We cannot know, but as he said in the *Realist* interview in 1960, "My work is probably as great a purgative as any analysis could ever be."

Nettleton would rather not talk about Jean Shepherd, but some who knew him would talk—some would throw brickbats and others thought he was a delightful teddy bear. Part of the enigma of Jean Shepherd was the inconsistent aspect he presented to different people and to the same people at different times. Jerry Tallmer, in his article written after Shepherd died in October 1999, quoted several people connected with the early *Village Voice*. "To Fred McDarrah, photographer of the passing throng in and out of the Village from the Beat Generation straight through to the present, Jean was 'a lovable teddy bear, a very sweet person who didn't have a mean bone in his body.'" Tallmer continues, "To Art d'Lugoff, also, Jean was 'a very pleasant guy—we used to sit in the Museum of Modern Art and schmooze about life.'" Then Tallmer quotes Ed Fancher, who, he says, knew Shepherd pretty well in those days: "He was a tremendously inse-cure guy, very narcissistic. Yes, I agree, he was in a way one of the world's great optimists, and he was also very generous in a way; he helped us [*Village Voice*] a lot." These are memories in the 2000s of Shepherd in the late 1950s—positive responses com-pared to the mixed reviews Shepherd got in later years when life may have taken its toll on the better side of his nature.

A MAN FOR ALL AGES

Shepherd's audience expanded beyond the earlier, very-late-night fans. The broadcasts before 1:00 AM accommodated younger listeners—more now vibrated to the special sensibility and attitude toward the world that he projected. A listener in a humdrum job, voicing a feeling shared by many, said that Shep-herd "served to remind me that there were people out there who were interesting and intellectual." Shepherd often spoke of his "listeners," using the word as though it was a badge or title, and they referred to him with affection as "Shepherd" and "Shep."

The few available photos of Shepherd in public in the earliest

New York days of the late 1950s show an adult crowd. One shot, labeled "in his *I, Libertine* days," catches Shepherd in a bookstore, microphone in hand, with dozens of people, none seeming younger than twenty; almost all apparently in their thirties to fifties and older.[49] Although most people think of Shepherd's fans as being mostly high school and college kids, memories to this effect are of the 1960s and 1970s.

Beyond his base of peers, friends, and older listeners, Shepherd wanted and needed a larger audience. Within a somewhat short period, what he was, what he did—became more easily encountered by a broader audience (Sundays 9:00 to 1:00 AM and then weeknights before midnight). From the late-night smoky-jazz-club context for the socially disaffected and those outside mainstream culture, Shepherd changed as his broadcast time frame shifted. Retaining his wide range of interests, activities, and artistry, he became somewhat (though not widely) popular and commercial, continuing his encounters with unusual and unexpected food for the mind, which, like escargots, he twisted out of shells and savored throughout his performing career.

Keeping his heightened sensibility and acute observation of the human condition, he refashioned his material for larger and more comfortable venues where more regular hours were kept— a more mainstream cult of curiosity, intelligence, and perception for a larger minority of like minds. Within a few years he was more easily appreciated and accepted (jazz on his broadcasts moved from the more esoteric such as Mingus and Brubeck to Dixieland and the funky), more tempered and honed, more tightly organized, without as much abstract expressionist rough edge—more widely available in more mainstream outlets in addition to radio—notably *Playboy*, books, TV, movies, and school auditoriums. This larger audience from all sources, he found, was composed of a large percentage of kids. To court his larger audience, Jean Shepherd used a number of techniques that encouraged a sense of community—a feeling of belonging to an in-group.

Whether his techniques for enthralling his listeners were carefully thought out as a game strategy, or whether he developed them more spontaneously, all we can know for sure is that they worked. The range of commentary and information he conveyed about himself encouraged the feeling that one knew him as an individual—a kindred soul. He used an intimate, conversational tone engaged in an ongoing thought process—the sense one felt that he was talking directly to each person, not performing from a prearranged script. He addressed his audience with "Hi, gang" and referred to them as "my listeners." Often when talking about a news clipping of some strange event (a "straw in the wind"), he would say that it was sent to him by "one of my spies." This encouraged listeners to seek interesting news items to send to him in hopes of also becoming one of that special group—one of his spies.

He used a variety of idiosyncratic words and phrases, which instilled a sense of bonding through recognition by the group, and he cultivated a sense of us vs. them by implying that "we" were part of an intelligent and perceptive minority, compared to the majority of "slobs." Sometimes he held a gathering, referred to as "a mill," and encouraged other activities that only those who knew the meaning of would understand.

In a seeming contradiction, he was both mentor (especially for the young) and a peer for all ages. He provided information and ideas as a mentor, someone listeners respected—he filled an intellectual void in their world—while at the same time he acted as a peer, who could understand them and discuss intelligent matters with them as an equal, thus aligning himself with his listeners, separate from all nonlisteners.

As his time slot got earlier, including Sunday evenings, Sunday afternoons, Saturday daytime, and earlier weeknights, his audience grew to include many more "kids" (especially those who didn't quite fit into the predominant kid establishment and mindset)—hip grammar school, high school, and college students in growing numbers added to his adult admirers. Many people remember first listening to Shepherd when they were kids, long after bedtime, hiding the transistor radio under the pillow—a clandestine and intimate experience of togetherness with him. Kids—and adults too—had that warm feeling of knowing that there was at least one kindred intellectual soul out there, somewhere, communing with them. Shepherd's style of knowing irony especially appealed to young minds that had reached the stage of doubting and questioning the world around them. He commented in a 1960 interview, "I'd say that the significant thing I've seen among kids is that the kids are *much* more aware than they ever were."[50] Recognizing the student connection, he sometimes referred to his extended comments as a "class" or "seminar," the current season as a "semester."

You know that. Good. We'll give you one point for that. Write it down. Let's see whether you get that. For those of you who are listening tonight—all of these questions will appear on the blue book exam at the end of the semester. So you might as well start taking notes, right?[51]

I get probably five hundred letters a week from fifteen- and sixteen-year-old kids, who write to me and tell me what they really think.[52]

When you get a thousand letters a week you begin to see a lot of interesting drifts of things—you see a tenor—anyway, this kid says [Shepherd reads in a stilted, kid voice], "Dear Shep, I listen to your show every chance I get... You and your jew's harp are a mystery to me. I am puzzled. To me, you're just another voice. I have never seen what you look like. Same with your jew's harp. Can you draw me a rough sketch of what a jew's harp looks like? I would like to play one. It sounds great. Yet it scares me.

"P.S. I do not think I am an outsider. [Laughs.]

"Cordially yours, Mark. I am ten and a half years old."

That's an actual letter.[53]

Fred Barzyk: Shepherd told me [that his audience was fifteen-year-old boys]. WOR was going to have an appearance by Shepherd for his fans. I can't remember where it was, but there were *hundreds* of kids outside, just waiting to *touch* him... Shepherd said [speaking in a low, conspiratorial tone], "You know—each one of them thinks they're the only one listening to me." He loved the adoration.

Gregory McDonald [television critic for the *Boston Globe*], who wrote detective stories—*Fletch*—he was a big Shepherd cuckoo. He grew up listening to Shepherd. These are the kinds of people—they're literary types, they're broadcast types, they're individuals. And some of the individuals unfortunately were quite weird. I think you had to be intelligent to listen. Had to have a good imagination to go along with Shepherd's story-telling—to be able to get into it. So that, I think, appealed to a certain crowd.

Herb Saltzman: Shepherd was the darling of the nerd—the kids who were out of the norm. The smart kids, kids who wore glasses, kids who didn't know how

to dress, didn't know how to get girls... I'm thinking of
my friend's son. He's brilliant. When I brought him to
the studio—WOR—to meet Jean Shepherd—he thought
he had died and gone to heaven.

Jean Shepherd's style and content on the air had always been
oriented toward the intelligent, literate, adult mind. His work
was on the highest level. He wanted to be a contender among the
Mark Twains, Ingmar Bergmans, and Norman Mailers.
Although he indeed had an audience of knowledgeable and
appreciative adults, his base more and more consisted of kids—
the hordes of adoring adolescents and college kids. With his
desire for recognition among the intelligentsia, this must have
rankled him. The kid fans had taken over, and he had to accept
that in order to continue his career on the radio. The kids idol-
ized him, but he did not always seem comfortable on a public
pedestal where he could be approached within striking distance.
The surfacing of his attitude in occasional little derisive remarks
about his adolescent admirers seems inevitable. In addition,
what really got to him was an over abundance of "cuckoos."

SHEPHERD CUCKOOS, CALLERS, AND LETTER WRITERS

Why do I get this stuff in the mail? Listen to this one.[54]

"Fan" after all, is a derivative of "fanatic." The peculiar
showed up, as they tend to do in any performer's life—Shepherd
seemed to attract a large share of especially strange people. The
older brother/mentor feeling and the direct communication that
Shepherd inspired attracted some listeners who had excess
enthusiasm. Possibly odd loners who had trouble connecting to
real people in their lives found Shepherd's special intimate style
attractive and they "glommed" onto him.

Would you like to hear what a real, genuine, cuckoo letter
sounds like—a real cuckoo-bird letter?[xxii] Want to hear a real
cuckoo—all right, will you please give me my cuckoo-bird
music. [Penny whistle type classical music with Shepherd's
wacky accompaniment—"ha ha ha who who who."] And now
we read to you from a cuckoo-bird letter of the week.[55]

Shepherd proceeded to read a letter in a "little old lady"

voice, which began rationally about people who had appeared on public stages impersonating him—then the letter descended into paranoia. On another occasion, he says he is reading an *International Psychiatric Journal* article titled, "Is Cuckoo Birdism on the Rise?"

> A cuckoo bird is not the same as a nut. Oh no. A nut—a true nutter—a true nut case—that's something else. You often wind up by throwing the net over 'em and hitting 'em—and hitting them on the head with a rubber mallet and all that. But a cuckoo bird is somebody who believes that butterflies are on the march. Or perhaps believes that she can obtain immortality by eating Grape Nuts. Now that's cuckoo birdism. Know what I'm talking about? Cuckoo birdism? Right.[56]

In another program, Shepherd talks about how every performer he has known has had some fans who think the performer actually reads their letters, knows them, and cares about the personal details of their lives:

> Once in a while you'll have the misfortune to actually run into one of these people in person at a show, see, and there'll be a lot of people coming up—you know, they want to talk to you about things—autographs or whatever it might be, see.
> I'm not talking about just Shepherd. I'm talking about all kinds of people. By the way, it might surprise you to know there are other listeners to my show other than *you*, friend. Which *always* surprises people. But you'll go to some place in person, and somebody will come up and say, "Hello!"
> And you say, "Oh, hello."
> "Well—ah—hello!" they'll say. "I'm Clarisse!"
> And you say, "Oh, yes, well, hello, heh, heh, glad to meet you. My name is Jean Shepherd. Is there—"
> Girl says, "What do you mean? I'm Clarisse!"
> You'll say, "Yes, well—well, is there anything I can do for you, Clarisse? Do you want—"
> "But I'm [bewildered tone] I'm—I'm Clarisse!"
> And you'll say, "Do I know you?"
> "Of course! I'm Clarisse!"
> By that time, of course, the guards, wherever they are, are beginning to edge forward, see, because they can recognize the cuckoo eye. The cuckoo eye is usually a kind of watery eye, where one eye spins faster than the other in its socket. This is

the cuckoo eye. They're beginning to edge forward and then
[laughs] they finally hurry this lady out with her shopping bag
that contains bones and feet sticking out of the bag.

They finally hurry her out and then three days later you'll
get this angry letter that says, "I always *knew* you were a
phony. To absolutely humiliate me, after what we've meant to
each other!"[57]

Barry Farber: He got into serious trouble one time
just by answering a fan letter from a thirteen-year-old
girl who then *invented* fantasies of Jean Shepherd
coming to visit her at night. And her father was an
Archie Bunker type. And you can just imagine the rest.
Jean was hard-pressed. Jean had some anxious moments
there because he had to prove the negative—that
nothing like that went on. That was another sermon
[told by Shepherd]: "Don't ever write letters to young
girls."

Fred Barzyk: He had to leave the Village [mid-1970s]
because somebody came in and trashed his apartment.
He and Leigh were living in this small apartment in
Greenwich Village and the police said, "Get out of
here." So they moved out of Greenwich Village because
somebody trashed their apartment. He attracted strange
people, and some of them weren't very stable. His stuff
was so special. The kids [who listened to Shepherd on
the radio] were going to be writers, television types.

William S. Forstchen, a science fiction writer who had bought
a house on Maine's Snow Pond Lake, realized that Shepherd's
summer cottage was there.[58] He knocked on the door. "Leigh
answered the door, I nervously mentioned Jean's name, and her
features just fell. The woman went pale, stuttered she didn't
know anyone named Shepherd." He explained to her that he
really was a neighbor and walked away after leaving a copy of
his book on the doorstep. "Then I heard that distinctive voice,
'Hey kid, come back here!' Jean extended his hand and then
offered a warm genuine apology and explained why Leigh pan-
icked. Their place in Maine was secret, known just to a few
friends. The previous year, someone had come to their home,
knocked on the door the same as I did, and when Jean opened it,
a crazy maniac had attacked Jean. He pointed out that I stood

nearly six and a half feet tall, had a fairly strong build, and well, one day I might realize that there are a lot of crazy people to avoid."

Shepherd, talking about phone calls to him at the station that got wilder and wilder toward the time of the full moon, spoke in mock-serious tones:

> I would like to tell you—all you nuts out there. A special message to the nuts who are with us tonight. If you have suppressed calling, you know—I understand that it's not easy being a nut and I understand that *suppressing* your nuttiness is one of the most difficult parts of being a nut. That somehow we realize [chuckles]—we understand that [plucked note on jew's harp] we—we won't get mad, it's all right. But tomorrow night, forget it! There ain't gonna be no more nut calls tomorrow night, okay?[59]

Shepherd in 1972 asked, "Have you ever wondered why I have a funny look in the eye, when this stuff keeps coming in over the transom?" As general manager of the station, Herb Saltzman, remembers, "They showed up, and we ended up having, I believe, to put a security guard into [WOR's offices]."

BOBBY FISCHER—SHEP CUCKOO

Call them cuckoo, call them strange—Fred Barzyk remembers, "The chess champion Bobby Fischer followed—he would stalk Shepherd. We called them Shepherd Cuckoos. [Bobby Fischer] would show up at all of his things and try to get his autograph, try to talk to him."

> And so, we would like to salute these mean people tonight... That's right, Bobby Fischer! By the way are you aware that one of the very earliest listeners—for those of you who don't know anything about Bobby, the chess player—used to come up here, you know. Bobby Fischer was one of the very first listeners we had. You know Bobby, the great genius—really. He gave me a chess set one time.
>
> And Bobby's a strange guy. He really is. I remember one night we were over at Grant's over here on 42nd Street. Can you imagine Bobby Fischer, world's greatest chess player—and you know Grant's is over here, and we're eating a hot dog, see, and Bobby—Bobby's just sitting there and he's looking

around, see. And I'm sitting there eating my hot dog and
Bobby Fischer the great chess player is eating *his* hot dog and
finally he says, "Lot of funny people in the world, aren't
there?"

I said, "Yes, Bobby, there certainly are." We didn't say anything else for the next twenty minutes. We just ate more pic-
calilli and thought about that.

Bobby Fischer, when asked at the age of fourteen why he
liked chess, I think he stated it well for all of us. Did you hear
what Bobby Fischer said? At the age of fourteen? Why he liked
chess? He said, and we quote, "I like to see 'em squirm."
That's Bobby. To the point, honest. Doesn't win many *friends*,
but he certainly wins chess games. Ohhhh! You better believe
it. So tonight we are saluting Fred Biletnikoff, mean Ben
Davidson, Merle Haggard, Dick Butkus, and Bobby Fischer —
some of the *mean* people. Yeah! Through man's soul, there
flows a deep, turgid stream. Yeah, it's full of beer cans. [Pause.]
There goes one now. A deep, turgid stream. And tonight we
take this opportunity to salute that other side of man...

He's gotten polite in the last couple of years. But it's the
same old Bobby. I can see that icy look in the eye. Of the guy
that likes to take your liver out, wind it backwards, and stick
it back in you — see what happens when the juice starts comin'
out of your ears...

Bobby used to come around here to the radio station a lot,
and we used to — very good friend — I haven't heard from him
in a long time, but at the time, he used to come around here
many evenings. [Shepherd talks about having coffee in a
restaurant with Fischer and another chess grandmaster one
afternoon. Fischer walks to the back of the restaurant to make
a phone call and the other grandmaster speaks.] And now this
grandmaster turns to me and he just looks me in the eye and
he says, "He's mean." [Laughs.]

I said, "What do you mean?"

"Oh, he's mean."

I said, "What do you mean? He's a great guy."

"Oh yeah," he says, "he's a great guy, but don't ever play
chess with him."

[Shepherd describes another time, walking with Fischer to
a grandmaster chess match in a New York hotel, Fischer referring over and over to his opponent as "stupid." Fischer,
according to Shepherd, is about seventeen years old at the
time, and seems to especially dislike this opponent. Fischer

slowly destroys this grandmaster in the first game and, in the second game, crushes him unmercifully within a couple of minutes. On the way back, Shepherd says, "Bobby—boy, you really—you really beat him!" "Well, he's stupid!"]

That's all Bobby kept saying. "He's stupid." As if he should know he shouldn't be playing. So I just thought I'd let you know, friends—that we oughta have to include Bobby Fischer, who happens to be a friend of mine, in the crowd of the *mean* people.[60]

VAST HORDES

At least three times Shepherd acceded to the desires of hordes that wanted their two seconds of fame—he devoted these programs to reading listener names. He kept one's interest with varied background music, sometimes mentioning cities and states and a few listeners' written words, adding his own comments, and varying the tone of voice, with occasional short asides.

Okay, gang. The time has come. That vast horde of mankind, anonymous, sitting out there in the great stygian darkness has at long last got its chance to shine briefly in the electronic sun. And [laughs] last year—as you know we did—it was just about this time of year, actually, we did the Vast Marching Horde of Mankind Show...in which, we—we've spotted over the time that we've been around, that the one great urge everybody has in this day and age is to have his name mentioned, somewhere. Have you noticed when the camera swings out there over the Steve Allen audience—what do they do? That's right. Vast waving of arms, and practically, hardly a day goes by but we don't get 7,922 letters that say at the bottom, "Please mention my name on Friday." We don't mention names. We're not in the name—we don't, you know? It's just not our scene.

And so tonight—are you ready? We have a gigantic stack of mail. These people out in the darkness—I will make no editorial comment about them. They're just there.

And if you can imagine them, marching past in this great, great ragtag mob, bearing banners that read "Excelsior." [Shep alludes to his record, *Jean Shepherd and Other Foibles*, in which the last track describes a parade of famous people and fictional characters, including Billy Budd carrying an "Excelsior" flag, and the record jacket cover drawings by Shel Silverstein depict a ragtag parade of humanity.]

Would you please bring me some Mankind is Marching Past music, Herb? [Slow march music starts. Shepherd laughs.] One guy already flubbed the dub. The first card I pick up, he says, "Please mention my name Friday." [Laughs.] And I clearly said, "Thursday." Yeah, there are people who miss every brass ring that comes their way. And here they come—that vast herd. That's it! *Make it big, Herb!*[61]

Jeez! The guy could be nasty. Maybe they deserved it. The more listeners the better, but the more listeners anxious for his attention, the more annoying he found them. A no-win situation—Shepherd knew all about those. Listeners were a vast, anonymous, marching herd—a horde, a waving of arms. Maybe some did not realize the putdown of "I will make no editorial comment about them. They're just there."

On a number of broadcasts and in numerous personal encounters, Shepherd was hostile toward adults and kids who tried to make personal contact with him. He wanted to be left alone. At other times, loving the adulation, he seemed quite friendly. For example, the former managing editor of the *New York Post*, Marc Kalech, reported on Bob Kaye's Shepherd website about two personal encounters during his college years: "I remember Jean was incredibly friendly and patient to me, a young idolizing fan."

Shepherd loved the adoration, but simultaneously wanted and needed to keep others at bay. In 1963 on a Long John Nebel radio program, discussing his performances in plays, Shepherd disingenuously puts this only in artistic terms:

As soon as you get involved with your public, your public loses interest in you—interestingly enough—as a performer. For this reason. I think many people are very wise in maintaining a large wall between them and the people who listen to them or who read them. For example, if J.D. Salinger were to hang around NYU and argue with the students, they would put him down the next day. They wouldn't read his stuff. They can't get to him. He's not available. He doesn't have any interviews, he becomes a mystic figure.

If you ever get to know a performer—his personal

attitude toward things—this is a wonderful argument in favor of isolation of the artist from the public...that since I really did bare myself on those late-night shows and *do* on my radio shows, that keeps getting in my way when people see me doing a performance.

"Isolation of the artist from the public." Shepherd put this in terms of himself as a performer, neglecting to articulate to himself, possibly, but definitively to the audience, that his real self did not seem able to let people approach him. Despite his intimate radio persona, he was so self-involved that he neglected his beautiful wife, Lois Nettleton, he wouldn't let Helen Gee get near him as a friend, and his actions made it plain to his male friends who observed him that he could not look past himself.

The intensity of Shepherd's introspective art seems inseparable from the intense self-absorption of the real Jean Parker Shepherd. The inordinately isolated persona appears to be the operating principle that enabled the performing genius. We have here a rare, crystalline purity, a fusing of cause and effect that elicits wonder, and a shiver down the spine.

But not just any natural-born self-obsessive could make what Jean Shepherd created. He was surrounded by adults, as well as by adolescent acolytes, who enjoyed the effect with little idea of how he did what he did—how he used the tools of his trade to make the complexity and artistry of his radio performance. Every night he improvised in sound and words—the twin tools of his art. It's time to think about sound in more detail. Time to realize that the well-orchestrated sounds he entertained with were composed and practiced—and that Jean Shepherd was the most sophisticated of one-man bands. It's time for a seminar.

PART IV

THE TOOLS IN HAND

Throughout his career, Shepherd was a master of the tools of radio—sound and those special sounds called words. He delighted in the nature of the medium, and we experience the very complex, personal, and entertaining art he created.

CHAPTER 9

BAHN FREI
Sounds

On the radio, sound is all there is. It comes in many forms, and Shepherd used all of them—the human voice, music, sound effects, and silence. Shepherd's broadcasts were compositions in words and in sounds. He hated when someone disparagingly and inaccurately referred to him as a "disc jockey." On the PBS program, *The Three Worlds of Jean Shepherd*, in 1968 or 1969—the date is uncertain—he described his work:

> They look at you and say, "Well, what does he do?"
> "He tells stories. He's funny. He talks about life."
> And they say, "Well, has he ever been on the *Ed Sullivan Show*?"
> And you say, "Well, no..." And ultimately, you find it difficult to explain what I do. I think that anybody who talks about life is not easily tagged. A man who tells one-line jokes—he's a comic. A man who sings songs—he's a singer.
> But a person who deals with life may do *all* of those. And so, when you try to talk about life, you have to sing—you've heard me sing "The Sheik of Araby" or sing "After You've Gone," because all these are ways to point out that life can't be talked about by just words. You've got to do it with silence, you have to do it with

beat and tempo, and rhythm. And it's tremendously exciting.

As Shepherd's radio program started, after the announcer's voice and that moment of silence filled with anticipation, on came that manic galloping theme listeners never tired of hearing, because it meant Jean Shepherd was here.

At the beginning and ending of virtually every Jean Shepherd broadcast his theme song—"Bahn Frei," which translates from the German as "open track" or "fast track," a full orchestral piece of wide-eyed innocent enthusiasm—provided an exciting ambience and seemed to announce great things to come. It began with a trumpet fanfare, as though calling racing partici-pants to the starting line. One could easily imagine horses trot-ting along at a fast clip. It had a "William Tell Overture" quality and was performed by the Boston Pops Orchestra (what else?). Its sense of self-important confidence and corn fit Shepherd's sardonic tone perfectly—it was glop, but entertaining glop.

Although one might listen to the catchy tune for years and not realize its genre, it is a frantically paced polka. On a program focusing on his high school summer vacation job as announcer on a foreign-language radio station, Shepherd played a typical polka, with yodeling and whistling on the record. "Did you rec-ognize that?" he asked those in the studio:

> That's the Jersey version of my theme!... One of the worst pieces of music I ever heard in my life! That actually is the *Jersey* version of my theme. A real foot-stomping *polka!*[1]

Shepherd played it again, and one recognized his theme song. He once described it as "the most dynamic piece of total medi-ocrity I ever heard in my life." At some time in the early 1960s, an addition is heard at the ending of his theme—his voice: "Ahhhh." It seemed to have a tone of slightly weary resignation, as though to imply "Well, I'm glad that's over and I can relax again." Its enigmatic quality puzzled many, as per the Alan Colmes interview/call-in show of December 1998:

> Shep: The music I played—that's a theme song, and yes, it's Eduard Strauss. One of the lesser-known Strausses. And, yeah, it's a—it's a—I played that because it's such a bad piece of music—that I thought it set the tone.

[Caller]: It's so corny but it's fun anyway, you know?
Shep: Fun is always fun.
A.C.: At the very end of that—and I heard it again tonight when we played it. That "Ahhhhh!"
[Caller]: That's a Jean Shepherd sound.
A.C. : Yeah—is that a dub or why is there that sound of your voice at the end of the recorded theme song?
Shep: Well, that's because I'm a mysterious person and I thought it sounded right there.
A.C.:...And I was wondering (if you were doing that) on purpose or...
Shep: Yes.
A.C.: Why is that?
Shep: Because I thought it was interesting.
A.C.: Ah huh.
Shep: It's like asking Picasso why he did the eye red—because it looked right!

Herb Squire, the engineer, who arrived at WOR several years after the added "Ahhhh," heard this explanation several times: The original 78 RPM disk of his "Bahn Frei Polka" broke or something and they couldn't find a replacement, so they had to take a copy from an old show in which Shepherd had said "Ahhhh." They tried to fade the volume down but didn't do it fast enough, so the "Ahhhh" remained. "Oh," Shepherd said, "don't worry about it. It'll make the kids—the listeners—wonder what's going on." One wonders what the true version of this Shep trivia is—why had they not just found another old tape without the mystery sound? To the end of his WOR broadcasting in April 1977, the theme continued with the "Ahhhh."

Shepherd at least once underscored the *Lone Ranger/* "William Tell Overture" connection when he played a very wobbly, orchestral version of the overture,[2] with himself accompanying it on the nose flute, at the end calling out, "Here he *comes*—the Lone *Shepherd!*"

One broadcast began with a recording of a woman describing and demonstrating how to call pigs. After this hilarious start, Shepherd implied that this was also the calling of his own audience to listen to him, using it to provide a sly and hostile commentary on his listeners. The distorted "William Tell Overture"—with Shepherd's manic kazoo rendition—followed this. This was sound at its hilarious best.

Shepherd also enjoyed an old radio program that used sound

at its scariest—*Lights Out*. He loved that program because it used sound inventively. He explained how the announcer told listeners to turn out the lights at the beginning of the show. Shepherd took pains to explain that in the theater there is the sense of being in a separate world where one can concentrate more easily on the performance than one can with movies or television. He considered radio to be a much more focused, one-on-one experience, commenting that each listener seems to feel that he or she is the only one out there listening to him. Shepherd described several episodes of *Lights Out*, in which the techniques of sound alone produced the tension, suspense, and grisly finish to the tales. He discussed radio sound effects with radio playwright Arch Oboler as a guest in late 1956. Oboler described a radio play in which a man jumped to his death from a high window. There were a few moments of silence as the man jumped, followed by the sound made by the sound effects person dropping a watermelon onto a hard surface from a considerable height.

Occasionally Shepherd played standard sound effects, such as those of a clock ticking on a program devoted to time. On the Christmas Eve 1965 program he read a long poem, "Rattling Home for Christmas," by Grant Reynard—his rendition was accompanied by continuous railroad sounds of steam, wheels, bells, rattling, and chugging. His great enthusiasm for flying came through in his June 17, 1968, broadcast devoted to World War I aircraft, in which he played recordings of several vintage airplane engines. He pointed out that the old airplanes had distinctive sounds that are no longer heard today, just as other artifacts of a culture have sounds, which disappear when new inventions take over. Thus, he suggested that sounds should be preserved the way pictures are preserved. Here again, Shepherd followed his familiar habit of noting easily overlooked bits of our culture.

One broadcast began with the "Bahn Frei" theme music, curiously distorted, and then one heard simple, sweet, bland, hypnotically repetitive, electronic sounds:

> The absolute had to happen. So much of the sound that we hear today is kind of dehumanized. Have you listened to those long hours of Muzak coming out of the loudspeakers? Do you actually picture musicians playing that? Is this a real bunch of guys sitting down there with timpani and trumpets and peck horns and stuff? Or is it just music by the yard! By the mile!

[Laughs.] —that stretches from here all the way to some galaxy beyond...on and on—on it goes. Data*tee*—the dirge of the nervous. They are afraid to hear the sound of their own inner voices...

I don't talk about recorded music much—this is not a disc-jockey show. However...this represents the very fascinating, and I think, to me—at least to me, a somewhat significant step. The album that you're listening to right now, is a special album that is called an "aural toy." That aural is spelled A-U-R-A-L. An aural toy—for infants.

These are children who have been born into the Muzak age. This is Muzak for kids—and I'm talking about kids—in this case—six to twelve months old. This is music to be played for them. [Laughs.] No—no—no—do you remember the old kind of kids stuff like "Tubby the Tuba," you know, that kind of jazz. Or Willie the Lion would sing a song, or Gene Kelly would sing "Little Red Riding Hood da da ta *da*." Oh no, that's not at all what this is. This is sound to soothe six- to twelve-month-old babies by. It's to be played over your hi-fi system, quietly, at room level, and as the infant lies in his crib, sucking his thumb, the woofers and tweeters carry peace and contentment to him. He will be a perfect adult twenty years later.

Perfectly attuned to the WPAT way of life. Perfectly attuned from dusk to dawn, quiet, easy, nonidentifiable music that sounds like any minute now it's going to burst into grand and glorious melody, but never quite does... You know it is peculiarly hypnotic, though? *Listen!*[3]

Shepherd was intrigued by nearly all kinds of music—from that played for babies to classical and modernist. Chapter 6 deals with Jean Shepherd and jazz—jazz from the contemporary cool, back to the inexorable banjo strumming and jug blowing of "Boodle-Am," the hairy-vitality song he loved to play. It is clear that, through all his connections in the early days, Shepherd was a knowledgeable and enthusiastic jazz buff. He not only played recordings of it on his broadcasts, but used its techniques, such as improvisation, in everything he did in the medium of sound. Jazz was not Shepherd's only passion in music—he also had a considerable background in the traditional music commonly referred to as "classical."

Shepherd sometimes played bits of traditional classical music records. He was proud of having played the sousaphone, a tuba designed for marching, in his high school band. He played double bass in the orchestra, and in an extended radio anecdote, he said he played bass in an all-city high school orchestra for 135,000 people in Chicago's Grant Park.

Shepherd's knowledge of music is confirmed by his friend, radio broadcaster of classical as well as jazz music, Ron Della Chiesa: "He was a great connoisseur of classical music and opera. He knew a lot about opera. Conductors, repertoire. That came from his early days in radio because he used to be on radio in Cincinnati—in *The Zoo Opera*. They used to come to Cincinnati and perform—Cincinnati had an opera company and its home base was the *zoo*." Della Chiesa continues, "He once did a show on that where the walruses were competing with the sopranos. It was a great show. When it came to classical music, he really knew his stuff."

At other times, especially to set a mood of dystopian disorientation, he might play a portion of Stockhausen ("Song of the Youths"—tape loops of children's voices and electronica), or George Antheil's *Ballet Mécanique*, with its jarring cacophony of siren, gongs, player pianos, airplane propellers, drums, bells, and assorted noise-making apparatus, just perfect for Shepherd's narration of steel mills and other discomforting environments. In 1959, he gave this eulogy on his broadcast:

> [*Ballet Mécanique* music.[4]] *Ohaaa!* Isn't that great? That music? *Listen* to that! You know that I know this little guy? Stop! *Stop!* I know the man who wrote this music. Hold it in abeyance there! He was one of the greatest little guys I ever knew, and he used to hang around the 57th Street Cafeteria.
>
> Hold it, and listen. The man who wrote this used to hang around the 57th Street Cafeteria. I knew about this piece of music. And I remember one day, see. I'm sitting there and I'm drinking a cup of coffee, and this little man came over, and I didn't know him—at the time. A little man came over and sat down and he had a scarf around his neck. He had a kind of a round, very boyish, kidlike face. *Wonderful* little man. He was about five foot five. He sat across from me in the Horn and Hardart and he had a tray full of food, and he says, "Mind if I sit here?"
>
> And I said, "No."
> And he looked at me. "Say, you're kind of familiar."
> I said, "Oh?"
> He says, "Yes, don't you do a radio program on Sunday nights?"

I said, "Yeah."

He says, "I'm a listener, put 'er there! My name is George Antheil."

I says, "George Antheil? You mean George Antheil who wrote this great music, *Ballet Mécanique?*"

He said, "Yes."

I knew—here was this little man. A man—I heard his music all my life! A great American composer! And he's standing in line like everybody else, see. We got to be very close friends.

Back in the early 1920s, he was an *enfant terrible*, you know? He was one of the people who made the whole world know about America. Did you know that? Yes, George Antheil. From Trenton! Yes. Ezra Pound, all of them. Gertrude Stein, Hemingway, the whole crowd, thought he was the greatest writer who ever lived—who ever wrote music. He was a wild little man!

By the time he was nineteen, he was one of the most famous concert pianists. But he realized that anyone—this is a thing you learn. And he had to write. He created a whole new career. When this thing was first done in New York—in fact when it was first done in Paris—the ballet you're listening to now—people got up and rioted. Cheered, screamed and threw things. Hollered, and Antheil still laughed. He was laughing about it one night in the Horn and Hardart on 57th Street. He says, "They were running up and down the aisles! Hollering, 'Get the cops, this guy is a madman!'"...

Here was this little man. [*Ballet Mécanique* sounds again, under.] And one day last winter, I saw him on Sixth Avenue in February. And I met him. We had a cup of coffee. George says, "I'll be seeing you." He walked down the street with his scarf, and his hair is sort of flying—in the direction of Uptown, and I went Downtown, and that's the last time I ever saw him alive. He died two days later. At fifty-five.

Hardly anybody knows, or said anything about what a great little guy he was. And this is what he wrote in the early 1920s. Can you imagine what fires were burning inside of this little guy? [Piano up.] *Ballet Mécanique*. Twentieth-century machine ballet! [Piano and other clashing sounds, pounding for a minute, then fading.]

...But this was George Antheil, who couldn't stop. This guy worked nineteen hours a day. Tremendous outpouring. And the last minute of his life, I know, he was as excited as he was the twenty-first year of his life. He was excited! He was contin-

uing to go! Like that—he did. I don't feel sorry for him. He
lived a *tremendous* life.

And he left behind, you know, which is even more important—'Cause that's, I suppose, in the end, what all of us want
to do—so that somebody, sometime, will walk along and say,
"Charlie Brown was here once. [Pause.] Charlie Brown was
once on this spot. He lived here once." Few people can ever
have this happen to them. Old George did.

A wonderful tribute. Note, that at the start Shepherd talked
about Antheil in part using the present tense—"I know this little
guy"—as if Antheil were still alive. This may well have been
conscious storytelling, drawing the listener into the present, then
the past tense made the death even more effective.

Shepherd liked some modernist music, but when it came to
the most pervasive music of his time, rock and roll, that was
another story. Shepherd spent a week in Great Britain with The
Beatles for his *Playboy* interview with them, which appeared in
February 1965. Through the years, he commented negatively
about 1960s urban folk music and rock and roll, though he
grudgingly admitted that there was some good stuff in it, too. He
seemed to especially disparage The Beatles, possibly because
they were such a large and unavoidable target.

Asked why *Playboy* would have chosen Shepherd to interview
The Beatles despite his obvious antipathy toward them, *Playboy*
publisher Hugh Hefner commented, "I suspect, quite frankly,
there were occasions when we would do that because it would
produce an interesting result. An obvious example of that is that
we sent Alex Haley, the author of *Roots*, to interview George
Lincoln Rockwell, who was a neo-Nazi." Hefner suggested that
"Using a very American guy like Jean, with his sensibilities, to interview The Beatles," was the same kind of inspired editorial decision. Besides the straightforward reporting of the interview,
Shepherd suggested in his introductory remarks to the article
that The Beatles were four regular guys who managed to take
their fame in stride, and he portrayed them sympathetically. In a
Limelight broadcast after Shepherd's week with them, he commented that they were treated like royalty, and that even *he* felt a
surge of pleasure when they invited him into their presence.

It should be mentioned, however, that in over five hundred
broadcasts listened to for this book, not one note of rock music
was to be heard, but he used many disparate kinds of music that
struck his fancy.

Would you please get for me in that...no, no, no, it's right
here, please get for me the—my cheap guitar music. Oh! It's
perfect for this—just perfect. And there aren't many things in
this life—believe me, daddy-o—that are perfect. Ah! That's
better—much better. Ah! The kids are gone, huh? The women
and children have departed.[5]

He enjoyed playing "cheap" and corny music at times (we'll
go into his "slob art" connection later). However, that "cheap
guitar music" wasn't cheap, but good classical guitar music.[6]
Occasionally, for effect, he did play corny orchestral music
(what we call "elevator music"). On a 1972 broadcast, after a
sample of 1920s popular music, Shepherd discussed why he
played corny music. (Remember that Shepherd's pleasures sometimes ran to things he loved to hate):

A lot of people hear me play this terrible stuff on the air.
And they think I *like* it! They really do! They think that this
is—No, I play a lot of stuff behind the various bits and stuff
that I do on the air because I think the pieces of music are so
incredibly bad that—they represent—let's put it this way—
another side of the output of man. [As we listen to more of the
same corn, Shepherd continues with great enthusiasm for how
great/bad the music is]... That is kind of a great rotten,
stinkin' record, isn't it? You want to hear the rest—listen to
this! Just put it on here! This is—this is—pop claptrap. In fact,
I think there should be a whole art form called "claptrap art."[7]

Sometimes Shepherd played recordings of the one-man band,
Paul Blackman.[8] (He accompanied these with his voice or one of
his instruments). The introductory comments accompanying the
CD re-release of the original recording described Blackman's
sound thusly: "His is a mongrel music, that veers now to the dia-
tonic, now to the flatted tonal style, respecting no modes and
arriving at no formal patterns, a music (to the ear) toneless and
disorganized." Blackman's instruments are enumerated as:
voice, kazoo, five-gallon oil can, doorbell, cowbell, pineapple-
can tops, wood blocks, and cymbal. The sound was happily and
skillfully amateurish and manic—no wonder Shep enjoyed it!
Around 1964, the Smith Street Society Jazz Band recorded a
song based on the Andrews Sisters' 1938 smash hit "Bei mir Bist
du Schoen." The new title and lyrics: "The Bear Missed the
Train" (say the two titles one after the other).[ii] Shepherd fre-

quently sang it—and the group who originally recorded it performed it on the *Shepherd's Pie* TV show. The lyrics include such silliness as "The bear missed the train and now he's walkin'."

Another Shepherd favorite was a Dixieland band with a style of controlled frenzy, The Sons of the Whiskey Rebellion. Shepherd played over a half dozen of their songs frequently through the years, usually accompanying with voice and his other quirky instruments.[iii]

He frequently sang, in ironic tones, a variety of songs that seem to have in common a simple, catchy tune: "Hindustan," "I'm the Sheik of Araby," "Yes, We Have No Bananas," "I'm Forever Blowing Bubbles," and "Yes, Sir, That's My Baby."

"Yes, We Have No Bananas" he probably liked for the contradictory words. "I'm Forever Blowing Bubbles" he occasionally did in extended renditions, obviously enamored of the fragile beauty of bubbles—aspirations bound to burst.

"Yes, Sir, That's My Baby" was his favorite, and one can understand why. It was unforgettable, and it was a quintessential example of slob mindlessness: the simple-minded idea of a relationship consisting not of human interaction, but just a cartoonlike, "that's my baby." The simple common phrase it repeats. The simple rhyme. The simple, catchy, compulsively repeated, tune of almost nothing but two notes—you can't get any simpler than that!

VOICE

Jean Shepherd knew how to talk: loudly and quietly, excitedly and wearily, profoundly, mock profoundly. There was a lot of mock profundity, which, in transcription, might seem pretentious or sophomoric without the ironic edge he put on it. We'll listen to "words" in the second half of the semester.

Shepherd often talked over music. When a disc jockey talks over part of the music or cuts off the end, it disrupts the aesthetic experience. But when Shepherd did it, he was not "playing a song," he was constructing an artistic sound collage, in which the music was but a scrap, along with his voice and other sounds. Other times, he didn't just talk over the music used as ambiance, he interacted with it as in "Blues I Love to Sing" and Nat "King" Cole's Rheingold Beer commercial. He often sang bits of songs, usually with an ironic, overly dramatic intonation. He also did fine scat singing, and sometimes played peculiar instruments in a jazzy, improvisational manner.

His vocal repertoire included a vast assortment of realistic, dramatic sounds (sometimes with an echo chamber), such as fireworks explosions, cars racing and backfiring, sirens in the distance coming to the aid of his friend Flick, who had his tongue stuck to a cold metal pole, boats bumping together, sounds of a roller rink, "the old man" working in the basement on the boiler, and trying to out-howl the neighbor's hounds, kid brother Randy whimpering, or snuffling his food like a pig, and Morse code. (Dit dahdididah dahdidahdit dit didahdidit dididit didit dahdahdah didahdit dahdidahdah dahdahdah dididah dididahdit didah dah didididit dit didah dahdidit. Ham operators will read this as "Excelsior, you fathead.")

NOSE FLUTE, JEW'S HARP, KAZOO

[Referring to the jew's harp.] That's the world's worst instrument. Oh, I *love* it, though![9]

Shepherd often accompanied music or commercial jingles—or played solo—on one of his favorite funny-sounding folk instruments: the nose flute (You make a note by breathing out through the nose and using your slightly open mouth as a resonant cavity, as in normal whistling.); the jew's harp (a.k.a. jaw harp), a metal contraption with a lyre-shaped frame, held near or against the front teeth, as one plucks a flexible portion, resulting in a twang sometimes heard in country music; and the kazoo, a child's small whistlelike instrument one hums into, with a resonating tissue giving a raspy effect to the hum. Each of these instruments sounds peculiar and funny and fits the quirky nature of so many of Shepherd's interests in sound.

Although he played these instruments extremely well, and the rhythm and general tone of the songs was recognizable, the sound was sadly out of tune—and that was part of the fun of his renditions. On one broadcast, he accompanied Mozart with nose flute. At a Town Hall concert, he distributed kazoos to each member of the audience, and after a short lesson, he and the audience rendered "The Sheik of Araby." On a trip to the Peruvian Amazon, in headhunter country, he played his jew's harp and kazoo with the local musicians.

Shepherd said that the jew's harp was good for accompanying hillbilly music and claimed he earned his first entertainment money at age fifteen, playing jew's harp for the Colorado

Cowhands group. The instrument, he said, was the loneliest and saddest, and he knew it was not to every listener's taste:

> They either like the sound, or they think it's a rotten sound. Now what is this sound? This is the jew's harp. Now I'm not going to play the jew's harp tonight, but I will tell you in answer to the question "Why do I play the jew's harp?" It's because the first time I heard that sound—I must have been about four—my life was turned into an incandescent flame! I could not stand it, it was so beautiful. [Laughs.] Well, I'm telling you the truth. It's a sad fact. Other guys are turned on by the accordion. And that's an incredible thought to *me!*[10]

On Lincoln's birthday in 1973, he commented that nineteenth-century political speeches were preceded by a little entertainment, and that Lincoln himself would play the jew's harp:

> There are actually written accounts of that around and I'm not ad libbing this or kidding you. The jew's harp, not an easy instrument to play, was mastered by Mr. Lincoln. And Lincoln himself never gave it up. Of course, the jew's harp is like any other religion—you can always try to get away from it—but you never really do—you've been formed by it.[11]

He described in a little-old-lady voice a letter accusing him of pandering, then went on:

> Well, she assumes there, of course—and I get letters like that constantly that I don't do this—or I play the kazoo or I play the Hogentwanger here, or I play my jew's harp because I am, quote, "pandering to somebody else," that this isn't the real me! Baby—this is the real me in *spades!*[12]

OTHER SOUNDS OF SHEP

Shepherd would bang on his desk to make some point, obviously enjoying the sound effect. When searching for something on that desk (or making listeners believe he was), he loudly shuffled paper. With all of his music-making techniques, he obviously practiced them extensively, was very good at them, and, in his own quirky way, took them seriously. Sometimes he asked listeners to identify "the mystery sound." One was obviously air squeaking through the stretched neck of a balloon. The clue: "That was not a balloon." Later in the broadcast, he commented, "You know, there's a guy in Dizzy Gillespie's band who plays a B-flat balloon."

KOPFSPIELEN

I'll award the brass figlagee with bronze oak leaf palm for the person who can rise above the mire of mediocrity of ordinary Saturday-morning-world-type-people citizenship. In other words, the blah, cream of wheat situation they find themselves in—if you can identify this tune. Listen carefully. See if you can identify this, Don. [He is speaking to the guys in the control room. Hollow thumping sounds for about ten seconds.] Okay. [Laughs.] Head thumping. Like I said, I've got a bad head actually. It goes out once in a while. I got it from playing football. It's a football head, they call it. The thing that you develop out there in the Middle West. *You guys have never heard me head thump?* Haven't you ever heard me head thump?

Well, if—I'll tell you what I'll do. After the newsbreak—at eleven o'clock, I'll go down...and I'll give you a little head-thump concert. Have you got any suggestions? Any—would you like to try it? Huh? Head thumping what? Lessons? Oh, well, no. You've got to start when you're young. It's much too late. It's like ballet dancing. No, seriously. It's a very difficult art...classical music is actually my forte...oh, I can hold a long note. You stick around. I'm probably the only person you've ever known who has performed, for money—for pay. The only person in the Western Hemisphere who has performed as a head thumper for pay. It's a very, very uncommercial art...

Other kids began to go out and take lessons in things like accordion. I somehow—I didn't do that. I can't explain it. My mother would have sent me out to take lessons on the accordion. I could have taken lessons in tap dance—at that age. I knew other kids who were. But I stood around in the kitchen with my mother, standing over the hot-air register, head thumping. This is a fact. My mother used to say, "Cut out that rotten—that thumping there! Now stop it! It's going to affect your brain!" And it did, of course. Everything a man does in his life affects him.[13]

During a 1970s syndicated broadcast discussing *kopfspielen*, he answered someone's written questions, claiming that he had a two-and-a-half octave range, could play a chromatic scale and even play chords. He then did a variety of accompaniment renditions, including slow Dixieland, blues, a razzmatazz performance of "Bill Bailey," and an extended rendition (with a modernist piece accompanying him) that he referred to as a "concerto."

He said head thumping was a basic example of a purely human form of music with no artificial intermediary. In case you're not aware of it, one holds one's mouth open whilst thumping one's head with the knuckles, the mouth cavity acting as the air chamber. (Shepherd would have liked that "whilst.") Thus his *kopfspielen* is "out of the inside of his head," while his word improvisations appear to be "off the top of his head."

This leads us to discuss in detail those sounds called "words." Considering how much he loved nonverbal sound, it might be difficult to decide which kind of sound Jean Shepherd preferred. Words are easier to show in a book, but we can't capture the varied tones he used either. He projected his mind in words—in the widest of ways, he hurled ideas—and he involved his listeners in the act by hurling invectives into the night.

CHAPTER 10

HURLING INVECTIVES
Words

Shepherd's love affair with sound started when he was a kid and lasted his lifetime. He talked and communicated in Morse code on ham radio. Twice in Cincinnati he was fired for too much talk. In the early New York "Sweetheart Soap" episode, he was fired for too much talk. Shepherd performed over five thousand broadcasts without a script and narrated his television and films. Several of Shepherd's friends have commented on Jean's love of talking, even in private conversation. Barry Farber's nephew was cornered in the WOR office and given a private program-length narration. Individual fans who encountered him after an appearance or in some other one-on-one circumstance were sometimes enveloped in a one-person, extended Jean Shepherd monologue. Herb Saltzman, his friend, and WOR boss for ten years, comments, "He loved hearing his own voice. So much so that it was an excess you could do without." Ed Fancher, founder/publisher of the *Village Voice*: "Jean talked a lot. Even when he wasn't on the air he was always talking. Most people who knew him found that fascinating and interesting—a great raconteur. In addition, he had problems with people because at a certain point they sometimes became tired of him. Self-involved." Helen Gee, his friend, discussing a personal matter: "Jean Shepherd, a nonstop talker, told me much the same thing but in many more words."[14] Jean Shepherd, the man who needed to go everywhere, know everything, be everything, needed to say everything, and never stop.

Beyond those listening face to face and those who tuned him in on the radio, Shepherd managed to project his voice even to those not expecting it by "hurling" it at them. "Hurling invectives" was one of Shepherd's best-known pieces of business (although only a couple have been located on tape as of this writing). He told listeners to place their radios facing out into the night on their windowsills, then turn up the volume. He then yelled an invective meant to startle and disconcert the neighborhood, giving Shepherd's listeners a whole set of gratifications: Express aggression without being any more serious than creating a minor disturbance of the peace. Do something covert and just a bit subversive—a collective prank. Startle and discomfort the uninitiated. Feel a sense of power. Feel a sense of participation, not just passive listening. Be part of a special underground group, forming and expressing a bond among them. Have a special connection to Shepherd. Help broadcast Shep (a kind of advertisement), spreading the word among the annoyed, and adding new fans among the intrigued.

> WOR, looking at it realistically, has realized that we must—nay, indeed all of us—you must have an outlet. You must, from time to time, tell them what it's all about. *Give* it to 'em! Don't stand still for *nobody!*
>
> Once again, the science of electronics brings deeper and richer meaning to your lives. Put your radio on the windowsill. In an unprecedented act of good will towards its listenership, in realization of its deep responsibilities as a purveyor of public good, WOR makes this service available to you exclusively. This is the only station you'll find an outlet for your aggressions, you'll find expressions for your repressions.
>
> [Shepherd speaks in low, conspiratorial tones.] Put your radio on your windowsill *now!* Do it now! [Pounds on desk.] Now! The loudspeaker pointed out—toward the neighborhood. You know that crowd out there. You know that gang. Of course you do. Put it out there. That's it!... And when I give you the cue, turn that radio up as loudly as it will go! We're going to use a very special kind of invective tonight. This is known as the "disquieting, with a touch of—morbid curiosity type." Which is type 23A, and a very difficult type to use. You can drop out now if you feel it's a little too strong.
>
> It's the—okay—radio on windowsill now! [Whispering.] Turn it up! Lights out! For heaven's sake, turn the lights out.

Turn the radio up. Pretend you're looking at television. Pretend you're asleep. Okay.

[Very loud.] Myrtle! This is the third time you've come home drunk again! What about the kids? What about the kids? I ask ya. How long is this gonna go on? How long?

[Cool jazz starts, as Shepherd continues.] Okay, get that radio back in real fast. [Sounding like an official announcer.] This is the Martin Block program. It's time for Make Believe Poolroom, friends, neighbors. Time to pick up your cues. Time to step over to the table and knock off a game of make-believe snooker.[15]

[Very loud.] You don't think for a moment you're fooling anyone, do you?[16]

[Very loud.] How long do you think you can get away with this? The jig is up![17]

[Very loud.] You filthy pragmatist![18]

[Preceded and followed by *Ballet Méchanique* music, Shepherd calls out an army sergeant's order.] All right, you guys! Fall in. The doctor will be along in ten seconds. The uniform will be helmet liner, raincoats, and GI shoes, and nothing else! Let's go! Boy, that'll bring the roses to their cheeks![19]

During the 1998 Alan Colmes call-in show, a caller said, "But you got me in so much trouble that night, 'cause I actually did it. And my mother came running down the hall and she stormed into my room and she started screaming at me. And I was lying on the floor laughing. I couldn't stop laughing. But it was worth it. You got me in a lot of trouble that night."

Shepherd responded, "Oh, that's good. Trouble is always good for the soul."

The caller asked, "But what did you yell? I forgot exactly what you said."

Shepherd: "*Drop the gun, you rat! I've got the drop on you! Move one more time and you're gonna get one between the eyes!*"

WORDS AND PHRASES

Shepherd hurled words at the unsuspecting and got listeners to consult their dictionaries. Just as Shepherd asked listeners to

look up "humor" in the dictionary, he told them to look up
other words. He got listeners to really think about the meaning
of what they heard and what they said. He often asked, "Do you
know what is it a—?" This sentence construction has an
amusing, childlike, or foreigner-speaking-English tone, which
softens what might otherwise have seemed too professorial.

> [Shepherd refers to a *New Yorker* ad for plastic molds in the
> shape of preformed parts to make sand castles.] "Precast
> walls, turrets, towers, keeps, corners, great halls, moats, and
> dungeons!" Does this kid know what a dungeon was like? No,
> of course not. Do you know what a dungeon was? Look that
> word up. It's a perfect description of most of your lives.
> [Pause.] Including mine. A dungeon. Down there in that dark
> keep. Do you know what is it a keep? Ohhhh—whither goest,
> oh, indeed, oh, oh—stop, stop in thy flight [Shepherd is getting
> excited.]—cut it out, History! Get *out* of here! Rotten old
> crummy history keeps marchin'. Tired of the whole *mess!*
> History! Have to do something about that![20]

On occasion Shepherd mispronounced a word—sometimes
for comic effect, but possibly because he was to some extent self-
educated through reading rather than extended, official, higher
education. Some of his pronunciations may also have been midwestern usage. He often used old-fashioned or archaic words,
probably because they were peculiar and a bit pretentious, and
very specifically, because they sounded funny—just as he liked
the sounds of funky music and odd musical instruments. Despite
his varied use of words and their sometimes slippery sounds and
meanings, Shepherd generally did not use puns—although he
once expressed dismay that he had used a particularly bad pun
as a guest on a late night television show. Some of Shepherd's
favorite words and phrases are collected in Appendix C
("Shepherdisms").

The name of Shepherd's (fictitious) newscaster of trivial
events, H.C. [or K.] Grubbage, was deliberately ridiculous in
order to undercut its pretension—and in one broadcast,
Shepherd associated trivia with the newscaster's name:

> It has been said that some people's navels collect lint, others
> don't—yeah, oh—it isn't every navel that collects lint. If you
> think that I'm being—I'm just telling you a medical fact—that
> it is not every navel, Nat, that collects lint. And it is not every

mind that collects—grubbage!—that kind of information is just called "grubbage." It's not really garbage, it's grubbage.[21]

A favorite phrase of many Shepherd fans is "Flick lives!" This referred to his buddy Flick from many of his kid stories. It may refer to the jazz phrase "Bird (Charlie Parker) lives," or to fans of the then-popular book series *The Hobbit*, scrawling "Frodo lives," referring to one of its characters.

> Hey, listen. I'm going to give you—all you kid-types out there—you have an assignment. If you want to cause a little problem out there. I want every one of you kids—under-ground-type kids—you're living in a whole great fantastic collection of yahoos who listen—to a man—listen every night to Cousin Brucie [a popular rock and roll disc jockey].
>
> I'll tell you what you want to do. Just put, wherever you can, in the school john or on the bulletin board, just one single line—just say, "Flick lives!" That's all. Say nothing. "Flick lives." Just let it hang there. On those Clairol signs on the subway, you know, where it says, "Only her hairdresser knows," you just write under there in simple, stark language "Flick lives."[22]

Remembering the old *Vic and Sade* radio program, Shepherd got pleasure in noting the characters' confused connections we are all afflicted with on occasion—the names of cities with the wrong state appended, malapropisms, mispronunciations, and the bizarre names of people referred to with utmost seriousness, such as: Fred and Ruthie Stembottom, Mr. Ruebush, Ike Kneesuffer, Miz Husher, Robert and Slobert Hink, Y.Y. Flirch, H.K. Fleeber.

And of course, Vic's lodge with its ludicrous name, "The Drowsy Venus Chapter of the Sacred Stars of the Milky Way," and the dead seriousness with which Vic took its every absurd ritual and rule. The lodge used an overabundance of ersatz Latin words in its ceremonies. Shepherd delighted in the funny sound of these words/names, and the goofy non-sense of them. The Latin stew is a mix of the authentic and the absurdly comical—dog Latin with a vengeance. An extended example came during Vic's rehearsal of the speech given to divest a lodge brother of membership (for nonpayment of dues, a ritual that had been several times previously performed for this same shameful member). In part, it went like this: "Harken to the words of our founder, R.J. Conc: '*In hoc spittle ponk, ad agricola nondisput-*

tannia honk. Sinus trouble dumbcock. Nomenclattia est.'" Sade,
forced into reciting some of the "Latin," horribly/comically mispronounced it (as many of us poor Latin scholars do).

Shepherd claimed that when a lodge brother of Vic's felt de-
spondent, Vic would quote some Latin that included the phrase
that would brighten the brother's spirit: *In hoc agricola conc.* This
was one of Shepherd's favorite phrases, often used with variations
to end an anecdote with the idea, possibly, of "Oh well, it's ridiculous, but what can you do? Life goes on!" Just as whatever said
in Latin sounds profound, the fake Latin, often with a bizarre La-
tinization of English, provokes a disparaging laugh. And there
was the funny sound of it and the unexpectedly understandable
English or almost English fragments encountered in the middle of
what was otherwise gibberish (such as "dumbcock").

One Shepherd variation was: *"Abracadabra, In hoc agricola
conc, in est spittle louk."* On August 8, 1968, after giving a
number of translations he had received (all, of course, bogus
interpretations) he said that his more extended version meant
"Don't spit on the radish farmer." Talking about a news item of
Druids being interrupted on their first day of summer rites, he
said, "Oh, *e pluribus unum, in hoc agricola conc, in est spittle
louk.* [Laughs.] 'Time, oh passeth in thy wounding, wounding,
tearing way. Pause but a moment and weep o'er me,' so quoth,
so speaks, the tiny man..."[23]

Writer Paul Rhymer's delight in funny-sounding names in *Vic
and Sade* was echoed in Shepherd's names for characters in his
stories, such as Wanda Hickey and Ollie Hopnoodle, and his
consistently goofy short story titles such as "Leopold Doppler
and the Orpheum Gravy Boat Riot," "Daphne Bigelow and the
Spine-Chilling Saga of the Snail-Encrusted Tin-Foil Noose,"
"The Star-Crossed Romance of Josephine Cosnowski and Her
Friendly Neighborhood Sex Maniac," and "The Grandstand
Passion Play of Dellbert and the Bumpus Hounds."

EXCELSIOR, "EXCELSIOR, YOU FATHEAD," AND SELTZER BOTTLE

Excelsior—the quintessential Jean Shepherd word. He varied
his usage of it at times, seeming not to want its significance
fixed:

From the *Morris Dictionary of Word and Phrase Origins*:

> Although New York's present nickname, the "Empire
> State," was occasionally heard in the nineteenth century,

the more popular designation was the "Excelsior State," from the fact that the state seal bears the word "Excelsior." This Latin word is the comparative of "exceslsus" and simply means "higher." It was apparently chosen as the state motto under the erroneous assumption that it was an adverb meaning "upward"...a favorite brand of Fourth of July sparklers bears this label... But the businessman who, about 1860, first labeled his new brand of thin wood shavings "Excelsior" wrought better than he could have dreamed of, for his brand name became the generic designation for this packing material.

Shepherd said that he got the term "Excelsior" not from the motto of New York State but from the Excelsior Fireworks Company. But this seems just a comic convenience for his Fourth of July show, 1975.

The prize Shepherd's old man won in a contest, the lamp in the form of a woman's shapely leg, was packed in excelsior.

Excelsior was the fictitious name of the publishing company for the bogus book *I, Libertine*. Shepherd asked his listeners to go into bookstores and ask for the nonexistent book. If the clerk at the store asked, "Who is the publisher," one was to respond by saying, "Excelsior, you fathead!"

Shepherd, on his record, *Jean Shepherd and Other Foibles*, in the last cut, titled "The Human Comedy," excitedly recognized famous people in the parade, and there was the Herman Melville character Billy Budd, carrying a flag that had emblazoned on it, "Excelsior." On the record jacket, Shel Silverstein's line drawings of a parade of odd characters walking over the edge of Shepherd's upper body, shows the man at the top of Shepherd's head carrying a banner with a strange device, "Excelsior." These references obviously refer to the poem by Henry Wadsworth Longfellow (1807–1882), "Excelsior." Because the word looms so large in Shepherd's legend—in his philosophy and in his pleasure in playing with the absurdity of the idealistic youth portrayed in it—it's worth reading the entire poem, which is reproduced in full at the front of this book. (Several parodies of it exist—notably ones by Edward Lear, A. E. Housman, and James Thurber, who illustrated a truncated version in his book *The Thurber Carnival*.)

All of the listed connections have some merit. But why did Shepherd choose to make it the important motto of his professional life? It fit perfectly with his consistent thinking embodied in the following:

> And of course, the aphorisms. The aphorisms are a substitute for really looking at the world or/and thinking about it. And so wisdom today has become a kind of mixing around shifting of all these various little aphoristic, jingoistic ideas. "Every day in every way I grow better and better." Why, this is obviously not true. Patently untrue. Every day in every way, each of us grows older and older. And the glands grow less and less active. The muscles grow less and less ready. Every day in every way, however, on the other hand, "I grow better and better." And the mind grows more and more like a concrete block—in most people's cases. Nevertheless, they repeat, "Every way, every day, I grow better and better."[24]

Yes, the notion, as implied in the Longfellow poem, that "Excelsior" somehow means "onward and upward!" represented for Shepherd the absurdity of the wide-eyed youth climbing foolhardily onward, pursuing the *idea* of success despite common sense. Everything was always improving, getting better, and if we only just carried on, we would assuredly prevail. Eternal self-delusion.

As in other circumstances, Shepherd did not exclude himself—in his promotion of one of his favorite sponsors, the Paperbook Gallery in the Village, he said that listeners who exclaimed "Excelsior, you fathead" to the cashier would be given a free pin with the phrase on it, and then he continued:

> You know what "Excelsior" means, don't you? We will not go any further. "Excelsior" has a really deep hidden meaning in our lives, and certainly in *my* life. As I lie on those snowy slopes, holding the sign up, with the touch of frozen North upon my brow, and the elderly farmer looking down on me— "You know what happened there, he died with the word 'Excelsior' on his lips." [Laughs.][25]

> And of course, what is the countersign? When you hear that password belted out at you, you just look the guy right in the eye and say. "Seltzer bottle, you slob." And you walk your separate ways. You never look back. Now, you want to know where that strange password comes from? [Pause. He reads verses from the Longfellow poem.] There now, you see where

that comes from? [Laughs.] Yeah... As you clamber up the icy slopes, reaching forever, reaching, grasping eternally, forever, at that shifting cloud of reason, that chimera that seems to just drift out of your reach each time you *grasp* for it. And it moves further and further away. Excelsior![26]

Defeated by one's own baseless optimism. The poem with its sentimentality is a quintessential example of what Shepherd referred to as "glop." Yes, "a banner with the strange device." The perfect Jean Shepherd ironic motto.

As for the "seltzer bottle" response one gave to "Excelsior"? It conveniently has the same "sel" sound as "Excelsior," linking the pompous word to the common, unflavored soda at the candy store, a two-cents plain—and the self-deluding pomposity of "Excelsior" should deservedly elicit a slapstick clown's squirt of seltzer in the face!

Across the street from where much of the present book was written, at Columbus Avenue and 81st Street, stands New York City's dignified Excelsior Hotel.

CROSSWORDS AND THE DICTIONARY

Shepherd made it into several *New York Times* crossword puzzles. He told listeners to check the newspaper's Sunday magazine for October 14, 1956. The clue for 45 Down was "Night people." The answer: "owls." July 28, 1971, 47 Down was "Shepherd of radio," the answer, "Jean." On October 7, 2000 (nearly a year after his death), 15 Across was "1983 Jean Shepherd film memoir." He would have been happy to see this, but unhappy to see *A Christmas Story* referred to as "memoir," when he insisted that it was fiction. With Shepherd's serious interest in the meaning of words, he spoke proudly on one broadcast:

> Have you seen in the current—in the current *New York Times* book review section, there's a big review on a dictionary of slang. Have you seen that? Well, there's a big review. It's the cover review, as a matter of fact. Well, I'll tell you, I feel like I've really made it now. I mean, I've really made it. And you know it—I never would have dreamed, when I was a kid that this could ever possibly have happened. I have made the dictionary. I'm serious. I am in the dictionary. On page 130 of the new slang dictionary. Wentworth and Flexner's *Dictionary of American Slang*.

That I have contributed a word that has become part of
American slang. It's a great feeling, you know, that you really
have—somehow—affected your—you know, your time, your
country, and I'm telling you this is a true story... Any of you old
listeners who might possibly think you know what phrase it
was, give us a call, and we'll award the brass figlagee with
bronze oak leaf palm. What a fantastic feeling it is to know
that you're in the dictionary, you know?[27]

Wentworth and Flexner's *Dictionary of American Slang*:[28]

creeping meatballism See **meatballism.** A somewhat
jocular though intrinsically serious criticism of
American politics, culture, education, or the like. Since
c.1955, pop. by N.Y.C. disc jockey and social commentator Jean Shepherd.

Also, the *Dictionary of American Slang* 1974 edition:

night people. 1. *People who work or live at night,
sleeping during the day.* 2. *Nonconformists.* Pop. by
N.Y. City disc jockey and social commentator Jean
Shepherd, c.1956.

"Social commentator." Yes, that's part of what Jean Shepherd
was—but he was more than that—he was a commentator on the
whole human condition. He observed, described, commented,
and evaluated—he responded with joy, wonder, irritation, and
despair—sometimes all at the same time. He had many themes
and variations—but as we will see, he never let us forget what to
do with our knees.

PART V
ENCOUNTERS AND
CONTENTIONS

Shepherd entertains us with amusingly expressed, idiosyncratic thoughts—his philosophy of life that, as we will see, is not all sweetness and light. Despite the effect of positive thought and amusement—the happy enjoyment of life Shepherd projected in his broadcasts—there is an undercurrent of what he would call realism, but which Positive Thinkers call negativism. The hostility, while usually concealed on the air, emerges throughout his activities, both professional and personal. He comments extensively on America, and on his us vs. them attitudes. As the man alone in studioland, he confronts his adversaries and renders unto Caesar—in his very special ways.

CHAPTER 11

KEEP YOUR KNEES LOOSE
Shep Philosophy

This is a rambling dialogue, isn't it tonight? Well, *life* is like that. Life is rambling. It does not have a beginning, middle, and end. Only in the movies does it have that. That's probably why people like movies. 'Cause their life just keeps flubbing along day after day. [Laughs.] You know, you figure the only person in the world who has a script is Peter Fonda. Somebody like that. You don't. You're just ad-libbing. And they never send you the right cues, and you read your lines bad. You go down to Barney's to get an Edwardian suit and you look lumpy in it.[1]

Of course, everything Shepherd did and said related to his "philosophy." In earlier chapters, I focused on special areas of Shepherd, giving examples of his various frames of mind. But here the focus is on the different aspects of his philosophy—not to say that it was particularly original, but that it was forceful and especially intriguing to listeners who received precious few ideas from other sources in the media. We can't know much of what was true or not in his stories, but we can understand much about his ideas and philosophy—the shape of his mind and attitudes—that were generally but not always consistent.

Jean Shepherd spoke and wrote a fictional autobiography of

a mind observing the foibles of human life, including his own. He asked listeners to recognize the foibles, to see that everyone had them—to revel in them and prevent themselves from being swallowed up by them, to laugh them into the open and thus be freed from being held prisoner by them. He had little confidence that we would prevail—as Shakespeare's Puck says, "What fools these mortals be." He described how, as a kid, he was setting up radio equipment and was about to get a large electric shock:

> I'm very diligently setting up a very, very, very memorable educational experience. [Laughs.] I think man walks right into the grinder always. I don't think man ever learns anything—I think he walks into each succeeding grinder with head up, with bands playing, and with the drum major out in front.[2]

Despite many Shepherd comments about walking right into the grinder, and the ultimate defeat of all of us, his fundamental attitude was a sense of wonder and joy.

> Oh, Shepherd's not complaining, not at all. There is not one single word of complaint you'll hear from me about life. Not one. I mean, I sit here looking at the raisins and I sit here looking at the dried apricots, I sit here looking at the vast, steaming, bubbling, hissing cauldron, the fruitcake of life, and I realize—I realize I've hardly scratched the surface...
> When I talk about the world around me, it isn't because I don't like the world around me or I am complaining. I am wondering about it. That's two different things. And wonder only comes out of involvement. They do not exist separately. The day that I cease to wonder about the world around me, that's the day I go into the insurance racket. Or I become a Broadway actor. And start reading other guys' lines. This is a thing which I don't want to ever happen to me. And don't assume that Shepherd is just sitting here complaining. No— Shepherd is marveling, as a matter of fact—I find it a fantastic thing that we are involved in.[3]

> You are scrabbling a bare existence out of this spinning orb, and look what is available to you! Let me tell you, once you get one little insight into what's available—you know![4]

He tried to get listeners to really *see*. "Look! Look!" he said constantly, "this is your life! Look at it and see it for what it is and live it as fully as you can." Whether during foreign travel, looking at what was five feet from him, or reading the small news items down in the corner of the last pages of the newspaper, or observing daily life, he showed how some minor incident could be a major life lesson. One learned about life by constantly observing and drawing lessons, because every moment was fraught with possibilities for insight.

> Now all of this might seem to you to be a mélange of nothingness—but isn't really a mélange of nothingness. Not at all. Because it is a mélange of our life, the existence we live. And if you're going to be fulfilled, you've got to live your existence out. You've got to play out the string. It's just the natural course of events.[5]

> Something that bothers me is to find a man who—who will walk away from things which are going on because he doesn't like them. This is—this is wrong—you should stand and look. You should watch this great crowd at the ball game, you should hear this guy hollering, "Come on, baby, hang in there!" This is all part of it, you know. You should go to the snake chucking. And just stand off and look. And if you do stand off and look enough you'll begin to have this great love of it all, which is an undeniable thing.[6]

He urged listeners to struggle to take in all the good and the bad and the indifferent—whatever life had to offer. But even a "love of it all" he would eventually undercut with irony couched in humor:

> Oh, hello there gang, how are you? Good morning, good evening, and good yesterday and good tomorrow, my friends, my fellow victims. Satisfaction will be guaranteed on this program. Your money back if not absolutely delighted within ten days, no questions asked. And we will award you bliss and happiness on your signature only. And you know how good *that* is.
> Yes, you have tuned in to The Seven Keys of Golden Happiness Hour. They will be available to you near the end of this program. Of course, we assume that many of you out there have been searching endlessly, have been searching throughout all of your time and existence for that great white light of truth and beauty which lies at the end of the golden rainbow of existence.

Hot dog! Well, tonight, you may just find it. Send your name and address to "Seven Golden Keys" in care of this station. You must be over twenty-one, and a registered art student. That's Box 6SJ7, Starlet, Hollywood, California.[7]

Yes, he said, there's all this great stuff, but we fail miserably to see it, understand it, and live life as full of wonder as we should. As he put it in another program, "The sad part of it is—we turn a continually deaf ear to ourselves," and thereby defeat ourselves.

But most men I know—almost, I'd say, 75 percent of their waking hours they are pretending one thing or another about what they are doing. Really, it is a kind of dream vision world that has hardly anything to do with the actual product that they deal with. If any at all. It's a sense of an abstraction piled on an abstraction piled on an abstraction, on an abstraction. A couple of days ago, a radio executive said to me, "I haven't listened to the radio for years." Well then, everything he *does* must be abstract.[8]

[Speaking of people who go over Niagara Falls in a barrel, or do other fantastic things.] Where are the Wondrous Willys? I mean, who really did it, by George, really *did* it? Ahhh—I guess what I need is a load leveler. I mean, I still bottom when I hit the bumps. With a big clunking noise, you know. And my tail pipe drags.[9]

We're all born butterflies. Each one of us. With these beautiful, magnificent wings ready to fly in the sunshine. For those slow barrel rolls and loops. And slowly, oh, ever so slowly we burn those wings off—in flame. And we wind up where we are now. Me sitting here. You sitting there. Both of us eternally hitching, hitching a ride along the US4 of life. Hoping that the next Howard Johnson's is going to have twenty-eight flavors—and only it's not about to happen. What are we doing? What are we doing? [Pause.]
You know, it's a funny thing. It's a funny thing. We lose our wings in the sneakiest way possible, and it's when we least suspect it's about to happen. You know, it's funny. I remember when I was a kid. I'm just this little kid, see, living on the South Side of Chicago. Let me tell you, it took *guts* just to *be* a kid on the South Side. We grew real hairy kids there.[10]

We were born butterflies Jean Shepherd told us—and we were accomplices in our own defeat. He would not let us off the hook:

> [Spoken with irony over the opening theme music.] Just a philosophical question. I mean, who does *who* in—in life? Or—and this is the worst question of all to ask—do you do *yourself* in? Aaaaa? "Oh no, it can't be! No, no, that's ridiculous! No, no! Society did it to me! Rotten, crummy, evil society!"[11]

> What I really want is...well, actually what I really want—I'd better not say this, it's still pretty early. Got kids with us. Women and children—all that stuff. All that jazz. All the impedimenta of civilization clinging to us—little leaves and stuff. I know—my eyes *are* narrowing![12]

Shepherd saw a lot of unnecessary foolishness around him, and it got him mad as hell. He talked about getting boiling mad more than once. He just could not remain calm when he saw mankind's continual failure to live up to his standards:

> Have you ever thought about the things that you got mad about? You were yelling and screaming about a year and a half ago? I'm a really—I admit this. I'm a congenital yeller. Oh, I'll tell you, I stalk around my office and knock over the plants and the people, and I bust the windows and yell and I'm yelling about some play I saw and I'm out of my—my eyes are bugging and popping out—some book I read, or some article I read. "Ah, come on—don't you see what they said in the *Post*? Holy *smokes!* Now look, look at this! What kind of idiotic—?" And I'll go on and you know, people go walking around, and guys are carrying cups of coffee and other people will be watering the plants—"What's—what's the matter with the nut over there—what?" And then, you know, five minutes later it's all gone. And then twenty minutes later again I'll be walking—I'll see a sign—"Oh—wha'—look—*look at that!* Look at that sign! Would you *believe* it? Look! Look, look at that—*look at that!*"
> Twenty minutes later I'm purple and I'm falling down the stairs and I'm going up the wrong escalator at Macy's, you know—yelling and hollering—and [laughs] and five minutes after it's all over again.[13]

One way or another or somehow, what we all get bugged by is an attempt to somehow express the inexplicable—whatever that is. You know—the little things—a little Brillo pad of something down inside each one of us. I suspect that some people's Brillo pad gets rusty very early in life and it begins to fall apart. You know how Brillo pads fall apart?—you see them dissolve in the sink, and they finally go down the drain, and that's the end of it? Well some Brillo pads that were born with that little Brillo pad cussed-ness—that little—well I suppose you could call it—you know it's been called many things—millions of things...

We're an engine. You know we really are! Whether we like it or not, we are converting food, we are converting sunshine and air and light. Things we see, things we feel—we're converting all these things into some kind of energy. We've never been able to quite define what that energy is, and what it should do—what that machine that we've got—why it's running. It's easy to see why automobile engines are running. It's easy to see because they're making the wheels go round, and the wheels take people around and that's the end of it. We know this or at least we think we—although I doubt whether any automobile engine if closely questioned—if any automobile engine could talk, and was asked why he existed, I doubt whether he could comprehend, [if he] would even... He would say, "I don't know!" because he does not believe in carrying people around. He says, "Is this all I'm good for? Driving along Route 6—driving along the freeway?"

Well, so ultimately we've got the same problem, you know. And everybody who is converting all this junk in his mind—the food comes in. You know, you eat just about as much food say as—name a great thinker of our world or a great doer of our world. You eat and devour and convert into energy as much food as let's say—let's say Bertrand Russell does, probably more. You see the world. You're just as much a part of the world as he is, and you observe it and feel about it. I think what frustrates most people is the sense that, whatever that flywheel they've got inside them—this thing—has never been hooked on to anything. [Laughs.] It's never—it's just running and it's an infuriating thing! And so somebody says, "Well, get a job!" All right. So he goes down and he gets a job at the bolt and nut factory, and he hooks his machine into that business. And there he is right there again, you know. He has no vested interest in bolts and nuts, and his machine just runs!

I think this is why artists often have trouble comprehending the walkin' around guy. Because artists are utilizing their machine in their own way, whereas the walkin' around guy— his machine is just running chi chi ka *chung* chi chi ka *chung* chi chi ka *chung* chi chi ka *chung*. And so you have poems about "the hellbound train." You do!

And so large numbers of people, on the one hand, will believe that if their machine runs cool and nice, and if it doesn't run over other people's machines, that they will receive their just rewards—after they're gone to that great graveyard of rusted machines. And then the Great Machine of All will hook them up to some kind of cosmic flywheel, and they will be connected into some kind of cosmic power belt, and they will be finally at home running their machine and running it properly!...

And so, being a machine, we're probably the only machine ever that has this little thing inside of him that says, "You got to get on the stick! You're lousing around! You're just fooling around! For crying out loud, get on the ball!"

What we have to do is ultimately sit in great audiences and watch other machines do real things. At least we can pretend they are, and so we read novels written by other machines about great machine lives—great machines that have had fantastic conflicts and have finally resolved them. We sit in movies... And ultimately we'll have to be content, I suppose, with watching actual machines make the scene, because if there's anything we believe in, it's machines—real machines, I mean real ones! Infallible! Yes, indeed! *In hoc agricola conc.* Wait till the first machine runs for alderman—*then* we're in business![14]

But using a facetious metaphor of kids, he both mocks and gets a serious point across:

I hung in there for a while but then I switched to Butterfingers. Now this was again, you could see I was veering off at the main track. You see, this is the way atheism starts. One does not start as an atheist, or a questioner or a nihilist right from the beginning. You start subtly—when other kids are eating Baby Ruth candy bars, you're eating a Butterfinger. Obviously an off-the-wall type of candy.

And you begin to defend it! Other kids were ordering chocolate malts—what was I ordering?—strawberry—and you defend it. Inch by inch, moment by moment, shard by shard, a man becomes an outsider.[15]

BILLION SHADES OF GRAY

Shepherd insisted that there were no ultimate truths. In 1972, he disparaged true believers this way: "And there's the one crowd who really *believes* that there is an *answer* to everything." People wonder what Jean Shepherd's religious beliefs might have been. He didn't talk about it much, at least not seriously—he once claimed that as a kid he was a Rosicrucian and then became a Druid. In a broadcast from 1960, he commented that the decade just begun was going to be unpredictable, startling, and wild:

> And I can tell you this from the letters that I get. That more sixteen- and seventeen-year-olders know more about the whole—the whole philosophy, the fumbling, the good parts, the bad parts. Incidentally, I'll tell you one of the things that bothers me about the so-called sick comic school is that it goes back to an old Western concept of good and bad. All good and all bad. That—that Mort Sahl could never admit that there could be something good about Ike. Or he would be dead. He could never admit it, that there is something bad about the hero's side, you see.
>
> While as a matter of the actual fact, there is no such thing as a—there is not even—there is not even the approach to a good or bad—in the solitary form. That the billion shades of gray in-between are the only things that actually work. That's the problem, you see... But I can see it slowly beginning to develop and—I don't know what the next five or six years is going to bring. I tell you this—whatever they bring there are going to be vast surprises in store for a lot of people. *Tremendous* surprises.[16]

Only three years later, he spoke about the disturbing aspects of American society in his radio eulogy following the assassination of John F. Kennedy. (A discussion and partial transcription of the eulogy appear in Chapter 17.)

Jean Shepherd's political feelings practically never emerged on-air. He didn't think one should speak much about public issues just because one had access to a microphone. He ridiculed the typical dumb actresses who would giggle for half an hour on some TV talk show and then pronounce on some important issue. In the following two excerpts, Shepherd emphasized the folly of all dogmatic stances:

> If you have any politically minded type friends, you know—the indignant Liberal or the shell-bound Reactionary—they both talk exactly the same, because underneath—underneath that simple, homespun exterior, there'll always beat the heart of a true Neanderthal. Doesn't make any difference what direction it takes, you know? [Laughs.] ...If you ever really were going to chase the money changers out of the temple, daddy, there would be no temple anymore. And so I'm sitting here and I'm roaring, you see, and I'm beginning to realize this is all part of the whole convention world [1960 Presidential Nominating Convention]. And these guys get up, and not one of them *really* is against sin, or really is for this or really is against that, because the terrible hard facts about the reality of men come through when you try to do any of these things. Did I ever tell you about the reform mayor who got elected in Chicago? Everything was great until he started to reform. Everybody elected him because he said he was going to reform, and three minutes after he got in, there were lynching parties being formed among honest citizens.[17]

> Interestingly enough today, the Liberals today are the banners. "I thought Shepherd was liberal"—and—well, I am. "And I thought Shepherd—is Shepherd *against?* You know—is he for the wrecking of our environment?" No, I'm not. I'm just discussing whether or not it's possible to ban something. That's all. It's not a matter whether Shepherd's for the environment or not. Whether you're for clean environment—has nothing to do with the efficacy of banning. So if you say, "Prohibition does not work, you can't ban liquor from the country," it doesn't mean that you're a drunk. Nor does it mean you're for drinking. It means that Prohibition doesn't work.[18]

But he was not always neutral regarding the day's issues. He referred to an article in *The Saturday Evening Post* that he had read, about poverty in America:

> Here's a letter which I thought should be conveyed to show this me-ism growing. Here is an answer. He says, "What is

your magazine trying to do?" This is a letter to the editor.
"What is your magazine trying to do? Undermine the peace of
mind with Socialist or Big Government propaganda?
Everyone knows that in a capitalist economy where everyone
follows his own profit-making motive, all society will auto-
matically benefit." At that point I will insert, "*Oh, yeah?*"[19]

The general tenor of his comments and considerations on the
radio gave the impression of a somewhat Liberal orientation, yet
with a reluctance to allow idealism to overrule reality. Shepherd
sometimes made fun of protesters and hippies, not necessarily
because he was against what they were for, but more because he
seemed to feel that their idealism and naiveté lacked the sufficiently rounded understanding necessary to take a stand and
assume that one could do a lot better in a complex and imper-
fect world. He said in one program, the public "would much
rather hear a pseudo folk-nick folksinger sing about poverty
than somebody who has spent the last year and a half in West
Virginia and *studied* the subject."
Jean Shepherd came of age in the 1930s and 1940s. His radio
career came of age in the mid to late 1950s, with his intellectual
and artistic interests fully matured and avant-garde (as a survey
of his areas of activity, friends, admirers in creative fields, and the
nature of his broadcasts at the time attest). As the era known as
the Sixties began, Shepherd, along with others of his generation,
faced a radical change in attitudes—a counterculture. As the
Sixties Reader puts it, "It was a time of excess—an excess of
love and an excess of alienation. It was a time of division—children from their parents, people divided from their country. It
was a period of moral and political enlightenment, and a period
of moral and political confusion."[20]
The craze for wearing buttons displaying one's attitudes—or
just anticulture whimsy—was a superficial, but possibly an
accurate, indicator of the era's swirl of strong emotions: PEACE,
BAN THE BRA, BLACK POWER, BOOKS MUST GO, SILENT
MAJORITY, GOD IS ON A TRIP, EFFETE SNOBS FOR PEACE, TURN
ON TUNE IN DROP OUT, J. EDGAR HOOVER SLEEPS WITH A
NIGHTLIGHT, THIS BUTTON IS JUST AN ATTEMPT TO
COMMUNICATE, I AM A HUMAN BEING: DO NOT FOLD, SPINDLE
OR MUTILATE, SUPPOSE THEY GAVE A WAR AND NOBODY CAME,
MY BUTTON LOVES YOUR BUTTON, KEEP THE FAITH, BABY, WE
SHALL OVERCOME, STUDENT POWER, HIPPY POWER, APATHY.
This was a different kind of avant-garde than the one

Shepherd had been a part of in the New York of the late 1950s, in terms of what many of the young were thinking, feeling, acting out—and even listening to. The 1960s were full of "Movements." Civil Rights, Anti–Vietnam War, Free Speech, Drugs, Women's Rights, Environmental.

Charles A. Reich, in *The Greening of America*, wrote, "There is a revolution coming," and spoke of "a change of consciousness."[21] This widespread cultural change bred immediate—and some longer-lasting—emotional attitudes. Despite this "revolution," Shepherd (other than his occasional antidrug, anti–"folk singer," anti–rock and roll remarks) seldom commented on the issues of the 1960s on the air—he seemed temperamentally uninterested in engagement with mass movements. He continued to criticize general and specific human foibles—thus, maybe more enduringly, the ways of thinking he fostered helped create sensitive, questioning thought processes in thousands of individual, one-on-one listeners.

Although he almost never commented on political or large-scale current events on the air, he did so from time to time in private. Ron Della Chiesa remembers, "He got very political there, during the Vietnam War. Against the protesters." This seems consistent with his anti-idealist stand—not that Shepherd was *for* the war—based on available broadcasts, his stand is not known, but in a 1972 program discussing an ad offering the ineffective, defensive World War II Maginot Line bunkers for sale as summer homes, he indeed made an anti–Vietnam War statement, albeit in a flippant way: "Just think of the great things that are going to be for sale when they finally cut out all this foolishness in Vietnam."

> **Paul Krassner:** He said that if there were ever an American version of Hitler, it would be some show business character. [Krassner comments that Shepherd would indeed deal with political matters at times on his show. "He would use some political event to segue into a childhood story."]

On one broadcast, Shepherd described his experience in a mass demonstration, riding a New York City bus filled with people going to the August 28, 1963, Civil Rights March on Washington. He didn't comment on civil rights issues, and he didn't go as an official "reporter," but just as another individual—thus he could participate in and observe the too-often

overlooked common-man experience that was of great importance to him. He spoke of the camaraderie and common
humanity of the people he was with—something no official
reports he was aware of even mentioned. This approach was a
subtle but effective way to express his social conscience. On the
fortieth anniversary of the March, in 2003, National Public
Radio, recognizing the special nature of Shepherd's viewpoint,
rebroadcast a considerable segment of his comments.

So at least on this one important occasion, Shepherd, who
would not take strong stands on the radio, took his stand by his
action, and then talked about this experience as he saw it. There
was some conflict within him, then, about this stance with
respect to serious matters.

> [Said ironically.] I wish I could be more serious about
> serious things. I wish I could get mad at the idea that they're
> sending out gold-plated hand grenades, you know. Real mad.
> And have a little button—"Suppress Selling Gold-plated Hand
> Grenades as a Lighthearted Executive Gift." "Disarm the Toy
> Industry." I wish I could do that, you know? I just wish I could
> get *mad* about the human condition, but I find it *exceedingly*
> funny.[22]

> **Barry Farber:** There was Left, there was Right, and
> there was Shep. He saw foibles where they existed. And
> of course they exist on the Right and the Left. I don't
> think he ever decided. I don't think he ever thought
> about it... Shep would just be very, very straightforward
> about everything. He didn't have an ideology. He didn't
> have an agenda. He would spoof someone on Welfare
> cheating, like he would spoof a greedy capitalist...
> "Shep," I would have loved to have been able to say,
> "do you feel that you are on the Right?" He wouldn't
> have answered. He would have considered himself
> philosophically way above answering something like
> that.

That attitude of being above it all might well remind the student of American literature of that savage wit of several generations before Shepherd, fellow midwesterner, Ambrose Bierce
(1842–1914[?]), whose best known work, *The Devil's Dictionary*, revels in misanthropic definitions of human activities.
Although Bierce's commentaries were far more caustic, Shep-

herd would surely have been sympathetic to the following words regarding politics attributed to Bierce: "My position as a looker-on enables me to see more of the game than the players do; that my indifference to the result makes me a better critic, that my freedom from political sympathies and antipathies gives my judgment an intrinsic worth superior to its current value."[23]

> **Pete Wood:** He never took sides on anything... I said, "How come you have so much talent—that you don't come down on the side of anything worthwhile?" In other words, I kept saying, "You don't crusade for *any-thing*... You don't take any stands, whatsoever. You're a great storyteller, but look how valuable you could be to try to preserve American values—things of that kind."
>
> And he would tell me over and over again, "Pete, I'm only going through this life as an observer. I have no desire to influence or change anything. I'm just going through as an observer."

In "Song of Myself" Walt Whitman wrote, "Apart from the pulling and hauling stands what I am, / ...Both in and out of the game, and watching and wondering at it." Occasionally, however, everyone is a bit inconsistent—Whitman, forty pages later in the same poem: "Do I contradict myself? / Very well then... I contradict myself; / I am large... I contain multitudes." [Ellipses in original.] Shepherd also stood apart—and contradicted himself. The consistency resided in mental involvement and close observation. Sometimes a usually suppressed attitude burst out, as in a response during the emotional weekend of November 22, 1963:

> **Jerry Tallmer:** The day John Kennedy was killed...all that day until that night...people came from all over to [*Village Voice* cofounder] Dan Wolf's office that night—to be together. And I was one of them...just talking—to grieve together. And in burst Jean Shepherd! So excited, full of fire! "Wouldn't you know! Wouldn't you know! It was a Fair Play for Cuba guy who did it!" [Lee Harvey Oswald, accused assassin, had connections with the Fair Play for Cuba group, an organization protesting the United States' treatment of Communist Cuba under Fidel Castro.] The *irony* of this thing. He made a big production out of it... The whole

idea that it wasn't some right-wing fascist but a nutcase of the left excited Jean very much. I can hear his voice saying it.

Tallmer also says that "It was Jean's compulsive diatribes, by the way, that sometimes had Dan [Wolf, *Village Voice* cofounder,] ducking out of the office when he spotted Shepherd coming in [late 1950s–early 1960s]."[24]

THERE'S ONLY ONE PROBLEM

Typically, Shepherd brought specific issues back to the problem within us. Although never put in religious terms, Shepherd frequently expressed an attitude not unlike a belief in original sin:

> There's only one problem, of course, in the end, and that is—why is mankind the way he is, and why is he so miserable? And that's been the subject of all the great literature since time began.[25]

> Why is it that we always discuss the results of some sickness in the human soul and we never really discuss the sickness? We discuss the war, and never discuss what brings about wars. We never talk about this. Endless pictures showing guys going through Normandy villages with the chicks, endless pictures of guys strafing other guys in planes, and this is supposed to be a big message, you know—"Be careful, war is bad."
> But nobody ever talks about the original thing that lies within all of us. Because you know, they started—they were having wars long before there were bad comic books... Are we a single creature, or are we not? That's a loaded question. Are we or aren't we? You have to decide, one way or the other. By the way, if you do decide, remember if you say we are a single creature, then all the properties are owned by *all* of us. Evil, good, bad, all the rest of it. We all have the same capacity and the same drives and the same urges. This, of course, is using the phrase "species" scientifically in this case.
> Just as it is impossible for you—if you were to walk out on the veldt somewhere, and there are seven thousand lions around—you're a pretty naïve scientist if you begin to believe that some lions are carnivorous and other lions are sweet, peaceful creatures that play violins.[26]

You see, the reason I told the women and children to get
out—and I feel very good about it now, since it's quite obvious
that the theme that came out was the thing that we had calcu-
lated would all along. That's that thin thread of the divinely absurd, which runs through *all* of the actions of all of us. You
don't think for a minute that—that countries, big countries—
big countries—I don't care—name any big country—really
wants to disarm? Do you really? Why—why that's—that's all
that history's ever been about—is wars and what happened just
after them. [Laughs.] No, seriously. It's—it's like telling some
guy whose whole world has been based on killing cockroaches
that from now on he's got to give up killing cockroaches.[27]

...and I might say that the same things that made that fistfight occur are *always* within people. Don't think for a minute
that they go away. You know we have this beautiful feeling
among ourselves—this is one of the great illusions of
mankind—and it is that he is a perfectible creature—like say—
a portable typewriter can be perfected. That next year's model
is better than last year's model.[28]

Last year's models were Og and Charlie, caveman types who
appeared in Shep tales from time to time. Og with the primitive
name, Charlie with the contemporary guy-next-door name.
They were a linked pair. They seemed to be minor bit players—
primitive comic relief around the edges of Shepherd's world.
They were not. Og and Charlie were central. They were "the
only problem," the sickness in the human soul, the things that
made fistfights occur. One identified with Og and Charlie—they
seemed so human. Yes—and they were brutes, not very far
above the lower forms of land dwellers. Without the interven-
ing evolution from lake dwellers through reptiles to primates,
we crawled directly out of the ooze. Jean Shepherd described
them:

There must have been the very first time when Og and
Charlie crawled out of the muck and out of the mire—that
ancient primordial lake from whence sprang all of us...and Og
and Charlie crawled out of the ooze and the slime.[29]

Jean Shepherd told listeners so entertainingly over the years,
in powerful fables, that Og and Charlie were us. Listen to one of

the more blunt portraits, told to a barrelhouse piano playing "Saint James Infirmary."

You know there was a historic moment that was recorded by one of the great physical anthropologists—at the University of Pennsylvania. And he has reconstructed it. I thought you might like to know about it. It was one of the *great*—it was the time that man became man. It was a very important moment. These two guys are sitting on the shores of this antediluvian lake...

Oh, you're interested in this story, heh? You want to know how we came to be? Oh, come on, that's not important, is it really? Course not. We are what are... I yam what I yam—all right, and that's—ne'er the truth was more betterly spoken than that. I mean, I am a war-peace-loving, hate-mongering carnivore. I am what I am and that's what I am. I mean, you know? I mean it's very difficult for a fox to stand in front of a group of rabbits and apologize for being a fox—when all the rabbits know that he's a fox. And all the foxes know that the rabbits are rabbits. It gets all quite convoluted. But these two guys are sitting there...

They were sitting there on the shore of this lake. For the purposes of discussion we'll call one of them Og and the other's Charlie. We do not know their actual names. It's been that long.

They're both sitting there. You know, an interesting thing about man in those days—he crouched more than he does now. He—which means that he was more honest. He didn't— he wasn't afraid to crouch down and show the rest of the world that he was afraid of the sky falling in on him. He didn't pretend by keeping his knees flexed, and so he just crouched, and he also knew, you see, when the sky *did* fall, there was nothing he could do about it, which is different—we pretend now that we *can* do something about it.

And eternally, every twenty years, the sky has fallen down and killed at least fourteen million. Now we like to pretend that we are twentieth-century man. This is, of course, modern civilized man. It's interesting to note that more civilized, modern men have died from the hand of his other—brother— civilized modern man than in all recorded history prior to 1900. I mean, we are getting to the point—of course, it is true that technology has its own particular fascination. Particularly when we apply it to the things that we *really* want. Like killing everybody. This is true progress—maybe. [Laughs.]...

But these two guys were crouched down. They were looking out over that dark, dark and placid sea. And they were crouched. They were legitimately and honestly crouched...

And then, one fateful afternoon, just after Charlie had come back from gathering a few clams down at the waterside, Og turned to him—looked at him for a long instant that went on for maybe six or seven years—just looked at him. Things moved much slower in ancient times than they do today.

Then, without saying a word he reached down, picked up a large stone, raised it above his head, and brought it down with a telling, fatal crash between the eyes of Charlie. [Long pause.]

In that instant, man became man. He ceased being a beastie of the field. He no longer could return to the world of flowers. Never again could he pretend he was like the clams. That moment modern man was born. That instant! It was the *great, great* turning point. And Charlie fell in a pool of blood. Og settled back on his haunches and continued to look out over the lake.

But they were seen—by another man, who crouched by his cave. He picked up a rock and moved into the shadows. And waited. Modern man had begun to progress.[30]

That was Og and Charlie from Shepherd's relatively early days, in a highly organized, brutal Fable For Our Time and All Time. What do we do about Og and Charlie? Are they just an isolated couple or are they symptomatic of the race? Were we still brutes in Shepherd's eye? Is this why he refused to take a more active political stand? If one has a profound distrust of the civilized behavior of all mankind, can one make political choices that, by definition, were determined by one group of those unreliable humans? Shepherd once talked about a class trip to Chicago's Field Museum of Natural History, seeing a scene of American Indians who ate the bodies of enemies, seeing a diorama of a dark cave with caveman, woman, and baby, with a slab of flesh off a slain animal:

[Shepherd is practically whispering, as though telling a scary story to kids around a campfire or huddled under the covers after lights-out time.] That male caveman looking over his shoulder at us, through the vast, unimaginable cavern—the tunnel of time. Inside of me flows the blood of a caveman! Somewhere—there's a tiny drop—someplace. Yeah, there's a— maybe even a—fugitive instinct—and that's the most important one—of all. [Pause.] We're about twenty years removed from barbarism—at any given time in history. I'll bet many a kid has thought his old man looked like a caveman.

Ever watched a pro football game with your eyes half-closed? [Pause.] Yeah! You see these great hulking beasts—covered with hair. Their eyes mere slits. When you see them going back to the huddle you can see a tribal ritual. They've gone back to the huddle to prepare further mayhem on the other tribe. Once in a while, there's a guy lying out there and he's been flattened in a play. Have you noticed the crowd *cheers?* The fallen victim of the other tribe. The next step, of course, when football really gets going, they will symbolically barbecue him. Drag him back to the huddle. [Laughs.] And they will remove his helmet, which will be his scalp. [Pause.]

The flickering flames outside the teepee grow dim. [He still speaks quietly, the storyteller weaving his spell as the kids peer over their blankets into the scary darkness.] The wind is picking up, coming in over the mesa. Winter cannot be far behind. Since the moon of the silver chariot, which comes just before the moon of the howling children—and just before the moon of the weeping mothers. And the moon of the crying wind. Yes. Winter can't be too far behind. It's coming up on us.

[The pure, clear trumpet begins the cheery innocence of the "Bahn Frei" end theme calling anew for the start of the race.]

Caught me right in the middle of a full flight, a full-blown, totally realized, unbelievably incisive imagination. [He jests ironically.] Well, what are ya gonna do, you know? Incidentally, even turtles are affected by time. I mean, right now, at this minute, the sand is blowing over the pyramids and wearing them down to a nubbin. They'll be nothin' left in maybe four or five eons. And where's it *all* gonna end? Well, that's a question that's been asked many times over and over again and will appear on next semester's work. So get your notebooks ready and we'll have the answers for you at that time. It'll be a lecture course, and there'll be three periods of laboratory work, including a work form.

[The music continues along its happy-go-lucky way as we wait for more words—forcing us to listen for content—receiving nothing but superficial gaiety. The orchestra crashes to its climax. Then Shepherd adds words in a halting, mock-primitive voice that puts him—and us—among the brute cavemen.]

This [Pause.] WOR. [Pause.] New York. Lester Smith and the news are next.[31]

The silence that followed for a long five seconds, then the high-pitched impersonal, soulless beep signaling the hour, emphasized the quiet chill in which Shepherd had enmeshed us all.

That, from 1972, was another of Shepherd's carefully crafted caveman tales—again a dark one (yet told with humor), revealing not an isolated moment of pessimism, but a theme woven throughout his work and philosophy.

Besides Og and Charlie, from time to time Shepherd suggested other metaphors for the human condition, among them charging bulls, whales that might turn mean, leaking boats, and electric rabbits caught at one's peril.

> By George, moment of truth here, frightening, you know, when you—when you face that bull, and the bull comes charging out of the chute, and all you've got between you and eternity is that big red bedcloth there, and you're holding it out and you've got a couple of little Boy Scout knives stuck in your belt, and he comes a-thundering along—he just comes a-thunderin' right at you. Then he stops! Yeah! Blows it right out through his nostrils. Starts pawing the ground. And you start backing up a little bit with your back arched a little bit the way you've seen in all those pictures—those bull-fight posters you bought three for a buck through *Playboy*. You stand there waitin' to get it. You know where you're going to get it, buddy. So you keep facing the other way, you know, kind of hoping that you're going to avert disaster. Which is a silly hope.
>
> Then all of a sudden he comes a-chargin' at you. He comes a-chargin' at you. You make a quick move to the left, a quick move to the right. He dodges to the right and then to the left, and goes rushing past you like a freight train. You are safe—for a moment. You take a deep breath, and light a cigarette. Where are my matches? Oh boy, that was a close one![32]

Here Shepherd described a scene from the *Alice in Wonderland* books, the exchange between Alice and the Queen about having to run as fast as one can just to stay in the same place:

> I'm sure that to many people this doesn't make sense—that phrase. Yet, if they look around they'll find that their life is a gradual running in place, and a gradual slipping backward, eternally. Whether or not sense is made is another question. In fact, I've often wondered if there's any sense in

anything... So get your harpoon ready, friends—here comes another whale.[33]

By the way, how are you doing with your bailing? Heh? Has it ever occurred to you that life is one long succession of work with the bailing can? Your own private bailing can—down there at the bottom of the boat—trying to keep the water that's coming in from lapping up around your knees. And is it water? That's another question we'd like to ask.[34]

...And a goal, perhaps, a point. We all have to have a point to pass—and look—one thing you got to learn—don't, for crying out loud—don't catch up with that—with that electric rabbit—this week. I mean, it's only a two-furlong race, and you catch up with that electric rabbit and all you're going to do is to get a shock, that's all, right down in your fanny. [Cheap guitar music.] That's no good.

So keep that old dream going, you know? I'm forever blowing bubbles. Bubbles in the air. How high they fly. Nearly reach the sky. [Shep is reciting these song lyrics slowly, quietly, pensively. Concluding theme music comes up under his voice.] And like my dreams, they fade and die. I'm forever blowing bubbles. Bubbles in the air. They fly so high—nearly reach the sky. And like my dreams, they fade and die.

This program was sent to you by the International Dream Bubble Bath Corporation of the Western Hemisphere. When better dreams are dreamt, when better bubbles are blown, we'll be the first to bring them to you. So don't lose sight of the rabbit, but above all, don't catch it.[35]

DREAM COLLECTION DAY

The following is an example of Shepherd's style in the late 1950s, his late-night extended musings on humankind's futile strivings—we forever have dreams and they are always thwarted (by life or by ourselves), and yet we never give up. We are *all* the guys carrying Excelsior banners into the snowstorm:

I suspect that at least fifteen percent of the population of New York City—particularly Manhattan—concealed someplace a pile of papers—the beginnings of the eternal novel. A poem, a play, "A thing I was gonna write once. And I am going to write it yet—you just wait and see!"...

I would like to know how many untouched watercolor sets there are in this town of guys who once, of women who once were going to take up painting. Thousands of tons of caked, hard, rocklike oil paints that haven't been touched since the Christmas of 1939. And the cracked guitars that are hanging in basements, covered with dust, that haven't been strummed since 1947—after the second lesson.

I have a feeling that these things are holding us down. Speaking of things that are holding us down, this is WOR AM and FM in New York. I have a suspicion that these are the things that if somehow we could clear the decks—get rid of all the glop—and admit once, to ourselves, we're not going to do it—and throw all this stuff out.

We ought to have a Dream Collection Day. You know how they have rag collection days, and old metal collection days? We ought to have a Dream Collection Day. Where everybody takes the half-finished model airplane out of the basement, the half-finished novel, the cracked guitar, the ancient watercolor set, and puts it out in front of the house. As a kind of public recanting, you see. Puts it out in front of the house for the salvage people to finally come and get. Everybody would have to do it together—all together, we'll clean out all these broken, old, sad, poor, wonderful, idiotic, debilitating, defeating dreams.

'Cause you know what happens, Jim—is that every time you go into the closet and you see that lump of paper back there, it looks out at you. Every time you go down to the basement you see that guitar, it looks at you. And it says, "Aha! I am your past." This is what Scrooge's ghosts, you know, were based on. "I was a dream once. Look what you did to it." That pair of hockey skates, that in a moment of impetuosity you rushed out in the fall of 1951 and you bought. You wore it twice—both times realizing that you had weak ankles that went all the way up to your ears—that are still hanging down there in the basement. "Aha!"

Let's clear it all away! Let's have Dream Collection Day! Let's get behind it and get rid of all this stuff! It's killing us! It's like John Osborne talking about the English Tradition. It's killing us. It isn't living any more! It's like dead tissue growing on us.

Let's get rid of all those portable typewriters—that'll never write that novel. Let's get rid of all those yellow sheets with all the notes for all the poems and plays. Let's get rid of those old guitars. We'll declare it a citywide holiday! Dream Collection Day!

We could all—we could all sit behind our windows and we'll watch these wagons go past loaded to the gunnels. Loaded to the gunnels with all the old glop and all the old, sad, decayed, past moments of glory. All the old—all the old, staring, vacant faces of the...ice skates that were never worn.

Dream Collection Day. What a magnificent idea! Magnificent moment. Maybe if we got rid of all these cigar boxes—full of charcoal pencils, those battered pads—from the life classes of years ago. Maybe it might start again. But what would happen, of course would be this. The day after Dream Collection Day, there'd be a guy walking down—walking down Fifth Avenue somewhere—maybe in the 90s—walking along there, the wind is coming out of Central Park—he smells just the touch of that sear, brown winter greenery with its strange excitement. And he would say to himself, "You know, what I oughta do is learn how to play the guitar!" And it would start all over again. It would start all over again. The whole business.

Three hours later, some guy would go into a stationery shop on Eighth Street, and buy four pads of yellow second sheets, two pencils, and he would go home and he would start to write. [Soft jazz starts in the background.] The first line would say, "The youth sat looking out over the town that lay like a small paper clip curved in the bosom of creased green earth." And it would start all over again. [Shep scats along to the soft jazz.][36]

Putting our dreams out for the trash collector—a kind of spring cleaning, after all—is almost a sunny notion compared with some of Shepherd's more pessimistic thoughts.

Tonight's program will undoubtedly contain material that is offensive to many of you. [Shepherd is about to tell a story.] I'll tell you this right away. It's in bad taste. Invariably the best embarrassing moments are. And let's face another thing—life itself is in bad taste. I mean, anyone who looks at life with a cold, unprejudiced agate eye of truth must realize that life is basically in *extremely* bad taste.[37]

Reportedly, Shepherd usually began his pre–New York City broadcasts with a line about "a tiny figure, tattered and torn..." Although the phrase was a rarity for the New York years, it occurred a few times; he began his June 16, 1957, New York broadcast with it, previously quoted, "And a tiny figure, tattered and torn, can be seen moving across the barren landscape. A giant load being pushed before him." In 1972, he used it again. One can see how he might think of himself—and the rest of humanity—as small, weak, ineffectual, battered by life, yet still struggling onward, undefeated. That he stopped using it as his refrain might indicate a decision that it was too much of a downer. That he brought it back occasionally perhaps showed his basic affinity for the idea—and maybe suggested a tip of his hat to his earlier radio days. Ultimately, Shepherd's message was a downer, in the sense that emphasized that in the end "you're gonna lose, friend."

> One of the funniest things that I have ever known—one of the saddest and I think, one of the most significant—of course I have a sneaking suspicion that almost anything that man embarks on there is a touch of sadness connected with it anyway. There is the in-built sliver of—well—frustration. The dream never quite comes up to the reality. Well, a friend of mine... [Shepherd is telling a story about a car racing mishap.]
> Have you ever stopped to think of all the business of mankind—all of the trivia—all of it—including all the great making of automobiles, all the fantastic operations that go on—what is it all about anyway? I mean, really. You eat, you sleep, and you die. This is about the extent of it, you know. When all of it is sloughed away. All the rest of it, as George Ade put it one time—George Ade said that fun is the few moments that you can forget that you're growing old and are about to die. And there's much truth to this.[38]

> Be the first in your neighborhood to admit total defeat. Come on, let's *go!* [Remember to read Shepherd's negative statements such as this with an ear for its jaunty irony.][39]

> [Shepherd asks for music, and sings.] Oh, life is tough. Ain't no way you can win. You're gonna lose, friend. No matter what you do, you're gonna lose in the end, dad. Bop bop *bop* bop *bo* bo*padooo*.[40]

More downers! Is there no hope? What do we do, Shep?

> Well, I used to believe that stuff—see, I was a kid—"Well, you know, that's easy enough to do. It's always easy to be prepared. All you gotta do is be prepared—you keep your Boy Scout knife with you." [Laughs.] You know there are actually people who *believe* you can be prepared for life? Many people believe that. It's one of the great, sad, misconceptions of existence. But they believe it. And if they wanna believe that I ain't gonna be the one to rock their little old boat made out of a sugar cube—which is quietly and swiftly melting even as they sit in the middle of it and holler, "I'm prepared!"[41]

LOOSE KNEES

Jean Shepherd's philosophy of life? When a kid asked Shepherd, "What's your plan?" he had often summed it up: "Keep your knees loose." What did this mean? It's good advice in many sports and refers to both offense and defense. Considering other Shepherd contexts, a baseball infielder was probably most relevant. If you locked your knees, you couldn't move as quickly in your defensive role against the oncoming ball in order to catch it. You had to keep your knees loose to be ready—to defend against whatever came your way in a game and in life.

> It's like the letter I got from this indignant fourteen-year-old kid. He says, "Shepherd, if it's all so rotten, what's your plan?"[42]

> I'll give you a word of advice. I'm beginning to produce a small booklet in my mind called, just simply, "Keep Your Knees Loose—The Education of a Twentieth-Century Man."[43]

> I thought you'd kind of like to know how it is out there, gang. Just keep your knees loose, keep your eyes open, and—like they say in the infantry, "Give them you-know-whats a low silhouette." That's right, keep everything low and move slow and easy down there among the roots. That's right—don't—you know. I don't have to tell you. You've gotten this far, you must know sumpin'. [Shepherd laughs.][44]

> And a kid wrote me a letter. He said, "Shepherd, I was listening to your program and I was caught under your spell and

then, five minutes after your show was over, I walked out into the sunshine and I realized that the world isn't the way you say it is."

That's *right* son. You're absolutely right. The world isn't the way *anybody* says it is—for *every*body. And therein lies the rub. The world is not the way it is—to each one of us. I have no idea what the world is to you. I am sure you have no real idea of what the world is to *me*.

There are billions of eyes that are constantly looking over this long spreading green globe—there's no correlating, there's no integrating—there is no—what is the other teachers' college—there were three words that were very important in teachers' college—correlation, integration—and—to correlate, to integrate—to *evaluate*—that's it! [Laughs.] The three catch phrases of the sociologist. Correlate, integrate, and evaluate. And how are you doing at evaluation these days?[45]

On July 2, 1960, Shepherd said there was no correlating, integrating, and evaluation, but certainly he couldn't claim that all he did was identify and describe. He pointed a finger— he evaluated. Summarize the Shepherd philosophy? We start out with two strikes against us: First, the world and death are against us, so we can't win, despite our illusions. It's all an exercise in futility. Second, the Og and Charlie in every one of us will defeat us. Yet, with the count 0 and 2 against us, we must fight the good fight despite the inevitable and seize possibilities from the glorious fruitcake profusion available to us. And we keep ultimate defeat temporarily at bay by keeping our knees loose.

Shepherd was obsessed with knowledge. He wanted to know and experience everything, he wanted others to realize how much he knew, and he wanted to expand other people's knowledge. His interests were indeed vast, but contrary to the impression that he seemed to know and understand everything about everything, several people have observed that in private conversations, he would bring up some deep literary or philosophical subject, but any pursuit of it by them might lead him to back away or reveal his knowledge as rather superficial. Larry Josephson comments that "Shepherd was a kind of a poseur. He talked about Kierkegaard, he talked about this and that, and he was kind of like an intellectual manqué. He wasn't really a *deep* thinker. What he was, was a great, *great* storyteller. And he had some insight into human nature—of a certain kind."

"By the way," Shepherd is quoted as saying, "you klutzes that are about to write in saying, 'Lay off the philosophy,' you can stop worrying. Tomorrow there will be an all-kazoo program."[46]

[As his shallow theme music gathers to its climax] I'm sorry—it was a silly program tonight. Then again, you're not often anything other than that yourself, friend.[47]

A guy wrote me a letter and he said, "Shepherd," he said, "it's obvious that the conclusion that I draw from your program is that in spite of all the way junk is—everything is—that it's still all basically all right and to be laughed at."

Well, I think [a bit whimsically spoken from here on] there is some truth in that. Yet on the other hand there is a large dollop of *untruth* in that. [Pause.] I don't know what conclusion is to be drawn from my shows. [Laughs.] In fact, I am wondering what conclusion there is to be drawn from *life*.[48]

BITTER

One might prefer to think that Shepherd's darker, negative attitudes only emerged later in his career, when life had begun to wear him down, but the early dates of some of the negative comments excerpted above belie that supposition. The positives and negatives expressed on the radio alternate over the years. A magazine article quoting him put it less entertainingly than his broadcasts do, but put it bluntly: "I'm not a cynic, I'm a realist. I believe that man's dreams are futile, but that life is joyful. I say enjoy the sad state of man. Laugh at it. Then existence will be sweet."[49] The problem seemed to be that, despite keeping his knees loose, this defensive maneuver was not enough. To continue the baseball metaphor, in the field of public acclaim, though he hit enough home runs in his own eyes, the fans and the box scores did not tally them. As his dreams for greater fulfillment continually failed to materialize to his satisfaction, evidence and testimony indicate a rising bitterness.

Herb Saltzman noted, "He was bitter. He was obsessed with making it as a comic. Which he really couldn't do. He was not a stand-up comic. Even though what he did was very funny. To

Shep's mind, he never really made it. That was the lament. He died not proud of his accomplishments but bitter, I'm sure."

After the great achievements and promise of his early New York radio days—remember how ubiquitous he was on the scene, as one editor had put it—Jean Shepherd's rising frustrations seemed destined to affect his attitudes in every aspect of his life.

Shepherd points at universal human foibles, and as he is an American—and an American humorist—it is America that is the special focus of his concern and of his derision. So next we concentrate on our country and listen to Jean Shepherd describe what it is about us that makes him so frequently laugh with exasperation and say, "Only in America!"

CHAPTER 12

ONLY IN AMERICA
His Country

Ron Della Chiesa: He was very pro-American—in what this country stood for... I remember once sitting down in the cafeteria and someone came over, putting Howard Johnson's down, and [Shepherd] resented that. He said, "That's typical of what you do here, in that elitist atmosphere here. What's wrong with Howard Johnson's? Howard Johnson was a great man." He went into this whole riff on defending that aspect of American culture. And I think he felt the liberals sort of put all that down because it was too American—too mom-apple-pie. In many ways, he was for a lot of that stuff.

I really miss his kind of talent—more than ever these days particularly, a lot of things that Jean said about this country that were a part of history and that he related to contemporary things—he had a great knowledge of history and civilization—and our place in it—and society.

Jean Parker Shepherd's main subject matter encompassed these United States of America, the country he loved, and which he defended against the frequent putdowns and disparagements heard in the 1960s and 1970s. (Later we'll get to Public Television's *Jean Shepherd's America*, the perfect title for the series.)

On a radio broadcast from March 2, 1961, he commented, "The only reason I say American is because I am an American, and know more about America than any other country." He frequently spoke about the special quality of Americans, especially about being a kid growing up in America. As America was his metaphor, he used his country for specific examples to express his view of all humanity's failed dreams, frustrations, and foibles.

In a talk sponsored by Young Adult Services at the Donnell Branch of the New York Public Library in 1972, he said, "I deal with American ritual... I write about things that most people know of in their lives and it's not yet recognized. I don't think in America we recognize America yet as having a specific, recognizable American *culture* as distinct from all other cultures." He went on to mention such rituals as Fourth of July celebrations, going to the prom, and standing on line in a department store waiting to see Santa Claus. He presented his tales within the context of what he saw as the special American institutions and customs he knew so well.

Why did he sometimes deprecate his country? He seemed to expect more from America and Americans because he appreciated the variety, the richness, the distinctness of what it was to be an American, and he was frustrated by the frequent failure of Americans to live up to their possibilities—and to his hopes. The potential was there, but life—reality—knocked over the applecart.

In a September 3, 1960, broadcast, he said, as a put-down, "*Only* in America!"[i] Words that come to mind that describe his attitude include bemused tolerance, acceptance and rejection, appreciating and disparaging, love and annoyance. On his return from a trip to Europe, where the buses were clean, Shepherd saw Europeans on an airport bus to Manhattan:

> I'm saying—these people are experiencing the same thing. And suddenly it began to be new to me. And I was very much aware of the dirty bus. I was very much aware of this gigantic traffic jam. I was aware of the—of the long stretch of ugliness that you run through when you come away from the airport. And you see all these gas tanks out there, and all this industrial area. I became very much aware of it—and yet at the same time very proud of it—and don't ask me how or why. I just kept saying, "I wish *somebody'd* swept up before these guys came." You have the feeling of an unexpected guest dropping

in, and you wish you'd taken your *socks* off the floor. I wish somebody'd *thought* about it. [Laughs.][50]

Describing a gigantic Times Square billboard advertising the movie *The Bible*, "Only in our time are we privileged to be so nutty." He went on to discuss other people's criticisms of America that he found erroneous, simultaneously disparaging the recent variety of stand-up comedians who made more of a mark on the nation's consciousness than he had.

> I was looking in the window of a record shop, and I see all these hip records, you know. All the guys that spend most of their time putting down the world we live in—and by the way, the attitude is quite common—that we are living in an extremely sick society. This is the feeling that you hear all the time...
>
> And I say this comes from really, primarily—it comes from a very bad knowledge of *other* societies! And I'm not certainly rationalizing *our* nuttiness by saying, "Look at how nutty they are." But I suspect that the nuttiness of the 1960s is not a U.S. phenomenon. Not at all...
>
> A couple of days ago I was at a party, and I mentioned this to somebody. I didn't—I was mentioning it that way but it came about—it built up to the same thing, and I said, "You know, I've traveled around, and I've got to say this, that I just—I like America. I just *like* it." And there was a kind of funny pause— this was a very hip party. It was kind of a funny thing. And somebody said, "Well, oh boy, how can you say that? How can you say that with all the things that're going on?"
>
> And I said, "Well, do you know what's going on around in any of the *other* countries?" Well, it doesn't seem to make any difference to most people. And I said, "Well sure, there's a lot of bad stuff going on, but for crying out loud—[laughs] you have to have a little—I suppose the word is—proportion." Many people have lost proportion today. They've lost a sense of proportion... We're very childish, you know? I think Americans are childlike—in the world we live in. We're like a large number of wonderful, fascinating sorts of bland, open-faced children—in the world.[51]

Many of Shepherd's stories about childhood and adolescence dealt with American rituals. Just before his television drama

Phantom of the Open Hearth was first broadcast, Shepherd told Martin A. Jackson of the *New York Times*, "I write about American ritual, which is largely unchanged, and I try to put my characters in a real milieu, one that we all live in."[52] Common bonds, not the abstract ones such as democracy, but homey ones such as the Fourth of July picnic, Thanksgiving dinner, and going to the prom.

Sometimes Shepherd mentioned a variety of American attributes. He referred to an American syndrome: the desire to be loved, and the American theater being obsessed with "How come you don't love me?" He also cited Americans using first names with strangers as an attempt to make people like us more. "The one thing that most Americans I know are afraid of more than anything else," he said, "is being alone." In the "Little Orphan Annie" section of *In God We Trust: All Others Pay Cash*, he commented that getting one's first membership card was a big step toward becoming a real American.

Assumptions are often wrong regarding what someone felt and believed, but in Shepherd's case, as he broadcast his ideas and views out there in public, our assumptions rise to probabilities and likelihood. There's some evidence that at least the early Shepherd regarded his fellow Americans (though not so much the women) with humor and affection. And of course, like anyone else, Shepherd modified his stances over time. He spoke of our "foibles," charming and lovable imperfections with which we are all sometimes afflicted at times. But he didn't always feel what one could call "affection." At times, he engaged in sharp criticism of people in general and Americans in particular.

At various times, obviously referring to himself, he spoke of the artist, the Greek chorus, the gadfly, and starlings:

> You can judge, really, a society very much by the *themes* of their artists—genuinely, their artists. 'Cause after all, the artist is supposed to not only reflect the society that he lives in, he is supposed to, in a sense, be a leader of that *society*. In addition to that, he is supposed to distill the *meaning* of that society. Now, that's what the artist does, really.[53]

Here Shepherd talks about the German film *Rosemary*, using it to discuss his role as Greek chorus:

> ... finding a lot of elements of Bertolt Brecht in this particular piece of work, which is to say, a very, very interesting

moving back and forth between a very strict realistic storytelling and then drawing back as a Greek chorus will—
drawing back and making a comment on what you have just
seen in the same terms as what you have just seen. If I play any
role in our society, my role is that of a Greek chorus. I am not
a featured player, I am not a star, I do not raise the dagger and
plunge it into the heart of the enemy. I stand in the back, and
once in a while, after the dagger has been raised and plunged,
I sing the long dirge, "Oh woe, oh woe, oh mighty, mighty
woe, oh time and man. Oh revenge, thou art sweet, and oh
revenge, thou shall destroy all of us."

Then the chorus rises and the lights go up and again the
action takes place. And this is a very necessary function. We
have in our society—we have somehow been able to bypass
the Greek chorus—the chorus which both explains the action
to the audience and to those who have just created the action.
This is what the Greek chorus always did. It provided an interesting frame to what was going on. Not only an interesting
frame, it provided a focal point to it.[54]

Now the only reason I'm bringing these things to you is
because I am perfectly aware that—oh—I'd say almost all of
the people—the percentage of people who are not involved in
daily brouhaha hullabaloo pursuit of whatever it is that makes
it possible to buy a new breezeway—you know, and etc., etc.,
etc., etc., ad infinitum ad nauseam you know, the whole jazz—
the rigmarole, the brouhaha, the *hoopla*.

Well most people are involved in that, you see. Well, by a lot
of tricks of fate, and inclination and probably—probably even
inherent-ness, I find myself *not* really involved in that. And so
I am, and have been enabled by the very nature of the slot into
which I have fallen—I have been able to examine minutely,
millions of things which most people—if they even see them at
all—don't have the time to fool with—they just throw it
aside—they don't go into it, you know. You know what I mean
by this? This is the role, I suppose you might call it loosely,
"the gadfly." Just fools around, you know—hollers. Sits in the
bushes and watches the stuff go by and shouts, you see.

Well, the thing about the non-gadfly—I concede this, is that
he is involved—I mean he is walking along the trail, you know.
It's like a great big wagon train and they're all plubbing along
there and suddenly he's out there in the bushes—who's not
really part of the train. Somehow he got off somewhere along

the line and he's valuable because once in a while he sees the Indians coming, you know, "Hey—Indians!" And everybody else, all busy hitting the horses and you know, fooling around with the water and stuff. And he keeps hollering, "Indians! Here they come! *Ohoo!*" Well, that's his job.

Now, it's a very important job, albeit, I can say, very unpopular, particularly if you happen to be an Indian. Oh—very unpopular. Also, it's very unpopular to the guys in the wagon train because half of them are asleep. It's easy to be there, you know, asleep and fooling around with the oats and stuff, and this guy keeps hollering, "Oh, it's no good—look at what's happening. It's startin' to rain! It's coming down! Get up the tops! *Look out!*" Well, he's unpopular on both sides. There's no question about it.[55]

Shepherd sometimes chose some usually disliked object or animal in order to identify with it—often to present himself as one who stirred up trouble. For example blue jays, birds known for their loud squawk, and the nearly universally disparaged starlings:

Now we've been kind of skirting the starling issue for the last couple of months. This issue came up on our program about a year and a half ago. Do you know—most of you probably do know that I'm a member of the Pro-Starling League of America.

I believe that starlings are much-maligned birds. And I feel that someone should speak on their behalf occasionally. There's too much one-sided argument today. You might not perhaps appreciate it, but starlings find *people* pretty messy. They have a lot of trouble with people. And it's all a matter of viewpoint. If you look at it from the starling viewpoint, you get a completely different picture of the way the world should be.[56]

As a gadfly, as a Greek chorus of one, and a starling, Shepherd was a made-to-order target for the "Great American Power of Positive Thinking."

You can see this is not the Norman Vincent Peale Show. [Over his opening theme, he scats a bit of wordless accompaniment.] It's the other side of the coin. [Scats again.] The Power of Positive Thinking, friends, often lands you in the slam.[57]

As he said in 1960, there are those of us who see life as a circus, and others who suspect we are no good. On the Alan Colmes 1998 interview, Colmes said, "And Jean, apparently you were once described as a professional scoffer. One clergyman warned his flock that you were a bad influence, especially on children." Shepherd responded, "You're talking about the late Dr. Norman Vincent Peale. I'm the only guy that I think was denounced personally by Dr. Peale."

There was no way Shepherd could think positively about one monumental "phonus balonus" American extravaganza he had the pleasure of attending. Nearly a decade after he originally broadcast the event, Shepherd obviously considered it a classic case of goofy America. On October 17, 1957, Mike Todd and Elizabeth Taylor had held a "little party for a few chums" at Madison Square Garden in New York City—18,000 invitations were sent out. CBS TV carried it live with Walter Cronkite. Jean Shepherd and John B. Gambling did the WOR play-by-play. The opening parade included Emmett Kelly, the famous clown, followed by, among others, jugglers, firemen, sanitation workers, rodeo performers, circus acts, a beer wagon, Scotch pipers, Texas Rangers, equestrian acts, folk dancers, and animal acts. The event has been described as including, "some of the biggest names in the fields of entertainment and journalism in the biggest fiasco in the history of show business."[58]

> What was the occasion? And I opened it up. I'll never forget, I opened it up and I said it would be just *fantastic*—and of course, you could hear the people yelling and hollering. It would be fantastic if we could pour plastic over the scene! Seal it! Just let all the air out of it. Seal it forever. All these people frozen right in the act. Frozen just the way they are now. Seal it. And bury it out on Long Island. Under 200 feet of loam. Just bury it out there—so that five thousand years from now when they discover it, this would be an archeological discovery to rank with all time. And they would know what the twentieth century was like. *Boy* would they know! Here it is! All lined up! All the *flimflam*, all the *sham*, the *hoopla*—oh yes, and now I'm really going to put you on—any guy who can tell me—this is the funniest one—and the saddest one.
>
> In the middle of all this, they euchred a famous United States senator—to give a speech—oh, yeah, that—that's what made this thing so—so—so—realistic in its evocation of our soc—of our time. Because it was obviously show biz phonus

balonus—it was *phonus balonus* all the way down the line, all
the way. It was plug-ola, it was cheap, it was just ridiculous. It
was orgiastic. Yet all the official people were in attendance.
And they were pretending what was happening wasn't really
happening. That, I think, is what made it *magnificent* to be at.
And so, up on the platform, in the middle of all this fantastic
hoopla—this cacophony—this brouhaha, the people were
yelling, and guys were stealing the cake they're throwing, and
guys pouring champagne from the upper deck down on the
guys on the lower deck. Everybody's mad—fistfights were
breaking out.

Well, in the middle of all this fantastic hoopla, this
cacophony, a senator is up on the platform—giving a speech
that was almost totally unintelligible. And he was a famous
U.S. senator, and you see, the whole thing was ostensibly in
favor of international relations. They had some big, high and
mighty theme that—nothing whatsoever to do with what was
going on. Which made it even *more* indicative or symbolic of
our society—our time.

People are constantly talking about things that have no rel-
evancy to what they're *really* doing. I mean all sides. Not just
American. I don't want anybody saying, "Yeah, rotten
society!" Listen, boy, [laughs] I mean every last country's got it
going, you know. Every last—oh, sure, guys are getting up
there, giving speeches in the Kremlin, and it has nothing whatsoever to do with the real life of the guy walking around in the
boondocks with a couple of potatoes in his back pocket, you
know—who hasn't seen two kopecks to rub together since
1915. You know, that kind of thing.[59]

The problem with misplaced priorities is universal. We participate in goofy extravaganzas or private waste of our lives. We
have no perception, no sense of what is important in life, and no
taste. We are mostly living in a howling darkness.

You're *alive*, you fool! You're alive and—that is about all
you can count on. You can hope for other things. You can
dream about other things. You can even believe in other
things. But what can you count on, that you can hold in your
hand? Yes, I am *alive!* [Bangs on desk.] And even that is sometimes questionable, right? It's becoming more and more so.
More and more, the dream is becoming a dream—a real
dream, and you're walking through it. It is as though you're

walking through an eternal second act, that was badly written by a second-rate playwright, and it's being reviewed by top-rung critics.

Did you see the ad—the full-page ad in the *New York Times Book Review* section? It was one of these ads that showed the typical ad-type housewife looking out of her typical ad-type housewife home. She's got that sharp, faintly aggressive, vaguely—neomaternal look about her. She's looking out, and underneath her—and underneath the great big old picture of this chick, the statement simply and clearly put, "A new way to learn how to paint by painting masterpieces right from the start!" You see, the great dream of America is—not to go from A through Z, but to go from A *to* Z in one gigantic leap. This is the dream of all of us. If somehow you could write a bestselling masterpiece novel, without ever writing the novel. This would be the ideal way to be a writer. 'Cause we believe in fame in America—we don't believe in achievement.[60]

As Shepherd made clear on September 10, 1960, that *phonus balonus* occasion at Madison Square Garden was not an anomaly, but merely an extravagant example of bad taste:

And—and oh, one point that has impressed itself upon me, and that is that we have a tendency to separate people from the things they create—including radio. A large number of people will say, "Well yeah, I mean, but the radio—the radio is terrible," and people—well, let me say—it's terrible because the taste of most Americans is pretty bad.

Shepherd writes in *In God We Trust: All Others Pay Cash* that "Mr. Doppler operated the Orpheum Theater, a tiny bastion of dreams and fantasies, a fragile light of human aspiration in the howling darkness of the great American Midwest where I festered and grew as a youth." Shepherd sometimes festered in America, and he would align himself with some other soreheads of the recent American past:

No wonder Don Marquis, and guys like Ring Lardner, and people like George Ade, guys who worked early in American culture, finally began to have a rather cynical and sardonic view of it. We have a very special kind of culture, you know, in America. It's laced with—with a—hope—curious thing—like any minute now you're going to make it all the way. On the other side, it's laced with a kind of hopelessness.

Most people in America feel a great sense of—deep-seated being cheated—when they see the stars on TV and they say wa—why not *me?* Why? They have a vague sense of being bugged when they see John Lindsey up there getting elected. This is all part of this special American thing. Most people in other countries accept—and it's part of the weakness of their system in many cases—the role into which they're cast. You know, a kid is the son of a peasant-hood, you know, he walks around and he goes in and eats his cabbage and he drinks his bad wine and sits down and belches, and that's about as far as he ever thinks.

He never thinks in terms of trying to become—Yves Montand. [Laughs.] He never sits and watches French movies and says, "Owww—why have I not gone *zis* way?" He just doesn't see it that way. But in America, every guy sitting in the seats vaguely feels that one day somebody's going to call him on the phone and it's going to be Daryl Zanuck. And Zanuck is going to say, "We've had our eye on you, Charlie, and we're doing the life of Charlie Witherspoon, and you're playing it." It's this peculiar combination of vulgarity, hope, dreams—who knows what?

No wonder we are now the basic spawning and breeding grounds for all kinds of demonstrations of one type or another—because we have a life that in a way lends itself to it. You know, it kind of encourages it. On the other hand, we have the Horatio Alger myth that is still with us, that any young man can work hard and go to school and wind up who-knows-what. And—it just isn't true! [Laughs.] It just isn't true! So we're bugged by it! We're *bugged* by that![61]

America makes soreheads of us—some of us because we can't achieve the dream, and others of us because we see that the dream is phonus balonus. Within this great Only-in-America land of ours, only a few perceptive individuals seem able to recognize the folly and foibles of Americans. And it isn't just Americans, it's *everybody*. Those of us (Jean Shepherd, me, and you) who see and *understand* are the "Tiny Embattled Minority."

Jean Parker Shepherd, from his high school senior yearbook, 1939. Calumet Room, Hammond Public Library, Hammond, Indiana.

Jean Shepherd, soldier, with his Signal Corps insignia on his lapel. This studio shot gives no clue to the way he would someday spin his army-life experiences into hilarious but sometimes heartrending radio tales. On occasion he claimed that he was in the Mess Kit Repair Battalion, Handle Platoon, ca. 1942–1944. Courtesy of Dorothy Anderson Martin and Mark Anderson.

Shepherd, still a mere tadpole in the radio business, in Cincinnati's WKRC publicity photo, taken around the time he was fired not once but twice for broadcasting "too much talk, not enough music," 1948. Courtesy of Dorothy Anderson Martin and Mark Anderson.

Shepherd broadcasting from Shuller's Wigwam restaurant, WSAI, Cincinnati, early 1951. After this Cincinnati program, Shepherd broadcast in Philadelphia before eventually coming to WOR in New York City in 1955.

Jean Shepherd's first known recording, made in 1955, includes comments by Shepherd and jazz performances. This record represents one of many of Shepherd's associations with the world of jazz in his early New York years. Jazz style was an important ingredient in his improvisational talk on radio.

Cover of *I, Libertine*, published in 1956, the Jean Shepherd hoax that became a "Turbulent! Turgid! Tempestuous!" novel by a non-existent authority on eighteenth-century erotica, Frederick R. Ewing. The book is in fact the product of a joint effort by Jean Shepherd, Theodore Sturgeon, science fiction writer, and Betty Ballantine, the wife of the book's publisher. Ballantine Books, art by Kelly Freas. Courtesy of Random House.

Portrait by Roy Schatt, suitable for framing, of
FREDERICK R. EWING
internationally known broadcaster, raconteur and author of **I, LIBERTINE**
A Ballantine Book   35c

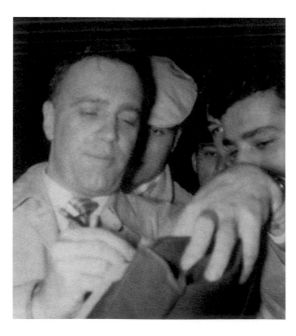

Flyer promoting *I, Libertine*, Shepherd posing as its bogus author, Frederick R. Ewing, 1956. Ballantine Books, Courtesy of Random House.

Looking nothing like the dissolute Frederick R. Ewing of the promotional flyer for the book, Jean Shepherd autographs a copy of *I, Libertine* during a gathering of his acolytes on the balcony of a Horn and Hardart Automat, 1957. Photo by Eugene B. Bergmann.

Screen credit at the beginning of John Cassavetes' first independent film, *Shadows*, 1957. Shepherd promoted the film, and his listeners, the "Night People," financed its making.

Poster for the jazz concert at Loew's Sheridan, Jean Shepherd emcee and narrator, June 15, 1957. Shepherd was emcee for several important jazz concerts during the late 1950s. He recorded his improvised story for the Charles Mingus performance of "The Clown" in 1957.

Record cover, Shel Silverstein's manic crew parading across Shepherd's figure, 1959. Close friends, Shel and Jean contributed to each other's works, for example liner notes and a book dedication from Silverstein and a foreword by Shepherd. The Electra Corporation; Silverstein drawing used courtesy of the Shel Silverstein estate.

Program cover for Shepherd's theater piece, *Look, Charlie*, art by Shel Silverstein, 1959. *Look, Charlie* starred Jean Shepherd, Shel Silverstein, Herb Gardner, and Lois Nettleton. Shepherd, Silverstein, and Gardner were close friends. Nettleton and Shepherd were married for about six years. Courtesy of the Shel Silverstein estate.

"One of the most prominent of the young American social critics and commentators..." Author photo caption for *The America of George Ade*, published in 1960, a book that Shepherd edited, and for which he wrote the introduction. Shepherd also demonstrated his kinship with Ade's sense of humor by enthusiastic readings of Ade stories on his programs.
G. Putnam's Sons.

Mephistopheles impersonating St. Francis, in the play *A Banquet for the Moon*, from a published description of the production, 1961. Contrary to the caption, in the picture Shepherd is on the far left.

Jack Betts, Lee Firestone, Jean Shepherd

Jean Shepherd looking out from behind a Dixieland band, the night of his premier broadcast performance at the Limelight café. Shepherd's Saturday night live broadcasts from the Limelight, February 15, 1964 through 1967 were very popular with those who attended as well as with many of his radio listeners. Copyright © Fred W. McDarrah.

Portrait of Jean Shepherd from *Playboy*. The magazine published twenty-three short stories, an article, and the Beatles interview by Shepherd. When a piece by him appeared, the "Playbill" introductory matter for the issue usually carried a new, current photo. The photo here was used for the June 1964 story "Harry Gertz and the 47 Crappies," Shepherd's first appearance in *Playboy*. Copyright © 1964 by *Playboy*. Reproduced by special permission of *Playboy* magazine.

Jean Shepherd in 1965 delivering cough drops to the Shapra Indians in headhunter country in the Peruvian Amazon. He is wearing the chief's headdress. During his radio broadcasts after his return, he played tapes of his jam sessions with the tribe members. Photo by Sol Potemkin, courtesy of his son, Greg Potemkin.

Shepherd's first book of linked short stories, described as "a novel," 1966. It contains the BB gun story, "Duel in the Snow, *or* Red Ryder Nails the Cleveland Street Kid." Some of these stories first appeared in Playboy. From *In God We Trust: All Others Pay Cash* by Jean Shepherd, copyright © 1966 by Jean Shepherd. Used by Permission of Doubleday, a division of Random House, Inc.

Newspaper advertisement for the two performances of Shepherd's one-man shows at Town Hall on New Year's Eve, 1968, during which he led the audience in a mass kazoo-rendition of "The Sheik of Araby." On the radio he would sometimes play not only the kazoo, but a jew's harp and a nose flute. He also had a talent for knocking out tunes by thumping on his head.
Collection of Pete Delaney.

Shepherd playing the jew's harp at the Overseas Press Club press conference in 1970, publicizing his *Jean Shepherd's America* television series for PBS.
Photo by Al Parker, collection of Andy Palley.

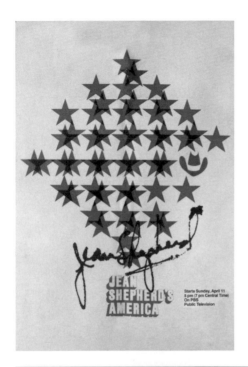

Poster for *Jean Shepherd's America*, a series of television programs done for PBS in 1971. A second series was done in 1985. The series boasted a largely improvised format, made possible in part by newly developed portable video equipment. Collection of Jeff Beauchamp.

Shepherd videotaping an episode of *Jean Shepherd's America*. Here he returns to the steel mill where he had a summer job as a teenager. Some of his most popular stories told on the radio were laid in this mill. Courtesy of WGBH, Boston.

Carnegie Hall program page for one of three annual Shepherd performances there, 1973. Collection of Pete Delaney.

Jean Shepherd, Bob Elliott, and Ray Goulding, relax over beers at a Manhattan restaurant, during a bachelor party for their colleague at WOR, engineer Herb Squire, 1975. Shepherd, as was his usual custom in any gathering, does the talking. Courtesy of Laurie and Herb Squire.

Saturday Evening, September 22, 1973, at 8:00

STAGGERWING PRODUCTIONS
presents

JEAN SHEPHERD

AT
CARNEGIE HALL

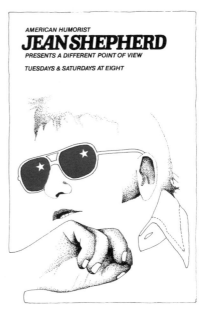

Shepherd's Pie television series, 1978: The set, opening shot of each program, into which Shepherd would do a silly dance and then begin the show; Shepherd mugging during a program; Leigh Brown, assistant producer, testing hamburgers on the "Chez Junque" episode.

Shepherd's Pie advertisement for the New Jersey Public Television series, 1978. Each half-hour program featured a number of Shepherd's favorite subjects for humor and satire.

Annual
**HAMMOND ACHIEVEMENT
AWARD DINNER**

A
U
T
H
O
R

H
U
M
O
R
I
S
T

JEAN SHEPHERD

TUESDAY, APRIL 7, 1981
WICKER PARK CLUBHOUSE
6:00 P.M. COCKTAILS - 7:00 P.M. DINNER
$17.00 Per Person
**TICKETS AVAILABLE: IN PERSON OR BY MAIL
AT ALL HAMMOND PUBLIC LIBRARIES**
Sponsored by
Hammond Rotary Club -
- Hammond Historical Society

Poster for the Hammond Achievement Award dinner for Shepherd. "This is the only picture of himself that Jean Shepherd can stand," wrote his wife, Leigh Brown, in 1980. Note his hat, the shape of which was used in the *Jean Shepherd's America* television advertisement of 1971.

Detail of the dedication page for *A Fistful of Fig Newtons* (1981), a book of Shepherd's short stories and articles with numerous drawings by him. Leigh was Shepherd's wife, Daphne was their dog, who played supporting roles in several Shepherd movies.

Doubleday and Company, courtesy of Random House.

To Leigh and Daphne—
Who share my bed, my board, and walks along the sea. May they never regret it.

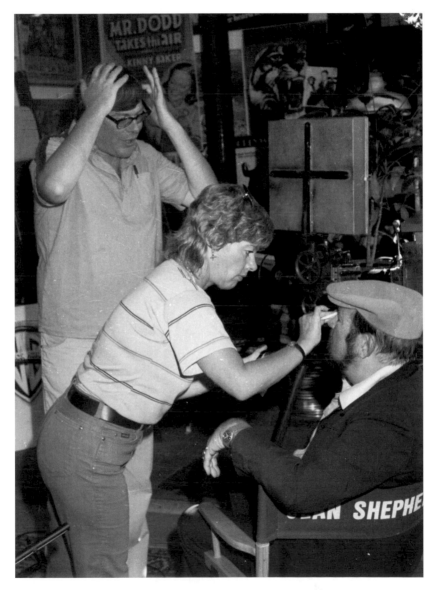

Director Fred Barzyk watches Leigh Brown, producer and wife, apply makeup for a WGBH Boston television production, 1983. Dan Beach, who took this shot, worked with Shepherd on several television productions and remained a good friend for over forty years. Photo by Dan Beach.

"Zippy the Pinhead" comic strip by Bill Griffith, January 9, 2000, a tribute to Jean Shepherd made soon after his death in 1999. This strip testifies to the importance of Shepherd's work for many creative people as well as for his legions of devoted fans, many of whom stayed awake listening, long after bedtime, captivated by Shepherd's voice in the night. Copyright 2000 Bill Griffith, used with permission of the artist.

CHAPTER 13

TINY EMBATTLED MINORITY
Us vs. Them and
Shepherd vs. Almost Everybody

At first blush, Shepherd appears categorically disdainful of slobs and everyone else except that small number of cognoscenti of which he is one. He conspired with his listeners to think of us vs. them—the rest of humankind was less intelligent and less sensitive. As usual, this is not the end of the story. Shepherd was far too intelligent and perceptive to hold such a categorical view. The fact of the matter is that he treated slobism with a rather light hand and looked at all points of view, his own included, with some skepticism. Nevertheless, with all that said, we would be foolish not to recognize that Shepherd considered himself fundamentally a superior minority of one.

> **Herb Saltzman:** Shepherd would transform himself in the middle of his monologue—he would lower his voice and you would be a fellow co-conspirator with him, with the "Night People" and Jean Shepherd. We're different from the people in the daytime. I'm different from Martha Deane, Dorothy Kilgallen, Ed and Pegeen Fitzgerald. [Very popular folksy talkers on WOR radio at the time.]

A feeling that Shepherd frequently cultivated was that he and the solitary listener were part of a very small band of insiders who really *knew* what was happening and what was hip. Everyone else was an ignorant slob. The secret message decoder of 1930s radio's *Little Orphan Annie* program was an insider's tool and made one feel one was part of a small group in the know. Shepherd numerous times referred to this decoder pin over the years, and the same year he recorded his story about it on his early LP, *Jean Shepherd and Other Foibles*, he talked in a low, mock-conspiratorial tone at the end of a Sunday night show about a decoder pin:[ii]

> Now come close to the radio because I can't talk up. Now you know as well as I do that there are people who dig and people who don't. I mean there is after it's all said and done—it's *us* and *them*—right?
>
> Okay. Well let me tell you what's been happening. A lot of *them* keep sneaking in on this. You know what I mean. Now look, I'm going to form a secret club. A decoder club. We are going to have a decoder pin, and there are certain portions of this program that we will send out only to people who have the decoder pin. We can say, you know, we can say things we can't say on the radio then. I mean really. Would you like to get into this club?... All of a sudden I'll say, "Okay, set 'em to B12, kids: 7, 32, 19, 8." Wow, we'll be on the floor!
>
> Now I'm serious. If you want a decoder pin, first of all you got to prove you're one of us... We've saved this until the very last because we know that the sheep drop off like flies. Block that metaphor, Charlie. They drop off like flies. Like candles in the wind guttering out against the terrible hard, cold blast of reality before this time. There's just us left. There's not many of us.
>
> Now you send me a card, see. And all you write on the front of that card is "Whoopee." "Whoopee!" "Whoopee!" On the other side you're gonna have to dredge something out of the past—a meaningful something—that we will know you are one of us who really *digs! Right?*... Then we can *really* do it! I mean, anything up to now has been preface—preamble. Prelude.
>
> And we'll send out all verbiage, see, all this stuff. I'll play the comb, I'll beat on my head and everything for the benefit of *them*. Then, about five minutes out of the whole thing, see, I'll send the message...[62]

There is no question but what we are a tiny, tiny, tiny embattled minority here, there's no question about it. That 97.999 percent of all portable radios tuned in today—all automobile radios tuned in are either listening to the beginnings of a baseball game or they're listening to the sound of rock and roll or they are listening to somebody playing a Bach quartet. Hardly anyone is listening to the mind of man in all of its mainly—all of its silliness, all of its idiocy, all of its trivia, all of its wonder, all of its glory, all of its poor, sad, pitching us into the dark sea of oblivion.[63]

You know, there is a trick to it—not really a trick—people do, some people don't. Some people have the ability to walk through life, to kind of absorb it, reflect it, and feel it churning inside them. Walk through life with the feeling that they have just been given the car for the first time by their old man, it's a summer afternoon, they have just learned to drive, and they are venturing out on their own on their first solo flight. All of their life they can keep this beautiful, beautiful clear memory forever. Then there's the rest of the people, the great horde of the disenchanted.

Of course if you're going to face it, there are those two types: the enchanted and the disenchanted, and the enchanted are the ones who, of course, are slowly but surely being ground under the heel, who will be eventually extinct. I got a letter from this guy, Jim, the other day, and he said, "Shepherd, you realize of course that natural selection and the evolutionary process will eventually make your type of man totally extinct: the questioners. The believers will finally win out in the end."[64]

Although he believed humor had love and understanding in it, Shepherd had little affection toward those afflicted with "creeping meatballism."

Mad magazine's April 1957 article, referred to in the magazine as the "Jean Shepherd Dept." quoted Shepherd defining creeping meatballism: "The average person today thinks in certain prescribed patterns. People today have a genuine fear of stepping out and thinking on their own. 'Creeping Meatballism' is this rejection of individuality. It's conformity. The American brags about being a great individualist, when actually he's the world's *least* individual person." After a series of assaults—on car tail fins, trying to buy a "size small," "custom" clothes off the rack, and fake Floridas, Shepherd ended the feature with:

> Once a guy starts *thinking*, once a guy starts *laughing* at things he once thought were very real, once he starts laughing at TV commercials, and once he starts getting a boot out of movie trailers, once he begins to realize that just because a movie is wider or higher or longer doesn't make it a better movie, once a guy starts doing that, he's making the transition from "Day People" to "Night People."
>
> And once that happens, he can never go back!

NEW JERSEY AND QUEENS (AND A BIT OF KENTUCKY)

Jean Shepherd, American, focused on several locations he loved to deride besides his hometown of Hammond. When he worked in Cincinnati before coming to New York, he lived on the Kentucky border. He sometimes spoke of those natives with amused scorn—as hicks and hillbillies. They all seemed to be rubes from the Kentucky backwaters of Rabbit Hutch or Dismal Seepage.

Shepherd loved to poke fun at people who lived in Queens, New York, and he referred to the "limbo of New Jersey." Both targets are common ones for snobbish Manhattanites. He's quoted in a newspaper article as saying, "New Jersey—the most American of all states. It has everything from wilderness to the Mafia. All the great things and all the worst, for example, Route 22."[65]

Shepherd's ridicule of New Jersey was another instance of making things real by particularizing his commentaries (often meant to encompass all of what the example represented). On a radio call-in show, someone asked Shepherd why he was so critical of New Jersey. He replied, "Jersey is the universal state in America."[66]

Responding to a listener for "always saying bad things about New Jersey" he did a salute and apology. The apology was tongue in cheek—adding insult to injury. In an entire program devoted to New Jersey:

> **I would like to salute tonight—Jersey. A typical aesthetic problem in Jersey has just surfaced—for those of you who don't know much about it. Have you followed the "Fat Mary"**

controversy? Oh! You don't know the controversy of "Fat Mary"? Well, for those of you out of town—this is a classic confrontation between the forces of good and evil in Jersey. The forces of Art and the Slob World are always coming into great conflict—openly in Jersey. You don't see it like this in other states.

And so here we have—from the *Newark Star Ledger*. I am quoting a piece that in a sense is the quintessence of Jersey life... It says there is a regulation forbidding a tavern to use the name of biblical characters. And so, it says that Fat Mary not only inflames the aesthetics of theologians around, but also this place, the building, is three hundred years old and once was George Washington's headquarters! Now it's Fat Mary's Bar and Grill. In fact, they have a big sign and it says "Booze and Bites." [Laughs.]

Oh, that's Jersey, that's Jersey! [Bangs on desk.] *Vitality!* I mean, there's a certain slob vitality to that. And so, we would like to salute Jersey tonight. It's *done* it again!

[After a WOR jingle for itself, and another commercial.] This is a show about Jersey—both pro and con. Remember! I'm not anti-Jersey. I *like* this vitality! There are those who feel that Shepherd is *against* the slob. Not at all! I think the slob gives *spice* and the piquant—just the piquant savoring of life. A slob in any crowd is that little extra spice, that adds to—oh yes, the natural. The natural habitat of the Jersey slob is either in two guys when they're having a lawn sale or standing in line at the Dairy Queen.

These are the two places he seems to function even better—than generally. If you go into a Jersey body shop—you see a lot of good walking-around-slobs in a Jersey body shop, you know—"Hey, what a wreck you got there, Irwin, ha, ha, ha. It's gonna cost Allstate, right, *huh*, huh, buddy? Right. Back into a *hydrant*, huh? Had a snoot full?" Well, this is typical Jersey discussion [laughs]—which, by the way, is the quote of an actual one that I heard one night. Ah—*wild!*

So I like Jersey. I love the Leaning Tower of Pizza at twilight. There's a certain uninhibited slobism about that, which I just love. There's a—and the motel reaches its greatest—greatest flowering along Route 206. You see some goodies. [Route] 46 has got some great ones. Yes, the Haven of Golden Dreams Motel is on Route 46. Three little sad shacks in a row and the weeds. [Laughs.] Hard right, next to the Carvel—and on the other side is a McDonalds. A place to spend those con-

templative hours. Yes, the Haven of Golden Dreams. Well, this
is part of Jersey life...

Oh, Jersey, oh thou gutsy state. Oh, Jersey, thy state with
human yeast, oh, Jersey, thy moiling state of incessant activity
and unbelievable slobs, oh, Jersey, thy great state stands as a
legend. In fact, I think Jersey itself is the most American of
states. Number of reasons. It has practically everything in it.
Yeah, on the one hand, Jersey is a beautiful state in certain isolated areas. On the other hand, you have areas of Jersey which
are *incredibly* ugly. I don't know whether you have driven
under the high-bristling, grayish sun of a typical Jersey day on
the Jersey Turnpike along about exit 12 and exit 13. You see
nothing but what looks like a moon—lunar landscape, that is
dotted with what seems to be wretched, burned-out hulks of
old tractor-trailer trucks [laughs] and belching furnaces.
They're belching noxious airs into the atmosphere—*AUUUU-
UUUU!* Purple smoke rises to the horizon. You look down into
the waters of the Raritan and you can see nothing but a long,
slow, gloopy, dark river of sludge. Moving into a larger body
of sludge known as the Jersey Meadows. Where even the toads
have to come up for air every five minutes...

[End theme music begins.] Which, incidentally, is the natural
business of Jerseyites—running motels, bars, and Carvel
joints. And so, Jersey, we salute thee tonight. Possessed of
devils, hounded by—a consistent sense of having just missed
out on history.[67]

One year Shepherd ran a mock election campaign with the
slogan "Let them eat Twinkies," and said, if elected, he would set
up giant fans along Manhattan's shore to blow the pollution
back to Jersey. Besides driving through it, Jean Shepherd had
many connections to New Jersey. His early overnight broadcasts
on WOR were from the Carteret, New Jersey, transmitter, many
of his television shows came from New Jersey stations, including
the performances he did at the New Jersey Museum in Clinton,
and he performed annually at Princeton University for nearly
three decades. Shepherd also lived on a small farm in
Washington, New Jersey, for a brief period in the mid-1970s.

WOMEN AND CHILDREN, ETC.

New Jersey and other geographical locations were not his
only targets. People, especially women, felt his sting, too. He

often quoted from letters received from people who didn't understand him and criticized him—especially "little old ladies." He read these with the voice of the cranky, little old lady:

> Like I received this letter that said in a testy voice "I'm *shocked* that definitely—I refuse to accept—I'm a veritable *pillar* of strength in our neighborhood. I am noted as one of the leading..." Oh, this terrible letter went on and on and on. "Will you please get that schizophrenic, raving Mr. Shepherd off the radio and put on some nice man playing nice music." Which, of course, is a schizophrenic manifestation if I ever heard it—in our time. A nice man playing nice music. And all the while, the tom-toms are beating just beyond the next dark cloud.[68]

Possibly in response to complaints from women who weren't the clichéd "little old ladies," on a 1966 show he commented that they could be any age, any sex, and that he used the phrase as a "generic" term because even more old ladies were perceptive and who "see what it's all about." Although he used terms and situations symbolically, again he got to criticize the particular group, and then claim that it wasn't really them, as when he also disparaged "women and children."

Women and children, in fact, bring up a much more serious subject for Shepherd, because they were not just generic. Shepherd's commentaries about women would be a rather consistently negative part of his publicly spoken attitudes. He did not seem to find them easy to get along with. And as for his own two children, he would, in his last will and testament, go so far as to deny their existence.

Sex and smut seem outside Shepherd's sphere in broadcasting. Inappropriate for his audience? Inappropriate for his art form? Conservative bent? A newspaper review of Shepherd's December 31, 1968, Town Hall concert performance indicated that his material was "blue."[69] Only occasionally on air would one catch a bit of innuendo, such as, "Let's really do it, baby!" Married-with-kids is not part of the focus of this book, but Shepherd, who married four times, seemed from time to time very antagonistic toward family life and sometimes expressed hostility toward women. He frequently commented that he would say something especially significant later in the program "when the women and children are gone," implying that the women would find the subject too strong or beyond their ken.

Sometimes Shepherd said things about women that are no longer politically correct, as the recent vogue phrase has it. Comedians tended to use such slurs in the 1960s (during which Shepherd also went through a phase in which he criticized "role reversal"). He obviously felt uncomfortable with the changing of sexual stereotypes. He believed in the old stereotypes—as in a broadcast in which, although he disparaged men for being childish and having a propensity to war, he also suggested that their sense of childish play and adventure resulted in their itch for creation and progress:

> So we're going to shoot this rocket up now, you know, with a guy in it. Everybody talks about it. All the scientific information we're gonna get. That isn't why we're doing it—we want to see if we can shoot a rocket up. It's like kids—when a kid is gonna do something. He's going to throw a rock up in the air to see how high it goes. He doesn't pretend, you know, that what he's doing is to measure air currents—or rocks—he just throws the rock—let's her *go*.
>
> Well, as man gets older, he does the same thing—he throws rocks up in the air—or he, you know, he breaks—which is the equivalent of war. But as he gets older, being mature, he has to learn all kinds of ridiculous rationalizations for it. This is a kind of maturity. We call it maturity. So, he invents all these economic things, and he invents all these—these wild, beautiful stories. Like, "We have to have—we have to have the information on the upper air currents—sporadic E-layer there—up around Van Allen Belt. Gotta *have* that information."
>
> So [laughs] we wind up—nobody knows why, you know—we wind up putting 87 billion dollars into a gigantic rock to throw...
>
> 'Cause this is the kind of talk that women I'm not quite sure understand. Because I don't think they have the same kind of itch that men have. That the itch that men have to—to throw things as far as they can be thrown. To fly up as high as you can fly. To jump as high as you can jump. All these things are tied up—oh boy—biologically, and everything else—with the problem of being male.
>
> Women don't have this problem—obviously. They have others.[70]

In the following excerpt, Shepherd addressed men vs. women, role reversal, motorcycles vs. cars, and—of course—New Jersey:

It's only within the last six or seven—maybe six or seven months. The trend has been growing. It's only within this past year or so that the actual exchange of roles—between the male and the female—has become a formalized institution—literally.

I don't know how much driving around you do. One of the more intriguing aspects of this time and place is in the exchange of roles in everyday life in America... I ride a motorcycle around. And when you drive a motorcycle around on the streets of New York, you have a much closer contact with traffic—in many ways, I tell you!—than you ever do riding in a car.

Mostly, most people when they ride in a car are just vaguely aware of this large vehicle. This large block of metal—this side, that side, you know, they drive along, and the car goes along on a pretty straight-line course. Driving an automobile is a pretty cut-and-dried operation.

But a motorcycle, on the other hand is—first of all—hated by everybody in cars. I'm sure for a lot of reasons. Boy, I'll tell you, more insane hatreds, by ordinarily sane people come out the minute they see somebody who is not behaving the way they behave.

That's like riding a cab—that's considered absolutely nutty. You know that I would say—I'd like to talk to a cabby, but I would be willing to bet—speaking of reversal of roles, that the cab used to be a thing that was really a thing for businessmen—hurried guys—I would say probably a good 75 percent of the cab riders today are angry chicks sitting in the back seat. Believe it. And I tell you by riding around the streets in New York constantly, and when you're driving along and when you're driving a motorcycle, you are not only aware of the car, you are aware of everything about that car, because you better be. One thing you get really attuned to, when you ride a motorcycle is sounds of cars. You can tell whether a car is going to be dangerous or not, often by the sound of it. You really can. There's a lot of things you learn.

But one of the most—I think significant things—is the number of people today—I'd say by far the majority of cars today, are driven by women with a man sitting beside them. They've completely reversed their roles... I'm talking about the date. The obvious date. And you see this—this steel-jawed chick sitting in the front seat on Friday nights, when you're riding along. And *boy!* I'll tell you they're *insane* when it comes to motorcycles. They *hate* motorcycles. Somehow the motorcycle is a—is a—particularly masculine statement—that really bugs this type.

But—oh yeah, oh yeah, I was almost killed by a couple of chicks in a car—who did *exactly*—I'll tell you how far the reversal of roles has come... These chicks wearing leather jackets. Of course the scene has been going on for years—but in a different way! Now they have completely taken the role.

I'm riding along on my motorcycle. I'm just going along, and there's a car behind me and to my right—you see—you know where everything is—and we're on a one-way street. Namely, Second Avenue. And we're going down Second Avenue. Just light to light, and without any warning my ears pick up this pshish-hihihi—the sound of the tires doing it— and sure enough, out of the corner of my eye I see this coming like a bat out of hell across my bow! These chicks are just cutting me off for the sheer kicks of it! They go *WHOOO!* And I go *SCHHOOO!* I'm pretty good on that little motorcycle now, so they couldn't really do it—they couldn't throw me up on the sidewalk. And these chicks are: "Marlon *Brando,* buddy?"

...So I yell, "Baby, you wanna fight? Come on back, you *idiots!*"

And they: "All right!"

I was ready to go! Sadly enough they chickened out. It would have been the first true fistfight![71]

After talking about how men generally will not "short stop" another person who is waiting for a cab—that is, try to hail one when someone else nearby started hailing before them:

A woman? Let me tell you—she goes, "Hey! Cab! Cab! *Cab!*" And it stops—it slues up—right out front. There's just no question about it. It's a peculiar kind of—I suppose you might say—uh—*barbarism*—in a way. They're not bound by those little subtle laws of chivalry.[72]

In a radio comment on May 29, 1975, gathering every man into his prejudiced camp, he said, "All males are male chauvinist pigs. Absolutely. And if he isn't, he's fakin' it."

The "Listen, Baby" monologues-as-dialogues Shepherd did from time to time displayed a disagreement and tension between him and an imaginary woman—he would try to explain his point of view to her (of course one only heard his voice). Sometimes it seemed that the man was to blame for the conflict. The woman noticed what the Shepherd persona complained was a misunderstood, unimportant detail. (Whether that detail, as we shall see in the following riffs, was a record player, some clams to be ordered, or whatever.) Quiet jazz usually played in the background, contrasting with the confrontation. Shepherd spoke in gentle, conciliatory tones. (The now politically incorrect term "chick" was common hip talk of the time—remember that Peggy Lee sang, "Chicks are born to give you fever.")

In the following, from an extended riff, Jean Shepherd managed the feat of making himself seem the psychologically inadequate one, although clearly, as seemed to be the pattern in these "Listen, Baby" pieces, he was also the more sensitive and perceptive of the two. One might consider these artful monologues as Shepherd speaking "truthfully" from the heart, though they are fictional set pieces—yet this one especially might well say something about the "real" Jean Shepherd's ambiguous and sometimes hostile attitude toward women—and life:

> What I said, I meant. And I want to say it once again. And it's this—that the thing that I—I dig about you more than anything else is that there are times when I say these things, because of what I am. [Pause. He speaks throughout in a slow, soothing voice.] Because of what I *am*, you know? Can you understand what I mean, chick? Can you understand that there are some guys who get—and can get involved—who really *are* involved. I have sometimes a terrible sense—a kind of envy for people who are dedicated to something. I mean even if it's their only—their crummy, lousy, rotten, money-grubbing *career*. They're dedicated to it. And it sometimes makes me feel—kind of funny—because then I wonder whether I ever can be really dedicated to *you*. And I know that this is silly because here I *am* [plaintive voice]. Do you understand what I'm saying? I'm not trying to say any more than *that*.
>
> Like the other day—but what difference does it make? All I say is that—is that sometimes when I walk down the street and I see these people living in these—these miserable little houses with their flowers growing out in front, and their bar-

becue pits. I can't get sarcastic about this, because somehow they're dedicated to their barbecue pits—and their Sunday papers—they're dedicated to the "game of the day." They're dedicated to their new Mercury. And I can't even get dedicated to *that*.

The thing that I am trying to say to you is that I understand sometimes that I must be *impossible!*—because of the things I say. That you can't *understand* why I say, and I can't understand them. And—and—like that time you said—you remember?—about a month ago, I'm on one of these things where in the middle of it all I say to myself, "What are you *saying?*" Look, can you put the crossword puzzle down one minute? I want to finish what I have to say here.

Do you remember a month ago or so when we were in the kitchen and I had gone off on something and you turned to me and you said, "Look—I'm *here!*" [Pause.] I didn't know what to say, you know? Because that's the final test. Well, all I got to say is, you know I understand and—I—I'm *grateful*, that's all. Because by rights you *shouldn't* be.

Because guys who can't get involved and who can't get dedicated are impossible guys. I've known about three of them in my life. One of them committed suicide. The other guy's living in Uganda. And I'm the other one.

I don't know what to say, you know, except—you know—*thanks*. And don't get mad about what—what the neighbors said about that record player. Because—if they come in and yell, it's *my* fault. I'll stand up for it. I'll yell at the landlord from now on. I guess it's about all—you know—I don't really *care*—they could throw the record player down the airshaft. No, I'm not saying anything about your *record player*. That is not at *all* what I mean. But this is silly. Now, now—let's cut it out. I am sorry I said things. [Then, in a very quiet voice.] No I'm not. Just don't try to understand what I've said. Because sometimes I'm afraid somebody's *going* to understand.[73]

Here Shep wants to order some clams, and she doesn't because of her diet. He complains that even when she does something for him, it's because she wants to do it anyway:

There was an article in the *Times* today, baby, and I'm going to sit here and I'm going to sit you down and I'm going to read it. It's about the changing status of women. [The] changing status of men is what they should have written the article about. Changing status of women, *my foot!* You know what? I'll tell you—most chicks today want to be treated as though they are tender flowers—and they prefer to act like King Kong.

You see, there's that neat split. You want me to pick up your handkerchief while you are kicking me in the duff—with a pair of hobnailed boots. Now which do you want? Now I can do either, and can take either. If you want me to pick the hand-kerchief up and swing the doors. If you want me to—to go around spraying chlorophyll into the corners, you know. If you want me to sweep—if you want me to polish the plants. If you want me to pet the kitty. If you want me to do all those things for you, I will be glad to do them for you. But you better *act* like you want them done.

As though—know what? Do you have any idea what chivalry was based on? You're always bringing up this chivalry business. I'm not *chivalrous*. My foot, I'm not chivalrous! Well, that's a matter of definition.

And look, you should talk about love. What are you?—Oh—crying out loud! Listen. I have come to believe that there is no such thing as love. That men don't know what love is, women don't know what love is. We've just got this word that floats around and it's confusing the whole issue. And I'm not talking about *clams!* So get the clams out of mind! *I do not want any clams!*[74]

MINORITIES

Occasionally Shepherd did some bit with a Japanese or Chinese accent that might offend, and for a while in the 1960s he did a few negative pieces about an obvious homosexual named "Mr. Chucky." On the other hand, he also did an army story about an effeminate soldier in the typing pool and the harassment he endured. It was an especially compassionate story about the gay-in-the-military situation. Was he a homophobe, or was he more sympathetic to homosexuality? We seem to have a contradiction in his attitude. In the following, is he expressing his true feelings, or is he trying to defuse possible accusations that he is a homophobe?

Here's one here you might like. This is De Wolfe Hopper talking about Oscar Wilde, and I don't have to tell you what

Oscar's problem was. And he says, "Oh it's all right, just as
long as they don't do it in the streets and frighten horses."
[Laughs.] That's really the way I feel about 'em myself.[75]

Shepherd's attitudes toward others seemed to be openness
and tolerance in his general commentaries (what he presented as
his philosophy), but when it came to specific groups and individuals, such as women, children, gays, middle America, the less
educated (radio engineers are a special case, as we shall see in the
next chapter), he tended to find the ways they were different
from what he would like annoying to the extent that can be
called prejudiced. On occasion, he seemed to realize that he held
a harsh and objectionable opinion, and he would back off, mod-
ifying the severity of his attack, but where did these attitudes
come from in Shepherd? He would undoubtedly have said that
his opinions came from his acute perception and analysis.
Others might more likely attribute his opinions to his early-
twentieth-century upbringing in the conservative Midwest, from
which, though he tried, he could never really free himself.

Beyond Shepherd's negative views on a majority of the
population, he sometimes suggested in his own amusing ways
what minor matters influenced him and what did not. Comic
strips—the funnies—are an odd but telling example of how
Shepherd could define himself both as a member of middle
America and at the same time insist that he stood aside from the
mob as a minority of one. Did the funnies influence Shepherd?
Listening to many hours of Shepherd suggests that they did not.
But he also clearly recognized their pervasive influence on
several generations of Americans if for no other reason than
their ubiquity. In that context, as one of those Americans who
grew up in the inescapable environment of the funnies, he could
not escape their influence. But it was not of the same order as
the influence that Dostoyevsky and Kierkegaard are said to have
had on the likes of, say, Norman Mailer. Thus he could insist in
the same breath that he was and at the same time was not
influenced by the funnies.

Shepherd talked and wrote several times about comic strips,
suggesting that they were not the best ways for people to get
their attitudes toward life. He obviously liked them, yet made
contradictory statements—at times he claimed to have never
read them, and at others insisted on their strong influence on
himself and others.

Running through the comic strips was a strong anti-art attitude—that ran through almost all the comic strips that people
really lived by. For example, I used to remember great arguments that my mother and father would have over relative vil-
lains—that Dick Tracy had. Whether B. O. Plenty was a better
villain than the Mole. This was the art that people really lived
by, you know. [A small slip—B. O. Plenty is the grizzled old
good guy in Dick Tracy.][76]

I was never hung on comic strips, like Joel Siegel.
Apparently, all Joel Siegel did as a boy was go out and drink
egg cream, collect baseball cards, play stickball, and talk about
the good old days. I did none of those as a kid.[77]

Shepherd read the funnies on the air during a newspaper strike,
just as New York City's Mayor La Guardia did years before:

And, good morning! By George, I've a special broadcast this
morning [laughs] and for the next half hour—this is Jean Shepherd. We're going to look at the funnies. As you know, the newspapers are not being delivered these days. I'm quite aware that
75 percent of Americans read, the first thing—absolutely the
first thing they read are the funnies. Every time the newspapers
arrive. This is a known fact. And I'm no different from all the
rest of the world. And, by the way, it's not just kids who read
funnies, either—it's people! Real people do. People every morning sit, they look at their old *Dick Tracy*, they look at their old
Blondie, and they know that the world is going on just like it's
always going on, and will continue to go on *exactly* that way.
So, good morning. Let's get at them—right now. [Laughs.]
I've gotten a little bit out of touch with Dick Tracy, but I've
maintained a kind of a running correspondence with
Dagwood. Here now is Dagwood and Blondie, and this, of
course, is from the *Journal American*. And everybody knows
Blondie. In fact, there's probably no more American comic
strip than *Blondie*. Because a whole—probably a generation
and a half of Americans—have tried to form their lives around
Blondie and Dagwood.[78]

Shepherd made a strong, yet ironic, statement about the
importance of comics in his column for the *Village Voice*,
November 14, 1956:

Briefly it comes down to this: I have begun to realize that my philosophy of living is based largely upon a firm bedrock foundation of comic-strip ideologies. This includes many subtleties of Right and Wrong or Good and Evil as evidenced in politics or just daily living. I find that many of my pronouncements upon issues of our time have tinges of dialogue left over from *Little Orphan Annie* or *Little Annie Rooney* or *The Little King* or maybe *Pogo*. And, I say, I'm not alone. Millions of Americans of my age bracket, the thirties, are obviously living in the same pulp-paper dream world where Right always triumphs over Evil, and Daddy Warbucks shows up invariably at the right perilous moment, just in time to have Punjab behead the Evil Ones. Punjab always does so without consulting such old-fashioned democratic relics as juries or judges or law books, and seems to function independently of even laws of gravity.

Shepherd thus commented on what a powerful force comics could be on American thinking—including his own. On one broadcast, Shepherd discussed how he and other writers had been influenced by comic strips, and went on to describe in detail the influence on him of one (one of his "roots"?) The following also shows Shepherd's sense of the absurd:

Would you guess what strip—as a kid—the one that I read most? Judging from my work? And that influenced me?

Who do you think I always looked at? Did you ever hear of *Smokey Stover*? [Shepherd is talking to his engineer or someone else in the studio.] You never heard of *Smokey Stover*? You never heard of *Smokey*? Okay. No way to talk to you then. You never heard of *Smokey Stover*. Well, maybe you called it something else... What was always said in the strip *Smokey Stover*? Did you ever hear the expression "Notary Sojak"? You have, or are you just saying that? Well, that was always said—every strip there was a little guy holding up a sign that said "Notary Sojak." Smokey Stover was the fireman. [Laughs.]

It was a completely maniacal strip. Had absolutely no real—well, among other things, above it was another strip that was written by—drawn by—the same guy, and there was a character in this strip who always walked around with a coal scuttle over his head. And he was always hitchhiking. What did he say all the time? "Nob schmaz kapop." [Laughs.] That's all he said—"Nob schmaz kapop." He was hitchhiking. Complete absurdity.

I remember one time it was explained in the strip—one of the characters asked the other character, "Well, how come he always wears that coal scuttle over his head?"

The other one says, "Well, he's prepared."

He said, "What do you mean—prepared for what?"

He says, "Well, he figures, you never can tell."

The other guy says, "What do you mean, you never can tell? Never can tell what? What's he prepared for?"

He says, "Well, he figures you never know when you're going to be hit by a meteor." [Laughs.]

There he stood. With a coal scuttle. For some reason or another, this hit my particular sense of humor. And I would have to say that among all the things that have influenced me—that probably influenced me as much as anything else. Reading that strip—I never missed it. It had a curious, maniacal sense of—complete absurd sense of humor. Nothing to do with preaching. It was almost like the—I'd have to say almost the Samuel Beckett of comic strips.[79]

SLOBISM

Shepherd liked to say that there were two kinds of people in the world, and then go on to describe the types, one of which was himself and a few intelligent, like-minded people, and then there was the rest of humanity, far below him. One of his favorite groups to disparage—obviously they were mentally inferior—were the kind of people who would put plastic pink flamingos, or their tasteless equivalent, on their front lawns. As he might have said, that was slob art in spades! Shepherd found the quirky mind of man—the absurdity of it all—perversely appealing. He was entertained by what he called slob art. He hated it/loved it/hated it. The phrase appeared in his broadcasts frequently, in his writing (his old man's prize woman's-leg lamp from his book *In God We Trust: All Others Pay Cash*), in a TV segment of *Shepherd's Pie*, and on the way to vacation in his movie *Ollie Hopnoodle's Haven of Bliss*. He referred to a "Praying Hands" salt-and-pepper set as an example of "pious slob art."

Well, I must tell you this [all said in ironic tones] I am *shocked*, I am amazed, I am disappointed, at the number of people with low, slovenly, slobish tastes. They seem to be pro-liferating, if anything. There are *more* of them, if anything. People who insist—who somehow pretend that they like bazoo playing, they like rotten crummy stories about Flick and Bruner fistfighting in the basement for snappy detective maga-zines, they like [extended laugh]—and you know, one of the saddest things of all is the lady, the poor, sad lady who writes a triplicate letter and sends one to the manager of the radio sta-tion, another one apparently to Saint Peter, and one to me.

And it said, [he goes into his little-old-lady voice] "And I would like to say that Mr. Shepherd is one of the very few people in public entertainment who admits that in the year 1965 he will attempt to do better and will think nothing but pure, clean thoughts. Thank God we have people like Mr. Shepherd around."

A little rotten piano music there, rotten piano music, please—that is not rotten piano music, but bring it up. Little rotten piano music there [player-piano type of "My Wild Irish Rose."] All right gang, let's go. Now let's all together now— [Shepherd starts singing] let's all practice thinking clean thoughts—*razzmatazz*. Let's all do some mental push-ups— *razzmatazz*. Let's clean out the shelves, let's pull up our socks, let's look with clear blue eyes to the future—razzmatazz. Let's sing of beauty and truth—*razzmatazz*. Let us play the lute of life—razzmatazz. With guts and bravado, with *presto agi-tando*, let us move upward and onward together rat*a*da! All together, now sing it out!

Rat*a*da ta *ta* da *da*—and every way in every day I'm doing better and better, bigger and taller, wider and fatter ta *da* da *da* la ta da*data*da upward and onward with you, ohhhh baby!

The trouble with Mankind is, he has a case of galloping slobism...and no matter where you go! You think we got a corner on S-l-obism? Do you really? [He reads a news report from Poland about one thousand ambulances rushing to assist victims of gluttony.][80]

In one broadcast he spoke of an estate sale that included a giant, full-color statue of Babe Ruth, a seven-story-high glass chandelier with fake candles held by brass fists, and an ele-phant's-foot umbrella stand:

I say you cannot give up on mankind if he's capable of this kind of stuff. I'm just talking about mankind in general. So anyway, I'm sitting there, where they've got this chandelier, and the auctioneer's up there—he's pounding away with a gavel, you know, and all of his assistants are bringing stuff up and he says, "And now we have number 172..."

Well, I'm looking at this thing and I think, by george, you know, you can't give up hope. Ya just can't give up hope...

Can you imagine what it would be like if mankind somehow disappeared from the face of the Earth tomorrow, and left all his stuff behind him? Just left it, you know—just—even better than that, I would *love* to see a pile of all the junk—just the junk of mankind piled up. I wonder how high it would reach, this pile—how big the base would be. How much it would weigh.

And how many hopes it would contain. How many. And how many distorted, strange, wild, beautiful, exquisite, circumscribed dreams. All piled up there—with those plastic streetcars and those leather whales, and those elephant toes. Oh boy!... Now lookit—if you really examine the case of the elephant knee, you will realize that there is a *logic* to it—there is a logic to everything. Everything fits—don't you understand that there isn't a single, itsy bitsy, wee tiny drop that does not somehow fit into the overall [pounds desk, goes "pttt!"] scheme.[81]

I saw a magnificent piece of slob art in Times Square, which is, by the way, where slob art can *really* be found. They had this three-dimensional rendering. This rendering has a little lard in it, too. [Note uncharacteristic pun on "rendering."] A three-dimensional rendering of Michelangelo's *The Last Supper*, and it was in color.[iii] Startling real-life color. And when you walked past it—you're supposed to move back and forth, see—not only did the eyes follow you, which, as you all know, is a big advantage in all artworks—when the eyes follow you—not only did the eyes follow you, but as you walked past this thing, Judas Iscariot—his finger pointed at the Savior. Just like that. He was fingering Him. What a *thing!*[82]

There was also "slob knowledge." He said his father believed many pieces of slob knowledge, such as the myth of the man who had invented a pill that, put in water and used as fuel, got incredibly high miles to the gallon, but "they bought him out"—

so it wouldn't get on the market. Shepherd said of his old man, "Logic had no place in my father's mythology."

From a broadcast that included an ad for Palisades Amusement Park in New Jersey, Shepherd includes himself as at least occasionally enjoying slob art:

> I must admit that I have a real weakness for amusement parks. Now a lot of people say, "Ah, what do you mean?" No—there is a strong streak of the slob that runs through me, and I must say I *love* this stuff.[83]

> On my show, for fifty weeks out of the year, I excoriate the slob. On my two-week vacation, I become an S-L-O-B in S-P-A-D-E-S. I become the—I have a pair of pink-green-blue-yellow-with-a-little-gold-stitching-on-the-side Bermuda shorts that you wouldn't believe. And I've picked them because they're exactly the *wrong* length... Of course there's a strong—a very strong mother lode of slobism that we all carry around with us. I think that it's a lifelong fight, you know, against that thing for most of us—to—to—oh *yeah!* It's terrible! I find myself liking things I should not like, and I find myself *not* liking things I should like. Constantly. Like I have a secret yen [whispers]—oh, this is terrible—*for Jayne Mansfield!* Oh! I fight against it![84]

On another occasion, he mentioned watching some "slob" sports show for "two and a half hours," and at other times said he watched the stuff he subsequently disparaged. Why did he watch it in the first place? He was outrageously exaggerating how much time he spent watching, or he enjoyed getting upset over it, or as research he could then stew over it and report back to listeners? Maybe he loved it so he could hate it. Or, to quote him, "I must say I love this stuff." It just might be that he recognized in himself a common, if not universal, human trait—he really did enjoy some things that, in his more sophisticated frame of mind, he realized he had to deride because of the simple, lowbrow pleasures they were. Let us say there was ambiguity in his attitude.

Surely a quintessential example of Shepherd's attitude toward slobs and the intellectual level of his fellow humans is this 1965 diatribe:

> Hey, have you had the sneaking feeling that somebody's playing a giant trick on you on the old-movie scene on televi-

sion? Have you had the feeling that they're playing the same ones over and over and over again now for the last month or so? What is it? Have they run out of crummy stuff now? Have they run out of junk—I almost said something more—have they? [Laughs.] Have they run out of it? And they've decided that they're going to only play the same six movies over and over again, eternally?

You know that they've found that slobs will watch no matter what they put on? That's the truth. One of the awful things you discover when you work in a television station is that the klutzes will look no matter what is on. So, ergo, it doesn't make any difference what is on! You know it's funny— have you read in the paper—it's a fact—and it really burns you up, and you begin to realize something about the nature of man.

Have you seen these pieces that poor old Jack Gould is writing all the time, and these various critics in the *Times* and the *Herald Tribune* about the terrible state of television? Well, I agree that television is the world's worst junk—it's awful. But you know the one thing they never get at? These guys should get right at the heart of it and say, "Let's face it, 97.9 percent of the world is composed of people with cabbage between their ears." This seems to elude guys like Gould. They don't seem to realize that there is a giant shark out there in the darkness—whatever that shark is—the *people* is a giant shark out there with *fantastic* stainless steel teeth who have an *insatiable* appetite, a *voracious* appetite for—*GLOP!* Just anything! Glop! It's got big, red-rimmed eyes, and it just sits out there and goes *Aaaaaah! Anything* you throw at it—goes *Aaaaagagaa! Waaaaaad!* Sits out there—*Aaaaah!*...

Samuel Johnson once said—or was it Johnson? Anyway, I think it was Johnson. Anyway, Johnson said, "It's *impossible* to underestimate the taste of the mob." [Laughs.] And now on the other hand, Gould would have us—he would say, "Yes, but you—you have a, quote, 'responsibility to raise the...'" Have you ever tried to raise the level of the Atlantic Ocean by spitting in it? Have you ever tried to put jacks under the Pacific Ocean and raise it about four feet? Have you ever tried to do that? [Laughs.] Holy *smokes!*...

A lot of people who write about TV and who yell about it, and who gripe about it—I think, are missing the point—that mankind is—in general—a big, fat, heavy, sweaty, slob.

[Shepherd speaking over the end theme] On all sides, you see the rise of the Neanderthal sittin' there with his slack jaw.[85]

Shepherd's attitude toward most other people seemed to be that they were Neanderthals. People who haven't the intelligence or sensitivity to feel decent emotion or involvement in life—as he put it, "the great mass of the population of people who are just moles."

I have come to the conclusion that there is a whole population of us who are not recorded in fiction, who are not written about, who are not moaned over nor discussed, and, in fact, in some ways are not even worthy of it—mole people. Are you aware that among us there walks—if that phrase covers their means of locomotion—a population of mole people, whose passions, if they can be called that, burn like a low flame on an ancient stove? Barely flickering, barely sputtering, a tiny almost extinguished spark of the divine flame of existence in life, and who, when in the heat of what, for want of a better word, we call flaming passion—are barely seen to move—the mole people.

You know what I mean by the mole people? The people who really are not capable of emotion—real emotion. Oh, they can get irritated when they are pushed in bus lines, and things like that, or when there is a busy signal on the telephone. They get irritated over the wrong things. You wonder even how they reproduce their own kind. Oh! Oh! Speaking of mole people, this is WOR AM and FM, New York, and we'll be here to midnight.

I'll tell you what the danger of the mole people is. You know what is it the mole people? These are people not really interested in—can't find it within their scope to become engaged in life—who can't reach out and grab the handle, and these are the people who are the quickest people to want to go to war. These are the people who love the idea of war, and all the rest of the things which make up for a kind of artificial excitement and stimuli which they would never get out of existence.

What scares me is that great horde of people who sit in the subways, and the only movement that you see stirring in their soul is when somebody steals their seat. That's the only time they ever have any excitement during the day, or when they hit their wife in the mouth. You know—that's the truth. There's a whole population of them. And it always baffles me to find writers and well-meaning people—you know—who march around with signs, who because of the fact that they are so involved with life, they don't seem to be able to understand the great mass of the population of people who are just moles.[86]

Of course, Shepherd hated the popular entertainment of the masses. He made clear that he and his intelligent listeners were above that. He proselytized for his pet enthusiasms in the arts—mostly arcane creators—fine but widely unknown, only appreciated by the perceptive. Shepherd had a large audience in radioland, but direct contact with only his engineer and maybe his producer, who seemed to have little interest in or knowledge of the creative arts, which Shepherd valued highly. This lack of an adequate peer communication frustrated him. As he put it in one 1966 broadcast referring at least in part to those in the studio, "To me an illiterate is a person who doesn't read. He may know *how* to read—that is irrelevant—to me. Knowing a skill has no meaning unless the skill is *used*." In one exchange, Shepherd discussed the poem about Richard Corey and then Miniver Cheevy. "You don't know who he is?" he asked someone in the control room. "Well, that's because you're illiterate."[87] Shepherd would have a lot more to say about those he worked with—they certainly did not live up to his standards, and he was quick to point it out to them.

THE GREAT NEW YORK BLACKOUT OF 1965

On at least one occasion, not on his own program, but with a mike open to all, Shepherd unexpectedly encountered an opportunity to disparage his coworkers in the midst of a common predicament.

A Shepherd fan, G.M. Frame, who nearly forty years after the fact finds his memory of a broadcast vivid, but not beyond possible fallibility in the details, remembers turning on his radio on campus at Rutgers University, New Jersey, and hearing the WOR staff reporting the loss of electricity throughout New York City and environs.[iv] WOR's transmitter was fine in New Jersey, and the New York studio was operating on an emergency backup generator, with the gasoline supply running low:

Perhaps around nine PM, Jean wandered in and joined the commentary. His tone was one of amused amazement at the scene, a typical Shep viewpoint. He crafted a word picture of the scene in the studio, something I don't recall anyone else having done to that point. As a dedicated ham, he obviously was delighted with the tabletop jury-rig system the engineers had put together. I recall his comment "Good old-fashioned American ingenuity; it's what won the war!" Suddenly a flurry of activity! In burst a breathless individual, who, having heard of the imminent demise of the generator, had driven in from New Jersey and raced up twenty-two or so flights of stairs at 1440 Broadway (of course the elevators were nonfunctional) lugging two jerricans of gas to keep WOR on the air. Shep was delighted: "A fan, a real WOR fan, from New Jersey already!" The others tried to interview the guy, but he was so winded that he could gasp out only a word every other breath. Shep could be heard chuckling in the background.

Mr. Frame remembers that the others on the air speculated and complained about the power grid failure. Shepherd commented on electronic complexities. When the others continued, the discussion degenerated "into acrimonious backbiting," and Shepherd "commented to the effect that people who weren't knowledgeable [about the issue at hand] had no business offering any opinions. It was clear from his tone that he regarded most of his broadcast colleagues as technological ignoramuses. Someone, perhaps Lester Smith or Barry Farber or someone like that, tried to pour oil upon the troubled waters, to suggest that they were all operating 'in the dark' here, and the floor should be open to all speculation. Jean's response was to turn the flame thrower of his contempt and derision in that direction."

Here is an event—unscripted because unexpected. Written scripts can mask egos and unpleasant feelings, but Shepherd's material on his programs was expressed as it was created, shortcutting much of the filtering process. There was joy in listening to an unscripted mind in process—the extemporaneous, refreshing openness bringing with it a *real* persona—with a propensity for laughing at his own wit, and for articulating his ego and occasional hostility. Here during the New York blackout, however, was an example of Shepherd when not on his own program, but coming unexpectedly upon a situation in progress. These unpleasant expressions of his ego toward the few people with whom he was in direct contact seem to presage his hostile ego outbursts in front of live audiences in his later years. The hostility, which Shepherd often put in the us vs. them category and kept on a lighter level, became at times Shepherd vs. the world—a much more serious misanthropy. His frustrations had perhaps been tempered in his early career by the still-viable dreams of fuller recognition of his talents. Increasingly over the years, however, these frustrations manifested themselves as those dreams were thwarted by the reality he knew was every man's fate and he began to recognize the approach of his own Dream Collection Day.

LOVE/HATE—A TINY EMBATTLED MINORITY OF ONE

On the air, Shepherd both loved and disparaged much of his background, and many of his enthusiasms, friends and colleagues, none of which measured up to his standards: Hammond, Indiana; New York City; America; trivia, slob art, and nostalgia; super-dramatic "glop" poems such as those of Robert W. Service; radio and television; and so much else that constituted his world. Everywhere he looked, he found much to disparage. And here again is the self-contradiction and the enigma—for all of that hostility in that embattled minority that was Jean Shepherd, when he went on the air in that little studio with his earphones on and a mike before him, his listeners heard a man full of life, urging us all to live to the full; his listeners were always amused, enjoying the outpourings of this man who reveled in all of existence!

Jean Shepherd reveled in the moiling brouhaha of the real world out there, but was alone or nearly so—isolated physically and intellectually in studioland with his mike, that small perforated piece of metal that he had to see as the extended ears of unknown numbers of unknowable listeners. Only his engineer, maybe his producer and an occasional other person were there in his visible world—and they were beyond him, behind a sheet of glass. As much as he may have found them inadequate, they were his only direct contact with listeners, and he needed the eye contact. Occasionally he also asked for and received a phoned-in ear contact.

CHAPTER 14

EYE CONTACT, EAR CONTACT
Engineers and Others

Shepherd needed to talk, but seldom did he want anyone to talk back. It is little wonder that of the four known guests he had on his program, his attempt at a dialogue with another humorist, S. J. Perelman, fell flat. Even so, for the man who could not stop talking, Shepherd needed evidence that there was an audience out there listening to the sound of his ceaseless voice. Listeners were the thousands of reasons for Shepherd's speaking life—the receivers of his unending monologues at the other end of his microphone—he sometimes had to be assured that he was making ear contact with people out there in the dark—in radio-land.

The very rare on-air phone calls usually involved Shepherd asking for a call. He could be heard, but the other end of the conversation was silent, or unintelligible—only occasionally one could understand the caller. In a September 1960 broadcast, he asked for a call from "a lovable woman," and one heard her voice—then he spoke to a listener who responded to a request for a "dynamic man." Once Shepherd talked on the phone with a "butt sniper" who took stuff from the trash left out at night, and on another occasion talked with a listener when the New York Mets won the World Series. In one instance, a wireless phone caller (before cell phones were common) approached a tunnel tollbooth and refused to pay, silence followed as he drove through the tunnel, then joy abounded as he emerged unscathed on the other side. Another time, Shepherd suggested that drivers at tollbooths pay for the cars behind them, and then described reactions of those drivers. One year Shepherd invited listeners to call and accept his Christmas greeting on behalf of the entire audience:

> All right now, I do this now symbolically for all listeners everywhere, personally—I wish you a Merry Christmas.
> [Listener] Same to you, Mr. Shepherd.
> [Shepherd] Thank you very much, Mr. Listener. And you're a splendid person.
> [Listener] Thanks a lot.
> [Shepherd] Thank you. [Hangs up the phone.] Now wasn't that a nice little ceremony?[88]

On more than one broadcast, Shepherd asked for a person to call him just so he would know there was someone out there—some human contact. As he once put it, "Everyone needs a cheer button in his life." Another time he asked for someone to praise him and say, "Yeah, Shepherd—for president of the world!" Shepherd continued, saying that he wanted just the smallest clue that somebody cared. Yes, Shep needed contact and approval.

> And I want one kid to holler in there, "Get up off the floor, Shepherd, and continue on with the show." [Shep has just read "The Face on the Barroom Floor"] I want to hear one little— that's the trouble with doing something on radio—you get no applause. A little applause here. Can I hear one—one guy applauding—and I'll continue. [Hits the table—one can hear glasses tinkling against each other.] Hear one guy holler "Yea, hooray, Shep! Wow!" Then I'll go on...
> Hello kid, okay, come on, let's hear some cheering, man. Come on, *hit it hard!* [We hear a kid's telephoned voice, "Yea, Shep!"]
> That's right! [Shepherd slams down the phone] Thank you. I will continue.[89]

Not only did Shepherd continue his broadcasts, and his broadcast-long monologues to anyone he could collar, but he could not stop talking even when alone at home—he would talk on amateur radio into the night. The obsession begun when he was a kid continued throughout his life.

Jean Shepherd (K2ORS[v]), talker—in person, on his radio show, and at night on his private little ham radio station. In addition, he spoke at the country's largest amateur radio convention three separate years,[vi] and in 1975, he hosted a half-hour educational video on ham radio satellites.[90] When he wasn't talking on ham radio, he was sending Morse code on it, and in 1976, he recorded the short, encouraging introduction to the American Radio Relay League's Morse code training tape. Incessantly talking to friends and strangers alike:

> **Bill Pasternak:** Jean would come on [ham radio] almost every night after his show. I guess it was 1970–71. He was just another ham radio operator who had an interesting job. Shep tried to keep his anonymity on the international band, but on the local band we all knew him, we'd all grown up with him.[vii] He was our mentor. He got a lot of us that he would talk to on the local ham radio—we grew up with him! We were his audience. We were now in our twenties and early thirties... We were the kids sneaking RCA radios under the covers to listen to him. [Sometimes a ham on the air would say,] "Hey Jean, I heard your show and you said such and such," and the conversation would continue, just as if it was the show.

Everything was the show—everything was Jean Shepherd in his never-ending communication with the world, using whatever format he could. It is no wonder that articles about him and radio tributes to him would have such titles as "The Talker," and "A Voice in the Night." Shepherd, in his isolated radio studio, had need of some human response he could also see. He had his engineer, his producer, and an occasional coworker or guest. But his ear contact and eye contact went much further than he would have expected. He would consider the radio engineers as mostly necessary evils, but they affected the quality of his performance, and his producer would become an essential part of his life in and out of the studio. She would go from being only a worshiper at his feet to being the emotional center without which he could not live.

ENGINEERS

The normal broadcast setup consisted of Shepherd at a desk and, beyond the glass window, both his producer and the engineer. Shepherd directed his broadcasts out loud as he performed them, explaining to his engineer what he wanted instead of merely giving silent hand signals. Just as he cultivated a feeling of intimate contact with his radio listeners, Shepherd needed to be involved in communicating with those in the studio. He needed personal rapport to do his work. There might be an off-hand comment, or a request for some kind of response to the subject at hand. Occasionally he looked for a positive nod: "Do you agree?" Shepherd's talking to somebody with whom he was in direct contact gave an added feeling to the broadcast of a real listener—direct communication.

> Did you like my song there, George? [Laughs.] Oh, *man!* Oh yeah. You really liked that, huh? [Shepherd had just done a funny commentary over a honky-tonk record] Sounds familiar, doesn't it, George? All right, you know. [Laughs.] Yeah, George. Every time I work with George I get down there where it really sweats, you know? Ain't no way to escape it. Have you noticed the different types of show I do when I'm with George or when I'm with Herb or when I'm with Matt? Really different scene.[91]

The engineer was Shepherd's technical and human link to his listeners. As Shepherd wove his spell, any break in the continuity could destroy it. Addressing engineers by first name allowed him to carry on a businesslike but friendly communication of what he wanted done—except when attention wasn't paid. Herb Squire, an engineer from mid-1963 to April 1977, commented on Shepherd's relationship with engineers in a 1999 WOR tribute to Shepherd (hosted by Joey Reynolds) that aired after Shep's death: "Jean was very exacting. He knew what he wanted. If you were an engineer in his studio, you had to pay attention because—you were his audience, and so, behind the glass, say in old Studio 3 upstairs on the twenty-fourth floor, I could do a show or one of the other engineers could do a show and our reactions to his material made or—you know—broke the material. If we laughed, he knew he was going in the right direction. If we did a thumbs down, he knew that things were not going as well as he planned." Asked if Shepherd looked you right in the eye all during his show, Squire replied, "Oh, yes, he needed the eye contact."

Squire was one of the very few engineers who got along well

with Shepherd. The rest of them did not understand what Shepherd was doing, and had little interest in the program except to do the minimum job. The engineer might undercut the essence of Shepherd's delivery, and he could do nothing about it. WOR's general manager, Herb Saltzman, comments, "His show required timing, and union engineers can be the bane of broadcasters' existence. Once they've achieved seniority, you have trouble firing them... The engineers hated him."

> **Laurie Squire:** Some engineers got him and some engineers didn't get him. And it annoyed the hell out of him to have assigned an engineer who didn't get him. Some of the engineers—we're talking the mid-'60s, '70s—were still the old sound effects guys from the 1930s and '40s who were putting in their time till retirement and just were—we used to call engineers like that "button pushers." They didn't care, they didn't listen to the content, they just pushed the button and that was it. And it irritated him because he played to the audience in the control room. Engineers had to maintain eye contact...
>
> I was taping a show and in the middle of the taping I got a phone call—my aunt died suddenly. Now you can picture, I was taping a humor show. I get this phone call—Jean knew what happened—and I'm *trying* to pay attention and trying... Jean literally said, "Laurie, I don't care if your aunt just died." He wasn't saying it to be mean. [It was like] "Pay attention to me!"

On occasion, Shepherd had a disagreement with an off-mike person. He was obviously friendly with some engineers, but though he sometimes may have been joking, over the years he showed a pattern of antagonism. It was his only means of getting back at those whom he felt were degrading his art.

> **And spring is a time of madness. It is, huh? Appreciate this. You even *see* among the engineers just a faint flicker of passion. Yes, they recall the days when they had *glands*.**[92]

He twice referred to an engineer in a derogatory tone as a "minion." Two Shepherd comments to a person behind the glass in 1971, typical of his caustic tone: "Well that's why he was a scientist and that's why you're a klutz;" "Only people with imagination have fears, so that lets you out." His frequent requests for answers to trivia questions usually resulted in the engineer not knowing, and his comments on some matter he considered common knowledge often resulted in a blank stare from the other side of the glass. He especially rebuked engineers for inattentiveness, frequently complaining on-air that an engineer had played a wrong song or missed a cue:

> Very good, Ralph. That was excellent. You played that very good. Certainly tell the pros around—he's playing it at the right speed and everything today—and—got it on. Didn't have to wait till Wednesday, like some guys. You know we got one engineer here—I give him a cue on Tuesday and by Friday it sneaks into my show the next time he's working with me. [Laughs.] He's got a reaction time of something like seventy-two hours.[93]

> You know, I kind of miss baseball season already, don't you, Corny? There's no—and it's terrible now. You come into this station here and the engineers have got nothing to watch. You know, the television sets are all turned off, and the engineers for the first time in months have been forced to listen to the programs that they're engineering.[94]

> That's right—there we go—bring it up just like—you know, like we're in the radio [business] here. Okay. We'll pretend this is the big time. I'll throw you hand cues, and—heh heh heh— you can *miss* 'em.[95]

In Shepherd's live commercial for Pottery of All Nations, apparently about to say "Pot to piss in," but with no intention of saying it in fact—he only had implied it. His engineer apparently thought he was about to say it:

> And if you don't have a pot to—uh—well, they've got pottery of all kinds there. Ah—They're down on Sheridan Square. Ask Larry. Say, "Hey, Larry, I don't—you have a pot?" And Larry'll say okay and reach up on the upper shelf around the back—they keep those in the back by—over the ovenware there. And you'll find a visit to the Pottery of All Nations is well worth it. They let you break things, and they have beautiful Chinese oriental imitation mandarin vases. Many things there—that are particularly indigenous to the art attitudes of

the upper Bronx and the upper areas of Fordam Road there, near Pelham Parkway...

Pottery of All Nations. It's the place to go if you don't have a pot to—[yells] will you quit cutting me off![viii] If I'm going to get cut off it's going to be *my* problem, not yours. You're just an engineer. You stay there and run that thing, will ya? One, two, three, four, off—for crying out loud—what *are* ya? That's the only good thing I've said tonight.

Well, for those of you who are interested, we'll get around this clown. For those of you who are interested in it, send your name and address to "Censor. WOR AM and FM, New York. Censor, W—." And you must be over twenty-one. We'll include—specially interesting for art students—fifty poses.[96]

In 1966, Shepherd talked about when he was working in Cincinnati (speaking in a kidding sort of way):

One day, one of the sneaky, rotten engineers—I've noticed that the engineers have the truly corroded minds. Something—basically *rotten* about many engineers. They sit there and they—Oh yeah!—I mean—year after year, they look in through the glass and they watch shows being done, and eventually they are totally immune to anything. Absolutely! I'm serious.[97]

Barry Farber: The engineers all hated him. They hated me too. They were disdainful. Don't forget—WOR was a galaxy of dynasties—McCann, three generations, the Gamblings three generations, Ed and Pegeen didn't need three generations—they *were* three generations. And nobody new came in. Jean was considered an outsider, even though he was in. So I was the first new guy who came in. The *young* engineers liked me a lot... Matt was a new engineer. And I said, "Jean, what's this all about?" He said, "Well, he hates me." [Farber says that Matt hated *him* as much as he hated Shepherd. Laurie Squire comments, "Matt could be obnoxious."]

I said, "Jean, so who gives a damn? He's like a porter carrying your bags. Carrying your words to the air. What do you care what a Pullman porter thinks of you?" And he said, "He creates a climate of negativity."

Jean would not put up with [the engineers'] stupidity. They weren't accustomed to being chided on the air. He used to chide everybody including the top executives. He was constantly looking for trouble.

> Life, as you know, is lived to the richest and fullest at the Limelight between the hours of ten and midnight. Wouldn't you say that, Matt?
>
> [Shepherd was plugging his live Limelight broadcast, and repeated with some insistence] Wouldn't you say that, Matt?
>
> You'd be surprised the people I know around here, Matthew. You don't know me long enough to know *why* I've survived here in this jungle. Oh ho ho *ho!* I'm an in-fighter. Now, let's try it again, Matt. Let's try that question again. Matt's the engineer down there who louses up the show. If you want to know who cuts us off all the time before we get to the end of our "Here he is...!"
>
> Now I'm going to ask Matt again. Matt—would you say that life is lived to the fullest—Oh, you wouldn't, heh? Well, I can see Matt's not going to get very far in this business—is he—[laughs] by George! Well, we'll be here from five minutes past—*We* will be down there, Matt. I don't know whether you will be, son, but—you'd be surprised—we've got a lot of openings out at the transmitter. And you know you spend your time all the time out at the transmitter fistfighting and making coffee. And—that just fits your personality, Matt.[98]

Shepherd two minutes later, talking about working at the transmitter on hot summer nights as he had done in his early days at WOR:

> My eyeballs were sweating. Your eyeballs sweat?—You wipe your eyeballs. And I'm sitting in there and I'm trying to be funny—and I'm being—you know, I'm being *me*, you know. I'm saying "Hi, gang, wow, whoopee!" And in the other room, just looking at me, glaring at me was this great stone-faced, angry, snaggle-toothed, stainless steel, psycho-edged engineer.
>
> Who'd been with the transmitter for a hundred and forty years and the only thing that warmed the cockles of his blood was the sound of an overloaded relay—popping out! And he hated all radio programs. And he would sit there and go, "Baa *yeah* bad*waaa* waaa*wa*."
>
> And he was always reading obscure Croatian newspapers, holding them up in my face to show he didn't care. Then he

would turn his back to me. And we would sit out there hour after hour, and I'd say, "Yeah, gang, this is WOR, ha ha ha ha, the *family* station, RKO General."

"Yeah baya*waaa*," in the sweat, the fantastic *hate* that grew out there!"[99]

BARRY FARBER

Broadcaster Barry Farber, one of Shepherd's few friends at WOR, considers Shepherd only in the most positive terms— genius, mentor, and friend, a man whose only weakness seemed to be an inability to compromise his strong will and ego to get further in the business. Farber seems immune to (or maybe unaware of) the various times Shepherd on the air made somewhat belittling remarks about him, as he did about everyone at the station. Maybe everyone thought Shepherd was "just joking." But then on at least one other occasion, as Farber was walking by during a Shepherd broadcast (June 21, 1968), Shepherd called out, "Hi, Barry—one of the *great* guys in this business, I'll tell you!"

LEIGH BROWN

Leigh Brown worked with Jean Shepherd as an assistant and eventually as his executive producer on many projects.[100] Born in 1939, eighteen years younger than he, she was a former professional horseback rider, according to the flyleaf of the novel she eventually published on the subject. She had been married from January 1958 until 1964, and had a daughter.[101]

> **Herb Saltzman:** She was a person who tags along. She was part of a willing—in today's terms, she would have been called a groupie, and looked like one. She was blond—dyed hair, short, kind of cute, and she was available to him and she was a gofer. Got him coffee, things on the air [until she became his producer]... She bought into the myth [that he was a genius].

Leigh as a gofer is a view of the early relationship between her and Jean, but she became much more, professionally and personally. Fred Barzyk, who has some of the earliest remembrances of Jean and Leigh together, beginning in 1961 when they came to

Boston to do a series of TV pieces for WGBH says, "This was the
first time I met Leigh Brown—in those days. She came up with
him. Obviously working with Jean. Obviously there was some
kind of a relationship going on." The business and personal relationship between Leigh Brown and Jean Shepherd was a complex
and important one—not as a matter of gossip, but because her
role also affected his creative life. She did not remain a gofer for
long. One might listen to many of Shepherd's radio broadcasts
and know much of his other creative works, but except for the
frequent, though easily overlooked, credit lines she got, one
could easily fail to realize her importance. She was his assistant,
constant companion, sounding board and creative associate, enabler, and emotional co-dependent.

As Shepherd's assistant, Leigh Brown, as Max Schmid put it,
"was his producer and just about everything else to him
including agent, from almost the moment they met until she
died. Leigh is an unheard presence on the show from around
1963 until the end of the run in 1977, making sure the kazoo was
on hand, fielding phone calls, shooing studio visitors, watching
the clock, taking notes (rating each show with a star system),
logging commercials, etc. Shep used Leigh and the engineer as his
audience when he was on the air."

Leigh was occasionally heard on air for a word or two, when
Shepherd so requested. A discussion about snakes and Ireland
prompted this on-air chat: Leigh: "All the snakes came to New
York to become policemen." Shepherd: "Oh really? I'm sure the
PBA would appreciate that crack." Another time, in the context
of Leigh being an animal lover, Shepherd had her say on air
"Awwwwww!" (in the tone appropriate for "How cute!")

Starting from sometime in the early to mid 1960s, Leigh and
Jean were "constant companions." (This was only understood
by a few who were close to them, and for good reason, because
to the best of our knowledge he was still married to Lois
Nettleton, although they may have indeed reached a parting of
the ways by then.) Shepherd apparently confirmed this one night
during his beginning theme music—speaking mock-dramatically
à la the opening of the old radio program, *The Shadow*, he
referred to himself as Lamont Cranston:

> Cranston's friend and constant companion, and continual
> producer, the lovely Leigh Brown, is the only person who
> knows to whom the voice of the mysterious Shepherd
> belongs.[102]

Because "constant companion" is a journalistic euphemism for "a person with whom you are seen publicly and regularly copulate extramaritally," as *The Faber Dictionary of Euphemisms* puts it, Shepherd may have been playing with the always unspoken but often wondered about sexual relationship between adventure heroes and the women associated with them in the pantheon of kid radio, TV, and movies—such as between Superman and Lois Lane, Roy Rogers and Dale Evans, and The Shadow and Margo Lane, who, in two opening sequences of *The Shadow*, was described as his "constant friend and aide" and "friend and companion."

Of course, as Shepherd's assistant, producer, and at some point editor and business associate, Leigh must have been with him frequently (constantly), and Shepherd might have been using the phrase in the strictly literal sense. Yet it is not likely that he was ignorant of the common euphemism, and referring to Leigh thusly seemed to imply the sexual context. What did he mean by this? Was he gloating publicly with an insiders' reference, expecting that his listeners wouldn't get it—the ambiguous commentary and veiled self-revelation hanging in the airwaves momentarily and passing into the ether—ungraspable—except on tape where it can be pondered indefinitely and without resolution? Had he inadvertently slipped further into personal truth than he intended? Shepherd usually went to extremes to hide personal information. For example, some of his close friends, though knowing both him and Lois Nettleton, were for some time unaware of his marriage to her.

We cannot know for sure what Shepherd meant, but we can be assured through evidence and commentaries that "Little Leigh," as he sometimes referred to her on the air, was a constant and most important companion, crucial to Shepherd in life and in art.

In Shepherd's art, Leigh served as his creative associate as well as a sounding board. Sometimes one could not tell if he was talking on the air to his engineer or to Leigh. Often he would ask a question, and when no one in the studio knew the answer, he would say, "Why do I know all this stuff?" Sometimes it seemed that he was asking Leigh, and if she did not know the piece of trivia out of the past (by the mid-1960s, Shepherd had been accumulating information for over forty years, but Leigh was only in her mid-twenties), he seemed to disparage her lack of knowledge, and on at least one occasion he excused himself for the apparent criticism by saying that to gauge the average person's general knowledge, "I use her as a litmus paper."

In a WNET television special in the late 1960s, Shepherd said
he wrote late at night, after his radio show, and used Leigh as a
sounding board to get reactions from an intelligent reader. A
later photo shows him standing, talking, while Leigh sits nearby,
writing it all down.[103] Fred Barzyk comments, "She had decided
that he was a genius, and it was under her tutelage that the man-
uscript for his first book was actually done. He'd had it in a
drawer—he couldn't sell it." Barzyk is referring to Shepherd's *In
God We Trust: All Others Pay Cash*. "He didn't have the time or
the patience to really do it. She was the kind of person who was
the editor who kept after him to get it done and to make it work.
So Leigh was responsible."

Barzyk emphasizes how important Leigh was to Shepherd's
being able to create: "Leigh was the tenacious one who tried to
keep it organized—tried to keep the space around him clear so
he could continue to do his thing... She always tried to clean it
up—clean up the act. She could rein him in. She was sort of his
enabler." Leigh kept it all together, kept him focused and protected from distractions, both personal and professional—the
keeper of the flame and the gatekeeper. In later years, various
people found her mediating between him and the outside world.

In addition to Leigh's importance for enabling and protecting
Jean, the two of them were tied together with emotional
bonds—not all of them positive. Despite all that Leigh did for
him, Jean was often unpleasant toward her:

> **Fred Barzyk:** He would say good things about her.
> The only thing that really bothered him was if she
> started taking center stage. If she got more highlights
> than he did—then he'd jump on her real fast. We were
> doing a show on the West [for *Jean Shepherd's America*]
> and Shepherd and I went, and Olivia Tappan, who was
> my associate producer, and Leigh, went in another car
> and they went in one direction, we went in another
> direction [to find good locations for shooting]. And we
> came back... So Shepherd told all the great things we
> saw. And it was Leigh's turn to talk about all the things
> that they saw. And he wouldn't let her get through three
> minutes—without jumping all over her to the point she
> was in tears. What she did was unimportant. And I say
> that with a *meanness!*

Shepherd was occasionally negative toward Leigh on-air. In

the first transcription, as a practical matter, he could not be telling his engineer to leave his post, so it would appear that he was speaking to Leigh Brown:

> Hey, you're really looking bugged tonight. I mean, what's the matter? Why don't you step out in the hall and let me continue the show and you can be mad outside.[104]

In one broadcast, Shepherd said that Leigh should get an award for whining, and on another show, he got her to whine in the context of saying that he hated whiners:

> Would you please whine for us Leigh?...[From the control room one can hear her whining.] Oh, that is sickening. I hate to hear a chick whine. For God's sake... I can't stand it. I hate whiners! [He describes what he says is a frequent situation in the office] And she goes — [one hears Leigh again from the control room whining] Oh! Nice little things go up and down my neck.[105]

By the early 1970s, Shepherd referred more frequently to Leigh in his on-air asides. Although his marriage to Lois Nettleton had ended, the years during which he was still married and Leigh was his "constant companion" must have been stressful for her, a situation possibly related to his 1971 book dedication for *Wanda Hickey's Night of Golden Memories—and Other Disasters*, maybe his first public acknowledgment of their relationship: "To little Leigh with love. I hope it's been worth it all..."

Fred Barzyk, as Shepherd's producer and director of so much of his television work in the 1960s through 1980s, has the strongest comments yet encountered regarding Jean and Leigh's emotional and psychological states. He discusses the period in the early 1960s when Jean married Lois Nettleton, although Leigh was already on the scene:

> **Fred Barzyk:** Here are two damaged people. I mean really dysfunctional people. Shepherd had married Lois Nettleton in the middle of this thing and again, with his vision of what his life was going to be—and that didn't last long once she started getting any kind of publicity— he had to be number one.
>
> The whirlwind swirled around him tighter and

tighter. And Leigh just kept hanging in, kept hanging in, kept hanging in. Being dumped on [as a] second-class citizen to the point where Leigh was told by Jean she had to give up her daughter—he didn't want that daughter. And she did.

Some contrary evidence makes the situation regarding Leigh's daughter unclear. Shepherd, at his 1970 Overseas Press Club conference, promoting *Jean Shepherd's America*, introduced Leigh to the audience, with compliments on her art of choosing the show's music, then introduced Leigh's daughter to the audience: "And this is her daughter, Elizabeth. Elizabeth, put your hand up. There's Liz." Laurie Squire remembers that from 1975 on, during her maximum time with Jean and Leigh. "I know that there was a lot of contact and Leigh was very proud of her."

The context for the following excerpt from the broadcast of September 27, 1972, was whether he had done a particular commercial, and is spoken with irony dripping with saccharine:

> Wait a minute, we want to get this straight from the producer here. Yes, little Leigh. Of *course* I did. Of *course* I did. I talked about J. and J. Miles [a sponsor]. Well, being on the phone is no excuse. I mean, for heaven's sake. Take the potatoes out of your ears, honey. Make like a listener—listen... [a few minutes later, as the end theme music plays, he asks what Walt Disney's Pluto Pup's name was changed to] Now I'm asking you *real* questions about our culture, and you sit in there with that dumb look on your face. Hey, you know, I know it's natural, but you shouldn't use it here. You're making everybody unhappy. I hate to see a grown producer cry.[106]

That Shepherd had truly insulted Leigh on the air, to the ears of tens of thousands of listeners, to the extent that she cried, is evidence of his mercurial attitude toward the woman he depended on and loved. Shepherd was sometimes cruel, yet sometimes kind to Leigh personally and professionally. In the broadcast from the day after his 1973 Carnegie Hall show, he gives the strongest of compliments regarding her ability:

> Now I'm going to credit where credit is due. I want you to listen carefully—all the lighting, many of the bits that were done in the show—including visual bits, the stuff that was done in the dark during the show—we did a lot of things

during the dark—we would cut all the lights and use lights and so on—up on the ceiling and so on—these were the work of a very creative person I never talk much about, and that's Leigh Brown. Leigh created the show... A really good producer— Leigh is really a *director*/producer. Yes. So she created the set... And it was beautifully done and I want to congratulate Leigh for this—publicly—for a change. And it was just a *great* job.[107]

At least from sometime in the early 1970s, Leigh and Jean began publicly expressing the care they felt toward each other. The dedication in Leigh's 1975 novel about horseback riding, *The Show Gypsies*, reads: "For Jean Shepherd... this fool's rainbow." On March 2, 1977, a month before his last WOR radio broadcast, Jean and Leigh married,[108] and would remain so until her death in 1998. Many who knew them assumed they had been formally married years before. The dedication in Shepherd's 1981 book, *A Fistful of Fig Newtons*, provides a touching image of a close family unit of three—including Daphne, their dog, who appeared in several of Shepherd's television and movie productions: "To Leigh and Daphne—Who share my bed, my board, and walks along the sea. May they never regret it."

Laurie Squire, Shepherd's radio producer from spring 1976 through his last WOR broadcast in April 1977, while Leigh dealt mainly with Shepherd's many nonradio projects, has insight into Jean and Leigh, based on both professional relationship and friendship. It may well be that by the time Laurie Squire met them in 1975, Jean had accepted Leigh's importance in his life and work and they had settled into a relationship in which Leigh could better hold her own:

> A very bright woman. Very short-tempered. Feisty... [Jean and Leigh] used to fight like cats and dogs.
> She always wanted to go beyond radio. She functioned primarily as the manager [of nonradio work]. She was a very, very smart lady. Very sharp. Interesting relationship. Very hot temper. An interesting combination because she could be—I have seen him meek in front of her. Meek is not the word I would use in front of Jean. He could be very quiet, more subdued.
> I think he liked to give the impression of being patronizing to women. Look at how much he really

invested everything of his life, of his work—into *Leigh*. So I think a chunk of it was all for *effect*. He liked to come across as the macho man in a sense. I found it a compliment that he referred to Leigh as "Little Leigh" and on occasion he referred me as "Little Laurie." Now normally a woman would hear that—"How could you stand that?" And from him it was an endearment. They were a very devoted couple... They were each other's staunchest fans.

[Laurie was asked if Leigh acted subservient toward Jean—which was the impression of some who knew them] She knew how to *play* her role, so maybe that's what they saw. I wouldn't call her subservient in any way. If that was the image that had to be portrayed—fine. I guess she did a good job at it... She was a very major person—and she knew how to handle his person-ality. And she knew how to handle Jean and his talent... She was a perfect match for him... They were very much equals.

They were Jean Shepherd. She sublimated, but she had a *very*—I can't emphasize enough—she had a very strong personality. And I think he admired that... Quite a temper. She could hold her own! The power behind the throne. He was the creative genius. She knew how to operate in the real world.

A year after she died, he died. I don't think he could live much without her.

Several people who knew Jean and Leigh have similar com-ments to make. Murphy Grimes, a long-time friend of Shep-herd's says, "She knew what buttons to push. She played him like a violin."

Jean Shepherd's relationship with Leigh Brown is the most prominent example of his wildly contradictory nature. Listeners nearly always perceived the Shepherd persona as the highly civ-ilized, literate, and caring, leader of the pack. The reality is that he could be a loving pussycat or a nasty son of a bitch—the enigma that places Shepherd in the same pantheon as all the rest of our Og-and-Charlie, flesh-and-blood heroes.

Within his isolated studioland world, Shepherd did know there were the others out there—the listeners he appreciated though sometimes found annoying, the engineer with the control button, and Leigh Brown, who formed such an essential emotional and professional bond with him. But there were others beyond his studio walls who had the power of professional life and death over him. He was not in total control, and for Jean Shepherd, that certainly meant trouble in whatever activity he engaged in. In his radio career, there was also the matter of the big bad bosses. They were the radio station administrators and the sponsors—those who made him push the "Money Button."

CHAPTER 15

THE MONEY BUTTON
Making Dough

One of the most significant signs here in New York is the sign
that flashes M-O-N-Y off and on—M-O-N-Y. You know that
I was in New York for over three months before I realized that
that wasn't a misspelling? [Laughs.] I had no idea what this
meant, and I just thought, well, it's New York, you know. I
used to walk up and down Broadway at two o'clock in the
morning and that thing would go M-O-N-Y. I said, "Why
doesn't somebody get that thing *fixed*? This is beginning to
bug me." MONY. MONY it would just flash and it would go
M-O-N-Y. [Said fast.] M-O-N-Y. M-O-N-Y. M-O-N-Y. [Fast.]
Underneath, it would say, 3, 1, 4—Unk! 3, 1, 5 M-O-N-Y, and
then there would be a little yellow pole or something that'd go
sha-sha-sha-sha-*cloc*, and there'd be a green star at the top—
drrrrrr—*cloc*, M-O-N-Y, and I'm walking along Broadway
trying to figure out—why weren't they getting that thing fixed.
Everybody's seeing it all over town! This misspelling! This is
awful! [Laughs.] Ah, you know—either you look at it, or you
don't. I find that most people don't. And those who don't
figure that those who do are a little bit out of their minds. [In
little old lady voice.] "What is this young man *speaking*
about?"[109]

We all need money, whether we like what we have to do to get it or not. Shepherd was in New York, where the money and prestige of radio was, but he was never happy about his relationship with those who paid him the dough. He showed his disdain for those who held the purse strings: WOR and his sponsors.

Shepherd did not seem averse to making money, and as a unique talent, he certainly deserved it, but he "had standards," and would not change his style or hide it from view. Barry Farber says, "All Shep had to do was, once in a while, play one commercial the way it was supposed to be done, or just once, smile at a WOR executive when he passed him in the hallway, and he would have been on his way to super recognition."[110] Farber says that Shepherd was the same off the air as on. In February 1964, Shepherd commented on the difference between being true to oneself and faking it when faced with the money people during a job interview:

> For example, if you're given a question that says, "What would you rather do—go to church, go to a ballgame, read a book, watch television—or go to the Playboy Club?"
> Which one are you supposed to answer if you're going to be a healthy individual of our time? Right! You hit it! You'd make a—that's right [laughs]—then you'd bring your little key with you. Yet if you really answered it truthfully, you're going to be put down as a nut—generally. Really. Especially if you write down "read a book"—oh, yes—that's a sick, introspective, non-crowd-oriented individual. Who will be a lot of trouble in sales meetings. [Laughs.]

Commenting on the "Advertising News" from the *New York Times*, he says, "The real news about how we're doing comes out of this one":

> A guy named Robert Alden writes this one. I do not know Mr. Alden except that he writes some awfully funny stuff. I don't know whether he knows he's being funny or whether he's just funny because advertising almost by definition is funny[ix] because it plays upon the hopes and fears and the giant calliope of man's inability to cope.[111]

The "Sweetheart Soap" incident of 1956, involved Shepherd's being considered not commercial—he told listeners to buy the soap, was fired, was sponsored by Sweetheart and rehired. After this brouhaha, he began attracting more sponsors. Many of them were products and services that he used and enjoyed, and he gave personal anecdotes and heart-felt recommendations. Listeners rushed out to buy a product because their friend and confidant had convinced them that it was superior. Decades later, some fans still remember Shepherd's sponsors fondly, quoting ads and singing the jingles like "Sooner or later, you'll own Generals." (General Tire often ran ads—they were part of RKO General, owner of WOR.) Some early sponsors who received the deluxe treatment included the *Village Voice* (he wrote for them), Paperbook Gallery, Marboro Bookstores, Art Students' League, Ying and Yang Chinese Restaurant, Prexi Restaurants, Marlboro cigarettes, Worth Perfume, Triumph TR3 sports cars (he drove one), Goggomobile (he drove one), Vespa scooters (he drove one), Rover cars (he drove one), Peugeot cars (he drove one), Lufthansa Airlines (he rode them), the Record Hunter, and the Electronic Workshop.

Just two examples of the close bond between Shepherd, his sponsors, and his listeners are the following. Bob Alden, who sold advertising time for WOR remembers, "I was there [at the Electronic Workshop] one day after Jean had done a commercial, and there was a steady parade of people coming in to buy what he was talking about." Another sponsor, the Record Hunter store on Fifth Avenue just above 42nd Street, Manhattan, kept a "Shep record bin" with LPs of music he played on his shows.

Shepherd was often quite derogatory and funny doing his commercials. Although sometimes he read the commercial straight, at other times he sang or played one of his instruments over a recorded spot. Maybe his way with commercials was the only method that kept his listeners' interest. He frequently had fun with Miller Beer, either with his own words, or by musically accompanying the jingle. Frequently he preceded recorded commercials with the command "Hit the money button!" or "Hit the whoopee button!"

> Hit the button! The escape button, please! [On comes a Miller Beer jingle, Shepherd's voice over] Have you ever been rained out at a cookout? Next time it happens to you, just bring the party indoors. Fill their glasses with Miller High Life Beer. Get 'em bagged. That party will swing from there on out. It won't make any difference if it rains or if it pours out there, or if fistfights break out in the bedroom—as long as you have enough Miller High Life, the Champagne of Bottle Beer on

tap—that party is going to go all the way. So don't worry about
the weather. Just be sure you have plenty of Miller High Life on
hand. In cans or in crystal clear bottles.[112]

Hey! Speaking of singing, do you have my favorite beer
commercial ready there? Big Herb? Hit it, hit it there! [Jingle
starts.] All right, let's go gang, before we get seriously involved.
Yeah. Hey, listen, friends, it's the weekend coming up, and that
is—a very serious time if you believe in beer and that means
you don't want to be caught like about the middle of this
weekend without any suds on hand. And if you're gonna lay in
a real trough full of genuine, vibrant suds, we can only recommend one—Miller High Life, the Champagne of Bottle Beers.
Miller, man. If you're gonna tie one on this weekend, tie it on
in style. Miller High Life. Do *do* beep *ou* [scats to continuing
jingle] on the go, you know. Miller High Life Beer. Once again,
it's the Champagne of Bottle Beer.

You can get it in the magnificent champagne golden can—
which makes a nice clink when it hits the sidewalk... And while
we still got you quivering out there, we've got another little ding-
dong for you—real quick. [Here comes another commercial.][113]

Asked by Alan Colmes in December 1998 about getting in
trouble with his sponsors, Shepherd claimed, "No, I never got in
trouble. In fact, that's why guys came on my show—to get that. In
fact one time I did a—I did a straight commercial for Miller High
Life and one day I got a call from the agency and they said,
'What's the matter, don't you like us? You're not having fun with
our commercials.' They wanted that." Herb Saltzman remembers
putting the Miller beer commercials on the air for Shepherd. He
said, "They understood what he was about. They were midwest-
erners, and when he met with them, he told them what he would
do for them—and he did it. I won't say he was single-handedly responsible for the introduction of Miller High Life in New York,
but he played a role."

Some sponsors seemed to like the fun, as Shepherd remembered it in 1998, and it appeared true of the Miller commercials,
but in a program from late 1965, several times during the same
program, he was considerably more acerbic:

Speaking of bringing it back into perspective, there is
nothing brings us back into clearer, cleaner perspective in this
world, than a good blast of commerciality. Believe me, I
learned long ago—when you are living in the land of Caesar,

you render—by George—unto Caesar what is Caesar's. Ya pay the piper. And so now, get ready to pay the piper for 120 seconds. Caesar is just around the corner. Here he comes with the message, by George!...

Speaking of idlers here, we have the—commercial people around—hanging around by the coffee bar there, ready to leap in and make a couple of bucks—and so, we will give them 120 seconds of their due. Stand by, friends—hang onto the handlebars, and hope for the best. Keep your knees loose. We'll be back in two minutes. The longest two minutes in radio. [Laughs.]...

Shepherd had to stop that one, boy! He was gettin' scared because if they ever backed him away from his radio show— what would *he* have left? So to prevent that terrible exigency happening, let us give the commercial people their due—for the next 120 seconds—let's waste time by listening to the natures, the beauties, and the glories of getting out and spending that cash. Right, friend? Next two minutes belong to Caesar.[114]

What did Shepherd have to stop? One wonders what happened to spook Shepherd into thinking he was in trouble! Later on the same program, talking about how people in the early days of radio thought the electronic waves in the air were like magic, he said:

People were beginning to say—all these words that were in the air were beginning to be—were rotting their brain. Well, little did they realize that they were actually speaking the truth. But in those days they—[laughs]. And speaking of brain rotters, let's give them a couple of commercials here. We'll be back in 120 seconds after this *fun* moment here.[115]

So in the beginning, Shepherd nearly lost his job for being noncommercial—but the more commercials he got, the more they annoyed him (especially as they were crammed into the short, forty-five-minute format). They were contrary to his sensibilities and they broke up the extended form of his style, even as early as the mid-1960s. In one program, with Shepherd in the middle of a story, people in the control room obviously frantically signaled to him to break for commercials. In mid-sentence Shepherd interrupted himself:

You want another one in there? Is that your problem? Another one, everybody? Everyone's all worried in there 'cause, you know, it's very hard to tell a story when everyone's worried about problems. So, I will make now a break, and then we will finish the story. Okay? [There is a break for commercials.]

You know it's like being up on the stage doing *Hamlet* and everybody can hardly wait to get to the men's room. You just cannot say, "To be or not to be." Actually, it comes out, "To *go* or not to go." That's the technique. You just gotta realize that—when you're being an audience, you either gotta be an audience, or you better be a nation of gentlemen's rooms go-er to-ers. There's no in-between.[116]

Speaking of the realities—you got a couple of those other little plum puddings in there? Oh yes, we've got a whole raft of them. So get a hold of your handle bars out there, friends. This is commercial time.[117]

After that introduction, Shepherd proceeded to read seven commercials in a row. Max Schmid reports that, in one forty-five-minute program in 1977, there were over fifteen minutes of commercials.

Has it occurred to you that the sponsor is the barnacle of the radio world? Just a thought. [Laughs.] I mean, clinging to the ship. [Laughs.] And occasionally dragging it down. And occasionally *becoming* the ship.[118]

Herb Squire remembers that the commercial time salesmen never really tried to sell time on Shepherd's show "because they couldn't get good rates. Basically, [John] Gambling made the station. Jean was never promoted [to sponsors]." Bob Alden, who started in 1955 shortly before Shepherd arrived, comments that he liked Shepherd and his work, but that other salesman not only did not understand what Shepherd was doing, but disliked the fact that he poked fun at the sponsors.

Although Shepherd continued to give enthusiastic, personal pitches for the products he liked, by the mid-1970s commercials tended to overwhelm his extemporaneous flow. Most of the clutter came from sponsors not linked to his show but to what Laurie Squire called "run of station spots," which WOR could insert in the schedule wherever it wanted—big, institutional, anonymous commercials jammed into his show, irrespective of the interest of either the sponsors or Shepherd.

> **Laurie Squire:** Radio at that point [1976–1977] started turning into big business radio. The salesmen did not understand the show. They rarely tried to sell the show, because they didn't understand it. For the most part Jean hated salesmen, primarily because they didn't understand what he was doing. Bob Alden was the exception…
>
> Whether the show was on tape or live we would stop the taping and literally go through all the commercials in one fell swoop. Obviously radio stations prefer that you break up your commercials—maybe three minutes here, then do show content, then do another three minutes. No—Jean would stop where he felt comfortable, and we literally would go through something like eighteen minutes of commercials. Just run the commercials straight through [one after the other].

Although commercials interrupted his style on his own broadcasts, Shepherd did quite a few recorded radio and television commercials heard on other programs, and occasionally on his own. On a broadcast from circa 1965, he introduced a recorded commercial playfully, an ad for the movie *The Face of Fu Manchu*, done by Shepherd in his typical, comically dramatic style (appropriate since he often read Fu Manchu stories on his show). Another sponsor was the *New York Times*, the recording starting with an announcer, "And now, here is Jean Shepherd," followed by Shepherd's recorded plug. *Car and Driver* editor Bob Brown comments, "Every third commercial that you heard was Shepherd. Because he had such a comforting, yet authoritative voice." A *New York Times* article of September 22, 1972: "Asked about his sudden new popularity with the world of commerce, he responded in Jean Shepherd-style with, 'sheer talent.'"

SPEAKING OF WOR

When Jean Shepherd arrived in New York in 1955, WOR Radio was, as an announcer preceding a Shepherd broadcast said, "the talk of New York." A promotional booklet years later put it: "The bond between WOR's audience and the WOR personalities who broadcast from their homes, such as the McCanns, the Fitzgeralds [Ed and Pegeen]… and Dorothy Kilgallen and husband Dick Kollmar, would last to the present day."[119] Others among the family of talkers were Martha Deane (a name used by three different women on WOR over the years), and three generations of John Gamblings.

> **Herb Saltzman:** OR was a family station. It's the greatest family station *ever*. [The people there were like a family], they were your friends. And that's why, for legions of women—a lot of women—growing up in New York—OR was their friend... We treated the audience—here's the key to it—like they were not twelve-year-old average mentality. We appealed to their intellect, to their intelligence, and maintained that... [Shepherd was considered an outsider.] He liked being that. Liked being outside the norm.

Though WOR was Shepherd's radio "home" from 1955 to 1977, he never seemed to feel part of the group. On the fortieth anniversary of WOR, in 1962, he commented that several well-known regulars on the station, including himself, did not feel they were part of the family. The next year, referring to countries and radio stations that were really quite different—if not the opposite—from the image they projected, Shepherd said:

> Now we refer to ourselves as "the family station." [Pause.] Forget it. I know this outfit—very well. *Forget it!* We just won't go any further than that! Just—just forget it! "The family" *in a pig's ear!* I almost said something else.

Of course, "family station" might have referred to the audience's perception, not necessarily to the WOR employees' feelings. Barry Farber, one of the regulars, comments that because various WOR talk show personalities had been around for so many years before Shepherd arrived, Shepherd indeed *was* considered an outsider—and because of the unusual nature of his broadcasts, he was considered a maverick. Shepherd the maverick sang over his opening theme one night:

> Oh, they're ever so humble, there's no place—like a family station. Be it ever so crummy, there's no place like home—with our single button carbon mike and our bad pre-amplifiers, with our lousy leaky studio, there's no place like home. Oh, WOR, we love you, even though you hate us—all the way down to the ground. WOR, we are masochists and that's why we love you.

Bring it up! All together, gang—yes sir, that's my baby, no sir, don't mean maybe, yes sir, that's my baby now. Oh by the way, oh by the way. [Kazoo.] Yes sir, that's my baby, no sir...[120]

[Again over his opening theme] I'd better give a disclaimer here very quickly before we get too deeply involved. Before you get sucked in—again. As you probably are aware, you've been sucked in many times in your life [laughs], by *George!* You're not alone, I'll tell you that. How do you think I wound up working *here?* [Laughs.] Doing *this!* Ohhh! That's another story. A sordid *rotten* story we don't even want to go into.[121]

On many broadcasts, he derided the station by blending the station identification into the subject he had just been discussing: [x]

Have you ever felt that in the vast punctuation system of life, you were but a small hyphen between two important words? Speaking of hyphens, this is WOR AM and FM New York, and we'll be here until—uh—you know.

Speaking of windows, this is WOR—as transparent as a sheet of glass, we are here to make dough. This is WOR AM and FM in New York, and I'll be here until one o'clock.

[Talking about Chicago gangsters who sold "insurance" to clothes-cleaning establishments to protect them from total destruction.] Speaking of being taken to the—this is WOR AM and FM New York.

Speaking of a hurting conscience, this is WOR AM and FM New York, and we'll be here until one o'clock in the morning.

Speaking of bad radio, this is WOR AM and FM New York.

Speaking of turkeys, this is WOR. [Said during his Thanksgiving broadcasts of several years.]

[On a live broadcast, Limelight show.] Speaking of dead elephants, that reminds me. What radio station is this? Come on, *hit it!* [Audience screams "WOR."] AM and FM, New York. The elephants' graveyard! *Ahhhhh!*

[After reading a Robert W. Service poem about saying good-bye to the old year] Speaking of wrinkled, seared faces, this is WOR. And we're in New York, of course.

Speaking of the frightening, this is WOR AM and FM in New York.

Speaking of slob art, this is WOR, friends, in New York.

Speaking of sickness, this is WOR AM and FM in New York.

Speaking of evil ideas, this is WOR, New York.

Speaking of intimations of disaster, this is WOR AM and FM in New York.

What a cacophony, gallimaufry, which reminds me, this is WOR AM and FM, New York. Silly, *idiotic* radio station!

Speaking of death, this is WOR AM and FM, New York.

Speaking of trouble, this is WOR. Holy smokes! [Single blast from his kazoo.] This is WOR AM and FM in New York. Wouldn't you like to have a station signature that's really angry? You know they have—they always have these pleasant little ones—you know [sings] "WOR, your friendly station."

You know that kind. You hear these singing station breaks all over. [Sings in jazzy, scatty way.] Who oh dada *da* da *da* dada *da* wawawa*waw*—your station for news bada*dawawa*. [Followed by kazoo sound.] I'd like to have a station signature—I'd love it just once if some station had a sense of humor about it. WOR.

Shepherd once commented that WOR could be spelled a different way by adding letters, not exactly saying but suggesting W[H]OR[E]. Beyond the mid-1960s, Shepherd became less openly sardonic and hostile toward WOR and his sponsors. His attitude never became friendly, but tended to settle for neutrality or less intense grumbling. The problems never went away, however, and the warfare never evolved to a truce—witness this comment after discussing famous monsters:

> And we want to salute all those monsters past and present.
> Including the present program directorship here at WOR.[122]

Showing the extent to which Shepherd was willing to express his hostility on the air, in a program devoted to describing "slob Christmas gifts" for sale, including cigarette lighters in the shape of bowling pins and pipes in the shape of privies, he interrupts himself:

> I don't know what's the matter with these earphones. Wait a minute. I'm going to try to fix them in there. I wonder if— yeah. I wonder if, Jerry, you can dart in and see whether they'll exchange this pair for another pair. Just run in there and ask somebody in there if he's got a pair of cans. And I'll plug this pair—the new ones—into this thing and get rid of these.
> [After a few minutes.] No, no, no, no, no, no. That's all they've got? Okay, forget it. Tell 'em that I'll buy 'em some earphones—poor little station here. That little dinky can he comes in and gives me, for God's sakes. That thing comes off a crystal set. [Laughs.] That's the $2.95 special that they make up in Japan and sell in plastic bags. [Laughs.] Ah, jingle bells, jingle bells—oh, this place. It gets worse all the time. Look, before we go any further, can I do a couple of commercials here, for real things here? Let's see.
> They don't have any others? Would you please say, "Shepherd says, 'You *must* be attempting a joke.'" Go ahead, you do it. That's an order. [After a commercial and more slob gifts.] Tell him I'm used to second-rate equipment but when it gets down to fifteenth- and twentieth-rate equipment, I draw the line.[123]

In "WOR Radio: 1922–1982, the First Sixty Years," several of the WOR dynasties such as the McCanns and the Gamblings got one or even more double-page spreads; some got a full page; Henry Morgan got half a page. Possibly indicating the extent to which feelings of disrespect were mutual, Jean Shepherd's photo shared a spread with several others, including Barry Farber, Joe Franklin, and Bob and Ray. Buried in paragraphs on other subjects: a one-sentence description of Shepherd and a half-sentence mention in passing.

Engineer Herb Squire says that until Herb Saltzman arrived, the WOR management was isolated from the day-to-day operations. Regarding Shepherd's comment during a broadcast that the WOR management didn't even know he had a show on the air, Squire reacted, "*That* is entirely possible!" Saltzman comments, "He knew I dug him. He knew that. And so he would come into my office as an oasis—a hideout where he could speak his mind—cry a little bit. He was a whiner. Definite whiner."

Saltzman further says that Shepherd and the previous general manager (who had fired Shepherd in 1956 and whom Shepherd hated) later became friends—Saltzman modified this to indicate that this was consistent with Shepherd's conflicted desire only to associate with the upper ranks. TV director/producer, Fred Barzyk has a similar observation, commenting that during a shoot, Shepherd did not want to sit with the crew—only with the producer. When it came to power and rank, it would appear that Shepherd did not want to chow down with the enlisted men, but preferred the prestige of the officers' mess.

Considering Shepherd's unending need to achieve the elusive professional and popular respect he deserved—to have his ego stroked—makes his associating with the upper ranks understandable. However, one might have expected him to be above such shallow matters, because, regarding his artistic concerns, his proper place, as he knew, was among the under-appreciated and the unsung.

Shepherd did receive recognition among his peers and among his fervent band of East Coast listeners, and with this circumscribed renown came the equally circumscribed rewards of prestige and money. Despite having a money button to push, the radio button was not enough for Jean Shepherd—not enough people in town and in the rest of the country knew about him. He had other ambitions. Ones linked artistically and financially to other media. Early in his New York career, and continuing over decades, for him this included the importance of "The Written Word."

PART VI

REFINEMENTS AND CONVERSIONS

Shepherd wrote extensively and continued radio in his special, increasingly formalized way until the medium, which had never had the prestige he sought, and which increasingly retreated under the onslaught of television, could no longer contain his ambition. During his radio work, and more extensively afterward, he created unique television and movies.

CHAPTER 16

MY NOVEL
The Written Word

Radio is ephemeral compared to books, magazines, even the daily newspaper. The words—they go into the air and disappear. Radio is unimportant; it is the medium of the masses to which intellectuals give no respect, and that fact was not lost on Shepherd. Written words are important—they are fixed, they are the form we remember and respect. We remember great thinkers from what they wrote. Even the spoken words of Aristotle, Socrates, and Plato we know because their words were eventually written down—we read them. On March 15, 1959, discussing his early reading experiences, Shepherd commented, "I found that *reading* and the excitement of an idea was to me the most *exquisite* of all excitements—*exquisite* of all excitements and the most difficult to explain to other people. Just the pure, bare, abstract idea!"

Among written words, books were the most important—the most official. Written words spread knowledge of one's activities more widely than oral forms. In addition, they increased one's income—both by themselves and if the rights were sold to TV or Hollywood. As Shepherd said, he was a storyteller, and "writing was a natural outgrowth of what I do." The subject matter he chose to write about, whether in fiction or nonfiction, was not arbitrary—he wrote about his constant themes and lifelong interests. What follows are descriptions of, and comments on, the books he wrote and his contributions to other publications.

I, LIBERTINE (1956)

The hoax that became a book began as an idea Shepherd articulated late one night in 1956.[1] He had complained about the assumption that lists—such as bestseller lists—were somehow reliable guides to the real world. He and his listeners invented and promoted the imaginary book, hoodwinking a surprisingly large number of "day people." More details can be found in Chapter 6. It is unclear to what extent Shepherd authored what was eventually written and published as a paperback, with a limited-run hardcover edition (The practice then as now: without some hardcover publication, there was little chance of getting reviews). Frederick R. Ewing was the fictitious author named on the cover. Theodore Sturgeon is usually named as the actual author. Betty Ballantine, the wife of publisher Ian Ballantine, relates that Sturgeon, rushing toward a deadline, did all but the last chapter—which she wrote to finish it off by the deadline, after Sturgeon fell asleep at his desk. She says that the entire book was written in about three weeks, and she credits Shepherd with a rough outline for it.[2]

The book is a farce about eighteenth-century London court life, the cover text whimsically exclaiming, "Turbulent! Turgid! Tempestuous! 'Gadzooks!' quoth I, 'but here's a saucy bawd!'" The cover art by *Mad* magazine artist Kelly Freas gave the informed reader a tip-off as to the nature of the enterprise. There's the leering roué in the ruffled shirt and cuffs, the blond with the outrageously immodest décolletage. The visible portion of the crest on the coach's ornate golden door in the illustration showed enough of the clue word, [EXC]ELSIOR.

The last portion of the afterword, supposedly written by Frederick R. Ewing talking about himself in the third person, reads:

> Mr. Theodore Sturgeon assisted nobly with the research, Mr. Jean Shepherd pushed and *pushed* at the author until he was, in the world of books, born; and last mentioned but first of all, the Night People whose battle cry is Excelsior, and whose humor and forbearance are really responsible for the work.

The "About the Book" paragraph on the back cover ends, "Greeted with unprecedented acclaim by the English press, *I, Libertine* is a novel which American readers will no doubt agree is destined to leave its mark in English letters."

Within three months of Shepherd's having perpetrated the on-air hoax, the book was contracted for, written, and published. In the *New York Times Book Review* of Sunday, September 16, 1956, David Dempsey knew the joke and wrote, "The book was coauthored by the team of Shepherd and Sturgeon." *I, Libertine* was a Shepherd idea, inspired by his themes of creeping meatballism, literary phonies, and bestseller lists. Within three months of publication, according to a magazine article titled, "The Rebellion of the Night People," it had sold "over 200,000 copies (mostly paperback)."[3]

THE AMERICA OF GEORGE ADE, 1866–1944 (1960)

Jean Shepherd edited this book and wrote the sixteen pages of the preface and introduction—an obvious labor of love.[4] The back cover says, "One of the most prominent of young American social critics and commentators, Mr. Shepherd has made a special study of the life and works of George Ade." The introduction deals with Jean Shepherd's important "roots"— short-form storytelling and humorous commentary on America. Further description and commentary are in Chapter 4.

THE VILLAGE VOICE READER (1962)

Several of Shepherd's articles were reprinted in this *Reader*.[5] He began writing articles for the *Village Voice* in 1956, soon after it started publishing. He said that the *Voice* was the first thing he wrote for. The first article, dated May 9, 1956, was about hi-fi. For a while, he wrote almost weekly. In August's "Quo Vadis?" he referred to "the wild events of the past two or three weeks, including *I, Libertine* and 'Sweetheart Soap' and the wrath of the Gods," that is, the hoopla over his commercial viability on the radio. In September's "Jazz It Up, Charlie," he suggested that, just as radio and TV programs got ratings, in the future, individuals would have ratings also. In October, he wrote a typical Shepherd short story—about his Uncle Carl. In the issue of November 14, 1956, Shepherd said his philosophy of living was based on comic strip ideologies, a subject he had had fun with over the years.

THE NIGHT PEOPLE'S GUIDE TO NEW YORK (1965)

Shepherd wrote only the introduction to this book.[6] It was a hymn to the great cities such as New York—none of which, he wrote, could be totally known, despite guidebooks such as this. Here he reiterates one of his overarching themes—the only way to really know something is through direct experience. As he puts it, "I hope this modest volume will prove to be helpful, but it is not the key. You'll have to find that yourself, and if you do, you'll be the first one who ever has."

IN GOD WE TRUST: ALL OTHERS PAY CASH (1966)

In God We Trust: All Others Pay Cash is the most important book Shepherd produced;[7] it continues to sell well in trade paperback. Here at last was his opportunity to express himself in a permanent and especially prestigious form—the published book—the first book that he had written from beginning to end. In addition, it contained some of his most popular stories. Shepherd modified some of his kid stories told on the radio, publishing twenty-three of them in *Playboy*, starting in June 1964. Some of the earlier ones became the core of *In God We Trust: All Others Pay Cash*. *Playboy* founder and publisher Hugh Hefner, who comments that Shepherd's stories were very popular with *Playboy* readers, recalls how Shepherd began writing for the magazine:

> **Hugh Hefner:** I was aware of his work and popularity on radio through friends who lived in the New York area. Most specifically, Shel Silverstein... Shel kept talking about various other talent that he thought belonged in the magazine. He kept talking about Jean, and what he had been doing was telling Jean to write— to put his material down on paper for *Playboy*. And Jean, to the best of my knowledge, had never written before. And he was reluctant to do it. What Shel actually did was sit down with a tape recorder and got him to *tell* some of his anecdotal stories as he did on the air. And then, in combination, edited that material, and that's what began Jean Shepherd's writing career.

> **Barry Farber:** [On Shepherd writing for *Playboy*.] He really loved that, and he could develop his themes, like the Red Ryder BB gun... He liked me because I could see

the allegory. He would question me like a professor: "What's the meaning of this?" "Well, Jean, this is like the eternal war between the younger and the older." And he liked that... He was very big on recurring themes.

Shepherd's first stories for *Playboy* were described in the magazine as "nostalgia" and "memoir" (probably to Shepherd's dismay), and the later ones were more accurately described as "humor." Hefner recalls that in the early years of *Playboy*, unlike other magazines, it used contemporary art for illustrations, and thus the reader might not at first know what kind of piece he was about to read, so the editor would choose a descriptive tag such as "nostalgia."

Why nostalgia? In the first place, Shepherd rejected the notion that he wrote nostalgia. In addition, given *Playboy*'s reputation as a girlie magazine obsessed with sex and a fancy lifestyle, it seems an odd category to choose. Shepherd's work for it never dealt with those themes but always remained consistent with his focus on childhood and the army. With respect to nostalgia, Hefner makes the following comment on a little-recognized characteristic of the magazine:

> **Hugh Hefner:** *Playboy* has *always* been a magazine steeped in nostalgia—in things romantic. Even in the very beginning, in the very first issue we did a piece on the Dorsey Brothers. We did a story on Red Grange... Retro, in a romantic sense, was a part of what *Playboy* was and has always been all about. So nostalgia is pretty much related to my own sensibilities. I think that my life has been a kind of a boy's dream.

Shepherd's stories of childhood and a boy's dream! A Shepherd-*Playboy* connection becomes clear. Of course, *Playboy* was always a highly respected venue for a writer's short fiction, but as short stories do not have sufficient importance in many people's minds, Shepherd put *In God We Trust: All Others Pay Cash* together and promoted it as his novel. His great pride in this is evident in the following:

> I did something today that you don't do very often in your life. I delivered to my publisher—I delivered to him the completed, edited, done manuscript of a novel that I have been working on for over three years, Skip [his engineer]. Handed it

in. And you have no idea what a fantastic feeling that is! And I mean a *novel*. I mean a *novel*-novel!

...There must be a hundred million guys in this country now, who say, "Boy, oh boy, if I could only get a—if I could only just get out of this damn rat race! If I could just get out of this damn ra—" Give me a little echo chamber. [Shepherd with echo.] "Oh, if I could just get out of this rat race rat race rat race. Ahhhhhh! *Rat race!* Aaaaaa! *Waaaaaaa!* Waaaaaaoh! [Echo ends.]

"If I could just get out of this rat race I'd write that novel. Boy! Boy oh boy! I'd put it! Don't think there ain't a book in me! I'd put it down! I'd turn this town upside down. They're scared of me. That's why they keep me tied to this—that's why they keep me—*aaaaaa!—Rat race haaaaa!* Yeah, they're scared of me. If they ever let me loose. If I hadn't run into this crummy chick and had seventeen thousand kids. If I hadn't bought myself forty-five Cadillacs and this crummy joint with the breezeway. Why the hell did I have to buy a *mountain?* Just because her mother likes mountains! *Aaaaa!* Ahaaaaarat race! Yayayayayayayayayaaa! *Aaaaaa!* When I write that novel! I even got the title. I got the title! *My Soul Is on Fire, Oh You Rotten Society, You.* Boy! Ah. Yeah, I'd start it out—I know just what I'd say. Let's see—uh—I know just what I'd say. I thought of it the other day. Damn it! Let's see—uh. I'd say, uh—I'd—I'd—I'd start out—say—uh—uh—uh—*All right!* I'll be right out! For crying out loud! *Rat race aaaa!*

"Boy, someday I'll spit out the whole damn thing—all of it. [Pompous music starts. Shepherd in pompous voice.] Then—I will stride over the landscape! An artist! I will take giant strides, devouring life! Ever upward! Ever onward! And never once will I look back and say, 'Yaaaaaaa!' No! Eugene Gant marches again!" [Laughs.] That's very good!

And I will not continue this fiasco, even if it is Friday night—unless one guy who's struggling to write a book or who always claimed that he's gonna write a book—will just call up—one guy! Just one guy. He's gotta give me the password—one guy! Gotta give me the password—and all I want him to say is "*Ya done it! Wow!* Wow! Ya really *done* it!" That's all...

Come on! I want to hear that guy!... All right now, I want you to say, "Shep, ya done it!"

"Shep, you done it!" [said the caller.]

Yeah! He did what?

"You wrote a book!"

Yeah! Wow! *I wrote a book!* Let's hear some more music!
Come on, let's bring it on quick! [Pompous music.] And once
again, man triumphs over his basic slothfulness. Man once
again triumphs over that innate urge to be a total slob. And just
lay around and drink beer and pick his teeth. Man has once
again done it—has built another pyramid! [Laughs.][8]

Shepherd referred to this book as "my novel." The full-page
ad by Doubleday referred to it as "Jean Shepherd's novel." It is
not a novel, any more than those literary classics *The Canter-
bury Tales* and *The Decameron* are novels. The short linking
chapters of Ralph the writer as adult returning to his home
town, to a bar—the traditional locale where tales are told—
talking to Flick, are obviously there to give the feeling of continuity, but the book as a whole is a series of short stories that
does not develop, either in theme or in character.

Ross Wetzsteon, who reviewed the book for the *Village Voice*
on December 29, 1966, began his long critique, "Relax, gang,
this isn't a novel after all. Or at least not a Novel novel... It's just
old Shep...telling a series of loosely related stories, each close to
forty-five minutes long, about childhood back in northern
Indiana." The "forty-five minutes long" comment obviously
implied that these were Shepherd radio stories, as per his forty-
five-minute-long broadcasts. Wetzsteon, obviously a big
Shepherd fan, lamented the fact that now Shepherd was telling
us, "After all these years convincing us that these people really
lived, that these things really happened, now he says he made it
up? He's just an entertainer?"

Wetzsteon, like many of Shepherd's listeners, seemed dis-
turbed to be told the truth. "Why get upset about it? Just
because he's too successful? But the privacy of our response to his
stories (which he's also spent years convincing us of) makes his
stories seem like both confessions and dialogues—in both of
which honesty is more or less assumed."

Wetzsteon also complained of Shepherd's cynicism, saying
that his particular form of nostalgia and his cynicism, "allow
him to 'see through' (or to not 'see through') without any real
commitment." The review continued with the complaint that
Jean Shepherd was extraordinary, but that he could have been,
and should have been, even greater.

The *Voice* review implied that the stories might be mere transcriptions of his broadcasts. Shepherd, discussing *In God We*

Trust: All Others Pay Cash on Long John Nebel's radio show
with fellow guests Bob Kotchner and Sanford Teller (January
1968), talks about this charge. A guest asks if Shepherd taped or
wrote out the stories. Shepherd responds, "Have you ever seen a
tape transcribed? Well come on now." Regarding a comment
about how true his written stories seem to the oral storytelling
tradition, Shepherd says, "Well you see, that's something that
I've always aimed at in writing, is to get—I feel that writing is a
substitute for speech—no matter how you write, you're really
substituting for a man talking to you. It's taken me a long time
actually—professional writing—ten to twelve years to attempt
to get the same feel—as a man literally—well—actually talking
to you. So a lot of people reading this: 'Well, you must have
taped that.' This is the last thing you can do."

Shepherd gave considerable thought to this relationship
between presenting stories orally and writing them down. In the
Realist interview of 1960, he said, "I feel that writing is a substitute *for* the voice, that *all* writing is; that writing came about
when it became evident that a guy could not talk to somebody
four hundred yards away, or five miles away, so he scratched out
things that stood for his real speech; that speech is the original
form of communication, and that writing is a secondary substitute for it." We see here how highly Jean Shepherd regarded his
primary medium—voice on radio.

Two examples—from the story about the Red Ryder BB gun,
and from the story about Ludlow Kissel on the Fourth of July—
show the rich, descriptive nature of Jean Shepherd's writing:

> Scattered out over the icy waste around us could be
> seen other tiny befurred jots of wind-driven humanity.
> All painfully toiling toward the Warren G. Harding
> School, miles away over the tundra, waddling under the
> weight of frost-covered clothing like tiny frozen bowling
> balls with feet. An occasional piteous whimper would be
> heard faintly, but lost instantly in the sigh of the eternal
> wind.

> The Fourth in question dawned hot and junglelike,
> with an overhang of black, lacy storm clouds. In fact, a
> few warm immense drops sprinkled down through the
> dawn haze. I know, because I was up and ready for
> action. Few kids slept late on the Fourth. Even as the
> stars were disappearing and the sun was edging over the

Lake, the first Cherry Bombs cracked the stillness and the first old ladies dialed the police. Carbide cannons which had gathered dust in basements for a year roared out, greeting the dawn. And by 7 AM the first dozen pairs of eyebrows were blackened and singed, and already the wounded were being buttered with Unguentine and sent back into the fray.[9]

In an exchange during the Alan Colmes 1998 interview, Shepherd talked about the special character of this book:

> Shep: Every good performer should sound like he is—like it's real. I've always worried about comics that get up and do material—"The other night I was riding on a train going to New Rochelle." And you know that it's material, and you know he didn't do it—he's just giving you material. Well, I always felt that what made a good performer—I was an actor. I'm an actor, you know. And I want my stuff to sound *real*. And so when I tell a story, I tell it in the first person, so it sounds like—by the way, that's the best way to tell a good story, in the first person—that it sounds like it actually happened to me. It didn't.
>
> It's a story I invented but I put it in first person so it would sound like—you know—a narrative, the guy telling the story. And, when I did this stuff people took me literally. They thought these things happened to me.
>
> A.C.: I always did to this day and today you're destroying a myth.
>
> Shep: Now, well, it didn't. I'm a fiction writer. I'm not sitting there doing a biography or an autobiography. Those are all *stories*... I invented those kids—they don't exist... There were no kids like that. I didn't know any kids with those names. I invented those kids.

According to the book's disclaimer, "The characters, places, and events described herein are entirely fictional, and any resemblance to individuals living or dead is purely coincidental, accidental, or the result of faulty imagination." Shepherd, often pushed into a corner over the years about the reality of his stories, insisted it was all fiction. However, conclusive evidence that kids with some of those names *did* exist in Jean Shepherd's childhood life is easily found in such sources as his high school yearbook.[i] He went to extremes to deny this reality in order to refute the idea that, rather than being a creative artist, he was *merely* remembering. He was a victim of his own success in creating the illusion of truth.

This book of fiction continues to captivate countless readers—in paperback, it has gone through dozens of printings.[ii]

THINK SMALL (1967)

This promotional hardcover booklet[10] for the Volkswagen Beetle includes art and words by numerous people.[iii] Shepherd's article—the longest in the book—titled "My Dream Car," an anecdote about wanting to buy an old car from a used car lot when he was a teenager, has nothing to do with Volkswagen. Here again we have Shepherd just doing what he wanted to do and turning his back on the commercial interest at hand.

JOHNSON SMITH & COMPANY (1970)

For this reprint, Shepherd wrote an appreciation of all the strange, goofy stuff offered by the original novelty catalogue in an essay titled "Mail Order America."[11] The products fascinated him, and the patrons ("Only in America") were chock-full of slobism:

> Johnson Smith & Co. is and was as totally American as apple pie; far more so in fact, since they do make apple pie most places in the civilized world. Only America could have produced Johnson Smith. There is nothing else in the world like it. Johnson Smith is to Man's darker side what Sears Roebuck represents to the clean-limbed, soil-tilling righteous side. It is a rich compost heap of exploding cigars, celluloid teeth, anarchist "stink" bombs ("more fun than a Limburger cheese"). The Johnson Smith catalog is a magnificent, smudgy thumbprint of a totally lusty, vibrant, alive, crude post-frontier society, a society that was, and in some ways still remains, an exotic mixture of moralistic piety and violent, primitive humor.

As Shepherd described it, the catalog was full of books of "lustful righteousness," of corny jokes, of get-rich-quick schemes. Also for sale were practical jokes of the "itching powder" variety, parlor tricks, and "its pages are jammed full of appeals to every human vice and fear. Cupidity, nobility, lust, piety—all are given equal space, and significantly there is never a sense of embarrassment or shame anywhere. Violence is taken for granted in almost every form of activity." Shepherd ended his nine-page essay by reminding us Americans what we are:

> Today this catalog is just a very funny coffee-table curiosity, because we are still too close to the life and times it describes. In two hundred years it will be a truly significant historical and social document. It might well be the Rosetta stone of American culture. Students of the future, in deciphering it, will learn far more about us through its pages than through any other single document I know of. Read it, enjoy it, and honor it. It is about us.

WANDA HICKEY'S NIGHT OF GOLDEN MEMORIES— AND OTHER DISASTERS (1971)

Wanda Hickey's Night of Golden Memories—And Other Disasters was originally published a chapter at a time in *Playboy* from 1966 to 1970.[12] It is a series of short stories that continued the *In God We Trust: All Others Pay Cash* mode of telling about Ralph's childhood and adolescence, but without the inter-chapter connecting links. In some chapters, Shep/Ralph is an adult in his Manhattan apartment, his memory is suddenly jogged, and the story begun: "True enough. In the gathering gloom of my Manhattan apartment, it all came back." As usual, Shepherd stories that seem nostalgic end in disasters, as the book's title makes clear.

The first chapter describes the next-door hillbilly Bumpus family that made life miserable for the Shepherd/Parker family, especially for "the old man." The highly anticipated baked Easter ham is on the Parker kitchen table and the Bumpus dogs invade and carry it off. In another chapter, Ralph's fighting top almost defeats a killer spinning top, the "Murderous Maria," until, at the last moment, "locked in mortal combat," both tops disappear down a sewer, lost forever. The "Ollie Hopnoodle's Haven of Bliss" chapter narrates the disasters of a family vacation.

The "Star-Crossed Romance" chapter undercuts the adolescent fantasy of sexual encounter with recognition of the reality that accompanies the dream—the potential for teenage pregnancy as well as a stunted marriage and a limited life. The temptation is strong: first Shepherd is enticed by unexpectedly delicious Polish cooking. (One might remember the discovery of unfamiliar foods in college-boy Shepherd's first eating of escargots that opened his mind to a world beyond. Here the tempting food lures toward the potential disaster of a closing down of that world.) Second, the sexual allure of Josie: "She wore a dirndl the way a tiger wears its skin. Her narrow waist flared suddenly into broad, sculptured peasant hips. Above a wide dirndl belt, her embroidery-laced puffed-sleeved blouse—stuffed fuller than the cabbage—billowed and rippled like the heavy white clouds that scud over Warsaw in the spring... It isn't often that a kid in the sophomore class has a date with an earth mother." At the dance, first there is fascination: "For some unaccountable reason, I discovered I was a consummate polka dancer." However, as he continued, repulsion arises: "Every third beat, feet rose and fell like great balls of concrete... I bounced and sweated, Josie clinging and hopping, ducking and bobbing as one born to the beat. As we danced she seemed to grow progressively more alien and foreign." By the end, Ralph escapes.

When he dates a rich girl in the next chapter, sexual desire encounters a different kind of barrier, as he realizes the unbridgeable gulf between himself on one side, wealth and beauty on the other.

Shepherd's mother provides the appropriate symbolism for the following chapter, as well as the whole book, when she sends him a box of old keepsakes from his childhood. He remembers fondly, but when his doorman sees him with some of the trappings of nostalgia, his pleasure is undercut by embarrassment: "Pouring myself a neat brandy, I began to straighten up the joint, ruffling through the still-untapped drift of effluvia that remained in the box. What further horrors lay here entombed? What as-yet-unrealized embarrassments?" Again, Shepherd has it both ways—his adult self waxes nostalgic over his kid paraphernalia (and the reader participates nostalgically), while at the same time he can once again disparage the fantasy of lost youth—then "I dragged my childhood to the hall closet."

The book's title chapter is devoted to the greatest event in adolescent life—the junior prom, in which our hero hasn't the nerve to invite the dream girl he wants to take, and invites the plain Wanda Hickey instead. Several disasters culminate in a nightclub where, after too much booze, Ralph and two friends vomit into the men's room toilets: "For long minutes the three of us lay there limp and quivering, smelling to high heaven, too weak to get up. It was the absolute high point of the junior prom; the rest was anticlimax." Shepherd, with mordant glee, has throttled the golden glow of our nostalgia—again.

The book is full of Shepherd's rich, comic nouns and verbs, and their attendant picturesque adjectives and adverbs. Many people must be enjoying this book, as the paperback long ago passed its twenty-first printing.[iv]

THE FERRARI IN THE BEDROOM (1972)

The Ferrari in the Bedroom[13] collects many of Shepherd's articles from *Playboy* and other sources, including the title piece from *Car and Driver* magazine. Nine of the twenty-one pieces had either already appeared or would appear in *Car and Driver*, so there is some car orientation to the book. The Johnson Smith catalog's introductory essay is reprinted here, titled "The Rosetta Stone of American Culture." This book could be described as a collection of comments, lampoons, and gripes.

The introduction, a reprinted article from *PS Magazine* of 1966, begins, "For the past eight or nine years (I have no idea under what circumstance I began) I have accumulated around me an enormous flowing collection of published Straws in the Wind. Almost from the beginning I fell into the habit of calling this ramshackle and growing mountain of crumpled, torn, dog-eared bits of paper my Vast File of Dynamic Trivia."

In the chapter "Lifetime Guarantee," Shepherd uses one of his favorite phrases, which he said he heard on the *Vic and Sade* radio program: *in hoc agricola conc.* The piece is about people who find that when life isn't perfect, it must be somebody's fault, because they thought they had a guarantee: "You will note that line at the very beginning of the Constitution which guarantees you the right to *pursue* happiness. Nowhere is it even implied that you will ever catch up with that particular electric rabbit, or even glimpse it in the distance amid a cloud of dust."

Shepherd said that he enjoyed drawing very much, and each chapter of this book has one of his line drawings.[v] The entire book seems mostly a way for Shepherd to put between hard covers a number of his lesser interests—the humor of his best stories is missing, but various Shepherd themes are in evidence and the reader can still chuckle at some funny stuff.[vi]

AMERICAN SNAPSHOTS (1977)

This book[14] features an introduction by Jean Shepherd, showing again the continuity of ideas and affinities he followed throughout his varied work:

> Don't let this book, this definitive collection of twentieth-century American folk art, get out of your hands. I say this for two very good reasons. First, it is a touching, true, Common Man history of all of us who grew and lived in America in this century, in addition to being very funny and highly informative. Second, it is a collection that will grow in value, both historically and intrinsically, with each passing year...
>
> Perhaps because of his very artlessness, and his very numbers, this nameless picture-taker may in the end be the truest and most valuable recorder of our times. He never edits; he never editorializes: he just snaps away and sends the film off to be developed, all the while innocently freezing forever the plain people of his time in all their lumpishness, their humanity, and their universality.

THE PHANTOM OF THE OPEN HEARTH (1978)

This is the script, with photos taken from the TV production,[15] based on several Jean Shepherd short stories from *In God We Trust* and *Wanda Hickey*.[vii] The video is discussed in Chapter 18.

Shepherd, in his revealing, detailed, twelve-page introduction to the book, describes the creative and production processes. He comments that one's illusion of the reality in written words is different from the illusion of reality in television and film, and that he "tried to combine the techniques of all three media" in the television production. His attitude toward his characters makes an interesting general artistic philosophy: "I can't speak for other writers, but in my own work I prefer never to editorialize on my characters, nor do I have my characters deliver sermons on the meaning of life; how sensitive they are, how all men must learn to love one another, etc., etc., which seems mandatory in what most critics call 'the serious film.'"

Contrasting his humor to that of the "one-line insult joke" style of some other television productions, he says that his humor "arises out of inflection, a character's attitude, the predicament he's in, and the constant struggle to remain afloat in a sea of petty disasters."

Shepherd discusses the technique of his narrative voice, a device used so effectively by others years later in the television sitcom, *The Wonder Years* (1988–1993): "The Narrator is actually the voice of Ralph, grown up, but at the same time he is somehow mysteriously in communication with the viewer. The viewer then becomes the second half of a dialogue between the Narrator and himself. The Narrator is both viewing the scene as it occurred or as he lived it and commenting to you about it, but never directly." Shepherd's claim of "theft" of this narrative device by *The Wonder Years* program is discussed further in the final chapter of this book as an example of one cause for his deep bitterness toward the world he had never been able to conquer to his satisfaction.

A FISTFUL OF FIG NEWTONS (1981)

This book is truly a miscellany,[16] and as with many of Shepherd's projects, he used a linking device between sections, this time consisting of his random musings while trying to get through a clogged Lincoln Tunnel heading from Manhattan to New Jersey. Short pre-chapters in italics lead into each chapter's subject or sometimes comment on the previous one.

The book combines a variety of Shepherd's subjects in a way that no other book of his does. The stories are not in chronological order, and concern college days, kid days, army days, and going back home after discharge from the army.

The stories are interspersed with musings and gripes—on New Jersey, on the "van culture" (youth-hippie comments), an article about "lemons," "crocks," and "baloney" for a car magazine for which his agent berates him for "biting the hand that feeds him." (Of course, the car magazine did not publish it, but one gets to read it here.) One chapter repeats the Johnson Smith novelty catalogue introduction previously reprinted in *The Ferrari in the Bedroom*, getting as much mileage as possible out of one essay. In a chapter referring to Marcel Proust, he compares Proust's cork-lined room with the enclosed solitude of the car he muses in while in a tunnel traffic jam.

In the final chapter, discharged from the army, he has that disastrous date with a minister's daughter, surprised by her taking him to a sleazy club she frequents. She gets drunk and throws up—so much for the sweet innocence of home one might have expected after saying goodbye to the miseries of army life. Then the italic section quotes W.C. Fields: "Judas Priest, what a gallimaufry" as an appropriate coda—a book with a last chapter that ends with the minister's daughter throwing up in a honky-tonk bar is not promoting nostalgia.

THE NEW JERSEY RESTAURANT GUIDE (1989)

A copy of this book has yet to be discovered.[17] Considering his usual attitude toward the Garden State, who knows what sort of introductory matter Shepherd may have written about New Jersey restaurants.

A CHRISTMAS STORY (2003)

The original stories that were the basis for Shepherd's 1983 movie, *A Christmas Story*, were republished as a tie-in to the twentieth anniversary of the movie.[18] Well aware of the material's perennial appeal, the book's press release states: "Gathered together in one hilarious volume, the humorous gems that the legendary Jean Shepherd drew upon to create the classic Yuletide film," while the flyleaf refers to "nostalgic Americana." The stories earlier appeared in Shepherd's *In God We Trust: All Others Pay Cash* and *Wanda Hickey's Night of Golden Memories—and Other Disasters*.

CAR AND DRIVER

Shepherd wrote monthly columns for *Car and Driver* between 1971 and 1976. The magazine's editor, Bob Brown, comments, "Jean wasn't exactly precise about deadlines." When Brown would call about an article that was due, he recalls, "Essentially he would start writing the columns while we were on the phone." As in many of his writings, Shepherd's tone was often less humorous than cuttingly harsh. He found some aspect related to cars that he could use to bring forth a favorite gripe— sometimes it was a news article, or a trip he took that inspired his lampoon instincts. He seemed to have had considerable freedom to write as he liked—some articles had little or nothing to do with cars or driving, and some are strongly critical of the auto industry and American car culture—the hands that fed *Car and Driver*. Brown notes that they were a good match; *Car and Driver* often took the same disparaging attitude, and the magazine "allowed [Shep] to do whatever he wanted, as long as there were wheels in it someplace. It was well received."

In one piece, Shepherd discussed an Iowa man who died and left twenty-three antique cars on his farm. He comments that the cars have this in common: "Each one was a stupefying Nothing of its day." Of the man's criteria: "Neither the superb nor the ridiculous, but the unobtrusively mediocre speaketh for the men of the time."

"The Ferrari in the Bedroom" article that became a book title is about a double-page, full-color photo ad for a bed in the shape of a blood-red Ferrari roadster: "I was looking at a true masterwork of Slob Art, fully worthy to stand beside the concrete Mexicans, the Seven Dwarf lawn sprinklers, and the Praying Hands day-glo reading lamp in the pantheon of true Slob Art."

Another article suggests, "The twentieth-century avant-garde is your average walking-around klutz. For centuries, it was the intellectual or the elegant society person who set trends. But no longer... Now the trendsetter," Shepherd writes, is "*Slobbus Americanus.*"

In a 1976 bicentennial article, "Happy Birthday, United States of the Automobile," the last paragraph says, "So take a good look at the world through your windshield down that great white line to eternity. Because it won't be long before museum-goers will look at the cars and streets in the backgrounds of circa 1976 Robert Redford films and think us as exotic as we do the scenes of 1876 Philadelphia or Williamsburg in 1776."

LOTS OF MISCELLANEOUS STUFF

Shepherd wrote stories and articles for many periodicals; as is common practice, many were reprinted in his books, which consist primarily of gathered (and sometimes reworked) material. Reprints of Shepherd's writings are still being discovered.

He began a series of articles on jazz for *Audio Magazine* in 1956, and wrote for *73*, an amateur radio-enthusiast magazine. For the March/April 1957 *Mad* magazine, his "The Night People vs. Creeping Meatballism" appeared, illustrated by *Mad* artist Wally Wood.

For *Playboy*, in addition to his twenty-three stories—he received their award for best humor and satire writing for four of them—he did one article about New York City and his interview with The Beatles, which appeared in February 1965. Shepherd: "I'm fortunate in that I work so hard at editing my work that I have never yet had a piece appear in *Playboy*—and I've had maybe fifteen pieces so far in *Playboy*, short stories—and I've never had one piece that the editors edited."

He appeared several times in the underground satirical magazine, th*e Realist*. At the other end of the spectrum, his humor piece, "When Schwartz Wiggled His Ears, *That* Was History," was published in the December 1981 issue of a periodical he earlier ridiculed, *TV Guide*. Sure enough, the story took a swipe at TV sitcoms. Shepherd's short stories and articles retained much of the special spoken quality of his broadcast tales in style and content.

His introductions for books such as *The America of George Ade, American Snapshots*, and the *Johnson Smith Catalogue* gave him the opportunity to articulate attitudes familiar from his broadcasts. His broadcast commentaries on our foibles and travesties, no matter how forcefully expressed, usually retained the humorist's enthusiastic joy in life despite human inadequacies and inanities. But when he wrote short nonfiction pieces for periodicals, usually making fun of some activity he disliked, the tone was loaded with sarcasm and griping, often festering at the level of the burlesques and lampoons found in the sophomoric *Mad* magazine.

This is not true for what he may have considered much more important work. In the 1970s, Shepherd wrote some occasional pieces for the *New York Times*. These nonfiction articles do not carry the heavy-handedness familiar in much of his occasional written commentaries. Possibly because of the august nature of the publication, for the *Times* he wrote with a more sophisticated sense of irony. Besides, rather than focusing on a subject he disliked, these were features about the sports he loved. Of course, he used the opportunities to pursue his usual themes.

Discussing the Indianapolis 500, which takes place each year not far from Shepherd's boyhood home in northern Indiana, two articles (May 25 and 26, 1974) reflect his lifelong interest in cars. One, titled "In Indiana, the Roar of the Motor Is Sweetest Sound," refers to his themes of the enthusiasms of ordinary people and the urge to flee the Midwest, and he comments that "the automobile means much more to the common people of the great plains of the heartland than it does to the city folk who huddle jammed together in the great urban East. It meant, and still means, freedom, mobility and, above all, a way out for lives that are often as monotonous as the landscape they are lived in."

In his article titled "If Catfish Is Worth So Much, What Would Ted Williams Get?" (January 19, 1975), Shepherd comments on the high-finance, team-hopping world of Major League Baseball stars. He discusses the television coverage of star Jim "Catfish" Hunter and writes, "There's one thing they'd better remember, though, about mercenaries. The British at Trenton found it out with their Hessians. High pay does not necessarily mean good play, especially when things are going bad, the ammunition is low, and the shades of night are gathering."

An article on the National Horse Show in New York's Madison Square Garden may have been inspired by Leigh Brown's passion for horseback riding. He reports on the rich attendees and the elegance of the women and the horses. He notes that the mustard that adorns a rich man's hotdog is the same sort that at the previous night's sporting event had topped those of the "red-faced yahoos."

His stance is that of the observer, with deep knowledge of the subject at hand, using his educated and perceptive eye for sharing the easily overlooked significant details. As his radio listeners knew, Shepherd loved to show off his broad expertise, and as Hemingway did, he delighted in instructing lesser mortals with his entertaining insights.

OTHER PEOPLE'S STUFF

Although he once disparaged doing "other people's stuff" instead of his own, he distinguished between the near-total freedom and creativity he had on the radio and the constraints of being an actor speaking other people's written words. (Early in his New York career he did some acting, but it was in addition to his radio work.)

For his listeners he enjoyed reading bizarre advertisements and news items that fell under the category of "trivia," "creeping meatballism," and "only in America." He read the Sunday funnies during a newspaper strike. He described cartoons he had seen. In addition, he sometimes read a bit of other people's stuff—stuff that amused him. On his pre-Christmas show of December 22, 1972, in one of his "silly moods," he sang *Pogo* comic strip creator Walt Kelly's takeoff, "Deck us all

with Boston Charlie, Walla Walla, Wash., an' Kalamazoo!"[19] He
often read the stories of George Ade and Sax Rohmer's stories of
Dr. Fu Manchu, which he obviously enjoyed for their exaggerated dramatic corn. (He gave them his mock-serious dramatic
renditions.)

He read a variety of poetry, from the funny to the serious.
Most of his interest in poetry appeared limited to the un-subtle,
idea-laden, quirky, and cleverly sardonic. He read some of Don
Marquis' *Archy and Mehitabel* poems. Mehitabel was a freewheeling, devil-may-care alley cat with loose morals. Archy was
a cockroach, her Boswell. Shepherd said he did a program about
them every year or two. He must have responded to Archy's
mordant and witty commentaries on the human condition.
Archy the clever roach banged out his observations letter by
letter on a typewriter, jumping on the keys with the top of his
head (creating poetry and prose, but as far as is known, no head-
thumping music).

Shepherd read "recitations" in his self-consciously, overly
dramatic fashion that perfectly fit the corn. As with the poetry,
he was entertained by the corn—the serious productions full of
platitudes and tears. He both enjoyed and disparaged corn—as
with trivia, slob art, and so much else, he succeeded in having it
both ways. It seems probable that he really enjoyed all the glop.
As he had said about his jew's harp playing, "this is me in
spades!" But that side of him was countered by the more intellectual side that told him he could not simply enjoy it with im-
punity—he had to disparage his predilections. A few of his
favorite readings include "Excelsior!," "Casey at the Bat,"
"The Face on the Barroom Floor," "The Hellbound Train,"
and "The Curfew Shall Not Ring Tonight." After reading the
last he commented, "Oh, that's a magnificent piece of glop, I'll
tell you!"

One of his favorite poets to read was Robert W. Service. In a
1959 broadcast, he commented that Service "had a bitter, cynical humor." Shepherd read Service in the dramatic style he
loved to lavish on this kind of stuff and did an entire record album of the poems in 1975, including such favorites as "The
Shooting of Dan McGrew" and "The Cremation of Sam
McGee." His short introductions to the recorded poems show
his admiration for kindred style and beliefs. For example, "The
best of Service's poetry told stories. He was a storyteller in almost everything he did, and oddly enough, almost every one of
the stories he told in his poems were based on people he knew."

Another introduction to a poem called "Ambition" captured Shepherd's own career aspirations—one wonders how much he identified with this. "[Service] was a confirmed skeptic on the one side of his writing—he really was torn right down the middle—on the other side he was an unabashed romantic. He was many things, but one of the things he really was, was a man who was against all earthly ambitions. He thought that all of Man's striving was ridiculous, even though he strove all his life."

A number of times he read the poem "Evolution" by Kentucky poet Langdon Smith (1858–1908) with its opening line, "When you were a tadpole and I was a fish in the Paleozoic time." The speaker at a fancy restaurant links himself and his love closely to their earlier selves sprawling "through the ooze and slime." One might well remember Shepherd's stories of brutish cavemen Og and Charlie, just risen from the muck and mire—as well as the ooze and slime. As one was intoxicated by the joy and humor in most of Shepherd's work, it was easy to overlook this darker side.

On Christmas Eve, after reading a long railroad poem with extensive railroad sound effects in the background, he ends the program:

> Wow! Only an American could have written that! This is the forerunner to Jack Kerouac! This is the forerunner to *On the Road*. In case you're interested, that was written in 1940. Just before the big war. "Rattling Home for Christmas," by Grant Reynard. "I just can't go home again." Pure American and a yard wide. You can hear echoes of Thomas Wolfe, echoes of Wordsworth, echoes of Edgar Guest, echoes of Jack Kerouac, echoes of protesters everywhere. "I can't go home again!" And you wind up blaming home. Somehow, it failed. Somehow, California didn't make it. Third Street didn't make it. Where do I go now? Merry Christmas.[20]

Shepherd devoted an entire program to reading two poems by T.S. Eliot ("The Hollow Men" and part of "Ash Wednesday"), three by Elizabeth Bishop, and three by Kenneth Patchen. He said how much he liked the poems, and expressed pride in his rendering of them (behind which he played haunting excerpts from the soundtrack of the film, *2001*). He commented that listeners must be surprised at the nature of this broadcast and he expressed pleasure in upsetting expectations—who would have thought that he would enjoy and read this material so different from his normal choices—and do nothing else on the air for forty-five minutes? He reread the first lines of "The Hollow Men":

> We are the hollow men
> We are the stuffed men
> Leaning together
> Headpiece filled with straw. Alas!
> Our dried voices, when
> We whisper together
> Are quiet and meaningless
> As wind in dry grass
> Or rats' feet over broken glass
> In our dry cellar

How about *that* for a station break for WOR in New York?[21]

Shepherd also had a serious interest in the Japanese poetry form haiku:

> After the rainstorm
> three fierce old women
> foraging for firewood.

I love the image of three fierce old women. We have all known fierce old women. [Laughs.] Have you ever wondered whether or not when a person gets very old, whether he or she really remembers the dreams, the things they thought, vaguely, in a shadow form, when they were young, the things that they thought would happen to them in life? Do they remember those things? Or mercifully, is there some kind of a sneaky eraser—built into man—that erases those dreams? Like the bubbles, you know, that "rise high in the sky and then like my dreams, they fade and die..."

Someday I would like to make an LP of really good haiku. And the thing, when you're doing haiku—in case any of you is interested in reading it—it's a very difficult thing. The first thing you have to do is erase yourself. Get your own little, miserable little ego and personality out of the way. Get it out of there! Do not act it! You must experience it. Do you understand what I am saying?[22]

Getting oneself out of the way was strangely divergent from Jean Shepherd's standard method of performing material.

VIBRATING TO NELSON ALGREN
AND HUNG UP ON NORMAN MAILER

Shepherd occasionally talked about contemporary authors such as Jack Kerouac and J.D. Salinger. His comments on Salinger were usually negative—concerning what Shepherd referred to as his I-am-so-sensitive school of writing. One author he did appreciate was fellow Chicagoan Nelson Algren:

> Nelson Algren is probably as close a—a blood brother as far as philosophical outlook on—on the world...as anybody I know in literature. When I say blood brother, I mean *to me*. If there is anyone whom I vibrate to it's probably Algren. And I'm sure that Algren vibrates to my stuff too, which is neither here nor there.[23]

In a program titled "Fake Shepherds," Shepherd, with amusing irony, comments on Norman Mailer, the author with whom he seems most obsessed:

> When people write to me and they say, "Your show lacks moral fiber. It lacks moral fiber and it lacks philosophical bases." Oh, I don't know. I don't know about that. I—I—you know, I—I—I don't know what this—does *Norman Mailer* have more moral fiber? Or has he just got a better press agent—louder, you know? Who knows? He writes good—but that doesn't mean you *think* good. Oh no.[24]

Jean Shepherd began writing for the *Village Voice* in 1956, soon after it was cofounded by Norman Mailer. Shepherd said he and Mailer used to see each other and talk. When Shepherd reached for a contemporary author for comment or comparison, he couldn't seem to avoid mentioning and disparaging Mailer (dozens of times over the years), who had already achieved literary renown, nationwide fame, and financial reward a decade earlier with his novel *The Naked and the Dead*.[25] Mailer continued to publish books and get himself into the media and consciousness of America.

Jean Shepherd and Norman Mailer both engaged in the process of expressing in their art their created personas—their

performing selves. But Shepherd remained confined in his isolated radio studio, restricted by all the limitations of conservative
radio broadcasting, talking to a few-score thousand fans along
the East Coast, while Mailer was free out in the world fistfighting and exploding in all public directions. Seymour Krim, an
author immersed in the New York avant-garde scene starting in
the 1950s and a friend of Mailer's, more openly expressed the
overbearing presence of Mailer than Shepherd seemed able to, in
an extended article originally titled, "Norman Mailer, Get Out
of My Head":

> It is Mailer the Individual who has now sizzled over
> Manhattan in a way that I imagine he always wanted
> (hell! that 95 percent of us would have wanted)... It is
> this essence, my identity in the world as a person, that is
> hurled into a tight knot by all the talk that swirls around
> me concerning Mailer-this and Mailer-that and which
> now triggers every protesting hope of my own
> birthright. If this is an indication of my own insecurity as
> a man, of my own marginal position on the New York
> status scale, of every wound and hangup of my own
> which Mailer now brings to a head because of his
> aggressive ubiquitousness in the literary-sexual-intellec-
> tual-avant-garde Manhattan environment where I must
> live my life, so be it.[26]

Shepherd was unable to make the big breakthrough—considering the number of times he referred to Mailer in negative
terms, one might reasonably wonder if jealousy was to blame.
Already quoted was Shepherd's response to the question of what
influenced him: "If you want to be really pompous—if you ask,
like—if you ask a guy like Mailer..." and another time he commented that Mailer would probably say "the great tragedians."
Shepherd's comment was not so exaggerated—decades later
Mailer wrote, "My mind was shaped at an early age, after all, by
the great Russian novelists."[27]

In his *Car and Driver* article about a man who left antique
cars on his farm, Shepherd said the man "dreamed dreams far
beyond the reach of any character ever invented by Norman
Mailer." Also from *Car and Driver*: "And like most of his
brethren, he has plastered his bumpers with stickers proclaim-
ing his various humanity-loving, poetic philosophies: 'Nader

for President,' 'Mailer for Mayor.' The whole puerile lot." On two consecutive pages in a chapter on role reversal and men's fantasies in *The Ferrari in the Bedroom*, Shepherd took swipes at Mailer. During a program on February 4, 1966, talking about a trip to Pompeii, Shep, speaking in the Italian accent of a tour guide, "And I can tell you they knew how to live in Pompeii. They knew more than Norman Mailer could even dream of in his best days." And, talking about the human comedy on March 23, 1965, Shepherd said, "Even you, Norman Mailer, you're part of the human comedy. Even though you take yourself awful seriously—and that's what makes you so *funny*."

Talking about the then recent custom of literary figures embracing boxing, after mentioning James Baldwin and George Plimpton, Shepherd commented:

> Oh, I expect a long, involved poem on Cassius Clay, as the true representative of the free spirit of the noble-hearted man. It'll be written by Norman Mailer, who will be fighting that same fight, and has been fighting that fight for years. So friends, you're a slob, huh? Come on, you know. Be a slob, I mean, eat your hamburgers, you know?—Yell and holler![28]

> We all live in a world—we've all had our own experience with sex—one kind or another. Does it have any relationship at all with the stuff that you generally read about it—in most novels? Of course not. Again, that's part of that fantasy world... In other words, fantasy fiction is really most of what we call serious literature. To me that is true fantasy fiction. Something like Norman Mailer's *American Dream* is fantasy fiction...up in front, some piece of total claptrap—like *The American Dream*—is treated *seriously*. To me this is genuine fantasy fiction.[29]

> **Dan List:** Shepherd had quite a shadow quality about him. How can I say it? When he was there he was there and when he wasn't there he was definitely *not* there. While Mailer was always there, even when he's *not* there. I always tried to strike a balance between the two of them—being *almost*, but not quite there.
>
> Shepherd had a quality—he would disengage himself, and a guy like Mailer wouldn't disengage himself if his life

depended on it... Shepherd had a tendency to fade into the woodwork—when he did whatever he had to do... He had a very diffident quality, and Norman is anything but diffident. I can't think of any more opposed people.

Fred Barzyk: He always said to me that he and Norman Mailer got into fisticuffs. Leigh wouldn't let him talk about it, but he said, "I cut that bastard up."

Norman Mailer, at eighty, about forty-five years after what would have been the circumstances, in an August 2003 correspondence with the author states, "To my recollection, I never met him," later amending to "I do remember Jean Shepherd, but only in the vaguest way." One might have expected some hostile retort about Shepherd, but maybe admitting only to the most vague recollection is the biggest putdown of all.

PATTERNS IN LITERATURE

In 1981, Jean Shepherd was undoubtedly proud to find that his story "Grover Dill and the Tasmanian Devil," from *In God We Trust: All Others Pay Cash*, was in an eighth-grade textbook, *Patterns in Literature*. At the end of the textbook chapter, students could contemplate Shepherd's literary qualities under categories such as Think and Discuss, Vocabulary, Thinking Skills, and Composition. The Shepherd story "Lost at 'C'" was used in a late 1990s literature textbook, *Patterns for a Purpose*. Other Shepherd stories found in anthologies include "Hairy Gertz and the 47 Crappies" in *The Little Book of Fishing*.[30] In this book, Shepherd's story was prestigiously nestled among thirteen contributions by the likes of Ernest Hemingway, Seamus Heaney, and Red Smith.

"HE WAS A REAL GUIDE FOR ME"

Talking about Shepherd's radio work, U.S. Poet Laureate Billy Collins remembers:

He was a real guide for me. One of the minor enlightenments I received from Shepherd was—I was just getting a little interest in poetry then [in Collins' adolescence] and he exposed me to Robert W. Service

for the first time. I didn't know Service. He read "The
Face on the Barroom Floor" and "The Cremation of
Sam McGee." That was a huge door he opened there to
Service. And probably some other poets I'm not
thinking of...

He was a *master* of narrative weaving. The way he
would—now I'm thinking back—the way he would
start a story and digress from it and find his way back
to the story was, I think, almost a model for some of
my poems. I tend to start in one direction and find an
interesting way to digress and then maybe return at the
end.

That was what kept you awake. You know Nelson
Algren—a quote from Algren about advice to novelists.
He said, "Make them cry, make them laugh, but most
of all make them wait." Shepherd would make you *wait*
for the conclusion of the story. He'd start out with a
fishing story about—there'd always be the narrative
thread, but then he'd go off into digressions about
movies and sociology and personalities in the story, and
sidetrack—subplots—but always he'd find his way
back. That was a bit of narrative structural genius, I
think, on his part. When you add that to the whole late
night mystique, then you had a really hypnotic
combination.

NUTTY FRUITCAKE

More than his spoken tales, Shepherd's written stories
abound in metaphor and picturesque modifiers—clusters of
comic nouns, verbs, adjectives, and adverbs. (Consider the Red
Ryder BB gun Christmas story—"waddling under the weight of
frost-covered clothing like tiny frozen bowling balls with
feet"—and the Ludlow Kissel Fourth of July story quoted
above.) Shepherd created a rich sense of a particular experience
with all the details that brought it to life. Even his story and
book titles tickle the imagination more with their whimsically
absurd irrelevancies (more concerned with appealing to the
mind's eye) than with direct descriptions of the material.
Although some of his articles revealed a more hostile side and
were not among his best works, his published writing remains a

permanent record of a fine humorist at work and illustrates his joy in partaking of the tasty "nutty fruitcake of existence."

Jean Shepherd's success with a variety of written-word projects and his involvement in movies and television provided some boost to his ego and bank account, and they probably also contributed causes for his comments that radio had begun to take up too much of his time. The pattern of his forty-five-minute broadcasts became more formalized, and he achieved masterpieces within the format before abandoning radio—see what he did with Mark Twain, and with the death of President Kennedy, in "Who Listens to Radio Anymore?"

CHAPTER 17

WHO LISTENS TO RADIO ANYMORE?
Later New York Radio

Some sense needs to be made of the changes in the nature of Shepherd's broadcasts over the years. Many people believe that he broadcast only on AM and only for forty-five minutes at a time. While it is true that this mode and program length predominated during the period from 1960 to 1977, Shepherd's mature radio work—in forms other than that just described—blossomed much earlier. Nevertheless, most listeners, familiar only with what can be called these later radio days, believe that the controlled and finely tuned style occasioned by that forty-five-minute format defines all of Shepherd's radio work.

The forty-five-minute broadcasts, however, are only part of the story. We know that in the 1950s he broadcast for hours at a time on both AM and on FM. What is important to note is not that one format is necessarily better or preferable to another, but rather that the length of his broadcasts and the time of day contributed to the style of his performance. Chapter 6 earlier in the book addresses his extended, late-night, more extemporaneous style. The few known recordings of this earlier period provide little-known examples of an artist working in uncharted areas of communication, creating his rough-hewn form as the listener listened.

That early period saw his most innovative and truly unique work.[viii] In any field of the arts, a new way of seeing—a new artistic vision—goes through an inevitable process. First comes the creation of a new and vigorous vision. (An example might be the early Renaissance.) The pathfinder breaks through, and it is exciting to be pulled along with him in his newly formed and therefore rough-hewn style—this was the jazzy, more extemporaneous, early Jean Shepherd. Then the innovator and those who follow develop a smoother finish and a more conventionally acceptable form. (The high Renaissance masters.) In the third phase (the Baroque and Rococo), the innovations are merely copied as an exaggerated, slick style with little substance. Shepherd formed his new style in his over-night and late Sunday-night programs, refined the style primarily in response to the forty-five-minute programming most people are familiar with, and never sank to the third level.

For several interconnected reasons, that earlier style changed in the very early 1960s. With the shorter broadcasts at earlier hours and wider audience (including large numbers of students), Shepherd's choice of jazz recordings changed. The early shows included more difficult, more contemporary jazz played for longer stretches, often by performers with whom he associated in the 1950s. By the early 1960s, this deep and important interest in more serious jazz gave way on his programs to the more easily understood and widely popular Dixieland and similar genres, which he often talked over and accompanied on his odd assortment of instruments. He obviously greatly enjoyed these genres—they were goofy, funny, and more entertaining to that segment of his new audience whose appreciation of jazz was less sophisticated.

Tapes of early 1960s broadcasts, with this shorter length, exhibit some—but not as much—of the same extemporaneous style, still laid-back, still full of spur-of-the-moment thoughts based on observations and anecdotes on which he based philosophical comment. But the effect was more condensed. Some later shows obviously exhibit more planning than do the earliest broadcasts. For whatever its goods and ills, the change resulted in a more widely acceptable form.

In 1960 and 1961, he also broadcast Saturdays and Sundays during the middle of the day. With the termination of the Sunday night shows, there would be a period of five months when he was only on Saturdays during the day. Shepherd made at least two comments regarding the time of day of his broadcasts. First when his Saturday morning broadcast was shifted to afternoon, he complained that at the new time, nobody would be listening to radio. Even for those who *would* listen then, Shepherd's style and content mixed with the hustle and bustle of Saturday afternoon the way fine wine mixes with Yoo-hoo. Second and more essential, when he regained the night, he soon commented on its importance to him:

> I can tell you this. That being on at this hour—between 11:45, quarter to 12—that period, from 11:15 to midnight is about as different—I can't describe it except to say that it's a completely different dish of tea! I've been doing for the last three or four years—ever since we left the nighttime, all night show—which was in 1956—I've been doing all sorts of—sorts of *half* daytime, half nighttime things. This is like returning to something that you haven't eaten for a long time but that you vaguely remember that you liked. And suddenly you're having it again, and it tastes even better than you thought it tasted...
>
> The time between 11:15 and midnight for me is about like a tiny drop of something that I'm used to having a glass full or a cup of. But the drop is so much sweeter because it *is* only a drop—that a cup would be too much now. That the drop is very important to me. A kid wrote me a note saying, "Shepherd, you sound since you got on the night show"—he said—back again at night—"you sound like a fish that's been flopping in the sun on a pier, that's been thrown back in the ocean by a kindly old Schraffts lady." Well, there's some truth in that.[31]

After that five-month gap in nighttime broadcasting, Shepherd began his forty-five-minute, late evening weeknight shows in early 1961 that would continue until spring of 1977. With a few time-slot variations, this was by far the form most familiar to most listeners.

An observation by Max Schmid regarding Shepherd's programs during the mid-'60s: "Sometime in 1964, two new elements are introduced. Leigh Brown seems to be in the studio all the time, and the Limelight shows begin. I can only speculate on Leigh's influence at that time, but Shep sounds truly inspired during this period." As we know, Leigh Brown played many roles in Shepherd's life from then on, including secretary, producer, editorial advisor, confidant, and eventually wife.

As the late 1950s had passed and the 1960s progressed, time on-air became less conducive to his earlier style—beyond 1960 the programs were earlier in the day and shorter, more broken up with commercials—the pace of Shepherd's delivery increased,

and the apparent pre-organized (though never scripted) character of his approach became stronger, probably necessarily so.
The longer broadcasts could afford less apparent order late at
night when the world moved to a cooler rhythm. Slow and free-
floating fitted neither the midday Saturday nor the short, forty-
five-minute format at night. One might also wonder whether
stream of consciousness and free association could be sustained
by anyone over a long career. Some tightening seems inevitable.
Despite the changes from his unique early style, Shepherd consistently created outstanding programs until his radio career
ended seventeen years later.

In 1964, he said he was happy to be shifted from 11:15 at
night back to 10:15, so that more people could listen. Kerr
Lockhart, a perceptive Shepherd listener, has this to say about
the time change:

> Clearly, a couple of things happened in the time shift.
> For one, kids started listening to the show in large num-
> bers. They began calling up. Shepherd became aware of
> them, and even addressed them from time to time. Also,
> there were more sponsors at 10:15. In fact the growth in
> sponsors from 1964 to, say, 1969 appears to have been
> exponential. By 1966, Shep has settled into a definite for-
> mat which governs about 75 percent of the available pro-
> grams. That is, he starts off with a news story or other
> odd observation. This often launches a musical or other
> random interlude. At 10:30 there is a station break, usu-
> ally followed by what is now called a "pod" of commer-
> cials. Thereafter follows what might be considered the
> "real" content of the show. If the show is going to be
> built around a story, the story doesn't begin until then;
> usually preceded by a lengthy thematic [introduction].
>
> Look at how many of his short stories have some
> brief contemporary prologue, in which an event or a
> modern phenomenon sends the narrator's mind back to
> his childhood (or other earlier life experience). That is
> more or less the outline he used in the forty-five-minute
> show—that is, when the show was built around a story,
> rather than simply being topical.
>
> One might think this was limiting, but like the sonata
> or the sonnet, the creation of a fairly standardized
> format seems to liberate Shepherd to do his most cohe-
> sive and best-organized work.

From February 15, 1964, through December 30, 1967, in addition to the weeknight studio broadcasts, Shepherd appeared Saturdays at the Limelight (what might be called a comedy club cum restaurant) in Greenwich Village, doing the show live on WOR from after ten PM to midnight. Many in this audience at the Limelight were his radio listeners come to see their hero live. He seemed to enjoy the audience reaction and played for crowd appeal, eliciting frequent, easy laughs, performing more for an adolescent mentality. A Max Schmid reflection on the Limelight broadcasts: "The Limelight shows bring us a different side of Shepherd the performer. The studio shows are intimate, but on stage, he's the class clown, the rabble-rouser, the cheerleader, and orgy instigator (and pretty testy about hecklers and talkers, too). It's on these live shows that the childhood stories and army stories seem to have been developed, and they were featured nearly every week in the later shows."

Shepherd, seeming less concerned with intellectual subtleties and mind-play before this live audience, became more exaggerated in his style, forcing too hard, needing a response from the Saturday night hamburger and soft drink revelers (sophomores and their dates). The mob laughed from the belly and the throat rather than from some deeper source within themselves. Even Shepherd's own laugh differed: his various studio laughs sounded natural, as though rising out of what he himself found amusing in the material—the Limelight Shepherd laugh sounded forced and embarrassed at having to cue the audience, as though prompting, "laugh *now*, gang!"

Comparing his two kinds of shows, on a 1965 broadcast Shepherd said there were those who preferred the studio broadcasts because they preferred thinking of themselves as being alone, with him talking only to them. He said that many people preferred the Limelight shows to the studio ones, and he suggested that this was because one was aware of a human response from the audience. This seems very disingenuous of Shepherd— he cannot have helped but be aware that it was not just audience response that made the Limelight broadcasts different. He had to know that his pensive, humorist self in the studio, tickling the listener's brain, gave way to milking the gallery for cheap laughs at the Limelight. Like a stand-up comic who had to keep the jokes coming (a live audience required an audible response), he spoke in a tone of voice that was not one-on-one as his studio broadcasts were, but with the forced intensity of someone entertaining a crowd. In these live broadcast performances, he often seemed to descend to the level of those stand-up comics he disparaged. Nevertheless, it was a professional, craftsmanlike, show biz style, and indeed, many enjoyed it.

On a 1966 studio broadcast, Shepherd separated the studio shows from the Limelight shows in a way that ranks them. On the assumption that he recognized himself as a radio artist, the following clearly distinguishes the primacy of studio work from the weekend furlough of what he tellingly called "just *fun* night":

> This, incidentally, is my last show of 1966—of the regular series. In other words, I look upon my Limelight show as a separate *entity*. You know, that's a separate kind of show. The shows that I do Monday through Friday have one kind of thing and my Saturday night show is just *fun* night for me, and I enjoy it tremendously and it's a big nightclub performance— we have a great time.[32]

Considering all those nights a week alone in a studio except for a frequently antipathetic engineer, one can understand why he enjoyed the response of a live audience. Fred Barzyk's comment about how Shepherd felt toward his young fans seems appropriate: "He loved the adoration." When Shepherd got going on a longer anecdote or story, and the audience kept its collective mouth shut, he produced Quality Shep. If, as Max Schmid suggests, the childhood and army stories developed through Limelight performances, that was also a dividend.

When the Limelight shows stopped at the end of 1967, Shepherd continued studio broadcasting on Saturday nights, at least through 1971, with a fifty-five-minute show without commercials (10:05–11:00). Instead of forty-five minutes broken numerous times for commercials, these were fifty-five uninterrupted minutes, and resulted, sometimes at least, in casual and extended riffs, similar to his earlier style. (His weeknight programs continued throughout and beyond, to 1977.)

TYING IT ALL UP AS "BAHN FREI" SWELLS UP AND OUT

During this period, Shepherd honed his style of apparently rambling, but actually circling around a topic. He said, "Rambling is not at all what I do. I take an idea, something that I want to say on a given show and I improvise around that theme, but I stick around that theme. If you notice, I always return to it at the end."[33] Bringing the diverse threads of his talk back and tying them all up at broadcast's end—just in time—was one of his most admired talents. With some of these timing triumphs, he ended his talk soon after the two-minute theme began under his voice—more dramatically, sometimes his final words merged in concert with the music of "Bahn Frei" exuberantly rushing to its finale.

WHO LISTENS?

As early as spring 1960, there were intimations of Shepherd's dissatisfaction with the general lack of regard given to radio:

> Guy says he listens all the time—see—this kid—he listens all the time. Actually, he's not a kid. This guy happens to be an assistant professor at Columbia—that's a kid, too, I suppose, in another way. But he's listening—he's listening all the time, and one day he's out with this chick, and the chick says to him—right across the table where they're having this little piquant Algerian wine—says, "Yeah, Shepherd's okay, but don't tell me he's practicing what he preaches. Look where he is—nice plush job on the radio, doin' what he likes to do—don't tell me he isn't nosing around with the wheels—*ha!*"
>
> So [he] says, "Well, yeah, well baby, the guy—he's been around a long time and look—look at the stuff he does, and look where he is on the dial, and look what time he is on the dial, and look—I mean, on Sunday night."
>
> And then the chick says, "Who listens to *radio* anymore?"
>
> The guy says, "I sat there for a while and drank some of my wine, and my wine wasn't piquant anymore."[34]

As in so much of Shepherd's talk, the tone of voice was important, so that a black-and-white transcription might imply no more than an unpleasantly hostile attitude, where indeed, in addition to having fun, he was also making a serious point. Certainly he was not "only kidding" in the following short pieces. But he made serious statements within the context of the great enthusiasm and joy he projected regarding his work.

> ...*silly* program. [Talking to his listeners.] Why'd you waste your time, for crying out loud! You could have been doing push-

ups and knee-bends. Here you were sitting around listening to *this* jazz. And *I* was doing it. Talk about wasting time![35]

Nobody worth his salt is listening to the radio at this hour of the night, I can tell you that. And I can tell you this—nobody worth his salt is *doing* radio at this hour of the night.[36]

Some people stopped listening as they moved from being students into adulthood. Certainly not because as adults they were less interested in the workings of his mind, or that the quality of Shepherd's broadcasts diminished—he maintained an extraordinarily high level to the end. Possibly the time of his broadcasts was no longer convenient with the changed activities of many adults—undoubtedly the television Shepherd hated intruded, substituting for the imagination the more easily pandered-to eye. In addition, his moving into media other than radio may have failed to bring some of his audience with him.

During the early 1960s, telephone call-in radio became popular and WNBC tried to lure Shepherd. Such a move would pay well, but Jean Shepherd had the right reasons for refusing, indicated during the Alan Colmes 1998 interview:

Well, I'm not a telephone answerer. That's when the telephone shows were getting big. And they wanted me to come over there and sit there, and answer phone calls and all that stuff, and I said, "No, I'm a monologist, for heaven's sakes! I don't want to sit there and talk to somebody out in Queens about the trouble he's having with his daughter's drug problem."

...And as far as I was concerned, I wasn't interested in going over to NBC to do that show and the day— they were trying to talk me into it. They called me up to have lunch one day, and the guy who was manager of the station—program director, actually called me, and he said, "I want to have lunch with you." So we went to this very elegant Italian restaurant on 49th Street right across from Radio City...when all of a sudden there was a big hubbub, and a guy came running into this restaurant, which was quiet and very distinguished and all that, and he shouted, "Oh my God, the president's been shot." [This was the day of President Kennedy's assassination, November 22, 1963.]

AN ELEGY AND AN EXCURSION INTO BEING A SOREHEAD

Barry Farber remembers that right after the John F. Kennedy assassination, "We didn't get on the air for four days. I didn't want to—I was too affected—didn't want to be on the air. Jean was furious. He came in—'For crying out loud, finally have something to talk about—*they took us off the air!*'"

The tape of what appears to be Jean Shepherd's first broadcast after Kennedy's assassination did not begin with the upbeat "Bahn Frei Polka" theme. He did not talk about the assassination the way others did—he spoke soberly, seriously, about what he saw and had long seen and talked about—indications in the United States of serious problems, why people do the shocking things they sometimes do. Some years later, he commented that he still had a tape of this show. Surely, he recognized that it constituted an extraordinary, beautifully composed elegy:

> Well, we're not going to use the theme song tonight and tonight we're going to talk about Mr. Kennedy and a lot of other associated problems and facts of American life, if we can.[ix]
>
> If you're expecting any great revelations or banjo playing tonight, I don't think you'll get it. However, I remember—wonder—it's difficult to say some of the things you have to say at times, but this has probably been one of the most significant—if not *the* most significant weekends that many of us will ever live through. And not just because a president has passed. But because of a lot of other associated things it says about American life, American attitudes, and American mores today.
>
> I remember the first time I heard about Kennedy, and I suppose many of you remember... I've always been a Kennedy man. And—for probably different reasons than you can always state—how you like a certain person—very hard to know all the personal things that make you lean towards a man—make you believe in a man, and so on. The one thing that I have always noticed about Kennedy, that appealed to me specifically, was that Kennedy was a *realist*. And being a realist in today's world is very dangerous. Because realism is not a thing that is easily accepted by Americans in the 1960s. And I always felt sorry for Kennedy because I recognized the fact that Kennedy did not give people a soft pap that most of them somehow wanted—on both sides of the political fence...
>
> [Shepherd talked about Kennedy's intelligence, humor, zest—all of which make people nervous. He talked about the problems of being a president in a democratic system.]

And I have a—tonight I have a feeling inside of me—there is a great sense of—apprehension—I suppose you might say—a kind of feeling of—I hate to say fear, because it's not that clearly defined. It's a kind of free-floating thing—a strange unreasonableness—a fanaticism that brought about this *unbelievable* weekend—is not only still around but is slowly beginning to grow in this land.

[Shepherd talked about getting anonymous letters and said that these *really* tell how people feel.] About a year or so ago I began to be aware—of a growing belief in violence in America—a growing impatience with the processes that are slow and painful, the processes of democracy—shall we say. I began to be aware of that, and that more and more people were beginning to see themselves as solitary, beautiful, lone, sensitive individuals—arrayed against an unseen, unthinking, grinding, totally an—insensitive society. You might say it's the Holden Caulfield syndrome—beginning to grow. Well this was fanned—this was fanned in a lot of ways, and I think it was part and parcel of the feeling today—that what I want is the most important thing in the world... Today, more and more, we are beginning to believe in *passion*—as a substitute for reason...

[He talked about the television broadcast from Arlington Cemetery.] Here was just this little, simple grave—and—it was just a hole in the ground—there was this little, simple bronze coffin. And there was a quick shot, which they cut away from. I don't know whether you saw this or not—but it was one of the most poignant shots of all. It was a little moment after the funeral party had left Arlington and—the cars were winding back up the drive over the bridge, back over the river to Washington. And the four soldiers were still standing guard over the grave.

You saw, coming down from the lower left hand corner, two workmen. Did you see them? Dressed in overalls? Just two workmen with baseball caps, and they were coming to do the inevitable. There was a brief shot of them. They walked up, and one of them sort of kneeled down, and he started to pick things up around the grave. He's beginning to do—what happens to all of us in the end. And they cut away from it very quickly. Maybe this was too much. I saw that—my God, how—how small we are. Even the *president* is—is no more, no different from us. Maybe this was one of the things that so profoundly moved me, and frightening about it, and at the same time, vaguely reassuring—it gave us all a sense of *unbelievable* loneliness...

Maybe this is why people rushed off to football games— although that's probably being kind to them. Because I believe that the—you know, I wonder whether the British would consider having a professional *soccer* game in London—the day after the king died. I doubt it. We're a different kind of people. This is not to say good, bad, or indifferent. Just very different. Sometimes you wonder just what kind we are. It was a terrible weekend. And I'm not so sure that we're not in for a few more in the next hundred years.

This is Jean Shepherd.[37]

As with Walt Whitman's elegy to Lincoln, "When Lilacs Last in the Dooryard Bloomed," the death of a president gave him the opportunity to express sorrow in a form that encompassed some of his recurring themes. And the workmen seen fleetingly in a corner of the TV screen was a fine example of what Jean Shepherd had frequently insisted—that the nearly unnoticed "cracks in the sidewalk" could reveal a truth. On that night, Jean Shepherd filled the Greek chorus role he had described for himself several years before as "drawing back and making a comment on what you have just seen." He must have worked through that weekend on what he would say, and he must have been proud, realizing this was a fine work of art. He ended the broadcast with his dire Greek-chorus prediction, then he paused and inscribed—with his voice—his name: "This is Jean Shepherd."

Shepherd's style that week was atypical. Instead of giving the feeling of an informal dialogue with listeners, he spoke *at* them, in serious essays on subjects connected to the American temperament—the subject of off-the-air diatribes, but previously treated lightly on the radio. He had indeed complained in broadcasts before about what he felt were naively unjust criticisms of his country by his countrymen. This must be understood in the context of the 1960s ferment—student unrest, civil rights struggle, civil disobedience, demonstrations, and riots in the streets. And America-bashing by Americans. Indeed, many Americans were criticizing America for not living up to its ideals. Shepherd admitted the problems, that America indeed needed to work to improve itself—but commented that other countries had even more problems, and that they were inherent in humanity. He seemed to feel that the criticism had created a climate that resulted in violence and assassination, and in part, he implicated the popular "seriously funny" comic satirists and commentators of the day.

Near the beginning of the second program he suggested that it was premature to express appropriate anger over the assassination—his voice was calm, his words well-reasoned, but the feelings behind them strong:

> One thing that I do feel about our time—and I think that eventually will be discussed by historians—is the growth in America of the new righteous people. [Not Left wing or Right wing, he said.] His belief that he has the message, his belief that he has the truth contained in the sacred vessel of his body. It's a kind of like a super, hyper-thyroid Holden Caulfield—with a good agent. And a great nightclub following. It's in a sense making paranoia pay... Do you have a feeling that all the laws have been passed because they're after *you*? Do you have a feeling that lurking behind every hedge is a guy who wants to belt you on the top of the head just because you're beautiful? Well, friend, there is a career awaiting you. Have you ever thought of becoming a top-flight nightclub comic and recording artist? And then eventually moving into the world of big-time social satire? Becoming famous?... One of the things that bothers me about our time is that for every—I imagine right now there must be at least thirty-five thousand writers who earn a living on one principle—proving to all the other Americans that America has the worst way of life in the world. The dishonesty, the hypocrisy, blah, blah, blah—whatever it is...I think it must be based on an unbelievable lack of knowledge of the rest of the world. In fact, most of the social satirists I have met have not been beyond the three nightclubs they work.[38]

Did Jean Shepherd have strong political and cultural opinions? You bet he did! What it took to bring them forth on the air was catastrophe—the death of the "man I respected more than *any* man I've respected, incidentally—in public life as long as I can remember being interested in public life." Shepherd ended this program with a tribute to Kennedy:

> Mr. Kennedy—I think in so many ways—almost—and this is a strange thing to say—almost embodied America. He was the embodiment of us. His attitudes, the way he was, the way

he talked, the way he moved. The look in the eye. And I think one of the great feelings of shock that all of us have is that his sense of—lust for life, his *enjoyment* of life—if you've seen him on these news programs that he did, his enjoyment of life—was something that we all felt, even subconsciously, and when he went, somehow a little bit of our life went too. Because, you know, life is contagious. And I think a lot us caught it from Mr. Kennedy. This is Jean Shepherd. We'll be back tomorrow night at 11:15.[39]

Jean Shepherd had been shaken by that assassination weekend and it showed—he continued for the rest of the week in this more somber tone:

> And here we are. For this week, we are dispensing with our loud and raucous and somewhat sinister theme. But I'll tell you this, we're not dispensing with our loud and raucous and somewhat sinister attitude.[40]

The Kennedy elegy program was not the only instance of Shepherd's carefully thought-out excursions into what might be considered spoken prose poems. From time to time, one can sense that he seemed to have more than just a general idea of theme in a broadcast. There would sometimes be a subtle tone of voice and sense of organization that one might well imagine arose not from a written script, but from a well-considered plan. Shepherd composed the following piece of beautifully modulated art in a broadcast on why he was noted for his anger:

> Now I must say, before we go any further, there've been a lot of people worried about why I am such a sorehead. About why, from time to time, I knock over the coffee table here in the studio, and why—you know—I've said some pretty rotten things around the water cooler...
>
> You've heard me from time to time here, on these very microphones, as Barry Farber says so indelibly. You've heard me from time to time [laughs]—these very microphones—well, I don't know. I think that we were using the microphone in Studio 6, actually, it wasn't this very microphone—this is a cheap one here, [noise of him banging on it] crummy microphones they used to use on those all-night—gee whiz! Hey, does this one turn on? It is, huh? Or does it say "Push"? Yeah, it says, "Push the button to talk." All right, I'll push. For

crying out *loud!* No wonder my ratings have been so rotten! Why didn't you tell me I was supposed to push the button on this thing?—to talk into it? Cheapies-ville all the way. 'Cause whenever I talk on radio here, it makes the juice out of the current—the transmitter go up—you know that—that's called "modulation." *Agh!* That costs more to do that than to go— [Silence.] That's right. [Laughs.] Didn't you know that?

As long as we're back on that subject. A lot of people have wondered—how is it you grow to be a sorehead. How is it, say, James Thurber grew to be James Thurber and not, say, Moss Hart, who never was mad at anybody. I mean—just wanted to make dough.

And how is it that Mark Twain, for example, grew to have that funny *look* in the eye? He did. And I'll tell you one of the reasons why he grew to have that funny look in the eye. Mark Twain, at one point was a riverboat pilot. Now, there aren't many things that are more irritating, frustrating, and that teach a man more *realism*, that convince a man of his basic— inadequacies—and also convince a man of how *small* he is than to be a riverboat pilot. Because the river's always sneaking and changing, and it tears the bottom out of the boat about every third or fourth day, sinks everybody on hand, and drowns them all without even a wink. Well, after a couple of years of this, you come East, and you just don't look at the world the same way that a guy living in an apartment in Brooklyn, you know, looks at it. Just not the same. Sixth Avenue does not swallow you up often. Just doesn't do that. And very few Staten Island Ferries are lost in the storm. Doesn't happen often.

Well, as a child, I had just such a thing happen to me. I became embarked on a course that was every bit as rocky, every bit as frustrating, every bit as *maddening* as the thing about learning how to be a riverboat pilot.

Have you ever read Mark Twain's *Life on the Mississippi*? Well, one thing that Twain talks a great deal about is learning how to be a pilot on the Mississippi. About these great pilots that he sailed with. And about how the old pilots could sit in the pilot house, and they could hear the sound of the paddle wheels—*dabadabadabadaba*—have you ever been on a riverboat? [Shepherd went on to talk about how kids in school, in order that they be constantly supported and encouraged, are led to believe that they are infinitely talented.]

You know it's been a long time since I've given a lesson to

the kids. Kids, are you listening? There is a *limit*, kid, to what you can do. Now you don't know it—and maybe you'll never find it out—but there *is* a limit, kid, in almost every direction you care to choose. Now, this is a very unpopular thing I'm saying here— [laughs] but I'm going to describe to you how it came to me one day.

I'm this kid, see. Now how these things happen, one doesn't know. How you drift, you know, along in life. How you meet the chick that you're going with. How you happen to—the random quality of life is inexplicable. But I can say, there was a kid living across the street from me. [Shepherd discussed how the kid got him interested in making shortwave radios. Shep at eleven years old got hooked. He met a friend's father who was a genuine ham operator. Shepherd became "a monk." He "found a higher calling." Finally, he got his license and could send Morse code at the fast rate of forty-five words per minute. And the end theme music has begun under his talk.]...

[I was] a lightning-fast operator. Then one night on forty meters, I met my match. One night on forty meters at three o'clock in the morning, I hooked up with a guy from Pittsburgh, and we got into a speed match. By 3:15 that morning, I was reduced to rubble. I met a guy who could send and receive well in excess of sixty words a minute—on forty meters.

It was then that I *knew*—out there in that dark river there are shoals, out there, there are people who can *really* do it. Somewhere there's a guy who can *re-a-ll-y*, really make it *move!* And that there are limits.

I can only say to the rest of you guys, you kids out there— you're lucky. You have not yet been put to the test. You have not, at three o'clock in the morning, met a guy who can *really* write a play. You have not met, at four o'clock in the morning, a guy who could *really* act. You have not met, at 4:15 AM, a guy who could send and receive above two hundred watts on forty, sixty-five words a minute in coded groups without even missing a beat for a half hour on end. And until you do, you are living in a *dream*—a dream. [Theme music finale, up and out.][41]

It may be worthwhile to examine how Shepherd achieves the effects in the foregoing monologue. Remember that Shepherd previously had said he was a sorehead because of all the infuriating things he saw around him all the time—that was why he was a sorehead at the moment. The main theme, however, turns out to be the humbling experience of discovering that somewhere there are those who are greater than we are—the experience of facing reality. How does he get from anger to humility—from sorehead to clear-eyed realist?

He begins, slyly, with the unexpected complaint about his microphone, demonstrating this current example of his being a sorehead. He proceeds with a series of digressions, each one impelled not by strict logic but rather by some aspect of the previous one, and the listener has the pleasure of experiencing the spontaneous development of the monologue and of an improvised, meandering journey. Then, as the airily cheerful theme music of "Bahn Frei" signals an end to the monologue, Shepherd pulls it all together with the moral of his tale: until one faces the sometimes humbling realities of life, one is living in a dream. Shepherd seems to suggest that anyone who has the courage to face such a reality, surely a frustrating experience, has a right to be a sorehead once in a while.

LATER YEARS AND EXTENDED STORIES

By the mid-1960s, Shepherd developed the extended stories more fully, and he produced many gems in the form. Several people describe Shepherd's manner from the 1960s on. Herb Squire remembers, "Every once in a while you'd see him before the show, he'd talk about something in the hall and lo and behold, that would become a topic for that night's show." Laurie Squire, observing from spring 1976 to the end of Shepherd's WOR radio days in the spring of 1977:

> There was no formal script. He would go through newspapers, he would clip out articles, clip out paragraphs—anything that might start the train of thought going. And he'd take a batch of clippings, and the records into the studio. He would tell the engineer, "Okay, when I hold up this finger I want you to play cut number so and so." He'd get very frustrated when the engineer would mess up on that, which of course happened. Once he was revved up he kept going, and then of course he'd lead right back to the point he wanted to make.

Ron Della Chiesa also observed Shepherd in action:

> You know he used a little piece of paper. I observed his paper. He knew exactly where he was going. [What did he have on the paper?] A little sketch. For example, "Signal Corps story," and then he would have names of people—Zudok, etc. And then he would use that as a frame of reference. And then he would have the ending. He would build the show in conjunction with the closing theme, which would be [played] under him, but in the meantime, during the course of the Signal Corps story or Zudok's house story, he would take you off on these other stream of consciousness paths, but he would always take you back into the main stream. In a way it was very symphonic, what he was doing. His work had movements. It had an opening, which was presto, usually the first movement of a symphony is very upbeat, you know. Then he would have an adagio—a slower part—a scherzo—upbeat—and then the finale. So you see, I think the influence of classical music is very strong in his radio work. The more I think of it, he knew how to shape it as a musical program too.

What was it like to see Shepherd in the studio? Martin Jackson, who met and interviewed Shepherd for a *New York Times* article in December 1976, years later describes the time he observed Shepherd at work:

> In a little manila folder—he had clippings and papers—it wasn't a script, but he had some notes. And he went behind the glass and Leigh was outside. And from what I've seen of other radio shows, pretty minimal production. It was Leigh sort of hovering, and an engineer, and Shepherd behind the glass... It was the standard sort of Shep show... He just sat, and he looked like [the photo by Fred W. McDarrah—Shepherd with earphones on, speaking into the mike, hand upraised]. A lot of those kinds of gestures. He really got involved and connected with the material. He wasn't casual about it...
>
> After the show he came across in a different way [from his earlier hostility]. He was much more friendly, much more chatty. He wanted to know what I was

doing, who I was. He had a group of schoolgirls—I can't remember why they were there... So Leigh escorted them into another office, where he spent ten minutes or so with these girls. He enjoyed being the center of attention. They took pictures of him and he made a few jokes. He liked that... And then Leigh took them wherever they went next... My memory of Leigh is that she was totally submissive and subservient to him. Really a beaten woman—I don't mean literally, but she really was his handmaiden. That was the relationship I saw...

I remember asking her at the time, "Is he married?" I didn't realize she was his girlfriend. She was introduced as the producer of the show. I thought it would be nice to put that in the article—where does he live, does he have children? She said, "No, no, no, not married." Nothing more. She didn't want to go there.

Behind-the-scenes anecdotes confirm the image one has of Shepherd at work. He excelled in a unique style of improvisation in his chosen medium. On the other hand, specific comments by Shepherd on-air express his displeasure with the way radio and television were thwarting his best efforts to prevail in his life's work as a radio artist. Radio in the person of the Federal Communications Commission cut off one conduit of his performance, and television was increasingly polluting the atmosphere, to radio's detriment.

Despite the scant audience for FM programming at the time, the FCC ruled that a radio station could not broadcast the same signal on AM and FM, so Shepherd's dual coverage of the airwaves had to cease in the summer of 1966:[x]

Did I give the station break here? Oh—this is WOR AM and FM in New York. This is the last time we'll be on FM, right? Ohhh. It's a poor, sad note. This is the last night we'll be on FM. [Said with irony.] Of course radio's moving forward. Now I understand we have some magnificent programming for you—on FM. I'm sure that—[Laughs.]

[Sings.] I'm forever blowing bubbles. [Laughs.] Ah well. Ah well. Progress often is a slow descent into quicksand.[42]

You know, speaking of cartoons—hold it there. Doesn't this sound like a cartoon? Just—just one minute there, will you. Keep that style. Everything must be done in style today. This is—this is all style. Our world is style. Let's face it. What is her name? Susan Sontag? Susan Sontag has said that "style is all," or was it Proust? Or was it Earl Wilson? Marshall McLuhan says, "the medium is the message." So don't care that you're getting junk out of the radio. Stop worrying about the junk that's coming out of it. What is important is that it's *radio*, friends. The medium is the message.

Don't complain about all that crud that keeps coming night after night out of Channel Whoopee! That's not the point. The point is it's *TV*. That is the message. And you know—that you all love TV of course. The medium.[43]

Did you see the—there's an ad in the subway? I'll tell you, we let out the truth in a lot of sneaky ways. There's an ad in the subway, and it says, "Now at last a real reason to hurry home." And it's an ad for a color TV set. That says something about family life, doesn't it? At last, there's a real reason on how to break away and why to break away from the Biltmore Bar in a hurry—get home to your TV set. Now you can see it in color. Now—does junk look any better in color—than in black and white?[44]

SYNDICATION ATTEMPTS AND "INTERNATIONAL JAWBREAKER"

> Time for Jean Shepherd, raconteur and commentator on the contemporary scene.
> —Announcer at beginning of a syndicated program

Attempts were made to overcome the shortcomings of local East Coast broadcasts and rebroadcasts (legal and pirated). Some of the programs were edited tapes from regular shows, others made especially for syndication. The shows were shorter, tighter, with breaks for inserted commercials. Apparently, Shepherd had mixed feelings about syndication attempts, possibly because he could see what shorter new programs, and editing of existing programs, did to the essence of his style. Barry Farber failed to convince him to try in the late 1960s:

Barry Farber: I wanted to syndicate Shepherd. He had all those forty-five-minute shows, and I reasoned that if you took a forty-five-minute WOR show—took

out the commercials—and he did very little padding,
and very little filling, but there was some excessive
laughter of his own, when he was deciding what to do
ten seconds after that. And if we just made every show
tight, it would be a *perfect* half hour show. And I
approached Leigh, and I had credentials in syndication.
I was syndicating myself successfully, and I wanted to
syndicate Jean—it was almost a labor of love—I would
reimburse myself and make some profit but I was going
to give Jean everything—just for saying yes. And he
didn't say yes. He never said no, never said yes, and
finally Leigh Brown, who I had a good communication
with said, "Barry, I don't think it's going to work."

Laurie Squire: Jean had wanted to do a more formal
syndication of the show because there were a lot of—
and to this day there still are—pirate copies. There was
a flurry of syndication of the show at that time... We met
[summer of 1976] with Jean and Leigh at a Chinese
restaurant. I remember we had drinks with the little
umbrellas and Jean had drawn up a little sketch of an
organizational title called "International Jawbreaker."
[His title for the group, consisting of Jean and Leigh,
Herb Squire, and Laurie Squire] And the objective of
International Jawbreaker was syndication of the Jean
Shepherd Show... We decided the product was going to
be taken from the WOR show, forty-five minutes. There
was half an hour of content, fifteen minutes of commercials...

Jean was the artist, Herb duplicated the shows... My
job was to *sell* the product, so I got hold of *Broadcast
Yearbook* and realized that the chief market was a lot of
college stations. I started calling up every possible college
radio station you could imagine... We charged very very
little. And it was *so* popular, they were able to afford us.
And it was a popular show. Primarily at that time he
was doing a lot of college performances. Herb and I
were doing the syndication. It was a two-person, mom-
and-pop operation.

You have been listening to Jean Shepherd, humorist,
author, and recipient of the Mark Twain Award for 1976.
    —Announcer at the end of a syndicated program

Although Shep made several efforts to extend the broadcast range of his radio work, his projects in other media such as television and personal appearances around the country made nightly broadcasting from WOR's New York studios a logistical problem. He insisted that almost all of his shows were live, but that if one were taped, it was done *as if* it were a live show, and there should not be any difference noted. By the 1970s, however, his professional life had become much busier:

> **Laurie Squire:** He would come into WOR a couple of times a week and tape several shows at one sitting... I know fans will say that's impossible, but *definitely* from the spring of '76 to spring of '77, primarily because he was tired of doing daily radio shows. ["Tired or too busy?" Laurie was asked.] That was the peak of other activity.

> **Herb Squire:** Those last few years, he was involved of course in the PBS specials and his books and so forth, so that took a lot of time. As a matter of fact when he was traveling for *Jean Shepherd's America,* he would be out of New York for weeks on end and basically in advance he would record shows—maybe a couple of shows a night and then go on and do a live show and then we would repeat certain of the better shows.

FAMILIAR ENCOUNTERS AND CHANCE ENCOUNTERS

Shepherd's son, Randall, recalls that in the early 1960s, after Shepherd had left the family, Jean visited his sister and him a few times in Princeton, where they lived. Then in the early 1970s, Randall worked in the same building as Shepherd: "My first job in NYC was in the WOR/RKO building at 1440 Broadway. I was an assistant recording engineer at a recording studio on the twenty-fifth floor called Good Vibrations... My being in the same building with Jean was completely coincidental. We had chance encounters in the building over the three years I worked there." Mere chance encounters must have been a disheartening experience for a son, and the statement represents a sad commentary for those who imagine Jean Shepherd as a real-life mentor. Once he moved on in life, Shepherd cut off the past, even if it was his own children.

"YOU BETTER GET OUT OF THAT DAMN MEDIUM"

By the 1960s, radio was in decline as television became
increasingly dominant. Barry Farber comments that, "Radio
was just bypassed prestige-wise by television. And Jean said
something I've quoted many times: 'You could be on New York
radio for many years and be widely unknown.'" Fred Allen,
radio and television comedian, emphasizes his dismay on the
last page of his book, *Treadmill to Oblivion*:

> When television belatedly found its way into the
> home, after stopping off too long at the tavern, the
> advertisers knew they had a more potent force available
> for their selling purposes. Radio was abandoned like the
> bones at a barbecue.
>
> Comedy has changed with the coming of television.
> The radio listener saw nothing: he had to use his imagi-
> nation...
>
> There was a certain type of imaginative comedy that
> could be written for, and performed on, only the radio.
> Television comedy is mostly visual and the most success-
> ful of comedians today are disciples of the slapstick...
>
> We are living in the machine age. For the first time in
> history the comedian has been compelled to supply him-
> self with jokes and comedy material to compete with the
> machine. Whether he knows it or not, the comedian is on
> a treadmill to oblivion. When a radio comedian's pro-
> gram is finally finished it slinks down Memory Lane into
> the limbo of yesteryear's happy hours. All that the come-
> dian has to show for his years of work and aggravation
> is the echo of forgotten laughter.[45]

In the 1960 *Realist* interview, Shepherd said, "Let's say I have
intimations that I'll never make it—because I'm on radio. If I
were doing what I'm doing now in nightclubs, I think I would.
If I were doing it on the *Ed Sullivan Show*, I think I would. But
radio—no. I'm saying that I'm backed into a strange corner
here—that if I can make four hundred people laugh on radio,
that's not much, it's not official." In the Alan Colmes 1998 interview, Shepherd puts it as strongly as he can: "In fact one night I
was going on the Carson Show and we were backstage. I was
with Carson. He said, 'Look, Shepherd,' he said, 'forever they're
going to think of you as a radio guy. You better get out of that
damn medium.'"

Despite the eventual realization that he was fighting a losing battle by persevering on radio, he continued to have hopes. In an April 1972 broadcast, Shepherd talked about and played a few samples of the Princeton University radio station's short humorous skits advertising his upcoming annual performance there. In one stroke, he gave a plug for his upcoming show, indicated that dozens of college stations carried his radio broadcasts, promoted himself for additional appearances and broadcast venues, and encouraged further radio programming that would use words rather than music alone.

He had obviously been discouraged by the overwhelming dominance of rock music on radio. He seemed not to like most of it, and saw that dominance as undercutting the potential of talk on radio. His fervent hope expressed in one program of that period was that "rock radio has had its day. And among a growing crowd they're far more interested in the human voice saying things—or doing things—than they are in the continuing sound of a reverb and a Moog, and somebody keening endlessly over the sound of a Fender bass... I'd say that within eighteen months you're going to be hearing a lot more in various above-ground media about the death of rock." Talk about wishful thinking!

Unfortunately for his ambitions and his expectations for the radio medium, rock and roll did not diminish, but expanded its presence on the radio dial—and as for talk, only a few talk-radio programs would do intelligent and inventive work. One can mention careers that would not have been the same without Shepherd's twenty-one years of stylistic genius. For example, major stand-up comics who have gone on to greater things in the 1980s, 1990s, and beyond. Some descendents might admit a family resemblance and others might self-protectively plead ignorance as to whence they came. What about the artistic influence of Shepherd's radio innovation? Disc jockey talkers such as Vin Scelsa and Jonathan Schwartz? National Public Radio's Ira Glass and David Sedaris? Garrison Keillor? The Car Guys? Harry Shearer? Conservative talking heads such as Rush Limbaugh? The funny nastymen Don Imus and Howard Stern? Sickos who'll remain nameless? In his later years, Shepherd witnessed a dominance of radio talkers who were crude, nasty, foul mouthed, and inflammatory. In an interview, he commented that he would not want to return to a medium in which one of the most flagrant polluters broadcasted. The crudeness reached this level described in the *New York Times*, April, 10, 2003: "The hosts... were fired after they broadcast a live account of a couple having sex in the vestibule of St. Patrick's Cathedral in Manhattan. The incident was part of a contest to see who would have sex in the riskiest place... Radio has become an industry dominated by three of four major chains, including Infinity [which, as owner of the station that broadcast the incident, had fired the hosts], that use rigid research to determine what listeners want to hear."

Near the end of the century, too late for Shepherd, there would be an annual talk-radio convention, a trade magazine devoted to talk radio, and several radio networks in the business of promoting and distributing a great variety of programs featuring talk. Many of these were politically conservative talk shows supported by ample conservative financing. According to the *New York Times* of October 11, 2003, one popular conservative talk-show host had an audience of twenty million people a week on six hundred stations nationwide, and a nine-year, $285 million contract.

Shepherd could not have thrived in such a world. He would not play rock and roll, would not be crude and inflammatory, would not do any shade of political commentary, and thus would not find an easy outlet in a medium controlled by popularity polls.

With the increasing popularity of television, many radio people had a difficult time staying on the air. WOR was still a major force in talk radio, and in the mid-1970s, the very popular creative geniuses Bob Elliott and Ray Goulding were broadcasting there.[xi] They sometimes talked with Shepherd at the station. Laurie Squire remembers, "They used to chat, and there was a nice respect going there. They used to talk—meet during station breaks... They would walk into the airlock between the control room and the studio and talk, or go out in the hallway, by the water fountain—that kind of thing." A 1975 photo shows Bob, Ray, and Jean having beers in a local Broadway restaurant, with Jean clearly doing the talking.[46] For the three of them, their glory days on radio were numbered.

Gerald Nachman, referring to the 1950s in *Raised on Radio*, writes, "TV was killing off radio headliners as efficiently as radio had dispatched so many vaudeville legends. Personalities and shows that people had listened to for their entire lives—ten, twenty, in some case almost thirty years—and with whom they had formed complex relationships, were snuffed out overnight."

Despite remaining on the air with much daytime talk into the 1970s, WOR radio announced its new format, resulting in personnel changes—most notably the departure of four principal news personalities.[xii] Herb Saltzman comments, "At WOR the newsroom was very important. We had the greatest selection of voices—John Scott, Henry Gladstone, Lyle Van, Harry Hennessey, Peter Roberts... [A new general manager] came in to 'youthify' the station and one of the things he did—he got rid of the whole nighttime block...of talk show hosts [and some of the announcers]." The *New York Times*, Monday, March 28, 1977, reported, "John Wingate, WOR reporter for 30 years;...Stan Lomax, a sports commentator for 43 years; Henry Gladstone, a newscaster for 32 years; and Jean Shepherd, famous for his impressionistic nostalgia monologues, which have been heard for 20 years, all resigned and will leave within two weeks."

> Radio seems to many people to not be show business, and it is true that many people in radio really aren't in show business—primarily in advertising, or the record business, or whatever it might be. But I'm in show business, and when you're in show business, as a performer, and as a writer, there's a time when you have to move on to other projects, due to the press of time.
>
> I'm sure this is—in fact I know this is what happened in the case of Mary Tyler Moore. The real reason that many people within the Mary Tyler Moore organization will tell you is that they want to move on to other projects, and the continuing doing of the Mary Tyler Moore Show has taken too much of their time. They've already done it; it's been a success, and that's as far as they want to go with it. Now they're moving on.
>
> That's the way I feel about what I'm doing. I'm delighted with my newfound time—which has immediately been taken up. I just want to assure you that it wasn't the station being instrumental in this, because this has been ongoing for about two years in my case... When you're doing five radio shows a week—five nights a week, forty-five minutes a night, and coming up with original material, for the most part every night, this requires an extraordinary amount of time.[47]

"It's a lot of time," Shepherd said of his broadcasts. "It takes a lot of effort and work—and it's very tiring." But back in Jean Shepherd's early radio days, we may remember, he claimed it

was a lot of fun and that he felt he had to lie when implying it
was hard work. The subject also came up in the Alan Colmes
1998 interview:

> A.C.: When I remember listening to you, the thing
> that strikes me most is how you would tell these great
> stories, and you would go off on these tangents and
> amazingly, while the last strains of the Strauss theme
> song were playing, somehow you'd bring all these dis-
> parate pieces together.
> Shep: Well, that was by design. And they weren't
> diversions, you know. When you say, "After all these
> diversions..."
> A.C.: Well, what I thought at the time were diver-
> sions, but obviously were not.
> Shep: No. They were the meat of the show. To me a
> good storyteller will almost always—if he's really a good
> storyteller—make it sound like he's hit upon the theme
> of what he's doing accidentally. So the audience sitting
> out there saying, "Gee, how did he get to that?" Well, he
> got to that because he planned it weeks in advance.
> A.C.: Yeah. I always got the feeling listening to you
> that this guy's just doing this off the top of his head. He
> walks in at five to eight, he sits down in front of a mike,
> and he talks for forty-five minutes. But that's nothing
> like what it was at all.
> Shep: Well, not at all. Some of the shows that I did
> that sounded the most casual, I'd work two or three
> weeks into it. And that was really my style. My style was
> an off-hand style. And I suppose in some ways that
> worked against me, because it made it seem to people
> who were listening that it was all accidental.

What ended was the broadcasting of an extraordinary fecund
mind that had kept stories and ideas—intellectual entertainment—going nonstop on radio for over two decades.

Although Shepherd grumbled even in the earlier days about
the lack of respect accorded his chosen medium, it should be
understood that he reveled in his radio program for the years he
was performing it. This is obvious from many of the transcripts
already presented. Only near the end of his radio career, when he
became totally disillusioned, focusing increasingly on other creative media, did he seriously disparage radio and his work in it.

Martin Jackson interviewed Shepherd in the WOR studio: "He came running up, practically steaming, into the studio, saying, 'Listen, I'm not here to talk about radio, I don't want to hear any of that "Excelsior" crap. I don't want to go back to the good old days. If that's what you're here for, you can leave now."[48] This was said when his twenty-one-year WOR gig still had three months to run. Then, in the 1998 Alan Colmes interview, Shepherd said bluntly again, "I hate to tell you this, Alan. I outgrew it. After all, when you've written and been involved with a major movie, and you're into movies, you don't go back and do radio." Comments by Shepherd's coworkers and friends of that time indicate that "outgrew it" in 1977 did not tell the whole story: he seemed bitter that—not for lack of talent or ambition—he had not been able to achieve more in radio. Radio had failed him.[xiii] Larry Josephson comments, "He was so bitter about being dropped by WOR that he went into denial and claimed that he was a writer, a novelist, and a this and a that and another thing and radio was just a sideline."

After Jackson's 1982 review of Shepherd's book *A Fistful of Fig Newtons*, Shepherd thanked him in a letter in which he wrote about radio, "Frankly I am delighted to be out of that thankless medium... My feeling about radio is that it once might have been a viable medium for a talented performer. And a creative medium at that. But no longer."[49]

In a talk on a May 2000 *Wired News* radio program, Max Schmid reflected that, "The tragedy of Jean Shepherd is that he was caught between two eras of broadcasting. Network radio died around the time he got started, and the technology for satellite syndication was developed after he left the air. As a radio performer, he was a regional phenomenon based in the East Coast signal area of WOR, and whatever tape distribution system could be managed (I don't know the details of the Boston and San Francisco broadcasts, but I assume it was by tape). *Playboy* articles and book sales, later PBS and movies, got national attention, but there was never a better guy in front of a microphone than Jean Shepherd, and it's a shame that he now [referring to the last years of his life] seems to be so unhappy with that legacy."

That legacy faded too easily in too many minds. Unfortunately, that ephemeral voice on the radio was too easy to forget, even by some people Shepherd had every right to think would have a part of him permanently in their minds. Author John Wilcock of the early *Village Voice*, who knew Shepherd, listened to him on the way to the *Voice* printer in Jersey in the late 1950s, and thought him "brilliant," now remembers little of him, and nothing of what he said on the air. Norman Mailer says he did not listen to Shepherd on the air, and he only vaguely remembers Shepherd despite what Shepherd remembered as conversations with him in those exciting, memorable late 1950s at the *Voice*. Dan Wakefield says, "Among the young people I knew—people just out of college, you know, people living in the Village or around Columbia [University]—everybody knew about Jean Shepherd... He was part of the conversation of people you knew. I later heard he was unhappy I hadn't mentioned him and his work in my book, *New York in the '50s*. I felt badly, as he certainly should have been in there... Who knows why I forgot... I was talking more about, you know, artists and writers in the *traditional* sense."

"Traditional" seems the operative word. Despite being an important presence in the creative world of his time, Jean Shepherd-on-the-radio—in that ephemeral medium—did not receive the recognition he deserved. Radio did not receive respect even when achieving the level to which Shepherd had brought it. Somehow, his voice was too much like the deepest and most intelligent conversations one had with oneself in one's head—it floated in the air—and was gone. It did not exist in a form one could see and grasp.

Of course Jean Shepherd knew of his tens of thousands of anonymous fans and he knew of the many people in the arts who were "listeners." But he could not know the extent of his influence and where it would lead in the lives of innumerable people—those whose outlook on life was changed for the better—who felt he had saved their lives! There were those who were inspired to go into writing or the media because of him, such as the *Realist* founder and publisher Paul Krassner, who remembers that Shepherd had influenced him to go into radio broadcasting. Another was broadcaster Larry Josephson, who says, "He kind of saved my life when I was stuck up in Poughkeepsie and drowning in loneliness and stuff, and he was a lifeline to what I thought was hip culture—New York City. Then, two years later I moved to the city. And I got to know him. He was on my BAI show once." Josephson, asked if Shepherd had also influenced his broadcasting, at first hesitated, then realized, "To the extent of just getting on the radio and talking. And I had this 'William Tell Overture,'" he remembered, recognizing that it was "probably suggested by Shepherd's theme—and talking over it, particularly at the end."

Others who would pay tribute in their art include Donald Fagen, former rock group Steely Dan member, who, about one of his songs, writes, "'The Nightfly' is a portrait of a late-night radio personality of the sort I used to listen to in my adolescence. The greatest was the monologist Jean Shepherd, who told magical stories of his youth in the Midwest."[50] Another who did so was comic-strip artist Bill Griffith, who declares in his strip *Zippy the Pinhead*, "His wit was like a life raft to me, adrift as I was on the sea of Levittown. I confess...I was a cultist...and Jean Shepherd was my guru. Who knows what deep subconscious effect his late-night loquaciousness had on me...?"[51] And how many others—such as U.S. Poet Laureate Billy Collins—were feeling, daily, as a kid back in the 1950s and 1960s, "I had to get my Shepherd fix."

By spring 1977, Shepherd's radio career was history, except for some short spots for CBS, NBC, and National Public Radio. (Which were like having a fine muralist paint miniatures on brooches.) He moved on to bigger—if not better—things. After all, as he once put it, "I'm an entertainer."

In addition to his writing, considerable projects in other media began during his radio days, such as his spoken word recordings, so closely related to the broadcast form. The major works involved movies and television, some also done during the same period as his radio broadcasting. Despite the change in media, Jean Shepherd's themes remained—his nonfiction work explored America and slobism, and his fiction, often using at least the trappings of nostalgia, usually left a distinct residue of mangled illusions. Think of those audiences, tears trickling, fondly remembering their own childhood, as they watch Shepherd's movie *A Christmas Story*—in which Santa kicks a kid in the face, and the kid nearly shoots his own eye out.

CHAPTER 18

I'M AN ENTERTAINER
Other Media

Although many saw Shepherd's métier as radio, from the beginning of his career he sought a wide variety of outlets for his creative talents. He sometimes complained that people in general, and the media in particular, quickly and permanently typecast creators, assuming that someone could not be good in more than one field at once. Although this may be true of many, Jean Shepherd indeed achieved good and distinctive work in several fields. Later in life, he would be so aggravated by those who focused on his radio work (and he tried so hard to boost his other work) that he belittled his achievements in that medium.

Beyond his work in radio—the medium in which he first achieved success and from which he increasingly tried to free his name—he had his writing. He gathered his short stories into books, the first of which he called a "novel." His articles were published widely and also anthologized. He made films that were visualizations of his already published stories. Each film contained several stories merged into a whole. He had television work (some of it also visualizations of his stories) that moved into nonfiction areas. In the latter, he apparently learned from the limitations of his early New York TV appearances, in which he merely faced the camera and talked. In the nonfiction works—primarily *Jean Shepherd on Route One*, the short series titled *Shepherd's Pie*, and the nearly two dozen episodes of *Jean*

Shepherd's America—he used television in a sometimes improvisational way as commentary on the American scene.

Shepherd was a great recycler of his own material into other media. There is a negative implication to this, but considering the immense quantity of material he created, the need to expose his work to other audiences, and the desire for wider recognition of his talent (with the concomitant financial rewards), recycling can only be seen as a response to reality.

The list that follows (mainly composed by Jim Clavin, maintainer of the Shepherd website www.flicklives.com) is not a formal analysis of such reuse, but an indication of some ways he did it, using the BB gun-for-Christmas story as a major example, which will be used to exemplify the stages his work went through. The first shot out of the rifle that "will shoot your eye out" ricocheted, barely missing little Ralph's eye, grazed his cheek, and broke his glasses. Shepherd said that he originally did the BB gun story as an antiwar commentary.

> Shepherd gets an idea that he develops and expands in a radio broadcast or concert. On December 26, 1964, he told the BB gun story—it was a Daisy brand he wanted, and he blamed kid brother Randy for breaking his glasses by stepping on them.
> The idea is used in a magazine article or short story. The *Playboy* story of December 1965, was titled, "Duel in the Snow, *or* Red Ryder Nails the Cleveland Street Kid." The model was now specified as a Red Ryder.
> The story is honed for his TV show or live concerts. His WOR TV *Jean Shepherd Show*, in which he practically word for word recited his Little Orphan Annie decoder story as previously rendered in other media, is an example.
> A studio or live performance version on record or audio cassettes is released. *Shepherd's Pie* cassettes of 1988 included the Red Ryder BB gun story.
> The work is formalized and legitimized in a book collection. The Red Ryder BB gun story appeared in the 1966 book, *In God We Trust: All Others Pay Cash*.
> A visualization of his favorite radio themes (such as "slob art") is filmed for his *Jean Shepherd's America*, *Shepherd's Pie* television shows, or elsewhere.

The story is retold on his radio broadcasts. Shepherd
   read the Red Ryder BB gun story from the book as an
   annual Christmas tradition.
Some of his "when I was a kid" stories are recombined
   into movies. Such as the 1983 movie, *A Christmas
   Story*, with its dominant story of the Red Ryder BB
   gun.
As the Red Ryder BB gun story evolved over the years,
   Ralph shifted the blame for the broken glasses to an
   icicle—this was probably to divert attention from
   Randy, a peripheral character here. The change from
   simple Daisy brand to Red Ryder model personified
   the rifle, so that Ralph could be seen hero-worshiping.

A component of Shepherd's creativity was his ability to use a
variety of media and maintain his distinctive vision at such a
high level. But a change in medium changes the nature of the
experience for the audience. The special quality of radio and
other aural formats in which Shepherd's mastery shone is that
mere sound conjures the image in the listener's mind. Although
the special quality of movies and TV is that the creator gains the
added tool of visualization, the audience loses the experience of
imagining. As radio lost its audience, Shepherd increasingly
chose TV and movies.

COMMENTARY AND OCCASIONS

Shepherd did occasional appearances in addition to his broadcasts, such as emceeing jazz shows and a radio jazz telethon, the
1957 live commentary on the Mike Todd party, and the 1976 live
broadcast from the top of the World Trade Center for the "Tall
Ships" Fourth of July celebration. He appeared on a variety of radio interview shows over the years, sometimes promoting one of
his books. Between 1981 and 1984 on NPR, he did over three
dozen commentaries on a variety of his pet themes, bits that varied in length from under two minutes to upwards of four.

THEATRICAL PERFORMANCE, ETC.

Back in 1960, Shepherd commented that "reading other guys'
lines" was of lesser interest to him than doing his own material—only to be done when he ceased to wonder about the

world around him.[52] A friend of Shepherd's gives interesting testimony in this regard:

> **Pete Wood:** He called me one time from New York—and this would be around 1961—somewhere in there. And he said that...as a radio personality he could not get on television. That he'd been trying and he just could not do it... I went up a couple of times to see him [from Philadelphia to New York, circa 1961]... He talked a lot about the fact that he was going to study to become an actor, and he was going to go into show business as an actor and he gave a lot of promotion about how he was going to do this show called *Destry Rides Again*.

Fred Barzyk remembers, "Shepherd always considered himself an actor. 'I'm an actor. I'm a *good* actor.'"[xiv] Despite his obvious desire for increased exposure (and money?), there were only a few instances of Shepherd's performing in the theater and possibly "reading other guys' lines." In 1957, Shepherd appeared in a "cafe show," a revue titled *Smalltacular*. (Indeed, he may have done his own material in this one). In 1959, he created the Off-Broadway theater piece *Look, Charlie*.

In 1961 he was busy on the stage playing Mephistopheles in *A Banquet for the Moon* starting in January,[xv] starring in *The Voice of the Turtle* in June, performing in a New Jersey production of *Destry Rides Again* in July, doing a summer revival of *The Tender Trap* in August, and appearing in *New Faces of 1962* in December (again, probably with his own material). A *New York Times* article said he "will be one of the principals" in *New Faces* and indicated that Shepherd would record some of his radio broadcasts only while on the road before the Broadway opening. He acted in 1963 previews of Arthur Kopit's Off-Broadway play *Asylum or What the Gentlemen Are Up to Not to Mention the Ladies*, which never opened. The above-mentioned seem to be Shepherd's only theater work. He also did the narration for various films and videos, and in the 1990s, he did the voice for the Orlando, Florida, Walt Disney World "Carousel of Progress."

LIVE CONCERTS

While still on WOR radio, Shepherd formed Staggerwing Productions with Leigh Brown as co-owner, apparently to manage at least some of his live performances.[53] (Staggerwing was an early type of airplane—a tribute to Shepherd's interest in flying.) Sometimes when Shepherd announced that he was to appear for a live concert, he included the running gag that he would perform his "Underwater Ballet." He included additional comments such as that the pipes were being installed, they'd paid off the cops, and he had a new sequined bikini.

A *New York Times* review of his New Year's Eve 1968 Town Hall performance described it as "blue," with off-color humor. He conducted a mass kazoo playing of "The Sheik of Araby." Knowing Shepherd, the kazoo seems perfect for performing in that august venue. He also appeared in concert at Carnegie Hall on October 17, 1972, September 22, 1973, and September 14, 1974.

"Jean Shepherd Plays Jean Shepherd"—his five-night (January 30–February 3, 1975) performance at the American Place Theater—began badly, according to the January 1975 *New York Times* review by Lawrence Van Gelder:

> As Mr. Shepherd's legion of devoted radio fans know, he can be a fine, funny, frequently spellbinding story-teller. As his readers know, he can be a captivating writer.
>
> But by choosing to read—rather than tell—what turned out to be the tale of a young boy who craved a Red Ryder Daisy air rifle for Christmas, Mr. Shepherd robbed himself of some of the keys to a successful performance.

The reviewer comments that when Shepherd put down his book and simply told a story, "It was short, funny and, most of all, well performed."

He appeared at One Sheridan Square, the Village Vanguard, and numerous other locations, especially on college campuses (including Princeton University annual appearances for thirty years).

Performing his own material before a live audience presented a different situation to the "entertainer." Instead of the seeming one-on-one radio effect, group interaction was expected and received. The Limelight broadcasts were his most conspicuous and frequent performances for live audiences, and comments earlier relate to the distinct differences in Shepherd's style before an audience.

A New Jersey Public Television videotape of a performance at the Clinton Museum Historical Society open-air theater provides a rare opportunity to see as well as hear Shepherd in action before an audience. (It was probably typical of this kind of Shepp-plus-audience affair, except for the major venues such as Carnegie Hall, where some simple set with lighting and sound effects were added.) This video opens not with the actual performance but with a lead-in of Shepherd seated at a picturesque pond, contemplating the scenery, ducks, and geese. He compliments Clinton, New Jersey, for having such a beautiful place, and walks down the street to the theater entrance. The use of himself as the performer heading toward the performance, rather than just beginning the video on stage, was typical of Jean Shepherd's style in all media. He insisted on making us conscious not only of the performance but of the reality surrounding it.

On stage, he begins with a series of anti–New Jersey lines, describing Saturday nights at the "Great Eastern" with Jersey-ites—"humanity moiling and boiling," buying anything and everything in sight. He encourages the audience to applaud: "Let's hear it for Jersey—what the hell, you've got damn little to cheer for!"

This beginning with a series of short, funny lines is similar to that of other stand-up comics. Then he segues into other material, such as "White enamel kitchen table with the little chips all around it... And if you put your nose real close—right on the surface of that table—it smelled like the vomit of thousands of kids. Now wait a minute, gang, that *is*, I grant you, in bad taste—ever had the sneaking suspicion that so is *life?*"

As the performance settles in and the audience quiets down, he moves into more extended, familiar material. The show ends with a return to New Jersey: "Gang, I've got to run. So out there in the darkness, get out there, go to the Dairy Queen, and allow yourself to fester as a true Jerseyite. Thank you."

RECORDINGS

Comedians from the 1950s and 1960s had garnered renown from their comedy records, and some even began their rise to stardom through these recordings. Shepherd's records, begun at about the same time, were not as successful. Despite their quality, they seemed to find most of their favor with those already familiar with his radio work. The original LPs are now collector's items.

Jean Shepherd into the Unknown with Jazz Music (1956)[54]

This first known album by Shepherd, not a comedy album at all, had remained among the missing until a copy sold in June 2003 at eBay auction for $1,995. Shepherd's comments alternated with eight musical pieces with titles such as "Socrates' Dream," "Voltaire's Vamp," and "Pride and Prejudice." One of the composer-arrangers, Mitch Leigh, later wrote the music for the Broadway musical *Man of La Mancha*. The jacket text (as it's in a style and content familiar as Shepherd's, he may well have written it) referred to Shepherd as "a true product of the twentieth century, nearsighted, fuzzy, but struggling bravely on into the unknown."[xvi] This recording, one of Shepherd's first published creative efforts, is discussed more fully (along with his collaboration on "The Clown") in Chapter 6.

The Clown (1957)

This album's title piece features Shepherd's improvisation to music by Charles Mingus, already discussed. In 1969, Duke Ellington, with his orchestra, narrated his version of "The Clown," in part improvising, in part using Shepherd's original improvisation.

Jean Shepherd and Other Foibles (1959)[55]

Shepherd's first full comedy album is a studio recording of finely honed renditions of his typical material, with no audience and no canned laughter. Shel Silverstein's drawings occupy the front and back covers, and he also wrote the liner notes. On the front, a motley parade marches across one shoulder of Shepherd, over his head (where the man on top holds a banner "Excelsior"), and down the other side. On the back, a parade moves around the foursquare sides, holding placards with letters sneakily spelling out backwards, "Jean Shepherd is a dirty rotten, one-way sneaky son of a bitch."

Side One:
1. "Peter Pain." Talks about the old comic strip ad, and ends with a typical Shepherd comment, that Pete was not promoting Ben Gay painkiller, but pitchforks.
2. "Judson-6." Recounts his calling a phone number scrawled in a phone booth.
3. "The Fun Funeral." An extended take-off based on an ad for funerals for modern Americans.
4. "For Men Only." He-man men's magazine taken to an

absurd extreme—with a real wild boar's–hide cover, plastic guts, broken glass, and blood.

5. "Fellow Americans." A phonus-balonus political speech with echo chamber and canned cheering crowds.

Side Two:

1. "Controversial-Noncontroversial Comics." A sardonic comment on what he sees as the then-popular crop of "controversial" comics who do not provoke controversy. See the description in Chapter 6.

2. "Monkey On My Back." The Cracker Jack candy slogan, "The more you eat the more you want"— being addicted to it as if it were a drug.

3. "Better Living." A short extension of the idea that scientists might create pills that induce the body's chemical reactions that create all kinds of delicious emotions.

4. "Balls." About Chicago White Sox fans, who "have known death every day of their lives, and it holds no terror for them." A classic Shepherd vignette: "Old Bill shakes off a sign, glances back toward second base where the runner's taking a short lead. He shakes off another sign—and everybody in the park knew that Deitrich had only two pitches—his slow curve and his wild one. He's already shaken off three signs. It was just the White Sox trying to play it out—you know— trying to make it look better—trying to make it look better for all of us. They represented not just Chicago, but the South Side! Do you know what it feels like to be a South Sider in a world of North Siders?" A story tinged with quirky un-reality, with a tale of humanity, full of illusions and futility, still acting out the dream.

5. "Credit Cards." Making fun of their ever-increasing proliferation in our lives.

6. "The Human Comedy." The final track: Shepherd watches the parade of humanity go by, commenting in part, as follows: Richard the Lion Hearted—"Hey Dick, hey *Hearted*"; Attila the Hun—"the little guy with the rug;" Jonathan Swift—"He's giggling. What's the *gag?*"; Billy Budd carrying a flag labeled "Excelsior"; "Hey, wait for me. I want to go—They never looked. Hey wait for *me!* Wait! I want to be *with* you! All the great people! *Wait! Wait!* I'm great too! Wait! *Wait!* They're gone."

Will Failure Spoil Jean Shepherd? (1961)

A live performance (with audience laughter) recorded in six cuts, Christmas week, 1960, at the Greenwich Village location, One Sheridan Square. Liner notes by Herb Gardner. Shepherd does not play to the audience to the extent he would at the Limelight a few years later. However, despite having complained two years previously, in *Jean Shepherd and Other Foibles*, that just naming a subject was not making a funny comment on it, in the opening track, titled "Purgatories," Shepherd says "Norman Vincent Peale" for the laugh. Peale was the enormously popular religious leader and author of such bestsellers as *The Power of Positive Thinking*. It is little wonder that Peale is said to have named him as a menace when one hears Shepherd continue on this cut: "Dr. Norman Vincent Peale... The greatest humorist America has produced! You see a twinkling in his eye, you know. He's pulling a fantastic gag on all of us." Shepherd's three-minute vignette ends with Peale in his luxurious office: "That door slams open. The light streams down." Shepherd screams the punch line: "'Peale, for God's *sakes*, what are you doing *now?*' It's *God*."

Jean Shepherd "Live" at the Limelight (1964)[56]

One should be able to listen to a few Limelight tapes to get the feel of this one. Liner notes by Paul Krassner. The record begins with Shepherd leading the audience to holler "Excelsior, you fathead!" He tells an Army Signal Corps story of laying wire from a plane, a story of drunken neighbor Brunner and his triangular donut machine, and a Chicago White Sox story.

The Declassified Jean Shepherd (1971)[57]

The jacket to this album has a caricature of Shepherd amid file cabinets, wearing an army uniform. The soundtrack includes Shepherd playing the jew's harp and thumping on his head. Group laughter indicates those tracks recorded with a Princeton University audience. This appears to be the only recording of Shepherd's done as an artistic whole, with a sense of beginning, middle, and end, with bridges between segments. It begins with a "man on the street" interviewer asking people if they like Jean Shepherd. The responses all give the impression that the interviewees don't understand the question, and/or don't know who Shepherd is. After extended stories, the record ends with the man on the street: "Do you know anything about Jean Shepherd, sir?" "Nah, don't."

Jean Shepherd Reads Poems of Robert Service (1975)[58]
For this Folkways album, Shepherd reads some of the more popular Service poems, with a short introduction to each. The album contains a booklet printing the poems, introductory text, and author description. Shepherd's short introduction to each poem is a serious comment on Service and the selection. Shepherd's renditions of the poems are similar to his super-dramatic radio readings and are accompanied by a tinkling piano.

Shepherd also did a 1983 recording for National Public Radio titled *The American Scene*, and in 1988 recorded *Shepherd's Pie*, seven "slices," cassette tapes of his readings of his stories, including the Red Ryder BB gun tale. Here Shepherd had even recycled one of his own titles from the TV series, *Shepherd's Pie*.

TELEVISION

We know how much Shepherd resented television. He saw it taking away his audience. He saw it as inferior to radio because it did not allow for the creative imagination possible on radio. He saw the commercial interests in television preventing quality work because they were pandering to the lowest common denominator. However, he realized that it was not going away and it was becoming more pervasive. Yet, in the beginning, he had trouble breaking into it. And in his early forays, when he did have a few small chances in New York television, he failed to sufficiently realize that he had to do something that was appropriate—rather than just look into the TV lens, which would appeal to his radio fans, who would be happy just seeing him do his radio thing, but perhaps not appeal to others.

> Did you hear what Les Smith said in the middle of his newscast? He's giving this commercial for *TV Guide*. And it came out of my monitor speaker like—like two little twin ice picks—*Schooo!*—and stuck right in the wall there. Right over Pegeen's cat picture—*Oing oing oing*—and hung there—the truth!... He says, "Yes, *TV Guide* will make you enjoy TV more because it will enable you to understand it—better." [Laughs.]
> Ah. I think the problem with TV is that most people understand it only too well. I mean, you know? [Laughs.] And so I say, "Yes, yes, that's right! Now if *TV Guide* would come out with an issue of what TV *really* means!" Oh, there would be

fighting—fistfights down in front of Rockefeller Center by three o'clock of the afternoon the magazine hit the stands. Foundations would crumble.[59]

Jean Shepherd hated the typical television broadcasting he saw, although he engaged with the beast from time to time. In his early encounters, on other people's shows, Shepherd had to battle insensitive circumstances or hostile forces.

He announced on an early radio program that he would be doing his first New York television bit on NBC's *Tonight Show*. One could imagine him on the TV stage set behind the curtain, waiting to be introduced. Maybe a bit nervous, hoping, expecting that he would be launched ever higher into the media heavens. Announcer Al Collins began his introduction to this show, gave Shepherd's name—and was interrupted by a "tour guide" passing through with a group on a fake NBC studios tour. Collins and the guide engaged in what was obviously a set-up plug for NBC and its studio tours. "Have you ever barged in on a show before?" This conversation lasted for nearly four minutes and then Collins said, "We're going to tour the local stations right about here, so stay with us." [Local station identifications and commercials followed.] Then Collins: "When we were interrupted, I was telling you about a guy named Jean Shepherd."[60] What a way to be mangled by a two-ton gorilla!

In the late 1950s, the investigative reporter Mike Wallace had hard-hitting, confrontational television shows. One saw only Wallace and his guest seated against a black background. With Shepherd as prey, Wallace was openly and consistently hostile. At one exchange, after a series of Wallace jabs, an exasperated Shepherd asked, "Have you *ever* listened to my show?" Wallace, admitting his lack of any basis for his nastiness, responded, "No."[xvii]

Shepherd's early attempts at performing on television in New York showed him, at least in some instances, doing his standard radio monologue. It did not work well. On one *Tonight Show*, while Shepherd tried to tell one of his stories as he sat on the couch with other guests, Victor Borge (who may have been bored, or resented that Shepherd was hogging the camera) constantly interrupted. On another *Tonight Show* appearance, guest host Ernie Kovacs (said to be trying to enliven a dull moment) had the screen split so that the top of Shepherd's perplexed and annoyed face showed over the lower half of that of Kovacs, whose mouth mimicked Shepherd's words.[61]

The Dissenters (Early 1960s)[xviii]

The Dissenters is said to have been a Philadelphia-based Sunday morning TV show on which Shepherd interviewed a person in the studio who held a belief in conflict with the mainstream. Reportedly, two such guests were Jules Feiffer and Paul Krassner, although when they were interviewed forty years later about the show, neither remembered anything about it. Considering the name of the show, and that it aired during the same period as much of the ferment regarding cultural and social conflicts, Shepherd and his guests must have had much to discuss; Feiffer as a commentator on social quirks and tics, and Krassner as a fierce critic of American society, culture, religion, and nearly everything else.

The Jean Shepherd Show (1960)

The only currently available remnant of Shepherd's short-lived TV show is the pilot's soundtrack. Some recall him seated on a stool against a black background, looking straight at the viewer, telling his typical radio broadcast stories, including the Little Orphan Annie Secret Decoder tale and other material. WOR's Herb Saltzman remembers, "I think it was only an experiment—which didn't do well." In these early New York days, Shepherd seemed to have forgotten the zany television work he had done before coming to New York. He was mistakenly trying to do his radio shtick in a different kind of medium.

Jean Shepherd, An American Humorist Looks at America (1962)

> **Fred Barzyk:** For us it was pretty radical programming. An Educational Television station which was doing Navy courses from Harvard, like physics, metallurgy, and all the rest—to have Shepherd show up and start doing this stuff...
>
> A local radio station, WHDH, for some reason picked up Shepherd and played him at twelve noon on Saturday... He sounded like all the *great* radio broadcasters I had known when I grew up in the Midwest... There is a whole history of storytellers [on the radio] that existed before Shepherd—but never moved to New York. I said, "I *gotta* work with this guy."
>
> Shepherd's audience was [young boys]. Girls—no! So I found a bunch of guys [at WGBH] who used to go under

the covers with a flashlight at night and turn on the radio and listen to Shepherd. That was how they grew up. That was their *Catcher in the Rye*. It was their way of hearing something different that their parents wouldn't understand... Why do you think I had such success getting Shepherd sold? Because all these guys grew up—the ones on the East Coast grew up listening to Shepherd—and that was like really putting money into their childhood again—to bring back an image. So it was real easy for me to sell... [Barzyk got these guys' help writing to Shepherd, who came up to Boston alone. They paid airfare and a check for one dollar.]

I convinced the engineers to give me one camera with a long cable that put him out on a dock right on the Charles River. So he stood up and I said, "You've got a half hour and we'll give you timing, and just do whatever you want to do." And so he did the two stories.[xix]

Matthew Callan reports that this show (July 30, 1962) has extremely tight shots of Shepherd's face—one sees almost nothing else. Shepherd tells the Little Orphan Annie story and one about realizing as a teenager that, instead of being the one having to endure the evening's blind date, *he* is the loser. Toward the end, Shepherd commented, "I've traveled pretty much around the world, and there are two really scared people in the world—the Americans and the Russians. They're scared for a lot of the same reasons, one of which is the fantastic immensity of the places they live in. You can get swallowed up in Russia like a cockroach on a football field. You can get swallowed up in America like an ant on an enormous baseball diamond. This produces people that, in a way, are afraid of their environment. Afraid of their climate."

Callan comments that, "What makes the show remarkable is a chance to see a relatively young Shepherd in action, and to get an impression of what his style might have been like in the studio, addressing an unseen audience as an intimate friend (although the 'rehearsed' nature of the tales makes them not as extemporaneous as his radio work)." So, at least into the early 1960s, Shepherd is still doing his basic radio act on television— fine for the fans, but not thrilling for other viewers. He needed to remember what he had done years before in his early *Rear Bumper* show.

Rear Bumper and Rear Bumpers

At some point, Shepherd must have realized that in a visual medium he had to do something more visual than just face the camera and talk. He claimed to have done visually inventive material in his pre–New York television days in his *Rear Bumper* program from WLW-TV Cincinnati (1953–1954?). In an interview with John Kronenberger of the *New York Times*, on June 3, 1971, Shepherd said:

> It was called *Rear Bumper*—it followed everything else each night and I'd come on for as long as I liked. One night I waited through one of the worst late movies ever made...jungle goddess in a plane crash...and I did the only logical thing. My theme came up—I had this beautiful opening—fade it out, and there's my face, full screen. I said, "Look, anybody who enjoyed that movie is not going to enjoy anything that I'm going to do. And conversely, any man with taste has already left us, so let's just part friends." And on came my theme again.

He did a similarly titled TV show (*Rear Bumpers*, 1969) for WGBH Boston: day-end, short, extemporaneous pieces.[xx] Fred Barzyk, who wanted to use Shepherd again for WGBH, asked him if he wanted to do a show like *Rear Bumper* for them. Barzyk remembers, "Again, I didn't pay him. I brought him up, he could do some things, and we would do these at the end of our program day. Our programming would end at eleven o'clock and instead of just going to the transmitter—and all that kind of good stuff—all of a sudden pops up—Shepherd. And he did about ten or twelve of these *Rear Bumpers*."

The programs are wide-ranging in subject matter, and sometimes play with the television medium itself. For example, Shepherd comments, "I like canned laughter. Wouldn't it be great if they put it on the Huntley and Brinkley show?" (A highly regarded and popular news program.) Canned laughter continues throughout the short. On another, Shepherd is heard as the camera moves though the WGBH studios. When the camera finally stops, it focuses on a reel-to-reel audio player, the obvious source of Shepherd's voice. At last, with Barzyk, Shepherd is having fun with the television medium. Commenting further on Shepherd in relation to TV, Barzyk says, "His expectations for *real* fame on television were quite large."

America, Inc.—First in a Series, *A Generation of Leaves* (1970)^{xxi}

A WNET Playhouse 1970 drama from WGBH, Boston, using a documentary style, one hour and twenty minutes long, *A Generation of Leaves* was narrated in part by Shepherd. Although Shepherd was not given the opportunity to do anything but narrate, the style and content of the drama as a commentary on American culture fit within the *Jean Shepherd's America* genre.

> **Fred Barzyk:** I had this other play I wanted to do called *America, Inc.*, which was a collage of a kid—'60s kid... I wanted to just do a reflection of the aimlessness of that particular group of kids. So we had no script. We would just go—"Where do you want to go?"
>
> The premise was—everything's going to be all right if you just listen to America, Inc., which is this wonderful company really making everything understandable. So you get these kids who are freaking out... America Inc., would say... "if you want more information write to America, Inc." We never thought anybody would write in—it was all tongue in cheek... Shepherd was my "stage manager" à la Brecht. So it's *Our Town* 1968 with Brechtian overtones. Meaning he tried to reveal the underpinnings, and separate you from the story of these guys and really make you think about the culture and how the culture is driving us.

In the beginning, Shepherd appears in a bare studio in close-up, talking into the camera, facing viewers just as his radio listeners picture him talking to each of them:

> Hello, fellow Americans. Fellow travelers on the yellow brick road of life... Have you ever had the suspicion that your life is on tape and that you're the victim of some really lousy editor? He's cut out all the great stuff—left you with nothing but all the dull junk like waiting in line at the cleaners—stuff like that, and your life just goes on and on, and the tape machine keeps running and you keep running, and—it ain't easy friends—being an American.

Jean Shepherd's America (1971 and 1985)

Public Broadcasting System did two series of programs that gave Shepherd's wide-ranging take on Americana—the perfect

TV vehicle for his particular attitudes. The first thirteen half-hour episodes were produced in 1971, the second thirteen in 1985, which included three repeats from the first series. Here was the American humorist commenting on his country from a power center of slobism itself—television (and doing it from the sanctuary of a nonprofit, educational TV network). They were all written and created by Jean Shepherd.

One of Shepherd's major complaints about television was its obsession with "format." Rigidity and standardization equaled death for Shepherd. He pointed out in a talk at the Overseas Press Club that each of his *Jean Shepherd's America* programs was different. He preferred to let the form emerge in process, generated by the nature of each show's content, as in a jazz interpretation.

The press kit stated, "It is the first time that series-length programming has been produced totally with a highly portable color video-tape system rather than film." Three technicians "hand-carry the entire system for location work... What they see, they videotape. It's as simple as that. There is no need to plan shots carefully in advance, or to prepare people for the camera. Things are recorded as they occur naturally... His technique is really a whole new approach to television, call it video verité. The point is spontaneous conversations, unplanned occurrences."

This is a bit overstated—the more spontaneous programs do seem to have only a basic outline and direction allowing for considerable improvisation, but some were obviously carefully scripted. The improvisation in his radio work that never failed sometimes faltered on television, but Shepherd and his producers seemed willing to take chances with the unknown, and that took guts. Fred Barzyk, the series production director, remembers:

> He was never going to appear in the show, but because the camera had so many technical problems, that was the only way we could get anything to be decent for the show... He wanted to be just a voice—as you look at all these things, and I was the one, because of all these technical things, who *forced* him to go on-camera.
>
> [Quoting Shepherd.] "We're not going to do any research. We're not going to know anything that we're going to do. We're just going to go someplace and we'll

find out what we're going to do. I don't want any research, I don't want any knowledge."

He just basically wanted to hit the road. What we did? I'll tell you exactly how we decided. He put out a big map and said, "So where do you want to go, Leigh, where do you want to go, Fred..." That's how the decisions were made. They were totally extemporaneous. They were freeform. It was uncertain what we were going to get. And Shepherd was *on* some days and some days he wasn't. And some days the camera worked and some days it didn't work.

Shepherd was seen at the beginnings and endings, frequently throughout, and he narrated the programs. Few people remember details of the 1971 series, and copies of these are not available as of this writing, but Matthew Callan, researching them at the WGBH offices, comments, "Even though Shep talked a lot, on camera and off, each episode also has extended quiet moments, where the camera will focus on some seemingly random bit of scenery. Despite the lack of talk in these scenes, they are very much Shep-like, since they focus on minutiae that seems unimportant to the naked eye—like a signalman waiting at a railroad crossing, or pieces of abandoned luggage on a train platform." Though always essentially himself, Shepherd sometimes played mock characters in the second series. Shepherd commented in an interview, "Instead of just going places and doing travelogues, what we do is go to different parts of America. But each place I go, I play another character. For example we did a show in Death Valley and I play this old prospector who is struggling across the salt flats with his mule."[62]

Some episodes seemed very slow moving, but slow moving often fit the kind of easy-going, contemplative mood Shepherd employed to indicate a broad range of visual and mental clues to his idea of the mosaic of America. Sometimes a slow sonata movement can tell us more than a frantic polka.

More problematic is the fact that, although the ideas behind the episodes were interesting, there did not seem to be enough to fill the half hour—the moment-by-moment was often weak in content, Shepherd's constant richness in detail, as heard on the radio, was sometimes missing, his narration seemingly uncertain and halting at times, and he appeared not to know what to say to keep it alive. This flaw could be considered the result of

Shepherd inserting himself into the proceedings—a frequent Jean Shepherd conceit—and one might think his ego was out of control, but it was not. Allowing for some ego in the act, Shepherd as Shepherd—on camera (or as narrator in *A Christmas Story*)—had a knack for creating a direct, real connection to the audience. Not that of a disconnected announcer voice, but of a specific individual engaged in personal communication. So Shepherd's idea to go places without preplanning, and Barzyk's idea to have him on-screen each caused its own kind of problem, but the technique of Shepherd being there as a voice (and sometimes on-screen) would lead to the technique Shepherd would use for most of his succeeding television and film work. The programs restated many Shepherd themes found in his previous work. The PBS capsule descriptions give an idea of each. (Parenthetical comments are the present author's.)

28 Flavors: Jean's tribute to Maine and fishing. (Shepherd sometimes talked on the radio about his love of Maine's distinctive inhabitants and landscape, and his frequent trips to his cabin on a lake in the Maine woods.)

Inland Steel: A visit to the steel mill in Hammond, Indiana. (Shepherd says, "I've never gotten over the overwhelming, fantastic sea of sound." Sparks of molten steel being poured, splashing like a waterfall, make the scene seem almost beautiful. He has come home again, to one of his high school summer jobs.)

The City of Los Angeles: A cross-country train ride. (Shepherd tells the story of Ernie, the soldier who got off the train for beer and couldn't make it back on, and says, "Behind each one of these great express trains is a crowd of shadowy Ernies, who always miss the train by inches—every train, their dog tags clinking in the long American night.")

A Bunch of the Boys Were Whooping It Up in the Malamute Saloon: Shepherd travels to Alaska. (He undercuts the wild, untamed-wilderness image of Alaska at the end, where, as he walks north off into the tundra, he looks at the ground and says, "Hey! There's a beer can here!")

There's a Lot More to Life Than a Hostess Twinkie: An ode to food. (The effect of the narration and the video is one of pure gluttony.)

The Bad Guys Were Back on the Shore, Shaking Their Fists: Jean takes the helm of a houseboat.

The Perpetual Swish of Windshield Wipers: An ode to the automobile and driving. (Shepherd: "I wonder how many people are on a road and don't know they're on a road. A lot of them are on a road and at the end of it, and they didn't ever know they were on a road. Do you have the sneaking suspicion that you're at the end of the road, and you don't know what to do about it?")

It Won't Always Be This Way: On the road in a mobile home. (After showing glistening new planned communities, the show moves to a ghost town called Independence. Shepherd: "It's funny that they named it Independence, because they had no independence. Once the mine quit, they were gone. Can you imagine someone digging up a piece of your stereo and putting it on display at the British Museum?... No matter how we live, we always think that someplace, somehow, there's a better way of life. It is the constant search for Paradise, Eden. And what do we get? Worn-out tennis shoes, busted pots, rusty nails—and it will always be that way. The wind blows through the broken windows, burlap curtains. I wonder who the lady was who put that up. One day, up on the moon, we're gonna be looking at the sky and saying, 'If only I could get outta this place...'")

From Its Ice-Cold Golden Depths Come the Echoes of Lost Battles, the Sound of Ancient Victories, the Noise of a Million Ballgames: Shepherd's classic tribute to beer. (The program begins and ends with close-ups of roiling waves of amber suds. He treats beer as a kind of American religious mania. He says one looks into a glass of beer and sees a million ballgames, moments, fights, victories. He tells of his father coming home from work and his mother has forgotten to restock the beer supply. There is a fight—Shepherd doesn't accept the verisimilitude of Edward Albee's plays where spouses argue over emasculation—they argue about beer and who takes out the garbage. "When you look at that glass of beer, you're looking at life itself—the mother of us all!")

Like Old Ahab: Jean flies a kite on a Florida beach.

There's No Place to Go But Up: Jean takes to the skies in his private plane.

Like All Inner Tube Specialists: Jean remembers his Dad, while on a beach in Hawaii.

Make School or Die: Jean is caught in a Wyoming snowstorm. (Apparently, the storm is unexpected, and the show has to be even more improvised than anyone had foreseen. We see him, cowboy hat tied on his head with a scarf, trudging in the windy snowscape. He remembers being bundled off to school as a kid on a snowy day. We see Jean in the "Little America

Motel." We see him dancing with a blonde—whom Barzyk says is Leigh Brown. While wandering through the motel's gift shop, Shepherd comments that, being snowed in, there is nothing to do but look at slob art.)

Mosquitoes and Moon Pies: A visit to the Okefenokee Swamp where Jean searches for his roots. (This is one of the most successful shows—both artistically, and in having momentum. It opens and closes at night with jittery shots of the moon. Shepherd recites the beginnings of one of his favorite poems, "When you were a tadpole, and I was a fish..." At the end, at night again, he comments that the swamp is where we all came from, and we'll all go back there. "I'll see you at the end of the evolutionary scale... I ain't never coming back. Bye bye, *TV Guide.*")

Filthy Rich at Last: Jean visits the rarefied atmosphere of the very, very, very rich. (Shepherd on his yacht, "Sinbad," acts the part of the proud, newly rich.)

Bourbon and Major Wilkes' Rocking Chair: The best of the ol' South. (Shepherd—"Colonel Beauregard Shepherd"—rides in on a white mare, as though it were 1858, and he a pre–Civil War plantation master—no slaves, just free men. From an evocation of the old, we move to the modern South, full of slobism accompanied by the brash music of "That's What I Like About the South.")

The Great American Tourist Trap: Shepherd's homage to tacky trash and the American tourist.

Cha-Cha Lessons on C Deck at 9 AM: A trip on a Florida cruise ship. (Shepherd comments that this vessel used to be a World War II troop ship, and we see old black-and-white footage of troops boarding her. The ironic contrast between modern-day vacationers and men going off to war is stark.)

Down in Death Valley: Jean follows the trail of the 49ers and meets some interesting characters.

The Devil on the Bayou: The Devil spends a weekend in New Orleans. (Shepherd as the Devil. Gluttony rears its voracious head. Shepherd, à la Toulouse-Lautrec, sketches a woman in a bar, and, joining the tail end of a small Dixieland marching band on Sunday morning, he plays his kazoo.)

I Love Cars, So There, Ralph Nader!: Jean watches his own car being assembled and takes a lap around Indy with racing great "Duke" Nalon. (After the glories of sports car racing and new convertibles, Jean cuts it all down to reality with a visit to an old car graveyard.)

Chicago, Chicago, That Toddlin' Town: Jean's ode to the Windy City.

Here Today, Guam Tomorrow: Jean visits a very distant American shore.

Was *Jean Shepherd's America* a bunch of individually self-indulgent, inordinately slow-moving, inchoate, failed graspings for the Great American Novel as Documentary? Or possibly, was it a few masterpieces of an incomplete, vast mosaic of this country, the very contemplation of which only a master, striving toward encompassing the unattainable vastness, would have had the temerity to attempt? The complete series can only be appreciated if one mentally steps back from the mosaic and visualizes it in its entirety, appreciating the courageous attempt, finding pleasure in the sometimes less successful results. When watching the programs, one needs to sit back, relax, and let it flow. McLuhan quoted Shepherd as saying his radio work was a continuing novel. *Jean Shepherd's America* is indeed profound in that sense.

A TELEVISION TRILOGY AND OTHER PROGRAMS

Phantom of the Open Hearth (1976), *The Great American Fourth of July and Other Disasters* (1982), and *The Star-Crossed Romance of Josephine Cosnowski* (1983) constitute a trilogy of fictions based on Shepherd's short stories. During the period of their production, he also did the nonfiction series, *Shepherd's Pie* (1978), and *Jean Shepherd on Route One* (1983).

Phantom of the Open Hearth (1976)

This "long-form drama" was a made-for-television movie of amusing short stories, loosely strung together with the recognizable Shepherd antinostalgia quirkiness and ending. An unusual feature for a fictional movie was that Shepherd appeared at the beginning and ending, as he did in *Jean Shepherd's America*, and would do in several subsequent filmed fictions.

In the opening, he talks about the steel mill's open-hearth furnaces, and one sees them in action. Shepherd explained in an interview, "It's a part of America that not many people write about and I don't know why, because most of America is an industrial world. Yet very little fiction is written about it. Very little drama is written about it—if they do, they call it a 'blue collar drama,' which is a real putdown. The father isn't a blue-collar worker, by the way, which is ironical. He works at a place he simply calls 'the damn office.'...They live in an industrial town. You know most of the people who live in industrial towns work in white-collar jobs in the offices, the tabulating departments and all that. Only a few work on the assembly line. It's *that* world that I write about really."[63] Shepherd is cribbing from his own biography here, in that he lived in a steel mill town and his father was a white-collar worker, a cashier.

Ralph delivers mail at the steel mill; his old man wins the lamp in the shape of a woman's leg; on "dish night" at the local movie theater, women (including Ralph's mother) revolt and throw gravy boats at a theater owner when they receive the same piece of china on dish night week after week; and Ralph has a disastrous prom night with Wanda Hickey.

This work is not only antinostalgic but harsh—one might say cruel (Shepherd would say "realistic"). It represents a more consistently bitter worldview than his earlier work. In his introduction to the published script, he wrote, "My humor is not the one-line insult joke of, say, *Rhoda* or *M*A*S*H*, but rather it is humor that arises out of inflection, a character's attitude, the predicament he's in, and the constant struggle to remain afloat in a sea of petty disasters."

In the introduction, Shepherd made an important statement regarding his technique of narrating a number of his productions, including the movie to be made several years later, *A Christmas Story*:

> The Narrator is actually the voice of Ralph, grown up, but at the same time he is somehow mysteriously in communication with the viewer. The viewer then becomes the second half of a dialogue between the Narrator and himself. The Narrator is both viewing the scene as it occurred or as he lived it and commenting to you about it, but never directly. He tells you, for example, what he thought at the time but not what he did, since you see that happening. He also makes oblique references to the ultimate consequence, in later years, of the action. This gives the script an added dimension of a life elapsed, and not just an isolated slice of time.

Shepherd also said the film received several nominations for Television Critics Circle Awards: Best Achievement in Comedy,

Best Achievement in Comedy Writing, Best Comedy Performance for James Broderick's portrayal of "the old man."

> **Fred Barzyk:** When he first started in, because we
> were representing Harvard and all the rest, he was sweet
> and wonderful and did all of his work fine. The *Rear
> Bumpers* were all right—no real problem. *America,
> Inc.*—no problem. It's when we started doing—after
> *Phantom*—he started to realize there was some success
> in this thing, that he started getting more and more con-
> trolling, and in *America, Inc.*, he lost more and more
> control. What happened was, here was a guy who nor-
> mally was used to going into a studio with a microphone
> and being in total control—giving up more and more
> and more as the crews got bigger and bigger and bigger.
> You know—"I don't want to sit with the actors. I don't
> want to sit with the crew. I want to sit just with you, the
> producer." It became "I'm losing control." And as he
> lost more and more control, he limited his access to
> people. So he would become very aloof. And he would
> become fearful—paranoiac about things that weren't
> going right.

Shepherd's Pie (1978)

In 1978, Shepherd did a series for New Jersey Public
Television that interwove studio pieces with short segments in a
fashion similar to *Jean Shepherd's America*. Here he came close
to using television as a visual realization of his radio work—he
combined an in-the-studio playfulness with humorous commentaries of the "Only in America" sort, using on-location footage.

Each program opened with an empty set, as though not yet
ready to go on the air, consisting of a foreground ladder in sil-
houette, a draped curtain, and a folding chair. Shepherd entered
doing a silly dance with his back to us, turned around, and the
show began.

The show focused on familiar Shepherd themes. In one studio
piece, someone threw him an obviously fake hand grenade, and
he responded, "We've just received this as another entry into the
Shepherd's Pie Contemporary, Memorial Museum of True,
Dynamic, Slob Art." There was a "Junkyard Waltz," with aes-
thetically caressing camera pans over junk, including slow-
motion junkyard equipment waltzing to Strauss music. He rated
"junk food," describing one burger thusly: "...has a certain pro-

letarian charm, a certain aggressive, peasantlike vitality—interesting aftertaste." He visited Fort Monmouth, New Jersey; and the barracks of the Signal School, where he said he went "through days of the Korean War."[xxii] As his army records show him in the service during World War II, in the previous decade, this may well have been an attempt to shave nearly ten years off his actual age, for public consumption.

Shows included a "crew member of the week," one showing "Leigh Brown of Washington, NJ" eating a hamburger. The end titles credited "kazoo solo by J. Shepherd."

The Great American Fourth of July and Other Disasters (1982)

Shepherd narrates as he drives a silver Rolls Royce, saying, "Oh God, I love I-95—all the way from the Maine border down to Tennessee Williams' house in Key West." A bit of steel mill footage, interrupted with Shepherd buying fireworks, leads into the fictional story of fireworks on the Fourth of July.

The film is a miscellany of Shepherd short stories strung together: a baton twirl that shorts out the whole county; Ralph losing a sack race; Ralph playing sousaphone in the high school marching band; and Ralph on a date with a blond beauty, realizing that *he* is the dreaded "blind date!" There is a tribute to one of Shepherd's favorite radio programs, *Vic and Sade*, in his mother's chain-letter washrag caper—and in sending her rags to Y.Y. Flirch of Fishigan, Michigan. For fireworks, Shepherd's old man presents his shoot-off like an orchestra conductor, and drunken neighbor, Ludlow Kissel, fires off a monster bomb that destroys his own porch.

The movie ends with the camera focusing on an American flag in an attic and Shepherd narrating a patch of indisputable *nostalgia*: "Americans measure their lives by holidays: Christmas, Easter, birthdays, Thanksgiving, the Fourth of July—like mileposts in the picket fence of the year that stretches on and on through our lives. But those holidays when you're young—they're the sweetest of all. You remember them forever. That great Fourth of July so long ago like all the others was gone—gone with the wind." There was no irony in his tone—but who knows what he was thinking. Maybe a nostalgia-laden coda was the price you paid when you moved from radio to the big world of television movies.

Jean Shepherd on Route One (1983)

This fifty-eight-minute show, produced in 1983 for the New

Jersey Network, was an extended put-down of New Jersey in particular, and America in general.

Shepherd drives the eponymous road and comments on the passing scene. "One word of caution, though. You cannot leave a diner without having a toothpick sticking out of your trap. I've always envied these truck drivers who go around with a match sticking out of their mouth. Oh, Lord, I love my fellow Americans. You just can't imagine the late Charles Boyer with a match sticking out of his mouth."

He refers to junkyards as "the compost heap of dreams," and "the ultimate collage—it contains *all* of life... Something that we have created in our time that future civilizations are going to marvel at. What *is* all this junk? What drove them to make it?... Above it all, the sun shines down on this curious barbaric beauty—that is, the eternal junkyard of all time."

He talks of going west on New Jersey's Route 22: "It's the true bastion of the slob road of America in full flower and it's got it all going... I would recommend to anyone who wants to know something about our planet—let's say he comes from Saturn, or Mars, or Indiana—just start at the mouth of the Holland Tunnel... And as the sun sets and glints and glows on the beautiful Watchung Hills, on the magnificent Route 22, remember you're traveling one of America's most complete works of living, surrealistic art, pulsing with true, deep, passionate, yeastlike life. It's all here. Hieronymous Bosch, Salvador Dalí, you have nothing on New Jersey's great and immortal Route 22."

The Star-Crossed Romance of Josephine Cosnowski (1983)

This long-form television story is subtitled "A Tale of Gothic Love." As the story concentrated on Ralph, not Josephine, a more relevant title might be "The Polish Wedding That Wasn't." The title of the original Shepherd short story as it appeared in *Playboy* magazine said it best: "The Star-Crossed Romance of Josephine Cosnowski and Her Friendly Neighborhood Sex Maniac."

As with other Shepherd television films, he appears in the beginning and narrates. We see steel mills. "My name is Ralph. I'm a movie freak." Shepherd with a White Sox cap on is watching a Polish art film—a woman dancer reminds him of Josephine. "It's Josephine Cosnowski! Did I ever tell you about Josephine Cosnowski?" This is probably the most direct TV/movie connection to his radio style of remembering his youth. There was also the connection to the middle-European population of Shepherd's boyhood neighborhood, and the multilingual radio program he said he announced for as a teenager. We are launched into the story of adolescent Ralph's lust for his new Polish neighbor, Josie.

As with Shepherd's other visual adaptations, several story lines interweave, with minor changes from the original short stories. Ralph is captivated by the voluptuous Josie (see her description in Chapter 16), and he likes Polish cooking, too; his old man wants to buy a used Oldsmobile; kid brother Randy does not want to play a turkey in the Thanksgiving pageant. More successful than in other Shepherd visualizations, the main story—Ralph and Josie—predominates sufficiently, and the whole comes together with sure craftsmanship. There is real development and plot—a work of art.

Although no discernible religion attaches to the Shepherd/ Parker family, one imagines a nonreligious Protestant background. Josie is Polish Catholic. Friend Howie, once a boy with potential, married too young to a Polish girl, now has kids, and is stuck consequently in a dead-end job and a dead-end life. Howie points out that Josie's script has Ralph headed for a Polish wedding, when all innocent Ralph wants is some Polish pulchritude. "Run for it, man! *Now!*" says Howie. Ralph recognizes the potential disaster and escapes.

As Shep the narrator says, "The moth had come close to the flame. There would be other flames, but that was in the future." Ralph escapes the Polish wedding, his mother saves the family from a bad used-car deal, and Randy is a great success as a turkey. Only we know, thanks to narrator Shepherd, that Randy's turkey triumph while still a kid will be the high point of his life. For now, it is Thanksgiving and all is well. The family dog is played by Shepherd's family dog, and at fade-out time, narrator Shepherd provides the glow that warms the cockles— *nostalgia* reins: "Those Thanksgivings at home were what Thanksgiving is all about. Mothers, fathers, brothers, the family dog, and Time, like a gray shadow pursuing us all. But those Thanksgiving drumsticks were the sweetest of all. Even Time can't rob you of those memories. They are forever."

Miscellany

A June 1962 New York newspaper article stated that Shepherd "is a headliner on NBC TV's *Today Show*." Shepherd appeared on a variety of other television shows, including those of Steve Allen, Merv Griffin, and Larry King, on *I've Got A Secret*, where he revealed he could head-thump a tune, and on

the *Tonight Show*, talking with guest host Ernie Kovacs. On
Sesame Street, he was the voice of Cowboy X. Shepherd also
participated in other projects, such as appearing in a PBS 1975
television documentary tribute, *Lenny Bruce Without Tears*.

In 1987, *Chicago White Sox: A Visual History, Hosted by
Jean Shepherd* was released by Major League Baseball. Decades
after he left the Chicago area for a career and life in New York,
Shepherd returned to narrate this one-hour video for the
favorite team of his childhood—the team he had frequently
described on the radio with a mixture of love and amused exasperation.

In the 1990s, Shepherd appeared for a few minutes on two
History Channel specials, one on the history of Thanksgiving,
another on the history of Christmas, with reference to his movie,
A Christmas Story. He also did some commentary on a video
about Babe Ruth in 1998.[64]

Credit Where Credit Is Due: A Bitter Story

Shepherd's influence on television can be seen most obviously
in the bittersweet, tender, and well-done situation comedy, *The
Wonder Years*, which ran from 1988 to 1993. A sensitive boy
lives through situations that teach him about life, narrated
throughout, with the introspective lesson at the end, by his adult
self, à la Jean Shepherd. And it is not just the storytelling style—
some specific Shepherd stories were used on the show, so he said,
without attribution. Jean Shepherd, reportedly, was bitter. In the
2003 DVD commentary for the Shepherd movie, *A Christmas
Story*, Bob Clark, its director/cowriter says:

> *Wonder Years* is a bitter story. They first auditioned
> Shepherd to do [the narration]. I introduced him to
> Spielberg. Steven was a big fan of *A Christmas Story*,
> and he wanted to meet Shepherd. So he had lunch with
> him—with his wife. And he called me and he said, "Bob,
> how did you [manage to] get along with this guy?"
>
> I said, "I know exactly what you're talking about,
> Steven, but Jean and I were together on this venture for
> ten years before, so we had a rapport, but yes, he's a
> [pause] —he's evasive. He's not nasty, just [pause, the
> thought left hanging]."

They rejected Shepherd as narrator. How close he came to a
major breakthrough in countrywide exposure and renown! *The*

Wonder Years, adored by millions, was on for five years and consistently has been seen in reruns ever since. The potential Great Jean Shepherd Popular Success Story was thwarted in good part by Shepherd himself.

MOVIES

The extent to which Shepherd rejected parts of his former self is manifest in Fred Barzyk's comment: "He wouldn't communicate with me after my usefulness was done. Once he moved on from television to the movies—he's not a television performer. 'Never has been radio.' It's all 'I'm a movie person.'"

As a movie person, Shepherd retained some characteristics of his television work. There is a blend of forms between television "long-form dramas" such as *Phantom of the Open Hearth*—with Shepherd narrating his stories strung together and appearing beginning and end—and what may more properly be called his movies, *A Christmas Story*, *Ollie Hopnoodle's Haven of Bliss*, and *It Runs in the Family* (a.k.a. *My Summer Story*). In these films, Shepherd narrates his strung-together stories without appearing on-camera.

A Christmas Story (1983)

Bob Clark, *A Christmas Story*'s director and cowriter, refers to it as "An odd combination of reality and spoof and satire."[65] The credits describe this 1983 movie as "Based upon the novel, *In God We Trust: All Others Pay Cash* by Jean Shepherd. Screenplay by Jean Shepherd and Leigh Brown and Bob Clark." It has grown to become beloved as a Christmas masterpiece. The movie is a series of antinostalgic disasters, focusing on Shepherd's alter ego Ralphie, who gets his hoped-for Red Ryder BB gun, and nearly fulfills the adult predictions that "you'll shoot your eye out!" A department store Santa disposes of nine-year-old Ralphie by shoving him down a slide with a boot to the face. (There is a cameo appearance by Shepherd and wife, Leigh Brown, waiting in line for Santa.)

When Ralphie gets pink bunny-rabbit pajamas, the Ralph-as-an-adult Jean Shepherd narrator comments that the aunt who gives the gift forever thinks Ralphie is four years old and a *girl*. (The scene is funny even without the in-joke allusion to Jean Shepherd's occasional broadcast comments that he has been annoyed throughout life by people assuming he is a girl because of his first name.) Laurie Squire comments that Peter Billingsley, who played little Ralphie, "was junior Shepherd. It was uncanny—that kid! Mannerisms, the speech pattern, everything was like a junior Jean. In the movie, when you're watching that kid act, it was like watching Jean Shepherd."

The movie features a number of comic scenes, such as Ralph's friend Flick, on a dare, getting his tongue stuck to a frozen metal pole. The old man receives, as a prize, an absurd woman's leg–shaped lamp and insists on putting it in the living room window. (Years later, a novelty company made reproductions of the lamp for sale.)

The look and feel of the movie, seemingly filled with holiday cheer and fondly remembered winter memories, cause people to wax nostalgic over it despite the nearly unrelieved string of misadventures. Shepherd claimed that he had wanted to call it *Santa's Revenge*.

The annual broadcast royalties probably set Shepherd up financially for the rest of his life. Shepherd's close friend, Ron Della Chiesa, reminded of the *Jean Shepherd's America* TV episode titled "Filthy Rich at Last," says, "He did become filthy rich at last, and it was because of *A Christmas Story*." The Turner cable TV network shows it round-the-clock starting on Christmas Eve. As Shepherd summed it up regarding the movie, "I'm fat and rich and money keeps rolling in."[66] Twenty years after it first appeared (and four years after Shepherd died), movie tie-ins proliferate.

The commentary accompanying the 2003 DVD re-release of the movie contains background information on the initially poor box office showing, and Shepherd's role in the making of the movie. Director/cowriter Bob Clark says that the studio waited too long to reserve venues for its original release in 1983, so at Christmas it was only in about one hundred theaters. (It is said that the movie studio only backed the making of it grudgingly, and did not promote it much.) Clark says that he read in *Variety* that during the Christmas Eve twenty-four-hour *Christmas Story* marathon on cable television one year, many years after its theatrical release, 38.4 million viewers tuned in for at least a part of it.

Although Shepherd claimed to have had major control, Bob Clark's commentary says that "[Shepherd] was there for the first two or three weeks [of the forty-day production], and after that I managed for Jean to go home. Loved him, but he was obsessive... It just was impossible."

The twentieth anniversary two-disc special edition contains

the complete movie in both full screen and wide screen, plus a feature-length commentary by Peter Billingsley (Ralphie) and Bob Clark, a documentary on the making of the movie, a history of the Daisy Red Ryder BB gun, a "humorous peek" at the making of the leg lamp, two interactive games, the original theatrical trailer, and a radio telling of the BB gun story by, as the package puts it, "the beloved narrator of *A Christmas Story*, Jean Shepherd." One wonders how Shepherd would have responded to being described as "beloved." Certainly some of his associates would choose a different adjective.

> **Fred Barzyk:** He [Bob Clark] was another one of these kinds of people who were drawn deeply to Shepherd. And he came to Shepherd and said, "I want to do *A Christmas Story*," and for Shepherd this was *big* because it was going to be a movie. Maybe at long last people will recognize *Shepherd*—as an important American icon. So he cut off all things with television. Didn't invite me to the set, he didn't do anything, even though we'd spent 1961 until the wee hours—he had moved on.

It seems that sometimes Jean did not play well with others.

Ollie Hopnoodle's Haven of Bliss (1988)

This 1988 TV film (the credits note, "a production of Pholly, Inc."), based on Shepherd stories, depicts the antinostalgic disaster of trying to get to a family vacation in the woods. Before the trip, the family endures the misadventures of getting ready, and Shepherd plays the role of the boy's terribly mean boss. Numerous disasters are inflicted on the family en route, but they enjoy browsing through a roadside extravaganza of "slob art." Ralph's old man, whose dream of "freedom" is looking out over the peaceful lake, must endure a rainy day when they finally arrive. Shepherd's frame of mind, when translated to the longer movie form later in his career, comes out rather mean-spirited. In Shepherd's world, there is certainly laughter, but as for the realities of the real world, there is no haven and there is no bliss.

It Runs in the Family a.k.a. My Summer Story (1994)

Shepherd's last movie combines stories from the books *In God We Trust: All Others Pay Cash*, and *Wanda Hickey's Night of Golden Memories*. It includes the obnoxious hillbilly Bumpus neighbors (surely nobody's idea of good-old-days nostalgia) and Ralph's near victory in a vicious top-spinning war, in which reality swallows the competing tops down a rain gutter. In a Shep opus, the past is seldom what one dreams it should have been.

THAT'S ENTERTAINMENT—REMEMBRANCE OF THINGS PAST

Shepherd had great dreams and expectations for himself on stage, in television, and in film, and he engaged in a large variety of projects—a mixed bag. He enjoyed his work in all these media, and he had a right to be proud of much of this work. *Jean Shepherd's America* is the great flawed television masterpiece, and *A Christmas Story* is the fine, perennial favorite movie enjoyed obsessively by millions.

In 1996, years after his last previously known published work of any kind, Shepherd was asked to write an article for a book commemorating the twentieth anniversary of *Videography*, a magazine for the professional video production industry.[67] He responded with a humorous piece, "Remembrance of Things Past," part fact, part comic invention, in which, near the end, he commented:

> But when I'm asked what I've enjoyed most, I must say big-screen movies beat them all. Sitting in the dark movie house, watching your work on the screen and hearing paying customers laugh is one of life's greatest experiences.
>
> Anyway, it's been a great ride.

Indeed, for Shepherd, his life had been a great ride. He worked and played in all the many fields of creative entertainment that interested him. Throughout his professional career, he produced an enormous quantity of work that people still enjoy. Despite his disappointments and frustrations, despite the many ways his work expresses his dissatisfaction and unhappiness— his bitterness—the final effect of Jean Shepherd's work on his audience is intellectual excitement and the joy of being alive to all experience. Take any and all of Jean Shepherd's work—read it, watch it, or listen to it—you will not cry and none of it will ever make you sad. You will grin at its cleverness, smile with its humor, and frequently laugh uncontrollably just because it's so damn funny.

He created a world. If his name were not on his works in all forms, one would recognize Jean Shepherd, humorist, everywhere within them—and that is an admirable achievement for an entertainer. Which might be enough eulogy for most entertainers, but not for ol' Shep—we need to play at his funeral.

PART VII
SUMMING UP TO A BOODLE-AM SHAKE

Jean Shepherd died, and his legacy in radio and other media gained an increasing following and widespread recognition. Instead of a funeral cortege, a parade of humanity passes by — not everyone carrying an Excelsior banner — but look at the confetti!

CHAPTER 19

THESE GUYS CAN PLAY AT MY FUNERAL ANY DAY

Boodle-am boodle-am boodle-am boodle-am boo.
Doodle-am doodle-am doodle-am doodle-am doo.
Break-a-leg break-a-leg break-a-leg break-a-leg now.
Shake-a-leg shake-a-leg shake-a-leg shake-a-leg wow.
I know this song don't mean a thing.
Just do that plain old Charleston Swing, when you sing,
Doodle-am doodle-am doodle-am doodle-am doo.
Boodle-am boodle-am boodle-am boodle-am boo.
　　　　　　　　　　　　—Dixieland Jug Blowers,
　　　　　recorded in a Chicago hotel room in 1926.

No wonder Jean Shepherd loved the grungy "Boodle-Am Shake" with its down and dirty banjo, violin, and jug blowing and played it over and over. Maybe it was the marvelous sound that he most enjoyed, but with his ironic turn of mind, he must have been aware of the special meaning of "I know this song don't mean a thing." The words *don't* mean a thing, but their sound complemented the kooky music—and the sound alone of the instruments and voice combined simply produced a mindless pleasure in a piece that had no other meaning. In a late 1950s broadcast, Shepherd, enjoying their "hairy vitality" as they marched enthusiastically, strumming and blowing bleary-eyed toward oblivion, said, "These guys can play at my funeral any day!"

Shepherd's outlook on life remained quite consistent throughout his career—balancing the seeming contradiction between a wonder and joy in life's possibilities, and inescapable failure despite our best efforts. He spoke often about foolish attempts to defeat the inevitable, and of course he was a victim of the very harsh reality he warned us of. We Americans know what our world's mundane obsessions and slobism do to true artists. Everyone has his list of tragic figures. F. Scott Fitzgerald, for example, and Orson Welles would be on most lists. Shepherd's ability to maintain self-confidence with his certainty of inevitable defeat is a contradiction. One must wonder how Shepherd could maintain what comes across as his supreme self-confidence in the face of his reiterated certainty that all human effort must come to a bad end. One suspects, in fact, that in his heart of hearts he saw the contradiction, and the buried awareness accounts for his sometimes anomalous behavior. This coworker and friend remembers what he considers a strong personality trait:

> **Barry Farber:** Jean never—he never—concealed an emotion... Jean Shepherd was Jean Shepherd twenty-four hours a day—not just on the *Jean Shepherd Show.*
>
> He became my mentor at the station. And he puzzled me in one way—I could never understand people who could have their way if they would only change something about themselves which should be very easy to change...
>
> Shepherd was self-destructive. If he had only done the commercials right. If he had attended a station meeting. If he had smiled at an executive. Didn't have to laugh at anybody's jokes. If he'd only smiled politely to an executive... If Shepherd had merely quit trying to destroy his career! You should have heard what he did to commercials—I wince! I couldn't understand—he—he was just like—he would spring the length of his chain and sink his fangs into a product that had committed no crime other than being his sponsor...
>
> And Jean eventually found expression in other areas—writing—television. So he was not a failure, but he always *felt* that he was a failure. If you compare him—flat field, sunny day—to the rest of us, he's a giant!

> A towering success, but I think inwardly he knew, com-
> pared to himself, and his potential—he felt like a
> failure!... He feared success. He feared any more success
> than he had. He could have had it *all*—just by changing
> his mode to the world—slightly—and—he didn't. He
> didn't want to.

Just after the finish of his radio career in 1977, Jean Shepherd
is quoted at the end of a *People* magazine article about him: "I
have often felt that I had a great lack professionally: the drive to
become famous. I like going my way." Maybe it was not the lack
of the desire for fame, but the compromises with one's own
integrity required—and, more important, a perverse contrari-
ness—which prevented greater fame and fortune.

By 1977, Jean Shepherd's radio days were over, except for
series of short pieces he did for NBC, CBS, and NPR. As far as is
known, Shepherd's creative work in his last twenty-two years
consisted in the main of a short series of half-hour comic programs for New Jersey public television called *Shepherd's Pie*,
Bumpers, a short series of two-to-three-minute television bits for
WGBH Boston, a second series of public television's *Jean
Shepherd's America* (ten half-hour episodes), and *Jean Shepherd
on Route One*, a television program in the *Jean Shepherd's
America* style. He published only one story and a few minor
magazine articles. (Other stories, not published by the time of
his death, may still be forthcoming.) He may have kept himself
busy in those last decades, but not much original work came out
of them, especially compared to the pre-1977 days, when,
among many other projects, he had been creating five forty-five-
minute radio shows every week for decades.

Sound as medium. Observation and imagination as tools.
Improvisation and collage as technique. Humor both in truth
and in fable as entertainment. Human foibles as content. Too
small an audience has enjoyed, and not enough of that audience
has understood, the quality and artistry of Jean Shepherd's
achievement. Much like writing a novel in installments under
the pressure of monthly periodical deadlines (as Charles Dickens
and Norman Mailer did), Jean Shepherd had to meet nightly
deadlines—and he met them at a very high level for twenty-one
years. His great talent went into writing, TV, and movies—but his
genius went into radio. That his major radio work lasted so long
was the glory. That it lasted no longer, the tragedy. The elusive
"real" Jean Parker Shepherd created the extraordinary per-

sonage "Jean Shepherd." He made himself into this persona for many thousands of listeners—people for whom Shepherd was such an essential part of who they were—and are—that others can only know them through knowing "Shep." No creator can ask for more.

Any book can only be a mere sampling of Shepherd's decades of creative radio broadcast effort and his work in other media. Just imagine the five thousand radio broadcasts alone—I want to hear them all for pleasure, and study them and transcribe them all, but the transcriptions would take up too many bookshelves. We watch the whole human parade—Billy Budd with his Excelsior flag and the rest of them (there's Jonathan Swift, giggling)—and the annual Parade of Humanity list of fans—all marching steadfastly into the night. We know we've seen some of the greats go by, but we know we will have missed a lot, because we have to stop watching the parade eventually. I hope I've stayed long enough at the curb—I hope I've listened, watched, and read enough—to get a reasonable, representative sampling.

Shep, I'm glad I've reestablished contact with you and gotten to know more about your art—better late than never. Out of the pieces I've found of the whole as I see it, I've tried to reconfigure all of Shepherd's work—especially the art of the Radio Shep and the Fictional Shep (and a "real Shep" pinned in quotation marks). I hope it's a recognizable image of the real Jean Shepherd artistic persona—one that, though Shepherd might sadly shake his head at it in dismay, might allow him to mutter to himself over the manic close of his "Bahn Frei" theme, "Yeah, he got a bit of me there, the fathead!"

At the time of Jean Shepherd's death in October 1999, I hadn't thought about him in a long time. Neither had many people in all likelihood. But I had retained a file with my collection of articles by and about him and, on a crowded bookshelf, my signed paperback of *I, Libertine*. It almost ended in a landfill. As my family began packing our over 7,000-book joint library for a move, I happened to glance into a wastebasket, into which my wife had tossed what appeared to be a trashy paperback novel ("Turgid! Tempestuous!")—seemingly not at all consistent with our serious-literature and fine-art book collection. It is more protected now in a sealed bag on a special Shepherd shelf.

Also, I still had a dozen reel-to-reel tapes of his early New York broadcasts, which I listened to until the aged tapes began to flake! Fortunately, there are many hundreds of tapes available from varied sources. Of Shepherd's estimated 5,000 broadcasts, there may always be some number that will never be found. They were never recorded, or they have disintegrated. But friends, coworkers, and fans almost certainly possess—buried in their attics—stashes of old reel-to-reels with additional, fragile magnetic memories of Jean Shepherd. He claimed he kept tapes of all his radio broadcasts. One wants to believe it is true and that they will appear—pristine, priceless, and available to all.

After he left WOR in 1977, he was generally dismissive of his radio work and of his fans, and kept repeating what most fans had never wanted to hear or believe—there were no kids named Flick, Schwartz, and Bruner. (We know there was less truth here than he wanted us to believe.) He was an artist who made it all up, left it for us, and moved on. Radio, the medium he loved, and which provided the perfect form for his unique talent, didn't allow him to flourish sufficiently. First, it gave outlet to his art, and then began to chop up and limit his style. Finally, as it lost audiences to television, it confined him to a smaller part of American cultural life than he had a right to expect. Thus, his attitude toward radio changed dramatically—early enthusiasm for radio's history and potential deteriorated into bitterness regarding its inability to better sustain his genius.

His fans were obsessed with his former radio work—they would not let him nurse those old wounds in peace. It was as though they were telling him that the final decades of his work were less valid.[ii] He responded in exasperation, in an egotistical bravado emphasizing his movie and video work and denying the value of his radio legacy.

Escape to other media altered without destroying his distinctive voice—somewhat the way a fine, creative jazz soloist could still be heard, but diffused in effect when absorbed into the corporate imperatives of a big band ensemble. By his late seventies, he had done good work in other media, had put up the good fight, climbing the snowy mountain carrying high the Excelsior banner, and had not gotten the recognition he deserved—yes, the inevitable happened to him, too, and he was not happy about his position in the world.

> **Fred Barzyk:** Happy!... The only time he was happy was when people would come up to him and say how great he was. *Then* he was happy... He *hated* Garrison Keillor [midwestern storyteller, creator of NPR's *A*

rie Home Companion and his popular books].
ed him with a passion because Garrison got all the
s and all the kinds of accolades Shepherd felt *he*
should have had.[iii]

Ron Della Chiesa: The person he was more embittered toward than anybody, I think, was Garrison Keillor. Keillor represented to Jean, I think, everything that Jean wasn't all about. Jean did not like the public broadcasting types, you know. He said, "Most of the women that I met in public broadcasting wore those little granny glasses. They were the women who never let you steal their algebra papers in high school, and now they're running public radio stations."

Herb Saltzman: And Shep didn't do as well as *he* wanted... I was his boss for a period of about ten years. And it was *painful*. Painful to see it...
  If I had to give you one summation of him as I saw him—a deeply unhappy guy... Once you broke him down and got him to relax, you would hear it...
  Shepherd was a mass of contradictions. His whole life was a contradiction. He would rail against the establishment—anti-establishment. *I, Libertine*. And yet he desperately wanted the acceptance of that establishment. He wanted to be recognized for what he truly was—a giant comic genius. He never got that recognition. At least to his satisfaction. You know, there were many guys who would have achieved his success and would have really been happy with it. He was never happy. I don't think he spent many happy times.

Responding to a comment about Shepherd's understanding that failure in some sense was inevitable, meaning that death is a defeat—but he said on the air that he believed in grabbing what you could out of life and enjoying it to the fullest—Saltzman commented, without hesitation, "He didn't *do* it! He was a profoundly unhappy man. There were times, I've got to tell you, I'd look at him and I said to myself, '*Look* at what he's *putting* people through!'"
  Shepherd on the radio insisted that he was never a complainer and that he enjoyed all of life—that he was happy and cool. Although he was not always happy, jazzman Jean Shepherd tried

to maintain an attitude that was hip and cool. In the literary review *Rain Taxi*, in a review of a summer 2000 book, *Cool Rules*, by Dick Poutain and David Robins, Jon Rodine wrote:

> They find that Cool is vastly contradictory in nature, placing high value on freedom and individuality, eschewing family ties and personal attachments, while at the same time playing a critical part in social and peer group acceptance, especially among young people. Cool maintains distance, an "ironic detachment," while at the same time caring about appearance, wanting to be noticed, unique. Cool may also be highly competitive while appearing not to care about competition, and may exist as an artfully designed effort to conceal effort itself. Cool wants while seeming not to want, tries while appearing not to try, appears "natural" while in truth being highly affected and artificial.

Although he was not always consistent, so much of this "cool" fits Shepherd. Pick an attribute: high value on freedom; wanting peer group acceptance; wanting to be noticed; wanting while seeming not to want.

THE MANY FACES OF JEAN SHEPHERD: A METAPHOR?

Complementing the many-sided and often self-contradictory aspects of Shepherd's stories, biography, and persona were the many faces he presented to the world over the years. Examining photos may yield some clues to the real Jean Shepherd:

The high school yearbook image of the conservative-looking fellow who appeared to be seriously expecting a middle-management position at the milk factory (1939).

The convincingly dissolute, invented Shepherd persona—the author of *I, Libertine*, Frederick R. Ewing (1956).[1]

The early New York radio Shepherd, clean-shaven, traditional-length hair, wearing a suit jacket, sometimes a tie—seen in newspaper articles and in publicity shots for the plays in which he appeared. He is wearing glasses—something he will seldom be seen with in public later—except tinted glasses (late 1950s).

The same clean-shaven Shepherd but now with crew cut, looking nothing like the Jean Shepherd one expects to find (early 1960s).

The hip-looking Shepherd, short hair, short, dark
   moustache, and beard thick around the chin and
   running pencil-narrow under his jawbone up to his
   ear. With his black turtleneck—the coolest of jazzmen
   (1964).
The classic Shepherd, again clean-shaven with
   traditional-length hair, on the job, earphones in place,
   body thrust forward, arm and hand outstretched
   toward us with forthright, exclamatory benediction—
   the full embodiment of his creative powers. This may
   be the essential photo of the Jean Shepherd persona
   (1966).[iv]
The Shepherd with thick sideburns stretching down
   under his jawbone (1971).
Thick, long sideburns and thick moustache, with studied
   garb that said he was a pack leader of the gang, a
   pretend older brother, with the professional-photo-
   studio look of the recognizable personality. Very
   different from the occasional image of him where he
   seemed to be smiling shyly (1973).
Thick, long sideburns, no moustache, tinted glasses
   (1975).
Full moustache attached to a narrow line of hair under
   his chin (1979).
The TV Shepherd with the full, black beard (1980s).
Finally, looking too much like an embittered artist, the
   retired-to-Florida, defensive, grizzled Shepherd (1990s).

We do not know why he changed his look so frequently and
so markedly over the years. He appeared to be at least a dozen
different people. Was he responding to the style of the times (for
his own pleasure or to better appeal to his audience); was he
trying on visual aspects of his artistic persona to discover which
outward manifestation might best fit the variety and complexity
of the creative forces he felt within himself; was he trying to conceal himself from others—or was he himself seeking a real Jean
Shepherd?
We can approach but never fully grasp the reality of Jean
Shepherd. The varied names and faces, the truth or fiction of
people and events in his stories and in his life.
A newspaper article about a successful businessman lying
might apply to Shepherd: "He had, like others with narcissistic
personality disorder, the constant fear of being unmasked as a

fraud, a sense that no achievement could relieve. Lying for him was a means to bolster his fragile self-esteem."[2] Barry Farber said about his friend Shep, "So he was not a failure, but he always *felt* that he was a failure." Recall his fear that no one would show up when he asked listeners to gather at the Limelight for a mill. Herb Squire, Shepherd's compatible and friendly engineer remembered, "He was a very private person and very insecure... He would say, 'Did I do a good job on that?' It was always—he would command the situation, but he was always, 'Did it really work?' Especially if it was a live performance. He was always a little—he'd need a little reassurance [such as] 'Yes, you did do a great job.'"

Truth, lies, distortion, artistic license, memory lapses, gratuitous fabrications in an unfair world of imminent defeat. Success, failure, and perpetual insecurity. An unreliability where one would like to find some truth, in a quintessential twentieth-century construct—many-faceted, translucent, a house of mirrors—a portrait of a twentieth-century sensibility—the improviser, performing the self he had created, wondering if it really worked. Tattered and torn, but still struggling upward, and, one hoped, never giving in.

Here is an irony, and maybe a metaphor. Jean Shepherd did financially well over the years—well enough to own sports cars, a small private plane, a summer home and a few other luxuries. He even made some of that money in radio, his finest creative field, but what really did it for him was the movie *A Christmas Story*, which made him rather wealthy. Two years after the movie opened, one episode of his 1985 *Jean Shepherd's America* television series was titled "Filthy Rich at Last." Although this, as well as other episodes, was done tongue in cheek with him playing a character, pleasure in the truth shines through. He acted the part of the rich man on his yacht, at one point singing, "I love money. Green, crisp, crackling money." The episode ended with him docking and heading for an exclusive club, a $10,000 bill appearing in the sunset sky with his voice over, "Ah yes, filthy rich at last. Thank God!"

Another metaphor. In a December 1997 interview, Shepherd said, "I miss New York enormously." Was this true? Yes, it must have been. He was the quintessential New Yorker who came from the outlands to the capital of intellectual pursuits—and found his home in the Big Apple. For a while, Jean and Leigh Brown lived in two locations in New Jersey; and they had a cottage on a lake in Maine, up I-95 and north of Augusta, to which they drove in the summers. Near the time Shepherd ended his radio career in 1977 and they married, they moved to Florida— first to a condominium on the beach in Fort Lauderdale.[3] Then in March 1984, they bought a house on Sanibel Island near a wildlife preserve.

As the "Bahn Frei" polka trots along eternally, and "Boodle-Am" words that don't mean a thing introduce the final chapter, there was Jean Parker Shepherd—no longer in the heartland, but on a tiny island off the Gulf Coast of Florida.

MORE ENIGMAS OF SHEP'S REALITY

I believed in Shepherd's apparent realities even though his frequent disclaimers in his books contradicted them—"the characters, places, and events described herein are entirely fictional." Then I found kernels of truth within the nutty fruitcake (the reality of the Warren G. Harding elementary school, for example), and I believed I had some grasp on the unsteady balance between his fabricated truths and real fictions. Then there was new documentary evidence such as the Hammond High Yearbook. There with the Jean Shepherd photo were his friends from his stories—not only Flick, but also Schwartz, Alex Josway, Eileen Akers, Patty Remaley, and Esther Jane Albery. Then the befuddling reality of what one assumed was the concocted archetype from his numerous kid stories—the unattainable high school beauty and heartbreaker, Dawn Strickland, also there in name and photo. Back in grammar school, surely the sixth grade teacher in his fictional story, with her peculiar name in the silly title, "Miss Bryfogel and the Case of the Warbling Cuckold" was a total fabrication. However, she was his real teacher with that real name; and a stranger-than-fiction Shepherd invention: in one of his television dramas one heard his voiceover saying that the high point of his (television) kid brother Randy's entire life was back in grade school playing a Thanksgiving turkey, but (real) kid brother Randall did a bit better than that after high school[v]—in 1947–48 he pitched for the Cincinnati Reds.[4]

Within Shepherd, the prophet of ultimate defeat had for all those years been in balance (in the same man and in the same art) with an insistence on seizing the day in spite of it all. He managed to couch his doom-saying in fine intellectual humor—in entertainment—the nose flute, jew's harp, and kazoo of absurd melodies.

We had been seduced by the fun of all that jazz. We—like the newspaper reporter who insisted that the sea captain who hated the sea was only joking—denied Shep's truths, somehow deluding ourselves into believing he was only joking. We should remember Shep's words:

> [Spoken with irony over the opening theme music] Just a philosophical question. I mean, who does *who* in—in life? Or—and this is the worst question of all to ask—Do you do *yourself* in?—Aaaaa? "Oh no, *it can't be!* No, no, that's *ridiculous!* No, no! It was *society* that did it to me! Rotten, crummy, evil society!"[5]

Toward the end of his life, Jean Parker Shepherd faced his own "Dream Collection Day." He wanted it all, grasping for the solid gold merry-go-round ring in every media beyond radio— high in the belief that he could create masterpieces in all of them that would achieve artistic, popular, and financial success. The final act arrived, and with it profound disappointment. Reality had not measured up to his aspirations and sense of self-worth. It appears that he succumbed increasingly to the more pessimistic side of himself—he seemed less able to hold the conflicts within himself in balance. From reports of his later public life, it appeared that ego and hostility sometimes overcame his better nature. In the distance is the exhortation of Private Sanderson: "Don't let 'em do it to ya." All of us irremediably flawed mortals still plagued by foibles—we remain Ogs and Charlies, fistfighting it out in the darkness.

THE LAST COUPLE OF YEARS WE DIDN'T EVEN SEE HIM AT ALL

Shepherd's long-time friend Peter Wood describes his observations of the later years, "His wife at the end, down there in Florida—she protected him and you couldn't get through to him. She would just say, 'Write or drop a note or something, he's not available.' She really kept people away from him." Herb Saltzman comments, "[Leigh Brown] really was with him through dark days. He got ill, and he was fat, he was a recluse."

> **Fred Barzyk:** He would cut—compartmentalize his life just like the wife and kids—didn't fit into his career?—goodbye. Now radio—I'm going to do the best radio. Now I'm doing television—who wants radio?— that was a piece of shit—I was *never* a radio person—I

was television. No, now I'm a *literary* type. Television?—now I'm a movie person—now cut off everybody. When there wasn't anything, he cut off everything. When he and Leigh were left alone he compartmentalized himself—into a prison.

Ron Della Chiesa: We really became good friends toward the last ten years of his life. We went down there [Sanibel Island] at least two or three times and we were his guests—just the four of us [Ron and wife, Joyce, Jean and Leigh]. He became very private. He was very embittered at times. [Shepherd and Leigh] virtually shut themselves off from people, particularly when they went to Sanibel Island. That's where Jean bought that home down there as a result of [the money he made from] *A Christmas Story*.

There was not much contact he and Leigh had with the outside world, except with his accountant... The last couple of years we didn't even see him at all. We knew something was wrong when—we would always send them little gifts, like his favorite coffee, and Joyce would call up and Leigh would answer and say how much they enjoyed the coffee and our card. And then one Christmas we didn't hear a word. And we knew something was up... We heard that she had passed away—we called and we didn't get any response. I think he was so devastated.

Laurie Squire: [The last time Herb and Laurie Squire saw Jean and Leigh was in the summer of 1991 in Florida.] He was working on a movie script with Steven Spielberg. We spoke to them through the years. After Leigh died I called, and he sounded like a broken man... He was crazy about her, very attached. She knew how to deal with him, how to run him, how to keep him going, how to keep him pumped up and everything. They were a made for each other couple.

Nancy (Leigh Brown) Shepherd died July 16, 1998.[6]

DREAM COLLECTION, NOSTALGIA, TRUTH, AND PRIDE

Brian Pearson, of northern Indiana, with a second home on Sanibel Island, has some valuable information, including what may be the final note on Jean's regard for his radio work: "Neighbors used to see Leigh outside all the time. She liked to do various yard work but was never too friendly. As for Jean, they told me you never knew what kind of mood he was in." Pearson relates what a neighbor of Jean's told him about seeing Jean some time after Leigh died and a few months before Jean's death: "Jean was on his front porch. They chatted for a while and Jean asked him to come in as they were talking about New York in general... On that day Jean spoke highly of his radio days [he played some airchecks of shows for the neighbor] and said he had boxes of airchecks in the garage."

Airchecks: boxes of tapes of his radio shows. Could it be that, Leigh gone (no one to take care of him), with nothing left to lose or live for, beyond conflicting emotions, not having to defend and rationalize his professional position, responding to this innocent neighborly friendship in his last months, Jean Shepherd allowed himself some nostalgia—and truth? Jean Shepherd may have finally been proud of his radio work. One hopes so.

In his last photos and in several descriptions by those who saw him then, he seemed to have neglected himself and his surroundings. His weight, his teeth, his grizzled face. Evidence indicates that he did not deal well with Leigh's death—there is a photo taken in the Sanibel living room of a small, partly decorated Christmas tree never taken down from over a year before, when she died. A number of Shepherd's friends say that Jean felt Leigh's death deeply and never recovered—Larry Josephson remembers talking to him by phone: "He sounded like he was falling apart. Her death really, I think, caused his death." Shepherd died of natural causes in a nearby hospital a little over a year later, October 16, 1999.[vi]

Bequests in his last will and testament indicate that Jean Shepherd remembered some of the more important parts of his life: Leigh, television and radio, and writing. The University of Pennsylvania School of Veterinary Medicine received $60,000 from the estate of Jean Shepherd to establish a scholarship for women in the name of Leigh Brown Shepherd.[7] Also receiving bequests were the American Federation of Television and Radio Artists Welfare Fund and the creative writing department of the University of Indiana. Shepherd left the remainder of his estate to two friends. His state of mind regarding another part of the will, made just a few months before his death, is unclear: despite the existence of an adult son and daughter, it affirms, "I hereby declare that I am not presently married and have no children, natural or adopted, living or deceased."

No matter how fast and well he ran, no matter how loose his knees, life caught up with him in the end, as he knew it would. But these matters do not affect his art. As he said when eulogizing modernist composer George Antheil, his art remains and that is the most important part. To know Jean Shepherd's work is to know a bit more about oneself, one's fellow humans, and about America—because one is a "listener." It is to have been taught by a master to observe, and as he said, "to correlate, to integrate, and evaluate." It is to have been shown how to appreciate life and to laugh. With all the negativity—the defeatism that seems such a strong undercurrent in Jean Shepherd's life and work—the overwhelming effect of what he said and made is a joyous and life-affirming work of art. Happy? Unhappy? Listen to any of Jean Shepherd's radio broadcast tapes and you will hear a happy man—a man full of joy in his work. At his funeral we play neither a dirge, nor the phonus balonus polka one never tires of hearing—rather we play "Boodle-Am Shake."

Let Shepherd have the last word:

> I can see, after I'm gone. Can you see them inscribe? What would you like to see inscribed on your headstone? Can't you just see, "Jean Shepherd—he died sustaining!" He died sustaining. Sustaining. Yes. It's going to be okay, baby.[8]

And, as he taught listeners to look things up, let's look up these last words:

> **sustaining program** A radio or television program that is supported by the station or network on which it appears and that has no commercial announcements.

> **sustain** 1. To keep in existence; maintain. 2. To supply with necessities or nourishment; provide for. 3. To support from below; prop. 4. To support the spirits, vitality, or resolution of; encourage. 5. to endure or withstand; bear up under: *sustain hardships*. 6. To experience or suffer (loss or injury). 7. To affirm the validity or justice of: *sustain an objection*. 8. To prove or corroborate; confirm.

Although, Jean Shepherd did a lot better commercially than just having a "sustaining radio program," the excessive number of commercials on his later programs probably did contribute to cramping his style and driving him out of radio. But more important, like so many of America's fine artists, each in their individually tragic ways, he was defeated in part by his success.

What is more significant, Jean Shepherd is now sustained (kept in existence, nourished) by respect and caring that might surprise him. Shepherd received many forms of recognition during his lifetime, and many others after he died. He was proud to be recognized, although some forms of tribute might not have been exactly to his liking. He received numerous awards. His hometown gave him its Hammond Achievement Award in 1981 while he was still alive to savor it. He seemed really touched by this—the letter of thanks from Leigh Brown Shepherd to the director of the Hammond Public Library, in part says, "There is no way I can tell you how much Jean Shepherd enjoyed his Hammond Achievement Award visit to the region. It was so special to him, so very moving, that other awards have paled in comparison."[vii]

That comes from the mellow Shep, but one might compare two responses toward Hammond that he made within a short period of each other. First, the positive response, from his letter to the Hammond newspaper editor:

> I'd like to thank the citizens of Hammond who awarded me (much to my astonishment) the 1981 Hammond Achievement Award... I have always felt grateful that I was lucky enough to grow up in Hessville [a section of Hammond]... It was a great place to be, especially for a kid, and I've always been thankful that I was privileged to know that country. For that reason, I have tried to capture as much of the Calumet region, its folkways, its landscapes, its fears and victories, in my work. My novel *In God We Trust: All Others Pay Cash* is laid in the region, and is truly a work of love by a native son.
>
> Jean Shepherd

Then, from a newspaper interview in Chicago the following year, regarding Hammond:

> A pit. Boring. I spent a good part of my life trying to leave here... You couldn't grow up in this area and be a sensitive kid. No way. The only reason I'm glad I grew

up here is I've got a real sense of reality: bad winters, crime, death... It's a place to see life... Don't you love spring? You can always tell spring in Hammond. The smog changes from gray to green.[9]

Earlier in that article, the reporter said that Shepherd several times had commented, "Oh, I'm only kidding, I love this place."

Years later, in 1995, he received an honorary doctorate from Indiana University Northwest.[viii] The Broadcasting and Cable Hall of Fame inducted him posthumously on November 13, 2000;[10] and on March 15, 2003, Hammond named its new community center in his honor.

Upon Shepherd's death in 1999, most newspapers did an obituary, including the *New York Times*, which did an extensive one, and a "News of the Week" article. Its Sunday *Magazine* paid tribute to him in its year-end issue devoted to the recently deceased—Shepherd shared the page with his old buddy Shel Silverstein.[ix] In part, the tribute says, "What he did was make literature—fresh, right in front of your ears—like a guy making pizza in the window of a restaurant."[11]

Ongoing tributes to his work take many forms. Both before and after his death, old fans came out of the woodwork, some with old tapes. Hundreds of these broadcast tapes and videos are available for sale and trade. National Public Radio produced a two-hour program (available on CD), "A Voice in the Night," featuring selections from Shepherd broadcasts and tributes from many of his peers.[12] A weekly radio program replays his old broadcasts, and an Internet site rebroadcasts his programs twenty-four hours a day. Several of his early comedy LPs have been re-released on CD. Several websites archive information, his broadcasts, and writing. An email discussion group is dedicated to his work.

Although Shepherd never received acknowledgement for his influence on the TV sitcom *The Wonder Years* (especially the adult narrative voiceover), Howard Gewirtz, the writer and creator of the 2003 sitcom *Oliver Beene*, with its adult narrative voiceover, acknowledged in a *New York Times* interview that it conjures up comparison with *The Wonder Years*, and testified to Shepherd's influence on him, commenting, "My mother used to listen to Shepherd on his old radio show every night on WOR in New York. That voice was memorable."[13]

Publications discuss his art and life. In 1986, *The Stars of Stand Up Comedy: A Biographical Encyclopedia* devoted an article to Shepherd,[14] and the 2003 book *Seriously Funny: The Rebel Comedians of the 1950s and 1960s* has a chapter divided between him and fellow radio-comedians Bob and Ray.

Shepherd's movie *A Christmas Story* looms large in his legend as perceived by the public. A play based on the movie is staged each November and December, in 2002 appearing in over sixty locations in twenty-five states and Canada. The script has also been published. The movie is still being shown Christmas Eve for twenty-four hours straight on cable television. It was issued in 2003 as a special two-DVD edition in celebration of the twentieth anniversary of its first opening, with both wide-screen and full-frame formats, a documentary describing the making of the movie, several special novelty tie-in segments, and the audio from old broadcasts of Shepherd reading tales found in the movie.

Several other Christmas Story commemorations occurred in 2003. The book *A Christmas Story* was published; drawn from two earlier Shepherd titles, it contains all the chapters upon which the movie is based. A novelty company, National Entertainment Collectibles Association, issued a dozen *A Christmas Story* items—including bobble heads, talking action figures, a lunch box, Christmas ball ornaments, Christmas lights (in the shape of tiny leg lamps), and the leg lamp in two sizes, no less. A clothing manufacturer marketed a half-dozen *Christmas Story* T-shirt designs. Finally, Macy's New York department store devoted all six of its windows facing Herald Square to animated recreations of scenes from *A Christmas Story*, with the appropriate audio track from the movie over each scene. The display, in which Santa propels Ralphie down the slide by shoving him with his big black boot, is altered: a Santa's helper does the deed. Obviously, Macy's Santa does not exhibit antisocial behavior in public.

Recognition continues in new ways. On September 18, 2004, well over a thousand enthusiastic visitors attended the daylong Jean Shepherd/*A Christmas Story* Festival at the Hammond, Indiana, Jean Shepherd Community Center. Dominating the day's varied activities, all afternoon hundreds of families waited in a seemingly endless line just to approach the tables chock-full of *A Christmas Story* tie-in merchandise—because tending those tables were four young men who as child actors in the 1983 movie had played Flick, Schwartz, Randy Shepherd, and Scut Farcas. The actors posed for photos and, signing stuff at a rapid pace, sold it.

Hammond's mayor proclaimed Jean Shepherd Day, though

more than a few in attendance undoubtedly did not know who that was.[x]

A CHRISTMAS STORY—LEGACY AS MIXED BLESSING

One can only imagine what comments Shepherd might have made regarding such "slob art" as action figures, bobble heads, and their ilk. Upon learning about this *A Christmas Story* tie-in merchandise, Shepherd's son commented, "Perfect! Just the kind of thing he spent his life mocking comes back to define him."

A Christmas Story movie and all its tie-ins—is this where it was all leading? Of course it is. Maybe it's "Santa's Revenge." Ask ten people who Jean Shepherd was and maybe two will know. Ask them all if they know of *A Christmas Story* and nine of them will know ("Oh, that's our family's favorite movie! We watch it every year."), but probably only a few will realize that the movie is a Shepherd creation, and that it is his narration one hears throughout. It is a very good movie—and only two degrees of separation from its original media: the movie based on written stories; the written stories based on tales spun live on the air. Yes, in his later years, Shepherd was proud of making movies—though his radio listeners mostly regard his twenty-one years of talk to be his most important legacy. Others, possibly the realists, have their own view, expressed by Flick (of tongue-on-pole fame),[xi] in the person of Scott Schwartz, the actor who played him in the movie: "Jean Shepherd will never be down in the history books as anything more than the writer of *A Christmas Story* no matter how many radio shows he did, all the books he did—it doesn't make any difference."

"It doesn't make any difference." Shepherd would probably have agreed—run-of-the-mill TV and movies, easier to understand and enjoy, tend to prevail, and the winners write the history books. Remember the grownup Flick, though; the barkeep, as described in Shepherd's book, *In God We Trust: All Others Pay Cash*—he was the one left behind, geographically and intellectually, in a dead-end job in Hohman. He never wrote a book, never made a movie.

PARADE OF HUMANITY

Official tributes and other public demonstrations are fine, but in addition, Jean Shepherd deserves parades as reminders and as celebrations. One can hear, faintly, a marching band approaching. Listen carefully for the B-flat sousaphone. Remember Shepherd's vision from his LP—it's the Human Comedy parade with the great figures of literature, such as Billy Budd—"You got a raw deal, Billy!" It's the annual Vast Marching Horde of Mankind parade of fans he named on several programs. In the following transcription Shepherd imagines looking out his window in the middle of the night and seeing a procession passing by. Was it the parade of Jean Shepherd's real/fictional life—was it a dream, were they illusions, shades out of his past?

> What do you think this is? Oh *no!* It's the old crowd! It's everybody again! It's everybody I've *ever* known again! Hey, there's *Esther!* Hey Esther. Esther Jane Albery. What's she doing beating a bass drum? There's—there's Alex Josway. Hey Al, *Al!* Oh, for crying out loud, there's *Gasser.* From the second platoon. Hey Gasser—I thought you were *dead!* Oh! They're all here again. All of them. I mean, why? Look at the confetti![15]

Look at the confetti! In addition to those who provide professional commentary and testimony about Jean Shepherd, many people have stories to tell and were affected by him in ways that do not often get mentioned in books. In contrast to some negative thoughts about Shepherd are hundreds of comments from ordinary fans regarding his positive effect on them. Here are a few admirers of Shepherd marching with their "Excelsior" banners. These few will have to stand for thousands who have written to message boards and other websites. At the head of the parade is Jim Clavin, maintainer of the flicklives website:

> I began creating this site in 1998 as an attempt to organize my personal "file of dynamic trivia." Seeing how many Shep fans are out there, I have decided to place it on the WWW for all to enjoy. The purpose of this website is to gather as much information as possible about Shep... His wit and humor which has entertained so many of us for so many years will play forever on those little transistor radios hidden beneath all our pillows.
> —Jim Clavin

When people write to ask for our Shep mp3 discs they often like to tell of where and when they were introduced to him. While the majority who write were WOR listeners, I think you'd be very surprised to find that he had/has fans from all over this country and internationally as well. Some have told me that they heard him on radio thru his syndicated shows. Others know of his books but are curious to hear what he did on radio. A few found him thru the *Jean Shepherd's America* shows or the PBS movies. Every Xmastime we're swamped with requests from fans who only know of him as the guy who wrote the screenplay for *A Christmas Story*. A hell of a lot of them are young people who weren't even born when Shep was on WOR—they found him thru ACS or were turned on by their parents (usually fathers). For quite a few years it looked like interest in Shep had declined, but now I think it's rising again, thanks mainly to ACS and the internet.

—Jeff Beauchamp of "The Jean Shepherd Project"

An elegantly composed message says that Shepherd's broadcasts taught the listener that observation and clear expression could be great rewards, that language was a vital thing when used both precisely and as spontaneously as one dared, and that the most sensible topic is the common—which is full of nuance, humor, and grace. Many people express how wonderful Shepherd was for them, selflessly giving of himself through personal contact and through his program. Among those tributes are comments of many who found Jean Shepherd a guide and a comfort throughout their teenage years, such as one fan who remembers how she was struggling to survive adolescence and that through listening to him, Shepherd gave her a sense that she belonged to a sympathetic group who understood him as she did. She comments, "He saved my life."

Among the positive testaments is that from Bill Pasternak, Shepherd's ham-radio friend, and himself a radio broadcaster, who, in the mid-1980s at a convention, was in a bind because the regular newscaster had not shown up to do a program on ham radio. He mentioned the problem to Shepherd, who said, "Oh, I did news at one time. I'll read it for you." Pasternak relates, "He sat down, rolled the tape recorder, and he recorded my newscast... Did it as a favor, never asked for a penny—that was Jean! His hobby was ham radio. This was ham radio, and he did it. He took [the script] and he read it cold—one read and it was done. I said, 'Thank you,' and he said, 'Hey, don't worry about it.' That's the kind of person—that tells you a lot about the person."

Tributes pop up everywhere: a first edition of Shepherd's *Wanda Hickey's Night of Golden Memories—and Other Disasters*, a former library book, has a bookplate stating "Donated to Dover Public Library, Dover, New Jersey, from the tuba section of Dover High School 1971–1972." A tip of my hat to the tuba players for their insider's reference to Shep and his high school tuba playing.

Well-known media people, coworkers, friends, and fans experienced Jean Shepherd's created and real personas. All have memories to share about this wide-ranging genius and complex, enigmatic man. Contradictions. Many fragments of an incomplete mosaic. Then there are stories such as this one of a fan (who wishes to remain anonymous) and his uncle, both good friends of Shepherd's for decades. This narrative, with its authentic feel of the vibrancy of living people, has captured interactions involving diverse circumstances, subject matter, and attitudes:

> [Shepherd and the fan's uncle] met in the early '50s in NYC. I am not sure of the exact circumstances. [My uncle] referred to their meeting as being strictly through the great god of dumb luck. It always seemed an unusual relationship to me when I was a kid, because they always seemed to argue. As an adult, I think that was the basis of the relationship—Shep could not win an argument with him, and this seemed to stimulate a sort of competitive nature in him. They were both extremely well read and equally stubborn. I can't speak for Shep, but I know my uncle sometimes took positions he did not necessarily agree with just for the sake of rattling Shep's cage. They sometimes went months and maybe longer without speaking, but it also was not uncommon for them to speak several times in a day.
>
> I first got to know [Shepherd] in the early '60s listening to his show. I met him for the first time when I was taken to a book signing. The topics discussed between the two of them were vast. I've heard them talk sports, politics, radio, philosophy, history—you name it, they discussed it. As for myself as a kid, it was always sports. However, as an adult I garnered a lot more respect from him—then our conversations revolved largely around baseball, comedy, acting, and subjects revolving around those areas.
>
> His general attitude was usually very positive toward

us, but I could detect that he could be very moody. On one occasion, I remember he was really grouchy—my uncle told him to go to hell and to give him a call if he ever decided to rejoin the human race. Neither of them suffered fools gladly.

My father had been a professional boxer and later a successful saloon keeper in New Jersey. ([Shepherd] and my father did not like each other—the old man used to refer to Shep as that "bullshitting son of a bitch from the radio.")

I attended what was to be his last concert in Clinton, New Jersey. After the show, I ended up having a very lengthy conversation with Shep, each of us telling long stories. Shep ignored Leigh and others who were waiting to go out to eat. You would have thought that these people were completely invisible or did not exist at all. All of his attentions were aimed at me. In all fairness, a good friend of mine was with me, and with me ignoring him on an equal basis. To this day my friend still kids me about the day he became invisible, but also states he was glad he was there as a witness, because had I told him of this evening he would not have believed it.

As for myself and my adult dealings with him, I always wanted to listen to what he had to say, even if I disagreed with him. I sometimes think he said a few things he might not have necessarily believed to test my mettle and if I had the balls to disagree. I did and I think he both liked and respected me for it. I found him a very good audience, at least for me. He knew my background included a lot of baseball experience and took delight in hearing about many of the baseball experiences I had. He also knew they were true, since he had been present at a high school game I had played in, that was the only game in history called because of the Easter Bunny. He had me repeat that story for him, complimenting me on the detail and accuracy of the incident. We talked a lot of baseball.

We spoke a good number of times after the Clinton concert. I know I called him a few times when he was in Maine and spoke to him a number of times while I was in Florida. A few times when I called, Leigh sort of whispered to me in the phone that it just wasn't a good day. She said, "The storm clouds are brewing."

On one of those occasions when I called and she had

answered in a sort of whisper, I said, "Hello Leigh. Is he human today?" She laughed and said, "Hold on, I'll check." I heard her say, "Someone is on the phone for you but wants to know if you're human today."

The next thing you hear is Shep roaring, "Who the hell wants to know if I'm human today? Give me that goddamn phone."

Before he got a word out I said, "Ooooh we sound grouchy this morning. Didn't we have our bran this morning?"

Upon hearing this I hear, "You son of a bitch, you're as bad as you're goddamn uncle," he laughed like hell, then hung up. He called me back a few hours later—we had a great baseball conversation.

[What about his dark side?] I can't be too specific, but his dark side—it was just something I could sense—you could just tell he had a real mean side. I always made it my business when I saw his mood was bad to steer the conversation back to something he liked or was passionate about.

Part of the reason I think he continued to like us was the fact that at no time did we ever ask him for any kind of favor. I think over the years he had more than his fair share of the "I knew you when" crowd.

We did have conversations on a number of occasions where I asked his advice on writing and performing comedy (I did standup for a long time). His influence was much more than I had ever realized. I was frustrated in standup, because while I wrote and performed well enough, I realized that what I really wanted to do was tell stories like Shep had done. I certainly have a ton of them. When I mentioned this he was, I believe, genuinely flattered. But his reply was, to keep writing and try writing plays or screen plays, that the way TV and radio is today, it would be impossible to do, as the element of time is such a factor in storytelling that I could never find a venue that would provide me the proper amount of time to do it right. He stated that if he were starting today, his storytelling career just would not happen. No one would ever give it the time it would take.

That extended description of a relationship with Shepherd encompasses the good and the bad, the delights and the difficulties, but leaves a rich and positive impression. Some other relationships with him, both familial and professional, proved far less pleasant.

NOT ONLY PRAISE

Fans by the many thousands have much to praise Jean Shepherd for. But there is also another side to being a kid in Shepherd's world. From the November 1, 1972, broadcast: "Oh yes, here's a message from *New York* magazine: 'If you're a New York City parent, heaven help you.' If you're a parent, heaven help you—I saw through that silly game early." Here is a comment from his son, Randall, forty years after his father left the family:

> This is what it was like being Jean's son, it was like what you hear about amputees; long after the limb is gone, they have periodic sensations of intense pain, and the source of the pain is described precisely in the limb the person is missing. Not at the stump where the connection was severed, but in the missing body. He was never here, but I could hear him on the radio every night. Listening to his show in the dark, I'm secretly thrilled it's my Dad telling the story, but his cab never pulls up at home afterward. I had a second-floor window at the head of my bunk bed, where I would listen to the show and then look out at the passing traffic in the night and wait. He'd tell great stories about being a kid with his old man, but I never saw anybody like that. He was always there on the radio having a great time entertaining the huddled masses by their radios, but he was invisible in the dark.
>
> And then there were the fans. People would discover I was his son, usually from someone else because I soon lost the taste for going public with it, and their eyes would open wide in amazement. Then they would launch into it; "I think Jean Shepherd is the greatest! I used to listen to him under the covers in bed every night when I was a kid. Gee, I didn't know he had kids. But he was terrific, telling his stories of what it was like being a kid, he must have been great to have as a Dad."

We note that Shepherd told the actor playing the father in his television movie that a year after the story, the father left his family with a young blonde. This replicated Shepherd's real life experience—Fred Barzyk remembers Jean once commenting that he was "his father's son."

> **Fred Barzyk:** They said I was *insane* for living with Shepherd [doing all those television projects]. I don't think there was anybody who could live with Shepherd for as long as [I did]... He was a child in many ways. The temper. Temper tantrums. The lack of maturity. How to deal with people. How to deal with life. There was an arrested childhood there that I still think comes from his father's [leaving the family] that really destroyed him. He needed to get it out. If you believe like I do, every artist has some really major handicap that forces them to throw all their energy into another direction so that they can get everything out.

Most creative people hate to have their mind and work dealt with like that—their creativity predicated upon the result of a psychological problem—and there are very few direct examples of this exorcising of demons in what is known of Shepherd. In an early broadcast, however, he had commented about a psychiatrist calling him, saying that he seemed to be "the most completely analyzed man I've ever met," and Shepherd commented that his work was "probably as great a purgative as any analysis could ever be." In a 1972 program, Shepherd said, "That's the one great thing about the human mind, you know. It's got a built-in eraser. God, would we be in trouble if it *didn't!*" No purge is ever complete, of course, and some writing on the psyche might have been done with indelible ink.

Too many people independently give negative reports about Jean Shepherd the man for the reports to be dismissed—making a grown producer cry was not an anomaly. As Shepherd always reminded listeners, we're all flawed. One might sometimes find an affinity between Shepherd and the Shep cuckoo, Bobby Fischer: "We oughta have to include Bobby Fischer, who happens to be a friend of mine, in the crowd of the *mean* people." Shepherd, writing in the introduction of the published script of his *Phantom of the Open Hearth*, described his dislike of the way a scene was being filmed: "I exploded. There were harsh, profane words exchanged. Actors cowered in corners. Rapidly my reputation as a Nice Guy went down the tube, and I was unmasked for the sonovabitch that I really am." When this passage was read to Fred Barzyk, the film's co-director and producer, he responded, "Gene, nobody ever doubted it."

Shep, somewhere, from some other view of some other truth, there are elements to be known of some other you that the inquiring part of us wants to know. Shep, you didn't want to have any of your personal life exposed—you claimed that your life was irrelevant to your art. Maybe in part that was a rationalization. People want to know the warts, the dirty linen, and the nasty substrata—they say it's part of the gestalt and gives a more understandable picture of the artist, and maybe in part that's a rationalization, too. But, Jean Shepherd, you made your art so inextricably a mix with your persona—your life—that no hammer, pliers, saw, or sword could undo such a Gordian knot.

What we find is not the Shep we knew when we first listened. Not the Shep discovered when reading the books and articles and seeing the television and film. Not the Shep anyone familiar with Jean Shepherd's work might expect. We find a Jean Shepherd in perpetual conflict with the world and with the self he wanted to keep separate—hidden like a mad part of himself locked away in the attic of his psyche.

Thus, we encounter a Jean Shepherd not only vastly more accomplished artistically than we may once have imagined, but at the same time we see a man vastly deeper, darker, and more damaged—which is both baffling and disconcerting. Disconcerting because we must realize that youthful, optimistic assumptions and enthusiasms may rest on insecure foundations—and we walk at our peril over cracks in the sidewalk.

AND THEN I SAID, "NOW I WILL PLAY FOR YOU"

Our perceptions of Shepherd swing back and forth like a pendulum in response to whoever is characterizing him. Good guy, bad guy, a sweetheart, a sonofabitch—and all of it true. Contradiction seems to define this extraordinary man. But in addition to fans, friends, coworkers, professionals, relatives, authors—all articulate, sophisticated, able to express themselves with subtlety and nuance—one small group (former headhunters in the Amazon, no less!) speaks simply and with great clarity over the decades through a broadcast Shepherd made the day after he returned from his trip to Peru. Jean Shepherd expressed what an extraordinary experience he had just had. He also described a scene that captured a number of his consistent attitudes toward life. Through the translator, he quoted the "natives" regarding the unique experience he gave them:

> After supper I took my—this is a very touching moment. I don't know how to describe it to you because of what happened. I took my jew's harp out, see—and I just took it out. They were all looking. They're just sort of smiling. And two little girls that attached themselves—tiny little girls about two or three years old that attached themselves to me, were holding my arm and sort of petting—just beautiful. They were just laughing—I'd look at them—they'd giggle. And they loved my beard. [Shepherd explains that the Indians have no facial hair but believe that their ancestors had beards.]
>
> I took the jew's harp and I said, "Watch. See." And I sat up on the table and I began to perform. I really did. I grin and they all laughed. I said, "Now watch." I held it up to my mouth and I went. [Note on jew's harp.] And there was a moment—and the kids giggled and Tahiddi [the chief] looked and Arushiba looked.
>
> "Now tell them I will play them—this is an *American* folk instrument." I said, "This is what the little people—the *natives* of America play." I said, "I'm a *native* of America. I'm not going to play a violin or an organ, or sing a hymn. I'm going to play what the natives—just like *you* natives." I said, "I'm also a native. I'm a native. And I play my instrument."
>
> So I played. [Laughs.] Here's what I played. [jew's harp of "You Are My Sunshine"]... And they were astounded!
>
> And I said, "Now I will sing this song to you." [He sings "You Are My Sunshine," then plays on his kazoo.] They couldn't *believe* it!...
>
> You have never seen—their eyes were shining—they loved it so, and then I took out my nose flute—now *that* thrilled 'em. [He plays on his nose flute. The Indians then sing for Shepherd, then two Indians get out their own native flutes and play.]
>
> Then I said, "Now I will play with you. Let's all sit in together—on a session." Well, they led and I followed with my jew's harp and my nose flute, and the three of us played and the crowd went out of its *mind!* We stayed till three and four o'clock in the morning playing and singing, and the translator had faded off into the darkness.
>
> They had never had anything like this in their lives before. Many white men come to them and give them medicine, white

men come and preach to them, white men come and *study* them. But no white man ever came to entertain them. [Pause.] And be part of them. When I left, Tahiddi said, "We have never seen this kind of white man." He just loved it. He said—to use his exact phrase, he said, "This is the first white man who has ever come to them who has *participated* with them. Who has done things *with them!*"[16]

ENDING(S)

There are so many possible endings. By quoting Shepherd, the ending could be described as the "how did it ever happen this way" ending, the "he died sustaining" ending, the "these guys can play at my funeral any day" ending, or the "how can I say it" ending. Where was it all going? Let's take it back to his description of one of his pre–New York television shows, the one where he described coming on even after "The Star Spangled Banner."

> ...about 928 guys who are watching their sets at that hour—that's about our total rating. And I'm looking out, and they're looking in, and we sat there and looked at each other for about two and a half minutes. Have you ever had your TV set look at you for two and a half minutes? I'm sitting there looking, and they're looking at me. For two and a half minutes. Then, finally, all I said is, "How did we let it happen to us?" [Long silent pause.] I sat there another minute and left. And that was the end of the show for that night. [Laughs.]
>
> I got about 948 letters from guys who said, "How did you *know?*" What do you mean, how did I *know?* It's right there in the middle of it all. I mean, all you gotta do is look around you, you know? Look around you right now! Is this what you were *striding* for? Is this what you were—you were *marching* towards, in the beautiful, green, gold sunshine of youth when you were—when you were striding over those green fields and looking up at the sun? Is this where it was—*of course*—*this* is where it was going.[17]

Where indeed was it going? The enigma of Jean Shepherd. The optimism and joy contrasted with the pessimism and hostility. The disappointments despite the triumphs. The great pleasure he gave his fans and the wounds he gave his friends and family. Shepherd's two children and their mother seem quite justified in their resentment toward this enigmatic man who gave pleasure to so many who did not know him, and grief to some who did. Both children have expressed their resentment and hostility over time—time, which does not heal all wounds. His son Randall comments on his father's inability to reconcile the humanity and humor of his art with the real life beyond the studio:

> **Randall Shepherd:** He wouldn't let his wife call him "Dear" when they were in a supermarket on the outside chance someone would recognize him and take him for a sap because he was married. And as for children, if anyone asked him if he had any, he'd say no. And if they personally knew of Adrian and me and pressed the question, he'd claim that we weren't his children, just some crazies making wild unfounded claims of paternity...
>
> He sat in the dark for years, alone in his studio, waving his arms, talking into the microphone and hearing only himself. He had the rapt ear of the night world tuned to his larynx. They were out there in the dark, under the covers, locked into the sound of his voice, waiting to hear how it would end. Of course he knew their story, he grew up in their life. But listening to himself talk, he came to believe that he wrote it, that it was his script, the work product of his mind. His ego got to him, it rose up behind him out of the dark and strangled him, it choked him off from everything outside himself that fed him. He died angry at the world for not understanding him, for not honoring his achievements as he felt he truly deserved. Yet he went to the end belittling his own best work in radio as beneath him, unworthy of his attention. After everything was said and done, what else was there?
>
> **Adrian Shepherd:** What I meant [in a previous email to a Shepherd email chatgroup composed of Shepherd enthusiasts] was my father was an A-hole as a father, and growing up I just never understood all of what was going on, with Jean never being around as a father or being home like most of my friends' dads were... I would hear about all of the great stories that he used to tell and that made me even more so want to get to know my

father, just to laugh with him and do all the things that the other kids would do with their dads. When I got older, I got bitter, but still very confused. Well, I *finally* got over it just within the past year [in 2003] and now I am listening to him on CDs for the first time, and need I tell you all, he's funny as *hell!* I am just glad that I came around to enjoying Jean's talent and what he has given to so many people, plus if you think about it, forgiveness and understanding is what it's all about!

At a luncheon gathering of a dozen or so enthusiasts to pay tribute in 2003, four years after Jean Shepherd's death, his daughter also attended.[xii] New plastic kazoos and nose flutes having been distributed to all, Shepherd's joyous theme song playing on tiny plastic speakers, and fans accompanying on their orange, yellow, purple, or chartreuse instruments, Adrian stood and, bearing her father's well-worn, deep red and blue metal kazoo he had long ago given her, she joined in the music.

The music of Jean Shepherd. After everything was said and done, what else was there? As information from Shepherd's family, friends, and associates accumulated, the unpleasantness emerged, tarnishing the myth of the Good Ol' Shep who fans knew as a richly layered friend. Reasonable people can ask how one can be such an enthusiast for the art of Picasso, Hemingway, and Jean Shepherd, when these creators could be so nasty to those around them. How does one separate the art from the life, the creator from the created? Why are so many creative artists such nasty people? Shepherd's friend, and WOR boss for ten years, Herb Saltzman, suggests, "Maybe it comes with the territory."

Broadcaster Larry Josephson, who had known Shepherd for decades, confirms observations of some others who knew him: "He only talked about himself when you were with him. That's all he ever talked about... I don't think Shepherd was very interesting off-mike. He was a monomaniac. He was always on... The first time I went backstage at Carnegie Hall—way before I was a radio personality—and met him, and hung out with him, I was disappointed because he didn't live up to his image—but most people don't. One of my rules—and most people's rules—you don't want to meet your hero. They very rarely live up to your image of them." Josephson suggests a cause for the problem: "I don't think it's possible to perform at the level that Shepherd did and have that kind of ego and drive—to be on the air five or six nights a week and yet be a sensitive, caring, loving human being.

You have to get up and concentrate the energy—drive, and whatever—to be a performer. It narrows your ability to give warmth and love to kids, women, and friends... I'm sure here and there there's somebody in the world who was a very great creative artist and also a nice person, but I can't think of anyone."

At the beginning of his thoughts on Shepherd, Josephson provided a summing up about creators in general, and Shepherd in particular: "I think that the most *important* thing about an artist is what comes out of the radio, or what happens on the stage or the screen. What they were as a private person is *less* important—it's kind of trivial—for the real junkies. I think Shepherd was an absolute *genius*. He was one of a kind."

Echoing what many creators have expressed (using a truism to obfuscate truth) is this from a newspaper article: "Leigh Brown tells me on the phone that 'Jean doesn't like to talk about his personal life. He thinks it has nothing to do with his work.'"[18]

I also fall back on the rationalization that life is short and it passes, but that art remains. The Art of Jean Shepherd. Overwhelmingly, my interest continues to be in his art. Maybe that makes me an art cuckoo—a *Shepherd* cuckoo. A certain heartlessness there—a certain amorality? Maybe, but there it remains, rock solid. See if you can hold in balance all three Shepherds: the creator, the mentor for tens of thousands of listeners, the deeply flawed man. As he would have it, one must grasp life's nutty fruitcake existence. Knowing all you know now, you can remain enamored and in awe of his work. The contradictions increase the sadness and the tragedy we understand to be the human condition. Pause, sigh deeply—it is all beyond quite understanding, which is part of awe.

I GUESS EVERYBODY HEARS WHAT HE IS HEARING

Let's see what Jean Parker Shepherd said circa early 1960. From the sound of his voice, he seemed to be reading this—whether he was quoting someone or it was his own material is unclear, but what is important is that he was saying something that he deeply felt about his obsessive need to talk—to communicate. There was "cheap guitar music" in the background and he spoke slowly, quietly, pensively:

> How can I say it? How *can* I say it? How *can* I say it? You know, when you've said it all. You still haven't said any of it. You really haven't, you know. You try to get it out—you try...

I'm looking out, and I see a white ship way off in the distance, trailing a long black streamer of smoke. And I saw a white cloud and gray gulls. I could hear that wind beating down from the north...

There was a kind of coolness in the air. There's always a coolness in the air in summer that says one day it's going to be winter. It's going to be winter. And in winter, there's always a softness you can find that says it's going to be summer. And so it shall be.

I'm standing there, and I'm trying to figure out how to say it to you. I can't. Never can. I guess that's the final frustration. That nobody ever can say all of it to somebody else. No matter how hard you try, no matter how much you want. In fact, I think that the more you want to say it, the least likely and the least able you are to do it.

I'm standing there, and that ship finally just disappears. Hear it? Did you get?—listen. Listen—you hear it? I've been trying to say it. What I have been trying to say all along. Yeah. There's not much time left. But you've got to hear it. You've got to be able to hear it. I guess you can't. I guess everybody hears what he is hearing. Nobody else can hear it.

Did you hear that? Oh yeah.

You know, it's going to be summer soon.

Yes. Yes.[19]

Excelsior.

ENDNOTES

INTRODUCTION

i. Note that the common idea of talk radio involves the broadcaster talking to listeners on the telephone, or a group of people discussing a subject on the air—and then taking phone calls from listeners. This was not Jean Shepherd. He talked by himself.

ii. Shepherd began radio broadcasting as an adolescent in the 1930s. His first major jobs were with radio and television stations in Cincinnati and Philadelphia in the 1950s. Probably his major claim to fame remains the 21 years he broadcast from WOR radio in New York City from 1955–1977. He also created television series, wrote stories and articles, made records, performed his own material on various stages, and participated in the creation of several movies based on his stories.

iii. These fifteen- to twenty-minute weekday shows, apparently starting early in 1955 and continuing into December, vary in schedule from weeknights at 11:15 to some at 5:30 PM. The *New York Times* radio schedule for February 26, 1955, 4:30 PM lists "Jean Shepherd, Disk Jockey (Premiere)." No information or description has yet surfaced regarding these programs, and the likelihood that recordings of them exist is slim. Dated tapes ("airchecks") of later broadcasts, made by listeners, exist by the many hundreds and are distributed through a variety of sources.

ENIGMA AND BRICKBATS

iv. Sometimes Shepherd began a show with a mock warning such as, "Tonight's program is in really bad taste," "Some really bad stuff tonight," or "I just have to warn you, it's going to be a bad one tonight." For readers who might fear that this book is going to contain some bad ones, remember that listening to Jean Shepherd is always a joyous, life-affirming experience.

FOIBLES: THE REAL JEAN SHEPHERD

v. The death certificate accurately establishes Shepherd's birth date—many secondary sources, such as articles and interviews with him, give varied years, all of which contribute to the illusion that Shepherd often sought to give—that he was a number of years younger than the facts prove. Ronald Lande Smith, author of *The Stars of Stand-Up Comedy: A Biographical Encyclopedia* (New York: Garland Publishing, 1986) in the book's preface, comments on the unreliability of information from many of his informants. He says that they "were either wary of revealing biographical material or didn't give a damn about posterity." He goes on to say, "In fact, the ultimate source was often unreliable. Performers are notorious for changing birth dates, forgetting career details, and embellishing anecdotes." Writing that he did his best to ferret out the truth, in the article about Shepherd he gives the birth date as two years later than do official records, probably having taken Shepherd's word for it.

vi. The uncertainty and confusion fostered by Shepherd regarding what was true and fictitious in his life stories are difficult to dispel. A number of those who appear in his stories are indeed based on real people (at least as far as their names). The details in the stories are far more likely to have been, at least in part, fabricated.

vii. Beyond the artistic trickery used to give the illusion of truth, there are other problems in determining accuracy regarding Shepherd. He often falsified his age and other personal and professional information in interviews. Despite his reputation for remembering, he also seemed to forget details of his past activities. There are also numerous reporting errors, such as a *New York Times* article of October 31, 1970, stating that Shepherd's theme song was "The Sheik of Araby." Though this was a favorite song of Shepherd's, his theme song (which sounded a lot like "The William Tell Overture"), played at the beginning and end of virtually every Shepherd program for twenty-one years, was the Eduard Strauss polka, "Bahn Frei."

PART I: FORMATIVE YEARS

i. Hohman is a street in Hammond; the street name and number are in the census information. Shepherd's BB-gun story (with the warning line, "You'll shoot your eye out!"), which he told as though true, but insisted elsewhere was fiction, gives the actual name of the street he lived on in its title: "Duel in the Snow, *or* Red Ryder Nails the Cleveland Street Kid."

ii. His father's newspaper obituary (August 26, 1956) and Shepherd's death certificate list his father's name as Jean Shepherd and his mother's as Ann Hetrich. In a Limelight show, Shepherd says his father's name was Jean Parker Shepherd, and that he was also referred to as "Shep."

iii. That Shel Silverstein wrote the song based on his friend's complaint about having "a girl's name" is likely, but unauthenticated.

iv. Morgan's comment thus derided Shepherd for making up much of his childhood stories ("lying"), when Shepherd, in other contexts, actually insisted that they were fiction.

v. "[*Little Orphan Annie*'s] extraordinary popularity owed much to the fact that in 1931 it was the only program for young children. It was, in fact, the genesis of the children's serial format." *Panati's Parade of Fads, Follies, and Manias*: New York: Harper Collins, 1991, 187.

vi. A letter from the Hammond Historical Society, May 28, 1971, to the Queens County Historical Committee gives Shepherd's teachers and years at Harding, and states that he graduated Hammond High in June 1939. Shepherd's photo and senior information are found in the Hammond High Senior Yearbook for 1939.

vii. A *New York Times* online story by Arch McKinlay states that Shepherd would take Randy's stories back to New York and refashion them on the air.

viii. Bill Pasternak, ham operator, comments about amateur radio in general, "We were the nerdy ones, we were the outsiders. We weren't outside playing baseball. I love [Shepherd's] description of kids like myself—we were the ones sitting around basements, tinkering with wires, getting the complexion of a fish."

ix. A glass radio tube used by ham operators—Shepherd frequently used the designation to label objects of all kinds.

x. Shepherd tells various stories about working at the local steel mill in temporary jobs as a teenager. He often claimed he still had a steel worker's union card. Fred Barzyk recalls the steel mill episode of the television series, *Jean Shepherd's America*, shot at Inland Steel in 1971—some steel workers remembered Shepherd working there.

xi. Soldier terminology for creamed chipped beef on toast, a gray, granular mush nearly universally hated: Shit on a Shingle.

xii. Fred Barzyk, TV producer/director and friend of Shepherd's, commented that Shepherd seemed to have an old knee injury from his army days. This may explain why he was discharged before the war ended. If true, no wonder he was obsessed with keeping his knees loose. However, my understanding of pole climbing is that, contrary to Shepherd's description, one indeed must keep one's knees slightly open so the climbing hooks remain in the pole and the climber does not come plummeting down. Thus Shepherd, to make his point, has turned pole-climbing logic upside down.

xiii. According to a 1967 issue of *Playboy*, this was scheduled to be the opening chapter of a new Shepherd book entitled *T.S., Mac.* In 1971 the title of the book (which would focus on Shepherd's army stories) had been changed to *The Secret Mission of the Blue-Assed Buzzard*, and was to appear in 1972. As of several years after Shepherd's death in 1999, it had still not been published, and four of these army-related stories remain available only in old *Playboy* magazines.

xiv. Shepherd's college experience—whether he had much, if any at all—remains one of those mysteries in his biography.

xv. The program was broadcast from Chicago, Shepherd's home area, but his claim remains unsubstantiated. Matthew Callan comments, "It was one of the first shows to directly—and sneakily—market to kids. It was essentially a vehicle for Wheaties, and is largely responsible for establishing that cereal's mythos in the public mind. This would explain, if Shep was lying about appearing on this program, why he picked this particular program to lie about."

PART III: THE GREAT BURGEONING

i. Matthew Callan comments, "What changed was that jazz went from dance-oriented music to a more artistic form—one that encouraged musicians like Charlie Parker and Dizzy Gillespie to explore a theme for many choruses."

ii. The heyday of modern improvisation was the 1950s and 1960s, when it emerged as a strikingly new force in entertainment. Its greatest popularity lasted only about a decade, but elements of it continued, including courses in schools, individual performers, and some improv groups appearing nationwide. *Whose Line is it, Anyway?*, a half-hour TV improvisational show that debuted in America in 1998 and is still running as of this writing, features a moderator and four performers, doing improvised vignettes based on an idea or simple prop. Of course, many "talk radio" shows are at least in part improvised. It should be noted that "live" call-in shows protect themselves from objectionable input by a few seconds of broadcast delay, permitting an emergency cutoff.

iii. Although some of the "Seriously Funny" people went on to other entertainment careers (Nichols and May into directing and other activities, and Bob Newhart into television sitcoms), as basic comic performers, the big names faded within less than a decade of their emergence, while Shepherd continued as a radio humorist for over 21 years, and continued in a similar vein into the 1990s doing new humor material at colleges and other venues (in addition to writing and creating television and movies).

iv. On pages 37–38 of the book, Sahl says he led the way for the new comedians, including Nichols and May, Bob Newhart ("and Jonathan Winters was in New York when I arrived there."). He goes on, "Most of the comedians came out of 'improvisational' theater, and they still use the word. I've never used that word, and I've never written a syllable except on the stage. I rehearse in front of the audience."

v. In the mid-1950s, it was Sahl, with his casual, conversational style and groundbreaking commentaries, who opened the way for the many comedians with their more personal style of the time. Many were clustered under the title "sick comics," and it was a time of sick jokes and the neurotic characters in Jules Feiffer's weekly *Village Voice* cartoon, "Sick Sick Sick"—all too varied a field for a single rubric. The back cover of *Ladies and Gentlemen—Lenny Bruce!!* quotes Bruce: "I'm not a comedian. And I'm not sick. The world is sick and I'm the doctor. I'm a surgeon with a scalpel for false values. I don't have an act. I just talk." —Albert Goldman, from the journalism of Lawrence Schiller, *Ladies and Gentlemen—Lenny Bruce!!*, New York: Random House, Inc., 1972.

vi. Many comedians gripe about their material being stolen. The fact that Shepherd's gold dust was floating in the atmosphere in the dark, on the ephemeral airwaves—which got no respect—may have made it more vulnerable for swiping, almost unnoticed (and perhaps, in the minds of the offenders, nearly guilt free).

vii. A promotional booklet, "WOR Radio: 1922–1982, the First Sixty Years," states, "At the end of the 1950s, WOR was settled into the era of the modern WOR, as it stands now [1982]. The talk format that composes the mainstream of WOR programming was established at this time. [A number of the talk-dynasty broadcasters, however, had begun on WOR decades before.] WOR ended the 1950s in the number one position in New York."

viii. Although he did play complete records (mostly jazz) in his earlier radio days, he was never primarily a record player ("disc jockey"). As he began to be erroneously described as such, inaccurately circumscribing his performance, and as he soon began playing only musical excerpts as part of his performance, he increasingly resented the appellation.

ix. Ed Fancher confirms that he called Shepherd to write for *The Voice*.

x. Exact times of some Shepherd broadcasts are uncertain. The Sunday night shows followed a short 9 PM newscast.

xi. In a 1965 broadcast he made an offhand comment which he did not relate to the Sweetheart Soap incident—but we might see a connection. He said that in his early days, he had been working at a new radio station located down in the police frequencies, and they had no sponsors. Someone got the idea of making up lots of bogus commercials, and this led to acquiring real sponsors.

xii. Gene Santoro in *Myself When I Am Real: The Life and Music of Charles Mingus* (New York: Oxford University Press, 2000, 127) writes, "The title track tinged Pagliacci with P. T. Barnum, and featured a semi-improvised narration by Jean Shepherd, a hip radio personality. Shepherd and Mingus discussed plot turns and moods, but the satirist was free to tell the tale his way. He changed Mingus's finale; instead of shooting himself, the clown dies onstage by accident, to the audience's oblivious ovation."

xiii. Currently no firm dates are available for these appearances, but the Cassavetes one, based on chronological evidence of the making of *Shadows*, would be early 1957, and evidence dates the others as pre-1960.

xiv. Reportedly, after the original version was shown to great acclaim among the avant-garde and some critics, Cassavetes extensively reshot it, revising the film into the only version known to have existed for over forty years. Author Ray Carney reports that he has uncovered a copy of the original—the Shepherd credit and cameo appearance also appear in this first version. Carney email to E. Bergmann, January 16, 2004.

xv. The night before his trip, Shepherd talked about a letter he received from a curator, suggesting that he not worry about the big animals in the Amazon, but rather the amoebas. Having a look at a copy of the original letter, from Dr. Robert Carneiro, an ethnologist at the American Museum of Natural History, allows direct comparison between a document and Shepherd's story about it—he adjusts the wording, but retains the details with absolute accuracy. As Dr. Carneiro's letter puts it, "If I were you, I'd start worrying about the amoebas you'll meet in your palm hearts salad at the Gran Hotel Mercedes in Pucallpa."

xvi. Greg Potemkin, son of Sol Potemkin, the photographer on the trip, relates his father's anecdote: Shepherd had loaned Potemkin his yellow rain slicker. The Indian chief's wife approached to touch it. Someone familiar with local custom prevented her—had she touched Potemkin, taboo rules required that he (and possibly his companions also) be killed. (Phone conversation with E.

Bergmann, January 30, 2004.)

xvii. Gay Talese, *New York Times*, October 11, 1964. The article, "Radio Sage Regards the Series as Stage of World-in-the-Round," states that Shepherd "was at Yankee Stadium to broadcast his brooding existential view of baseball over armed forces radio to hipster American troops overseas."

xviii. "Here's a story Shepherd tells," Fred Barzyk remembers, "and I assume is absolutely true because Leigh [at the time, Shepherd's producer] was there. He did a show—one of his radio shows—talking about *Dr. Strangelove*, [the Kubrick film] and he was talking about how the [film] was really a polemic and it really wasn't irony. He gets a phone call the next day from Kubrick. Kubrick wants to see him. Kubrick comes in. Leigh said she was there. Comes in with his scrapbooks to show Jean all his credentials and how— what he's doing and how he's doing it. His *mother* was a big fan of Jean Shepherd and she called up her son to let him know that her favorite on-air personality had dumped on his movie. Kubrick made the effort to come all the way there. Needless to say, Kubrick didn't win."

xix. Discussing *A Thousand Clowns* in an article/interview of March 30, 1968, in the *Sunday Record* (Bergen County, NJ), writer Edward Norton reports that Shepherd said the use of his life in the play and film led to a lawsuit against Herb Gardner.

xx. Jean's son, Randall, in an email to the author, April 2003, states four marriages. This would be, chronologically, the brief one, the one to Randall's mother, Joan Warner, the one to Lois Nettleton, and finally the one to Leigh Brown. Details of the first one are elusive.

xxi. According to the article by Shaun Considine on Nettleton in *After Dark* magazine, November 1972, "Seven [years] of which were spent married to disc jockey-author Jean Shepherd."

xxii. For a while (after his radio days), to those mailing in critical comments about his work, Shepherd sent from his 1978 television show, "Shepherd's Pie," a signed certificate titled "t.v. coo-coo." (An unabridged dictionary shows no "coo-coo," but "cuckoo," besides being a common European bird, is defined as "a crazy, silly, or foolish person; simpleton.")

PART IV: THE TOOLS IN HAND

i. Raymond Scott created several record albums of electronic music to be played for very young children. Shepherd played the album *Soothing Sounds for Baby, Volume 2, 6 to 12 Months*.

ii. A band member reports, "We recorded 'The Bear' in 1973 and sent promo copies to everyone we could think of, including Shep. He sort of adopted it and would kazoo along with it night after night. We corresponded and eventually appeared on one of his TV shows. We even booked him on a few concerts (without our band). 'The Bear' originally appeared on an LP titled *But First* that went out of print many years ago, but we still sell the album, as a cassette, for $12 plus $2 S&H and now available on CD for $15 plus $2 S&H. If you would like to buy it, send check or MO to Muskrat Productions, 169 South Main Street, #377, New City, NY 10956."

iii. The trombone player was Shepherd's flying instructor.

PART V: ENCOUNTERS AND CONTENTIONS

i. *Only in America* is the title of a 1958 book of commentaries by Harry Golden.

ii. Just as his friends would sometimes note that what he had been talking to them about would emerge on the air (as though he had been dress rehearsing it with them), on occasion, whatever occupied Shepherd in his real life outside the studio would be the subject of a broadcast. (Naturally, he often discussed on the air what was happening to him and around him—the more interesting items, for those in trivial pursuit of Shepherdiana, are those not related by Shepherd in an on-air reference, but pinned down through comparative chronologies of his far-flung activities. An example of this is his offhand, ironic broadcast comment in 1966 about having a little button, "Disarm the Toy Industry" (quoted in Chapter 11), which repeats the opening line of the written BB-gun story in his 1966 collection of stories.)

iii. "Michelangelo's *The Last Supper...*" is another rare Shepherd slip—it's da Vinci's painting.

iv. "Tuesday, November 9, [1965,] approximately 80,000 square miles of the Northeast, a total of eight states, falls into darkness, as the triple conductor line fails. Begins with a faulty relay in Canada. Toronto, the first city afflicted by the blackout, goes dark at 5:15 PM. Rochester follows at 5:18 PM, then Boston at 5:21 PM. New York, finally, loses power at 5:28 PM. The failure affects four million homes in the metropolitan area, and leaves between 600,000 and 800,000 people stranded in the city's subway system. Late in the evening, around 11 PM, President Lyndon Johnson calls New York Mayor Robert Wagner to offer assistance. 'Like a pinched aorta,' journalist Theodore White later wrote, the blackout 'caused an entire civilization to flicker with it.' By midnight, more than 90 percent of subway passengers are freed. By 4:44 AM the next day, power is restored to Manhattan." —Blackout History Project, blackout.gmu.edu/events/timeline.html

v. Every ham operator has a unique call sign—K2ORS was Shepherd's.

vi. Dayton Hamvention, pre-1980, 1980, 1985.

vii. Pasternak says, "It was hard for him not to [reveal who he was on ham radio] because his voice was too well known. Especially after [*A Christmas Story* came out in 1983]. Local stuff tends to be like a party line—twenty people on the telephone. And it's more social. International ham radio is more formal."

viii. Although a tape-machine, seven-second-delay system is generally used on talk radio, Herb Squire, who engineered Shepherd shows says, "The only time, to my knowledge, that the delay was used...was for the Shepherd shows from the Limelight on Saturday nights. It was felt that a foul remark from someone in the audience might be a problem... Jean never had the delay machine used during his studio show." He also says, "As far as the offensive material for spots, it was all a setup! We used to have fun creating these effects." As for having fun setting up interplay between Shepherd and engineers, though this obviously happened between Jean and Herb, who were friends, animosity on the air is unlikely to have been anything but deadly serious between Jean and the majority of engineers who hated him.

ix. Occasionally Shepherd would suggest some semi-seriously expressed universal truth based on some observation, such as these two related to advertising/self-promotion: the more outrageous the claim, the worse the product; the bigger the postage stamp, the smaller the country.

x. Scores of these put-downs have been heard on a ten-percent sample of the estimated 5,000 broadcasts Shepherd did for WOR. He may have done this hundreds if not thousands of times. Not atypical is that on his December 17, 1965, show, in which he is talking about a news story of a bulldozer that had started moving, driverless, inexorably down the street, destroying fire plugs and a convertible: "The thing they were always afraid of—that big bulldozer had gotten free, gotten loose on that street and ran right over— right over the Cadillac. That great, inchoate monster of evil—which reminds me [pause], this is WOR AM and FM New York."

PART VI: REFINEMENTS AND CONVERSIONS

i. Among the pieces of evidence is the Hammond High School 1939 yearbook with photos and names of some of the kids in Shepherd's stories. His dedication in *In God We Trust: All Others Pay Cash*: "To my Mother, and my Kid Brother and the Rest of the Bunch" further obscures distinctions and conflates real and fictional—his mother and kid brother are real, but what about "the Rest of the Bunch"?

ii. In addition, for the National Library Service Shepherd recorded his reading of the book onto discs as an audio book for the blind.

iii. Printed on the front endpaper: "Compliments of your Volkswagen Dealer."

iv. The back cover, however, is a disaster: It misspells Leigh Brown's name, Hammond/Hohman is misspelled as "Holden," and the text refers to Shepherd's "nostalgic Americana" and "nostalgic Indiana muse," apparently preferring wording that might lend a commercial boost at the price of Shepherd's firm beliefs.

v. In the same drawing style, to help promote Prexi restaurants, a sponsor, he had earlier drawn for reproduction a still life of restaurant condiments, printed on the backs of the paper placemats.

vi. The author photo on the back cover, taken by Leigh Brown, apparently was taken when they were shooting an episode of the television series *Jean Shepherd's America*.

vii. The colophon page indicates, "The Phantom of the Open Hearth was produced for Station KCET/28's 'Visions' series, Barbara Schultz Artistic director, by the Television Laboratory at WNET/13 and the WGBH/2 New Television Workshop."

viii. E. Bergmann's opinion, backed by evidence in the book—best supported by comparative listening to extensive broadcasts in each style. "Most people seem to like the shows from the era when they started listening," said Max Schmid, May 22, 1999, on www.bobkaye.com.

ix. A measure of Shepherd's grace under the stress of his shock at Kennedy's death is that in these programs he contained his emotion through the formality of his presentation—and the dead president was referred to as "*Mr.* Kennedy."

x. Amateur radio authority Bill Pasternak comments that in the 1950s, hardly anybody had FM receivers: "The only way you could keep a radio station on—an FM station—was to simulcast to AM. There was no other way to do it because there was no audience and nobody was going to spend the money for advertising. FM was just an extra thing you could throw in."

xi. According to the WOR promotional booklet: "All the way through the turbulent 1960s, WOR continued its solidity and strength. The rock and roll era changed many New York stations into music stations seemingly overnight, and others found themselves buffeted by television."

xii. The WOR promotional booklet naturally put this in the most benign light, talking diplomatically around their action of summarily eliminating some long-time, popular broadcasters: "From an outsider's view, WOR looked as strong as ever in the mid 1970s. The station stood number one in revenues and audience, but this wasn't conclusive evidence that all was going well... In August 1976, Rick Devlin took the job of vice president and general manager of WOR. Coming into WOR, Devlin was faced with a complex set of problems: 'We had to modernize WOR, change the audience, at the same time not lose the existing audience, and build on and bring in new people to WOR.' Management feared that what had happened to several other so-called grand old stations could befall WOR. The radio media had changed with the new era in the 1970s. WOR, in turn, must recognize change in society. A change in programming was inevitable. At this time, a careful reshaping began to take place. The basic talk formula would remain, but some changes of content and pacing would have to take place within the programs themselves. Some personality retirements would occur at this time."

xiii. This is not a simple, straightforward story. Although Shepherd was obviously bitter about his enforced separation from WOR, the fact that producer Laurie Squire reports him doing multiple recorded shows and very few live ones in his last WOR year seems to indicate a certain disengagement as other media vied for his attention. The decline of radio in the public's entertainment patterns seems a factor that affected Shepherd as well as WOR.

xiv. Two reviews mentioning Shepherd's acting have so far surfaced: Howard Taubman of the *New York Times* wrote of *A Banquet for the Moon* on January 20, 1961, "Jean Shepherd, who used to speak on the radio for the night people, is a smooth, sinuous M." The reviewer of a revival of *The Tender Trap* (for the August 28, 1961, issue of the New York theatrical paper the *Morning Telegraph*) did not care much for the other performers, but wrote, "Jean Shepherd is no Ronnie Graham [of the 1954 Broadway production], though he tries hard enough to put the bachelor role over believably." The failure of Kopit's *Asylum* to open after previews in 1963 ended Shepherd's attempts at acting, as far as can be determined.

xv. As an example of the annoying confusion wrought by Jean having a "girl's name," a publicity photo for *A Banquet for the Moon*, shows four people. Shepherd as Mephistopheles impersonating St. Francis, on the left; then a man; then two women. Only three names are listed: the man's, a woman's name, then "Jean Shepherd," on the mistaken assumption that the second woman must be the "Jean." Shepherd, for all his getup and his hyper-dramatic gesture, goes unaccounted for. (*Theater Annual*, 1960–61)

xvi. The photo of Shepherd with microphone and headset on the back is one of the few showing him wearing glasses. By the late 1950s, he had switched to contact lenses.

xvii. E. Bergmann remembers the interview. The following information is from www.museum.tv/archives/etv/W/htmlW/wallacemike/wallacemike.htm, Wallace's two similar interview shows: *Night-Beat* (1956–1957) and *The Mike Wallace Interviews* (1957–1959). ["The show lasted only through 1958," according to the website's text.] "Using only a black backdrop and smoke from his cigarette for atmosphere, Wallace asked pointed, even mischievous questions that made guests squirm. Most were framed in tight close-up, revealing the sweat elicited by Wallace's barbs and the show's harsh klieg lights."

xviii. The organization that retains copies of old programs, as a service to the industry, does not keep programs before the mid-1980s. Despite reports of *The Dissenters* from several sources, neither Feiffer nor Krassner remember it.

xix. Dan Beach, TV production coordinator for *Rear Bumpers* and other Shepherd WGBH television, says, "Fred spent countless nights with Jean and Leigh, nursing, cajoling, begging, and soothing the irascible. Surely *someone* would have brought Jean to TV. Fred had the vision to do so and hung in there through tantrums and insults and negotiation and philosophical arguments. Fred somehow brought Jean's brilliance to television, something Jean was proud of though he seldom admitted it. The video legacy of Jean is due to Fred and I think it's very important that he be recognized." Statement on www.flicklives.com

xx. "Jean Shepherd came to WGBH-TV in Boston in 1965 as a Rockefeller-Artist-in-Residence, where he created twenty *Rear Bumpers*, a series of short features that ended each day's programming." Quoted from the *Jean Shepherd's America* press kit.

xxi. This fine piece of television is locked in WGBH Boston vaults, but copies can be seen at the Museum of Television and Radio in New York and Los Angeles.

xxii. As previously indicated, official papers show Shepherd was discharged from the army in 1944, five years before the start of the Korean War.

PART VII: SUMMING UP TO A BOODLE-AM SHAKE

i. Ham operator and friend Bill Pasternak also noted the same thing: "In the times I met him off the radio—off commercial radio. He didn't sound any different in person. What you heard was the same person."

ii. Shepherd's early listener and friend Jules Feiffer commented that the earliest Shepherd radio work was "brilliant," but that, as Feiffer put it with one of his favorite metaphors, Shepherd never seemed to take the next step "in his creative dance."

iii. Keillor tells stories about a hometown, Lake Wobegon, and some compare them to Shepherd's stories about Hohman. Both published such stories in book compilations. The similarities and the differences— the comparisons— angered Shepherd. Keillor is quoted in *The New York Review of Books*, November 6, 2003, page 60, with a description of what it was like to stand before an audience, and to know one's voice carried at the same time to radio listeners—something akin to what Shepherd must have felt: "Standing at stage center with your toes to the footlights, you're as close to a thousand people as you can conceivably be... such intimacy on a grand scale is shocking and thrilling and a storyteller reaches something like critical mass, passing directly from solid to radio waves without going though the liquid or gaseous phase. No script, no clock, only pictures in your mind that the audience easily sees, they sit so close."

iv. This photo, seen on the dust jacket of this book, was taken of Shepherd in action during his broadcast on November 30, 1966 according to photographer Fred W. McDarrah. [Phone conversation with E. Bergmann. December 17, 2003.] The photo was later used for a 30" x 43" "Personality Poster" which Shepherd advertised for sale on the air, spring 1967.

v. Some ascribe Shepherd's negative depictions of Randy as envy of Randall's sports prowess, which exceeded that which Shepherd would claim for himself in later years. It is reported that when back home in Hammond, Jean pumped Randall for stories, which he would then elaborate on in his broadcasts. (Whether or not this is true, it is not the bare bones that make the art, but how they are fleshed out.)

vi. The *New York Times* obituary of October 17, 1999, starts: "Jean Shepherd, the New York radio raconteur whose rambling jazzlike monologues on the air puzzled many but delighted fans over two decades, died yesterday. He was believed to be at least 70." The equivocation regarding his age illustrates the general lack of consistent and reliable information about Shepherd caused by his own propensity to falsify. When a ham operator dies, he is referred to as "a silent key."

vii. Consistent with Shepherd's sardonic attitudes, he wrote ironically in his acceptance letter of July 2, 1980: "Of course, I am delighted to accept your invitation to be the recipient at the second annual Hammond Achievement Award dinner. I can't tell you how delighted I was when I received your letter, since every artist or performer or whatever has a secret, usually unfulfilled desire to be at last honored in his home town. In fact, yours is the first letter of any sort that I've ever, in all the years, received from Hammond, good or bad. I have always had a sneaking suspicion that an undercover Select Committee of watchful Hammond citizens was operating successfully to keep my books, short stories, TV shows, and any mention of my name out of the records of the town, for their own sinister purposes."

viii. Doctor of Humane Letters, May 15, 1995, from the University Commencement Program, 1995. The program's description of Shepherd contains much misinformation ("Born July 26, 1929," which would have had his army service begin just before his thirteenth birthday) as well as other information that may well be true: "He returned to his native soil [after army duty] to study engineering and psychology at the Indiana University Calumet Center in 1949 and 1950." As previously noted, his memory for the dates of his New York radio work was inaccurate. The program (apparently taking Shepherd's word) gives "from 1958 to 1976." Dated broadcasts and other documentation show this to have been 1955 to 1977. The program's opening paragraph comments that Shepherd "entertains with a distinctly midwestern viewpoint that gently highlights the foibles and strengths of the human spirit."

ix. The photo with the article shows Shepherd, not as himself, but as the nonexistent author, Frederick R. Ewing.

x. Amy Stocky and Shane Bugbee, creators and organizers of the event, bowed to present realities by promoting this first major Jean Shepherd Festival as "*A Christmas Story* Comes Early!" Through a variety of thoughtfully planned means, attendees were exposed to some of Shepherd's other work. Part of the event proceeds will go toward establishing a permanent Shepherd exhibit at the Community Center.

xi. Schwartz remembered when he was a kid on the *A Christmas Story* set: "[Shepherd] loved to talk and people loved to listen to him. He was enjoyable to be around. He could make anything interesting. He could tell you a story about a pen and he would describe this pen for forty minutes and make it interesting." Twenty years later, Schwartz says that when people find that he played Flick, "I get, 'Can you stick your tongue to this pole?' and 'I triple dog dare you!' I get all of it."

xii. Held at a restaurant in Princeton, New Jersey, November 9, 2003. Adrian commented that in addition to his kazoo, her father had given her, as a child, her first Barbie Doll. Shepherd seemed to keep up some semblance of fatherhood while his children were young, but in later years, at least for public consumption, went to the extent of denying their existence. Daughter Adrian seemed to achieve some accommodation to this—a generous feeling under the circumstances of her father's denial of paternity even in the opening page of his will. What were Shepherd's thought processes and acuity of mind when he signed that will during his decline only months before his death? And finally, with relevance to his life in art, what other personal and creative matter might forever remain in obscurity, beyond our knowledge and comprehension?

SOURCE NOTES

PREFACE
1. June 21, 1968.

INTRODUCTION
2. November 1972.
3. Death certificate, Lee County, Florida.
4. June 1957.
5. New York: Pantheon Books, 2003, 272.

ENIGMA AND BRICKBATS
6. March 15, 1959.
7. *Jean Shepherd and Other Foibles*, The Electra Corporation, 1959.
8. From Jean Shepherd Memorial Message Board at www.keyflux.com/shep.

FOIBLES: THE REAL JEAN SHEPHERD
9. September 29, 1965.
10. In a letter to E. Bergmann, September 27, 2001.
11. Death certificate, Lee County, Florida.
12. *New York Times* obituary, October 18, 1999, and petition by Shepherd's son and daughter in the probate division of the Circuit Court of Lee County, Florida, January 21, 2000.
13. Date unknown.
14. February 3, 1975.
15. From the dust jacket of the biography of Miller: Jay Martin, *Always Merry and Bright*, Santa Barbara: Capa Press, 1978.
16. New York: Random House, 2000.
17. Cambridge, MA: Harvard University Press, 1960, 175.

18. December 30, 1965.
19. Death certificate, Lee County, Florida.
20. New York: Doubleday, 1966.
21. New York: Dodd, Mead and Company, 1972.
22. Shaila K. Dewan and Jesse McKinley, *New York Times*, March 9, 2004.
23. Bruce Weber, *New York Times*, March 9, 2004.
24. See *Drawing Hands* lithograph, 1948, by M.C. Escher, reproduced in Bruno Ernst's *The Magic Mirror of M.C. Escher*, Ballantine Books, 1976, 26.
25. January 14, 1971.
26. December 16, 1998, radio interview, WEVD.
27. Cambridge, MA: MIT Press, 1964; Reprint edition, 1994, 303–304.
28. Undated excerpt from NPR tribute.
29. September 21, 1969.
30. November 1971.
31. *Chicago White Sox: A Visual History*, Sports Collectors Edition, 1987.
32. Interview with Anne Ligouri on WFAN, December 20, 1997.
33. Information releasable under the Freedom of Information Act; Shepherd's army record shows "Dates of Service: July 20, 1942, to December 16, 1944."
34. February 26, 1965.
35. *New York Times* book review, June 20, 2000.
36. New York: Oxford University Press, 1971.
37. Quoted in Henry Hart, *James Dickey: The World as a Lie*, New York: Picador USA, 2000, xii.

PART I: FORMATIVE YEARS

1. August 29, 1964, Limelight.
2. 1930 U.S. Census Bureau.
3. 1966, syndicated.
4. Newspaper obituary, August 26, 1956.
5. *Realist*, #20, October 1960, 11.
6. *The Three Worlds of Jean Shepherd*, PBS-TV, 1968 or 1969.
7. *Realist*, #19, July–August 1960, 13.
8. Pascal, *Design and Truth in Autobiography*, 135.
9. *The New York Post*, December 8, 1964. Jerry Tallmer, "The Radio Talk Jockeys."
10. July 28, 1965.
11. July 20, 1966.
12. Nachman, *Seriously Funny*, 77.
13. *The Hammond Times*, October 16, 1955. Earl Wilson reporting.
14. June 16, 1957.
15. NBC *Tonight Show*, June 1957.
16. April 1960.
17. September 10, 1960.
18. Garden City, NY: Doubleday and Company, 1978, ix–x.
19. May 1, 1968.
20. From emails to author.

21. February 15, 1962.
22. July 19, 1967.
23. May 14, 1966, Limelight.
24. Date unknown.
25. November [28?], 1969, syndicated.
26. January 28, 1965.
27. August 9, 1965.
28. December 24, 1975.
29. December [19?], 1963.
30. June 4, 1960.
31. March 1, 1961.
32. From official photo of Shepherd (featuring his name and the Cincinnati WSAI call letters), circa early 1951.
33. From several sources, including Shepherd's son, Randall.
34. [1966?], syndicated.
35. "Evolution" by Langdon Smith (1858–1908).
36. July 3, 1960.
37. From the Archives of the Broadcast Pioneers of Philadelphia; a photo of a Shepherd broadcast, with Philadelphia's KYW sign behind him, circa 1953.
38. January 24, 1953.
39. *New York Times* feature article by John Kronenberger, June 3, 1971.
40. April 10, 1960.

PART II: HERITAGE AND ENDOWMENT

1. [1972?], syndicated.
2. 1976, syndicated.
3. November 1972.
4. March 12, 1960.
5. March or April 1960.
6. May 2, 1959.
7. June 21, 1968.
8. February 15, 1962.
9. E.B. White, Irvin S. Cobb, and Will Cuppy quoted in Max Eastman, *Enjoyment of Laughter*, New York: Simon and Schuster, 1936.
10. *Now Here's My Plan: A Book of Futilities*, New York: Simon and Schuster, 1960.
11. April 10, 1960.
12. April 1960.
13. From *The New Dictionary of Thoughts*, New York: Standard Book Company, 1954.
14. Ross Wetzsteon, December 29, 1966.
15. "Edited and introduced by" Jean Shepherd, New York: G. P. Putnam's Sons, 1960.
16. Minneapolis: University of Minnesota Press, 1997, 1.
17. Berkeley: University of California Press, 1998, 4–5, 7.
18. Hilmes, 271.
19. July 9, 1960.

20. Mary Frances Rhymer (ed.), New York: Seabury Press, 1976.

21. December 27, 1974.

22. *The Realist*, "An Impolite Interview with Jean Shepherd," October 1960, 11; and "An Impolite Interview with Henry Morgan," July–August 1960, 13.

23. July 9, 1960.

24. March 1, 1961.

25. July 3, 1960.

26. September 23, 1960.

27. July 3, 1960.

28. July 19, 1967.

29. April 1959.

30. July 29, 1966.

31. July 29, 1966.

32. March 1, 1961.

33. On a Long John Nebel program, January 1968.

34. September 21, 1969.

35. July 31, 1960.

PART III: THE GREAT BURGEONING

1. November 10, 1972.

2. From *New York in the '50s*, Boston: Houghton Mifflin Company, 1992.

3. *American Heritage Dictionary of the English Language*, 4th edition, Houghton Mifflin Company, 2000.

4. Jeffrey Sweet, *Something Wonderful Right Away: An Oral History of the Second City and the Compass Players*, reprint, New York: Limelight Editions, 1987. (Originally New York: Avon Books, c.1978.)

5. From an article/interview in the March 30, 1968, edition of the *Sunday Record* (Bergen County, New Jersey), by writer Edward Norton.

6. New York: Harcourt Brace Jovanovich, 1976.

7. New York: Welcome Rain Publishers, 2001.

8. From multiple sources, including John Kronenberger's *New York Times* article, "Jean Shepherd Tells It Like It Was, Maybe," June 3, 1971.

9. September 1960.

10. June 4, 1960.

11. June 10, 1965.

12. August 20, 1965.

13. Reprinted in *The Village Voice Reader*, edited by Daniel Wolf and Edwin Fancher, New York: Doubleday, 1962.

14. January 23–24, 1953.

15. *The Nat Hentoff Reader*, Da Capo Press, 2001.

16. Available on *Louisville Stomp: The Complete Sessions of the Dixieland Jug Blowers*. Frog DGF6, England, 1995.

17. Recorded February 13, 1957, according to information on the re-released CD. Audio CD October 25, 1990.

18. "Bahn Frei Polka," (Fast Track Polka) Boston Pops Orchestra, Arthur Fiedler, Conductor, c.1948.

19. Adelaide Hall, singer, with the Duke Ellington Orchestra (between 1923 and

1929). The song version Shepherd used is on CD AJA 5092, *Ladies Sing the Blues*, Academy Sound and Vision Ltd., England, 1992.

20. June 16, 1957.
21. June 1957.
22. *Wishing on the Moon: The Life and Times of Billie Holiday*, Penguin Books, 1994.
23. S.J. Perelman—a tape of part of this talk exists; Arch Oboler & Herb Gardner—heard by E. Bergmann; John Cassavetes—see *Shadows* by Ray Carney, 22.
24. London: British Film Institute, 2001, 22.
25. *Shadows*, directed by John Cassavetes, Gena Enterprises, 1960 (Fox Lorber Home Video, 1996).
26. New York: Faber and Faber, 2001.
27. December 31, 1959.
28. September [3?], 1960.
29. From typescript of an article for the newspaper *The Villager* at the time Shepherd died, October 1999.
30. September [3?], 1960.
31. 1972.
32. As relayed on the air by Shepherd and confirmed by Farber.
33. September 16, 1965.
34. February 4, 1966.
35. March 12, 1960.
36. June 1966.
37. September 7, 1965.
38. August 22, 1964.
39. [Spring 1964?]
40. October 23, 1969.
41. 1965, syndicated.
42. Interview in a Chicago humor magazine, *Aardvark*, 1963.
43. March 15, 1959.
44. New York: Simon and Schuster, 1960.
45. New York: Simon and Schuster, 1961.
46. Now available as a CD from Collectors' Choice Music, reproducing the original cover and the back, including Gardner's notes. Additional liner notes for the CD by Joseph F. Loredo.
47. April 1972.
48. *Newsday*, Long Island, New York, November 1977.
49. Photo by Gene Dauber in *The Great American Newspaper: The Rise and Fall of the* Village Voice, Kevin Michael McAuliffe, New York: Charles Scribner's Sons, 1978.
50. *Realist* magazine, October 1960, 18.
51. Date unknown.
52. July 10, 1965, Limelight.
53. January 14, 1971.
54. 1972.
55. April 1972.

56. May 29, 1975.
57. Fall 1970.
58. Correspondence on www.flicklives.com.
59. August 12, 1965.
60. November 1971.
61. [Late 1960s?]

PART IV: THE TOOLS IN HAND

1. January 25, 1973.
2. "William Tell Underture" by Arturo Mouscanini and the Happy Mice. Written by "John Charles Fiddy" and "Otto Fieben," Hollywood: Sonoton Music.
3. October 5, 1965.
4. By George Antheil, BMG/RCA Victor #68066.
5. Date unknown
6. *Rey de la Torre Plays Classical Guitar*, Epic Records #LC 3418.
7. February 1972.
8. *One Man Band: Paul Blackman*, Folkways Records (now Smithsonian Folkways Recordings, FA 2605, 1957.)
9. April 8, 1965.
10. 1976.
11. February 14, 1973.
12. August 6, 1965.
13. March 12, 1960.
14. Helen Gee, *Limelight: A Greenwich Village Photography Gallery and Coffeehouse in the Fifties*, University of New Mexico Press, 1997.
15. November 1957.
16. April 28, 1957.
17. May 13, 1957.
18. Undated.
19. July 15, 1965.
20. July 3, 1960.
21. [Early 1966?] syndicated.
22. December 11, 1967.
23. July 2, 1960.
24. September 23, 1960.
25. April 9, 1960.
26. February 10, 1972.
27. July 3, 1960.
28. Thomas Y. Crowll Publishers (editions copyright 1960, 1967, 1975).

PART V: ENCOUNTERS AND CONTENTIONS

1. June 6, 1972.
2. April 1972.
3. March 19, 1960.
4. March 12, 1960.
5. April 9, 1960.

6. June 4, 1960.
7. December 11, 1967.
8. Early 1960.
9. July 3, 1960.
10. November 25, [1958?].
11. January 24, 1966.
12. June 1957.
13. March 15, 1966.
14. November 2, 1965.
15. December 30, 1974.
16. July 2, 1960.
17. July 3, 1960.
18. January 7, 1971.
19. February 1964.
20. James Haskins, Kathleen Benson, Viking Penguin, 1988, 1.
21. New York: Random House, 1970, 4–5.
22. March 24, 1966.
23. From the *Ambrose Bierce Site*, the "Bierce on Politics" page, www.donswaim.com/bierce-election.html.
24. Jerry Tallmer, article in *The Villager*, October 1999.
25. March or April 1960.
26. June 1964.
27. February 19, 1962.
28. July 2, 1960.
29. July 19, 1967.
30. July 31, 1960.
31. November 1972.
32. Early 1960.
33. October 5, 1965.
34. June 1964.
35. 1960.
36. November 22, 1959.
37. 1972.
38. June 25, 1960.
39. July 29, 1966.
40. September 11, 1970.
41. January 6, 1971.
42. June 4, 1960.
43. February 22, 1961.
44. November 12, 1967.
45. July 2, 1960.
46. Quoted in *Harpers Magazine*, January 1966, by Edward Grossman.
47. November 22, 1972.
48. August 12, 1965.
49. *Cue*, January 1961.
50. April 29, 1960.
51. April 6, 1965.

52. From December 19, 1976 issue.

53. 1966.

54. April 1960.

55. February 22, 1962.

56. June 16, 1957.

57. June 21, 1968.

58. From *Movie Collector's World*, Pete Delaney, April 8, 1994.

59. March 15, 1966.

60. September 18, 1960.

61. November 8, 1965.

62. March 15, 1959.

63. July 2, 1960.

64. April 1960.

65. From *Newark Sunday News*, January 11, 1970.

66. From Larry King radio call-in show, March 10, 1982.

67. March 22, 1977.

68. March 1, 1961.

69. From *New York Times*, January 1, 1969.

70. February 19, 1962.

71. [February?] 1964.

72. February 8, 1965.

73. April 10, 1960.

74. July 31, 1960.

75. August 20, 1965.

76. July 20, 1966.

77. December 17, 1975.

78. December 14, 1958.

79. 1972.

80. January 4, 1965.

81. February 19, 1962.

82. December 11, 1967.

83. Date unknown.

84. August 6, 1965.

85. April 19, 1965.

86. February 21, 1962.

87. October 17, 1974.

88. December 22, 1972.

89. Summer 1966.

90. *Oscar and the Ham*, 1975, The American Radio Relay League.

91. 1977.

92. May 2, 1973.

93. April 19, 1965.

94. October 24, 1969.

95. August 9, 1965.

96. February 14, 1964.

97. 1966.

98. August 20, 1965.

99. August 20, 1965.

100. Numerous radio references, interviews, and credit lines for TV shows and movies list Brown.

101. From *Contemporary Authors*, The Gale Group, volumes 65–68.

102. September 29, 1966.

103. *People Weekly* magazine, September 19, 1977.

104. July 20, 1966.

105. October 30, 1969.

106. September 27, 1972.

107. September 23, 1973.

108. Certificate of marriage, March 2, 1977 (at Key West, Florida).

109. September 3, 1960.

110. Audio tape from Friends of Old Time Radio Convention, October 2000.

111. March 1, 1961.

112. July 19, 1967.

113. Date unknown.

114. Late 1965, syndicated.

115. Late 1965, syndicated.

116. Late 1964 or early 1965, syndicated.

117. October 8, 1965.

118. 1966.

119. "WOR Radio: 1922–1982, the First Sixty Years" [64-page undated booklet, c.1982].

120. August 20, 1965.

121. May 31, 1966.

122. June 27, 1968.

123. November 22, 1972.

PART VI: REFINEMENTS AND CONVERSIONS

1. New York: Ballantine Books, 1956.

2. Information regarding the outline and writing of *I, Libertine* is from an interview with Betty Ballantine by Lester Nafzger, November 14, 2000.

3. *Saga* magazine, January 1957.

4. New York: G.P. Putnam's Sons, 1960.

5. Doubleday, 1962.

6. Bantam Books, April 1965.

7. Garden City, NY: Doubleday and Company, 1966.

8. February 4, 1966.

9. From *In God We Trust: All Others Pay Cash*, Garden City, NY: Doubleday and Company, 1966.

10. Copyright 1967, Volkswagen of America, Inc.

11. Chelsea House Publishing Company, 1970.

12. Garden City, NY: Doubleday and Company, 1971.

13. New York: Dodd, Mead and Company, 1972.

14. Ken Graves and Mitchell Payne, Oakland, CA: The Scrimshaw Press, 1977.

15. Doubleday and Company, 1978 (Doubleday/Dolphin paperback).

16. Doubleday and Company, 1981.

17. HDL Pub., 1989.
18. Doubleday (Broadway Books), 2003.
19. Walt Kelly, *Songs of the Pogo*, Simon and Schuster, 1956, 146.
20. December 24, 1965.
21. June 28, 1968.
22. September 11, 1960.
23. June 4, 1960.
24. Date unknown.
25. Rinehart and Company, New York, 1948.
26. *Shake It for the World, Smartass* (reprint; The Dial Press, 1970).
27. *Modest Gifts*, Random House, Inc., 2003, vii.
28. August 6, 1965.
29. August 9, 1965.
30. Introduction by Nick Lyons, edited by Will Balliett, 1994.
31. February 27, 1961.
32. December 30, 1966.
33. National Public Radio's *All Things Considered* Shepherd tribute of October 1999.
34. April 1960.
35. November [17?], syndicated.
36. August 22, 1964.
37. November [25?], 1963.
38. November 26, 1963.
39. November 26, 1963.
40. November 28, 1963.
41. January 6, 1965.
42. July 28, 1966.
43. July 28, 1966.
44. July 19, 1967.
45. Little, Brown & Company, 1954.
46. From the Squires' personal collection, taken during a bachelor party for engineer, Herb Squire.
47. March 1977.
48. Extensive December 19, 1976, article in the *New York Times* Arts and Leisure section, about Shepherd's *Phantom of the Open Hearth* television drama.
49. Sunday *New York Times Book Review*, February 28, 1982. Letter from Shepherd to Jackson, April 26, 1982.
50. In the DVD liner notes to the September 2002 reissue of his album, *The Nightfly*, Warner Brothers Records, 1982.
51. Strip for January 9, 2000, subtitled "Random Memories." It is reproduced in this book.
52. *Look, Charlie* reference in Chapter 7; *Voice* review the *Morning Telegraph*, June 29, 1961; *Destry in the Playbill*; *New Faces* from *New York Times* article, December 3, 1961; *Asylum* from *New York Times* article, September 13, 1962, press releases, and *Village Voice* articles through March 7, 1963.
53. Sources include Carnegie Hall program of October 17, 1972 and back flyleaf

of Leigh Brown's novel *The Show Gypsies* (New York: Mason/Charter Publishers, Inc., 1975).

54. Malibu, CA: Abbott Records, Inc., 1956.
55. Now available as a CD from Collectors' Choice Music, reproducing the original cover and back with the liner notes by Shel Silverstein. Additional liner notes for the CD by Joseph F. Loredo.
56. New York: Quote Records Corporation.
57. The current CD by Wood Fire is made in France, reproducing the front but not the back of the original.
58. Florida: Folkways Records, 9754.
59. March 1, 1961.
60. Audio of the telecast recorded by E. Bergmann.
61. From *Ernie Kovacs: Television's Original Genius*, A JSC Production, 1982 VHS.
62. From WGBH Boston radio, on Ron Della Chiesa's program, March 14, 1985.
63. From WGBH Boston radio, on Ron Della Chiesa's program, March 14, 1985.
64. *Babe Ruth: The Life behind the Legend* Home Box Office, VHS and DVD, 1998.
65. From 2003 commentary for *A Christmas Story* two-disc DVD special edition, Turner Entertainment Co., 2003.
66. Alan Colmes interview, 1998.
67. Brian McKernan, editor, *The Age of Videography: Twenty Years That Changed the Way We See Ourselves*. New York: Miller Freeman PSN Inc., 1996, 63–66.

PART VII: SUMMING UP TO A BOODLE-AM SHAKE

1. Photo by Roy Schatt, 1956, uncredited author photo on the back of the book.
2. *The New York Times*, August 5, 2003, by Richard A. Friedman, M.D.
3. From a letter sent by Leigh Brown, "Agent for Jean Shepherd," October 22, 1980.
4. Earl Wilson column, October 16, 1955.
5. January 24, 1966.
6. Florida death certificate for Nancy Leigh Shepherd.
7. From the university website; originally in Shepherd's last will and testament, dated May 10, 1999, Lee County, Florida.
8. 1957.
9. Eric Zorn, in the *Chicago Tribune*, April 1982.
10. From www.broadcastingcable.com, "A Baker's Dozen of Excellence: B&C Hall of Fame Poised to Induct Class of 2000."
11. Obituary dated October 17, 1999; "News of the Week" article titled, "Kabuki Radio: 'Creeping Meatballism' and Other Peculiar Riffs on America;" *The New York Times Magazine*, January 2, 2000.
12. Narrated by Harry Shearer, produced by Shearer and Art Silverman.
13. From March 19–25, 2003, article in weekly "Television" section.
14. Ronald Lande Smith, Garland Pub., 1986.
15. September 4, 1960.

16. September 16, 1965.
17. April 10, 1960.
18. John Kronenberger reporting, June 3, 1971, *New York Times* Shepherd article.
19. [1960?]

ANNOTATED LIST OF INTERVIEWEES

Bob Alden (WOR Radio time salesman): Began working at WOR in 1955, shortly before Jean Shepherd arrived. (Phone interview with E. Bergmann, September 29, 2003.)

David Amram (musician, composer): Classical and jazz musician, composer and conductor, close associate of Jack Kerouac and other Beats. (Phone interview with E. Bergmann, February 16, 2003.)

Fred Barzyk (TV director, producer): WGBH Boston television director and producer of Jean Shepherd television films, *Jean Shepherd's America*, and other broadcasts. (Interview with E. Bergmann and M. Callan, May 5, 2003.)

Dan Beach (TV Production Coordinator): Friend of Jean Shepherd for over forty years, Production Coordinator for several Shepherd WGBH television programs. (Email correspondences, 2002–2003, with E. Bergmann.)

Bob Brown (the editor of *Car and Driver*): A Shepherd listener, who, while editor, asked him to write for the magazine. They became friends, and Shepherd also did the announcing for a number of *Car and Driver*–sponsored car races. (Phone interview with E. Bergmann, December 17, 2003.)

Ron Della Chiesa (radio broadcaster): With his wife, Joyce, were friends of Shepherd and his wife, Leigh, beginning in the Boston PBS days in the early 1970s, and became very close to them in the last decade of Shepherd's life. (Phone interview with E. Bergmann, March 31, April 17, 2003.)

Art D'Lugoff (concert promoter): Organized the Billie Holiday jazz concert of June 15, 1957 among many other major musical performances. (Phone interview with E. Bergmann, November 19, 2003.)

Billy Collins (U.S. Poet Laureate, 2003): Jean Shepherd enthusiast since 1956. (Phone interview with E. Bergmann, May 20, 2003.)

Ed Fancher (*Village Voice* cofounder/publisher): Invited Shepherd to write for the early *Voice*, friend. (Phone interview with E. Bergmann, July 21, 2003.)

Barry Farber (talk show personality): Friend of Jean Shepherd starting in the early 1960s when Farber began at WOR where he and Jean were considered "outsiders." Farber has continued to be a talk show host into the twenty-first century. (Phone interview with E. Bergmann, March 7, 2003.)

Mort Fega (jazz disk jockey): Far-out jazz disc jockey, who broadcast overnight in New York in the 1950s and 1960s, and continued his work in other venues for several decades. (Phone interview with E. Bergmann, March 12, 2003.)

Jules Feiffer (cartoonist, playwright): Radio listener and friend of Shepherd's in the 1950s and 1960s. (Phone interview with E. Bergmann, December 8, 2003.)

Helen Gee (founder/owner of the Limelight café): Friend of Jean Shepherd beginning in the late 1950s, founder/owner of the original Limelight photography gallery and coffee shop. (Interview with E. Bergmann, June 6, 2003.)

Murphy Grimes (friend): A long-time friend of Jean Shepherd. (Interview with E. Bergmann, at Shepherd gathering in Princeton, NJ, November 9, 2003.)

Hugh Hefner (founder, editor, and publisher of *Playboy*): Published twenty-three short stories, one article, and The Beatles interview by Shepherd in *Playboy*. (Phone interview with E. Bergmann, April 22, 2004.)

Martin Jackson (author): Interviewed Shepherd and wrote the *New York Times* article about his TV film *Phantom of the Open Hearth* and reviewed for the *New York Times Book Review*, Shepherd's *A Fistful of Fig Newtons*. (Interview with E. Bergmann, May 9, 2003.)

Larry Josephson (radio broadcaster and producer): Host and producer of numerous radio programs, Josephson is responsible for the revival of interest in Bob and Ray. He and Shepherd were friends for decades. (Phone interview with E. Bergmann, February 3, 2004.)

Paul Krassner (founder/publisher of the *Realist*): An early listener, who interviewed Shepherd for the *Realist*, and was his friend. (Phone interview with E. Bergmann, December 20, 2003.)

Dan List (*Village Voice* columnist): Rally master of the *Voice* sports car rallies in Washington Square Park for several years— Shepherd did the announcements for the audience. (Phone interview with E. Bergmann, September 29, 2003.)

Norman Mailer (*Village Voice* cofounder, author): Writer for the *Voice* at the same time as Shepherd. (Response to a letter and a question list from E. Bergmann, August 6, 2003.)

Bill Pasternak (radio broadcaster, ham operator, friend): Producer of a weekly amateur radio newscast, TV news engineer, author; knew Shepherd in person, but primarily through talking to him as a friend on amateur radio. (Phone interview with E. Bergmann, December 14, 2003.)

Brian Pearson (northwest Indiana radio broadcaster, fan): Provided many pieces to the puzzle of Jean Shepherd. (Emails to E. Bergmann, June 2003.)

Herb Saltzman (WOR Radio general manager): Merchandizing manager, later general manager (Shepherd's boss) for Shepherd's last ten years at WOR. (Interview with E. Bergmann, May 27, May 30, 2003.)

Scott Schwartz (actor, Flick in *A Christmas Story*): As a child actor spent weeks on the movie set of *A Christmas Story* in 1982. (Phone interview with E. Bergmann, December 12, 2003.)

Randall Shepherd (Jean's son): Named after Jean's kid brother, Randy. (Email correspondences with E. Bergmann, 2003.)

Herb Squire (WOR Radio engineer): Engineered many of Shepherd's shows from 1967 to 1977, friend. (Phone interview with E. Bergmann, September 24, 2003, and subsequent emails.)

Laurie Squire (WOR Radio producer): Shepherd's radio producer from 1976 to 1977, friend. (Phone interview with E. Bergmann, September 25, 2003, and subsequent emails.)

Jerry Tallmer (author, *Village Voice* columnist): Author. Wrote off-Broadway theater reviews, and knew Shepherd in the early *Voice* days. (Interview with E. Bergmann, October 29, 2003.)

Oliver Trager (author): Biographer (*Dig Infinity!*) of stand-up jazz comedian Lord Buckley. (Phone interview with E. Bergmann, March 13, 2003.)

Dan Wakefield (author): Creator of the book and documentary, *New York in the 1950s*. (Phone interview with E. Bergmann, February 13, 2003.)

John Wilcock (author): Helped establish the *Village Voice*, wrote its early column "The Village Square." (Phone interview with E. Bergmann, August 21, 2003.)

Pete Wood (friend): Listened to Shepherd's Cincinnati broadcasts and was a friend of his starting in Philadelphia, 1951. (Phone interview with E. Bergmann April 7, 2003.)

LISTENING TO, WATCHING, AND READING JEAN SHEPHERD

The sound of Jean Shepherd, in hundreds of broadcasts, is widely available in several formats. A number of videos, several of Shepherd's books, and many articles by and about him are also available. The sources below are accurate at the time of publication.

> *Mass Backwards* program broadcast by Max Schmid on WBAI 99.5 FM, Tuesday mornings (Shepherd usually at 5:15 AM).
>
> www.wbai.org streams its programming, including *Mass Backwards*.
>
> Schmidco, operated by Max Schmid, sells hundred of audios of broadcasts, as well as some videos. Max Schmid, P.O. Box 3449, Astoria, NY, 11103.
>
> www.flicklives.com: Run by Jim Clavin, the major Jean Shepherd website archives the most recent *Mass Backwards* Shepherd programs and summaries of scores of *Mass Backwards* rebroadcasts. Also at the site are enormous amounts of well-organized material by categories, including news, playbills, ads, photos, and reviews; articles by Shepherd; and articles about his life and career from the *Northwest Indiana Times* and elsewhere.

Jean Shepherd Project, through Jeff Beauchamp, found at
their email address, fatheadcentral@aol.com provides
audios on CDs.
shep-archives.com: Maintained by Charles Hayden,
includes hundreds of audio files.
jeanshepherd.blogspot.com   continuously   broadcasts   Jean
Shepherd programs.
WBCQ, 7,415 kHz shortwave, check for schedule.
www.skybird.org plays Shepherd on Friday during
evenings.
NPR (and its affiliates) offers their two-hour tribute to
Jean Shepherd "A Voice in the Night" as a premium
on CD.
www.keyflux.com/shep, run by Jim Sadur, has a variety
of materials on Shepherd.
www.bobkaye.com/Shep.html, run by Bob Kaye, has a
variety of materials on Shepherd.
www.eBay.com usually has a number of Jean Shepherd
audios, videos, and miscellany at auction.
Some audios and some videos, including *Generation of
Leaves: America Inc.*, can be seen/heard at the
Museum of Television and Radio. New York: 25 West
52nd Street, New York City; (212) 621-6800. Los
Angeles: 465 North Beverly Drive, Beverly Hills; (310)
786-1025.
Some audios, visuals, and other material may be forever
lost, and some are currently inaccessible in the archives
of PBS, WGBH, NPR, and other entities.
Various book and video stores and websites carry
Shepherd material. Copies of his books are available—
from very inexpensive paperback and hardcover
versions, to first editions and signed copies. His hoax
turned into a real book, *I, Libertine* is usually
available in paperback and hardcover originals,
starting at under $100 for the paperback. Books
containing forewords and introductions by Shepherd
are also available used. Back issues of publications in
which Shepherd articles and stories originally appeared
are also for sale, but most stories and some articles are
collected in the books.
Various websites contain tributes to Shepherd. *Time*
magazine's website has an extensive article.
Hammond, Indiana, and various other organizations

contain Shepherd tributes and other material on their websites.

Of an estimated 5,000 or so Jean Shepherd broadcasts originating in New York, only about one quarter have surfaced as of the publication of this book (other than the last two Philadelphia broadcasts, none of Shepherd's radio work prior to his Sunday night New York program in 1956 has yet been found). Although some may be lost forever, newly discovered recordings of old broadcasts continually emerge, mostly from listeners who recorded them when originally broadcast. Please report such heretofore unarchived material (especially of the overnight and Sunday night broadcasts, from 1956 to 1960) to the author through his publisher or to www.flicklives.com.

SHEPHERDISMS

Night People

Trivia

A tiny figure, tattered and torn (humanity—himself included—the worse for wear, but still struggling onward)

Straws in the wind (a hint of some new idiocy, usually found in a news article)

Creeping meatballism (conformity—a common American defect)

Excelsior! (battle cry)

Excelsior, you fathead! (friendly battle cry)

Seltzer bottle (response to battle cry)

In hoc agricola conc (ersatz-Latin silliness)

We're living in par-less times (or parlous times)

Hurl an invective (a mildly hostile voice in the night)

I will award the brass figlagee with bronze oak-leaf palm (the silly sound of "figlagee" derides the whole idea of awarding medals for supposed achievements—usually, for Shepherd, the award he will give when he asks for the answer to a piece of trivia.)

I will award the brass figlagee with aluminum palm (less commonly used form—possibly more prestigious, possibly less)

Keep your knees loose (defensive maneuvering as philosophical imperative. See Chapter 11, describing Life According to Shepherd)

Hang loose

Hold it in abeyance

I winkle (he wonders what game his aunt had been playing when she'd say it, and what the significance was of the funny-sounding phrase)

Slob art (many American culture items—think plastic pink flamingos on the lawn)

Glop (term for pretentiously overwrought ideas, prose, and music)

Time, tide, and the affairs of men

A vague, fugitive notion

Just walking around, scratching

Hit the money button (here come the recorded commercials!)

Hit the whoopee button (see "money button" above)

Fistfight (said as though it represents the primary brutishness within us)

New York is a summer fistfight

Fellow sufferers (life is tough)

Fellow victims (life is tough—we're all victims and we're all perpetrators)

I suspect... (I really believe...)

You know... (common monologue filler, often used to nudge his engineer into increased participation by directing a comment or question to him. This also helps promote the feeling of his listeners that Shepherd is speaking not to an abstraction, but to real, live people whose minds are engaged with his.)

As a matter of fact... (maybe fact, maybe not)

It's true! I'm not exaggerating! (often said when inventing or exaggerating)

I'll never forget... (total fabrication may follow)

Effluvia

Flick lives!

6SJ7GT (ham radio tube—whenever he needs a code designation for anything)

Bring it up big! (the engineer should significantly raise the volume)

Take umbrage

Feckless (as in "I was a feckless youth")

Without feck

Festered (as in, "I festered as a youth")

All that jazz (a group of like items, recalling his jazz interests and orientation)

Razzmatazz (often used when scatting along with some song)

Gallimaufry (a W.C. Fields word—a hodgepodge, usually of human tumult)

I'm this kid, see... (begins many stories about his childhood)

Holy smokes! (just about as rash an expletive as Shepherd ever uses on the air)

Ahhhh! (snuck in starting at some unknown date at the end of the "Bahn Frei" theme)

INDEX